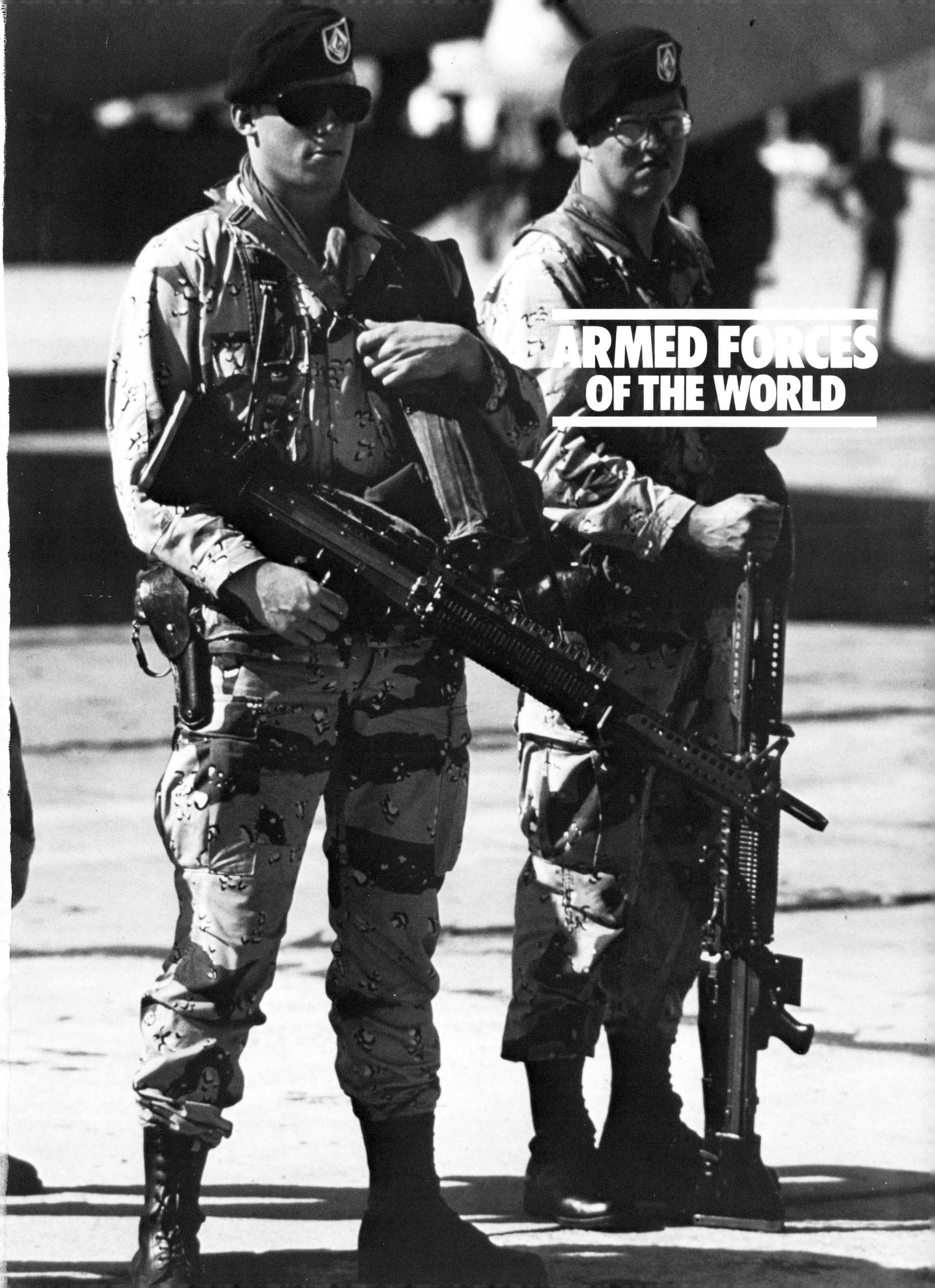

ARMED FORCES OF THE WORLD

2

ARMED FORCES
OF THE WORLD

**CHARLES MESSENGER
ANTONY PRESTON
ANTHONY ROBINSON**

Bison Books

This Edition First Published in 1985 by
Bison Books Ltd
176 Old Brompton Road
London SW5
England

ISBN 0 86124 210 6

Printed in Hong Kong

Page 1: The Red Beret is almost universal as the symbol of airborne forces.
Page 2-3: The nuclear carrier USS *Enterprise* (CVN.65), the world's largest warship when built.
This page: The AH-64 Apache attack helicopter shows its capabilities.

THE ARMIES
Charles Messenger

THE FIGHTING SHIPS

Antony Preston

THE AIRCRAFT

Anthony Robinson

INTRODUCTION

While the defeat of Nazi Germany in May 1945 may have spelled the end of Europe's most devastating conflict to date, it simultaneously raised the curtain on an era when the divide between the Soviet Union and her erstwhile allies was to grow seemingly ever wider. An initial policy of simple non-cooperation in the administration of now-divided Germany was followed by a series of events that not only raised international tension but, on occasion, also put world peace at risk once more.

The West reacted by forming the North Atlantic Treaty Organization (NATO) in 1949, following the unsuccessful Soviet blockade of Berlin the previous year. The first Supreme Allied Commander Europe (SACEUR), General Dwight D. Eisenhower, was appointed in December 1950, at the end of a year that had seen the invasion of South Korea by her Communist neighbors. It was NATO's intention that Europe would not be the next battleground.

NATO divided Europe into three sections: the Northern Flank encompassed Scandinavia, Denmark and Schleswig Holstein, the Central Region the remainder of Federal Germany and the Southern Flank Southwest Europe. The Soviet Union's Western Theater covers these areas, and is divided into three Theaters of Military Operations (TMO or TVD in Soviet parlance). The Northwestern TMO covers Scandinavia and the Baltic Coasts, while the Western TMO equates to the NATO Central Region. The Southwestern TMO is based on Bulgaria, Rumania and Hungary and is concerned with Italy, Greece and Western Turkey.

The 1950s brought the gradual realization that conventional forces alone might not be sufficient to counter a Soviet war machine seemingly unfettered by the budgetary constraints of a Western economy that had still to adjust to peace. At about the same time the Warsaw Pact, formed in 1955 following the admission of the Federal Republic of Germany (FRG) to NATO, had closed ranks and demonstrated its resolve by invading a member country, Hungary, in 1956 when it threatened to declare military neutrality. NATO's reliance on the nuclear deterrent in place of modernized conventional arms, the policy of Massive Retaliation, was being reconsidered by the end of the decade, while the formation of a multinational Allied Command Europe Mobile Force (ACE Mobile Force or AMF) ensured that Soviet aggression would initially be met by conventional arms.

A crucial element in the so-called Cold War which developments in the 1950s had precipitated was intelligence, with both superpowers engaged in a constant information-gathering process. One example of this, the operation of high-flying American U-2

spyplanes over Soviet territory, was abruptly terminated and an international incident precipitated when Gary Powers fell victim to a surface-to-air missile in 1960. Yet it was aerial reconnaissance that alerted the United States, two years later, to the establishment of Soviet missile bases in Cuba. President Kennedy's unequivocal response, the threat of all-out war, was the closest the world had yet come to World War 3. The folly of regarding nuclear weapons as substitutes for conventional arms was recognized by the adoption of a Flexible Response strategy, a mix of nuclear and conventional weapons providing counters to a number of possible Warsaw Pact gambits. The United States and Soviet Union were not alone in possessing a nuclear deterrent; France removed theirs from NATO in 1966, a decision that forced the removal of Supreme Headquarters Allied Powers Europe (SHAPE) from Paris to Mons in Belgium.

Since the early 1960s, the Soviet Union has re-emphasized its intentions on a global scale with the subjugation of Czechoslovakia (1968) and the invasion of Afghanistan in 1979. The United States' withdrawal

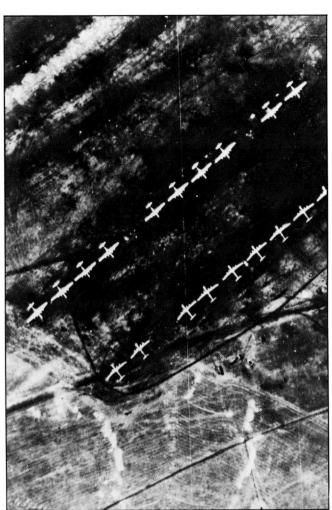

Left: Admiral Sergei Gorshkov, architect of Soviet naval power.
Above: Spy pilot Gary Powers and (right) one of the photographs he obtained in 1960.
Below: Soviet military supplies en route to Cuba, 1962.

Above: Soviet and US delegates continue SALT II talks in 1977. The treaty, though agreed, was never ratified.

from Vietnam after a long, vain and bloody attempt to stem the tide of Communism in Southeast Asia failed to dampen its determination to conclude Strategic Arms Limitation (SALT) treaties with the Soviet Union. While the interim SALT I agreement was signed in Moscow in 1972, seven subsequent years of delicate negotiation finally came to nothing when the US Senate refused to ratify SALT II following the Soviet incursion into Afghanistan.

In the nuclear sphere, the United States continues to rely on its Triad of land, sea and air-launched weapons, believing that this combination provides the greatest insurance possible against pre-emptive strike. Although President Carter's 1977 decision to scrap the B-1 bomber threatened to remove one option from the equation, the project's reinstatement by the Reagan administration and the planned introduction of a 'stealth' bomber by the 1990s suggests that the flexibility afforded by manned bombers will now remain a foundation-stone of US nuclear policy.

The likely battleground for a conventional land conflict would seem to be Western Europe, where NATO and Warsaw Pact troops and armor face each other at a constant state of readiness. This scenario has brought into play not only armor, infantry and artillery but also their airborne counterparts, notably tankbusting aircraft and helicopter gunships.

The main Soviet Army strategy is considered to be the pre-emptive strike, by which NATO command, control and communications (C^3) systems would be quickly immobilized before tactical nuclear weapons

could be brought into play. Crucial to this is the Soviet Operational Maneuver Group (OMG), which would aim to make good the success of any initial attack with assistance from air and heliborne troops. The US reponse is known as Airland Battle 2000, in which heliborne and mechanized forces aim to knock out this Soviet second wave, crossing borders to do so if necessary.

The growth of the Soviet Navy under the direction of Admiral Sergei Gorshkov since the mid 1950s was finally being matched in the 1980s by a parallel expansion in the US Navy. The shifting balance of sea power, which saw mass obsolescence strike the US Fleet while the Soviet Navy commanded the lion's share of military expenditure, was reversed by President Reagan's pledge to equip a 600-ship navy and the impending retirement of Admiral Gorshkov himself. It remained to be seen how far the pendulum would swing the other way.

The weapons and organizations described in the pages that follow are indeed impressive. Yet it is by no means certain that the information contained herein has not already been superseded by the multi-million-dollar arms race that, for all the efforts of politicians, seems all too frequently to outstrip efforts for multinational disarmament. It is certain, however, that the equipment described here will play a major, if not a decisive, part in any future conflict.

ARMIES
OF THE WORLD

CHARLES MESSENGER

Previous page: Soldiers rapelling from a Canadian Armed Forces UH-1 helicopter. In British military parlance, the technique is termed abseiling.
Below: Canadian infantry launch an attack from their Grizzly armored personnel carrier.

THE ARMIES LINE UP

In order to make a comprehensive evaluation of the armies of World War III, it is necessary to have an understanding of the higher command organizations of the two alliances. Clausewitz's often quoted dictum that war is a continuation of national policy is reflected in the structures of both, in that the highest policy making bodies of each are political rather than military.

NATO is headed by the North Atlantic Council which is made up of representatives of all member nations. These can either be permanent representatives or national ministers, dependent on what there is to be discussed. The Chairman is the Secretary General, appointed on the approval of all member states, and is currently Lord Carrington, Britain's former Foreign Secretary. All decisions are taken by common consent rather than majority vote. Below this comes the Defense Planning Committee (DPC), which is also chaired by the Secretary General and consists of a permanent representative from each of the member states in the integrated military structure, which excludes France. Below these two bodies come the civil and military structures. The former consists of a number of committees ranging from political and

economic affairs, science, armaments, nuclear planning and communications. The latter is the Military Committee, headed by a President, at the time of writing General Sverre Hamre of Norway, and a Chairman, Admiral Robert H Falls of Canada, as well as a Deputy Chairman. Each nation has a permanent military member who sits on the Committee, except for the French, who have a military mission and exercise a watching brief. The role of the Committee is to make recommendations to the Council and DPC on military matters, and to give guidance on military questions to Allied commanders and subordinate military authorities.

Below the Military Committee come the three major NATO Commands – Allied Command Europe (ACE), Allied Command Atlantic (ACLANT) and Allied Command Channel (ACCHAN). The last two named Commands are essentially maritime and outside the scope of this book. Allied Command Europe is commanded by SACEUR through SHAPE at Mons in Belgium. He is always an American, and is currently General Bernard W Rogers. He has five subordinate commands under him. To cover the Northern Flank is Allied Forces Northern Europe

Left: Soviet ASU-85 85mm tank destroyers.
Above: Soviet Naval Infantry dismount from a BTR-60P APC.

(AFNORTH) with Allied Forces North Norway, Allied Forces South Norway and Allied Forces Baltic Approaches under it. Headquarters is at Kolsos in Norway. Allied Forces Southern Europe (AFSOUTH) with headquarters at Naples, Italy, has five subordinate commands – Allied Land Forces Southern Europe, Allied Land Forces Southeastern Europe, Allied Air Forces Southern Europe, Allied Naval Forces Southern Europe and Naval Striking and Support Forces Southern Europe. The ACE Mobile Force is also directly under command of SACEUR and has its headquarters at Seckenheim in the FRG. Furthermore, the United Kingdom Air Forces Command (HQ High Wycombe, England) is also under SACEUR's direct control.

This leaves the Central Region, the focus of attention for this book. The Command responsible for this is Allied Forces Central Europe (AFCENT), which is based at Brunssum in the Netherlands. Under it come two army groups and two tactical air forces. The northern part of the region, with attention fixed mainly on the North German Plain, is covered by the Northern Army Group (NORTHAG) and supported by 2nd Allied Tactical Air Force (2 ATAF). Both headquarters are located at Rheindahlen near

Moenchen Gladbach in Germany. NORTHAG has four national army corps under command, reading north to south, I Netherlands (NE) Corps, I German (GE) Corps, I British (BR) Corps and I Belgian (BE) Corps. In the south is Central Army Group (CENTAG), supported by 4 ATAF, with headquarters of both at Heidelburg. The four corps under command of CENTAG read from north to south as follows: III(GE) Corps, V(US) Corps, VII(US) Corps and II(GE) Corps.

The main difference between the Warsaw Pact and NATO higher command structures is that, whereas NATO defense policy is formulated as a result of consensus among the member states, that of the Pact is dictated by the Soviet Union, with the other member states having little influence. On the surface, nevertheless, this essential difference appears blurred. As NATO has its Council, so the Warsaw Pact is headed by the Political Consultative Committee, which has political representatives of the Pact member countries on it. Although, it is supposed to direct all Pact cultural, political and economic activities, it seldom meets more than once or twice a year, and has never been involved in major decision making. Below it appear the Combined Secretariat and the Permanent Commission. The former is responsible for logistics and armaments, including research and development (R&D) within the Pact,

Left: Soviet T-55s on the march.
Above: Soviet BMP mechanized infantry combat vehicles.

while the latter makes foreign policy recommendations to both the Political Consultative Committee and the Permanent Commission. There is also a Committee of Defense Ministers made up of the Defense Ministers of all Pact nations and always chaired by the Soviet Defense Minister. It is significant that all these bodies are based in Moscow. As for the military side of the higher organization, the Combined Supreme Command is headed by the Supreme Commander of the Combined Forces of the Warsaw Pact, who is always a Russian, and is currently Marshal of the Soviet Union Viktor G Kulikov. The Combined Supreme Command was based in Moscow until late 1971 when, as a sop to the other Pact members it was moved to Lvov in Poland. In peacetime it exercises command over all Russian ground and air forces based in the three most western Soviet Military Districts, all Soviet ground and air forces based in the satellite countries and all GDR air

and ground forces. In wartime, other Pact member forces would also come under its command. Its staff, including the Chief of Staff, is overwhelmingly Russian, although officers from other Pact countries do serve on it. The Supreme Commander also chairs the Military Council of the Warsaw Pact Forces, which is there to advise him on planning and operational aspects, and is made up of representatives of the member states.

Thus it will be seen that the Soviet Union exerts an iron grip on the Pact as a whole. Furthermore, the Supreme Commander is also a member of the Soviet Main Military Council, along with the Soviet Chief of Staff, 1st Deputy Defense Minister, 1st Deputy Chairman of the KGB and the Minister for Internal Affairs, and hence the Soviets can also influence the Pact through this route as well as through the Soviet Minister of Defense.

Under the Combined Supreme Command of the Warsaw Pact come the TMOs, and below them fronts. Each TMO has its own air force, made up of ground support, interdiction and helicopter elements, as well as an air defense force (PVO). Fronts equate to the NATO army groups. Thus the Central European Theater of Military Operations is likely to have three fronts, North, Central and Southwestern, which would be activated in wartime. As it is, the peacetime organization is very much built round the Groups of Soviet Forces based in the satellite countries. The most important of these is the Group of Soviet Forces Germany (GSFG), which is made up of five armies, comprising in total ten tank, ten motor rifle and one artillery division, as well as an air assault brigade. The headquarters of GSFG is at Zossen-Wunsdorf outside Berlin, and this would become the TMO HQ in wartime. Also under command of GSFG are two tank and four motor rifle divisions of the People's Army of the GDR. The Soviet Central Group of Forces based in Czechoslovakia (CGF) has two armies (three tank, three motor rifle divisions). The Soviet forces stationed in Hungary are known as the Southern Group of Forces (SGF), and its headquarters in Budapest would probably become the HQ of the Southwestern TMO. In Poland the Soviets have two motor rifle divisions based in the west of the country which make up the Northern Group of Forces (NGF). The NGF would be incorporated in the Central European TMO. As for the Northern TMO, two Soviet divisions are permanently based near the border with Norway, and the remainder would come, in time of war from the Leningrad Military District and the Baltic states.

All the Warsaw Pact armies are conscript, with the period of service being two years or eighteen months. For the Soviet Army the period is two years and conscripts are called up twice a year in May/June and November/December. Service is broken down into four six month periods. The first six months will see the conscript doing his basic military training and learning his trade, be it tank driver or radar operator. During this time conditions are harsh. If he is a combat soldier as opposed to a specialist he will carry this out in his combat unit, and then spend the next two perfecting his skills, and the last handing his expertise over to his replacement. His noncoms are made up of approximately one third regulars and two thirds conscripts like himself, who have been selected for special training after their first few weeks service. His officers will be for the most part regulars, although a number will be university graduates who have qualified as reserve officers and are serving for one to three years. The regular officers will have served between three and six years at a military academy before being commissioned, and will receive further training at advanced academies and staff colleges as they proceed upwards through the ranks.

In the past, two weaknesses of the Soviet Army have been made much of in Western writing. The first is the lack of initiative allowed at middle and lower levels. It has always been contended that the

Above: Warsaw Pact troops with SA-7 Grail surface-to-air missile launchers.
Right: Soviet soldiers in Afghanistan.
Below right: BTR-60Ps in typical attack formation.

rigidity of the communist system would not countenance any deviation from the official line, and that this was reflected as much in the armed forces as any other sector of Soviet society. This, however, is no longer so. During the past decade, the Soviet High Command has realized that too much rigidity conflicts with the fast moving battle which it is intending to fight. The middle and junior commanders are therefore being encouraged to use their initiative very much more than hitherto, and this is likely to grow further in the years ahead. The other is the Soviet lack of experience in action since 1945, something which was a popular accusation in the late Sixties and early Seventies, when the US Army was experiencing much high intensity fighting in Southeast Asia. For a start, Afghanistan, with upwards of 120,000 Soviet soldiers being stationed there at any one time, is providing valuable operational experience. Furthermore, the Soviet missions to Third World countries often find themselves embroiled in local wars, which gives them not just experience, but also the chance to handle and evaluate Soviet military equipment in active service conditions. Two prime examples are the campaign in the Ogaden between Ethiopia and Somalia in 1978, which produced important lessons in the value of heliborne operations, and the Middle East, where Soviet advisers in Syria gained particular experience in the effectiveness of their air defense systems during the fighting in the Lebanon in 1982.

The quality of the armies of the other Warsaw Pact members is more questionable. Probably the best is that of the GDR, the most enthusiastic nation other than the Soviet Union about the Pact. Training and approach, as well as tactics, in the other armies

Above left: Canadian infantry dismount from a Bell UH-1D.
Below left: Soviet infantry suppress a strongpoint with AK-47 assault rifles and 30mm grenade launchers, supported by BMPs.
Above: Infrared goggles enable the soldier to see at night.
Top right: US troops in Vietnam.
Above right: US infantryman with M-16 Armalite rifle.

Below: US soldier training with a laser fire simulator.

Above: Dutch YP-408 wheeled APCs.

mirror the Soviet Army, and much of the equipment used is Soviet, which gives the Pact a distinct advantage over NATO in terms of commonality of weapons systems. Nevertheless, there is a distinct political question mark on their will to fight. Apart from in the GDR, relations between Soviet troops stationed in Eastern Europe and the local populations are lukewarm at best. Indeed, the Soviet troops are allowed little contact with their 'hosts'. It may therefore be that the Soviet Union will not commit satellite armies to the offensive unless it is forced to do so. There is also the danger of unrest within Eastern Europe, which may force the USSR to keep troops stationed there.

NATO's main problem is lack of standardization. This is not just in equipment, but in tactics, organization and training. While the US, British and Canadian Armies are all-regular, the remainder are largely conscript, with varying terms of service. Thus while, the German conscript serves for fifteen months, his Belgian counterpart, if posted to Germany, has only an eight month term. Within the Central Region, the two largest ground force contingents are those of the FRG and the USA.

The US Army went through a difficult period in the Seventies. Although Vietnam had given it extensive operational experience, much of it was not applicable to Europe and the emphasis in approach had to be radically changed. Vietnam had also been a chastening experience. The growing unpopularity of the war had isolated the US Armed Forces and morale

suffered, and the incidence of drug taking and 'fragging' rose alarmingly. The decision to end conscription and move to a volunteer army also took time to implement, and the early volunteers were of low caliber. Budgetary restrictions meant cutbacks, and these together with the recession resulted in US servicemen abroad, especially in Germany, finding it difficult to make ends meet financially.

In the past few years there has been a radical change. The Army is obtaining a much higher quality of recruit and much effort has gone into improving terms and conditions of service. A further move to raise morale has been the introduction of a regimental system, whereby a soldier will serve as much as possible with one particular unit, on much the same lines as the British system. In addition, the Cohort Scheme, provides for companies of recruits to do their basic training together and then be posted *en bloc* overseas, so that they will continue to soldier with one another. The adoption of the Airland concept as official doctrine has instilled the Army with a much more positive sense of purpose, and recent and ongoing equipment improvements are resulting in a more dynamic force.

The armed forces of the Federal Republic of Germany, the Bundeswehr, came into existence in 1955, when the FRG was made a member of NATO. With the spectre of the first half of the 20th Century there to haunt them, the government was determined that never again would the armed forces be allowed to dictate policy. Emphasis was therefore placed on the concept of the 'civilian in uniform', and the fact that the Bundeswehr was an entirely new force with no connection with its predecessor, the Wehrmacht. A further constitutional point is that the Bundeswehr is strictly for defense of the homeland and will never be operationally deployed outside the borders of the FRG in pursuit of national policy. With these restrictions it might seem that the result would be an ineffectual force, but this is not so. German soldiers have always been first class and, although they only serve for 15 months, they quickly reach a high standard of training, and are led by professional officers and senior noncoms. In terms of equipment, too, much of it is home produced and among the best in the world.

The other two volunteer armies, those of the Canadians and British, are both very professional. Although the Canadian contribution to the Central Region is small, one brigade group, which is the CENTAG immediate reserve, it is nonetheless valuable for that. Canadian troops have also had much recent experience in peacekeeping operations overseas. The British Army, too, is finely honed. Continuing operational experience in Northern Ireland, although in many ways frustrating, does have one bonus in the valuable experience it gives to junior commanders, both officers and noncoms, and this was amply demonstrated in the 1982 Falklands Campaign. The latter also confirmed that British Army training in general was on the right lines and provided a useful operational evaluation of weapons systems.

The other NATO armies are all conscript. They also suffer from continuing budgetary problems, which makes the procurement of high technology weapons systems more and more of an uphill struggle. This is most marked on the Southern Flank, where Turkey, although a very loyal member of NATO, possesses an army with largely obsolescent equipment, but lacks the money to modernize on her own. The same, too, can be said for NATO's newest member, Spain. The other problem on the Southern Flank is Greece. Her continuing feud with Turkey over Cyprus does result in difficulties in cooperation between the two. Nevertheless, the will is there.

The problem of standardization of equipment is one with which NATO has grappled since its inception. The root of it lies in the fact that, being a democratic organization, its members are there largely for reasons of self interest. When it comes to weapons and equipment, there is an understandable concern to maintain national defense industries. Yet, there has been some progress, both in terms of collaborative projects and agreements such as that on the standard NATO small arms round, which is currently 7.62mm but is soon to change to 5.56mm. NATO, however, will never reach the level of standardization of the Warsaw Pact.

There is also independence of thought in tactical concepts. Thus, in the Central Region, while all national corps observe the policy of Forward Defense, there are different interpretations of it. While the Germans understandably obey it to the letter and will not give ground until forced to do so, the other national corps take a slightly more flexible approach. One other difficulty is over language, but this is also the same for the Warsaw Pact, where, although the official language is Russian, many of the Soviet recruits from the more farflung Soviet Socialist Republics cannot speak it. With NATO, the official language is English, and this is spoken at all integrated headquarters. Within the national corps, the national language is spoken, and with corps of different nations fighting side by side, the requirement for liaison officers who are bilingual becomes most important. One area where standardization has made much progress within NATO is over staff procedures and the majority of operational procedures are now common for all member armies.

When considering the relative strengths between the two alliances, it is difficult to be precise in terms of numbers of men and weapons equipments. Indeed, estimates vary enormously. To give but one example, NATO believes that it is outnumbered by as much as 3:1 in tanks in the Central Region, whereas the Soviet Union will only admit to a very slight advantage in its favor, arguing that NATO estimates do not take into account those tanks in storage. Any figures thus given can only be approximations.

On the Northern Flank, the Soviet Union has two motor rifle divisions permanently stationed facing a single Norwegian brigade. In time of war, she could reinforce these with an additional seven divisions from Leningrad, which would give her a total of some 1700 tanks and 2000 artillery pieces and mortars. NATO meanwhile could field a total of some 13 infantry brigades, but these would be for the defense of not just Norway, but Denmark and Schleswig Holstein as well. In the Central Region, including indigenous forces based in national territory, but excluding those in North America, NATO has available some 39 divisions, with 7700 tanks and 4550 artillery/mortar pieces. Opposing these are 95 Warsaw Pact divisions with approximately 25,000 tanks and 17,500 artillery/mortar pieces. Eight divisions (1250 tanks, 1550 artillery/mortar pieces) in Italy face 17 divisions (4300 tanks and 2700 artillery/mortar pieces) in Hungary, while Greece and Turkey in Europe can muster 25 divisions (2900 tanks, 2850 artillery/mortar pieces) to oppose 33 Warsaw Pact divisions (6900 tanks, 5700 artillery/mortar pieces) in Bulgaria and Romania. Finally Turkey will have to defend her eastern border with the Soviet Union with 12 divisions (1000 tanks, 1800 artillery/mortar pieces) against 19 Soviet divisions (4100 tanks and 4000 artillery/mortar pieces).

It would seem, therefore, that NATO is seriously

outnumbered on every front, but these bald figures do not give the complete picture. For a start, only those Soviet divisions stationed in other Warsaw Pact member states are maintained at close to established strength, along with her eight airborne divisions. Of the 67 divisions based in European USSR, about half are maintained at 70% strength, and could be brought up to full establishment in a few days. The remainder are kept at less than a third of established strength. These also could be fully mobilized within days. The remainder of the total standing force of some 175 divisions would, apart from those stationed on the Sino-Soviet border and in Afghanistan, take much longer to mobilize and would have obsolete equipment. Furthermore, there is the question of the reliability of the satellite armies. In particular, Romania, which has always taken a very independent line, might well decline to join in military action, which would remove her nine divisions from those facing Greece and Turkey.

NATO also has a number of its divisions and

Below: Infrared jammer on a UH-1H helicopter.
Bottom: British Scorpion light tanks firing by night.
Right: Canadian West German built Leopard 1.

corps at less than full strength. While the US Army in Europe (USAREUR) requires four brigades and some individual reinforcements from CONUS, the frontline German corps are almost up to strength. 1(BR) Corps, however, relies on a full infantry division being deployed from the UK, and for unit reinforcements to bolster its three divisions in place in Germany. 1(BE) Corps relies on the third brigade of each of its two divisions being mobilized in time, and 1(NL) Corps has to mobilize one of its three divisions from scratch. However, the US Army could fly across a complete corps of three divisions, III(US) Corps from CONUS in a matter of days to reinforce the Central Region, and there is also France, whose strength has not been included in the calculations so far. Although, she is no longer part of the NATO military infrastructure, she has made it very clear that a Warsaw Pact invasion of the Central Region would be a direct threat to her and that she would give military support to NATO in that event. At present she is restructuring her forces to create a Rapid Action Force of one light armored division and four antitank infantry divisions with significant helicopter support, one of whose roles would be to provide indepth support to NATO forces. This would be a valuable addition.

If the Warsaw Pact intends to launch an attack against NATO territory, it must decide how much warning time it is prepared to give NATO of its intentions. The more divisions it mobilizes, the stronger its forces, but this will take time, and will be a major indicator to NATO. In turn, therefore, it will allow NATO to deploy more forces before hostilities break out, which will make the Warsaw Pact task that much more difficult. NATO planners are fully aware of this and consider that there are three possible scenarios.

In the first, which is currently seen as the most likely, there will be a period of growing tension, at some point during which the Warsaw Pact will begin to mobilize. NATO will do likewise, and the two alliances would sit and glower at one another. At this point the tension would cease rising and probably drop. After a period of time, NATO would withdraw most of its forces from their deployment positions, and it would be then that the Warsaw Pact would choose to invade. In other words, they would sacrifice strategic for tactical surprise. Alternatively, NATO might receive a seven day warning of the outbreak of hostilities. This would allow both sides just time enough to mobilize their first line reserves and deploy them. Finally, the third option is where the Soviets may decide to sacrifice force for surprise and initially use just those divisions in the GDR, Poland, Hungary and Czechoslovakia, which are, of course, virtually fully up to strength. In this event, NATO would receive as little as 48 hours warning, and, given this, the Soviets would catch the Alliance while it was still deploying, which, in itself, would be a force multiplier.

The next question is the means which NATO would have at its disposal in order to obtain warning of an impending attack. There are several. Some indication of Warsaw Pact intentions would probably be obtained from the political signalling during the period of tension. Warsaw Pact deployment is also likely to take place under the guise of field maneuvers. However, any NATO or Warsaw Pact exercise involving over 25,000 men in Europe must, as a result of the Helsinki agreements, be notified to the opposing alliance. Thus, large scale maneuvers by the Warsaw Pact in a period of political tension would be regarded with grave suspicion by NATO. If, however, the Warsaw Pact failed to inform NATO, there are other ways of detecting that they are taking place. One method would be through the US and British Military Missions to East Germany. It was originally agreed at Potsdam that the Soviets, British and Americans would exchange military missions within the zones of occupation in Germany. This has never been rescinded and, although both sides impose rigid restrictions on the activities of these missions, they do provide a very useful window into the enemy's camp. Information might also come from espionage, defectors or refugees.

There are, however, a number of surveillance devices which can be employed. Intelligence satellites (Intelsats) are being put up in increasing numbers by both the Soviets and Americans, and much intelligence can be gained from the pictures which they transmit back to earth. Many people believe that they are so effective that nothing can be hidden from them. This, however, is an exaggeration and they do have their drawbacks, and there have been many examples of this during the last decade. They failed to detect the Egyptian preparations for crossing the Suez Canal in October 1973, and led to an incorrect estimate of the number of Cubans on the island of Grenada prior to the US invasion in the fall of 1983. These are but two incidents. Nevertheless, they are an invaluable intelligence tool. Coming closer to earth, there are the so called 'spy planes'. The Lockheed U-2 is still in service, and has now been joined by the TR-1, which is a derivative and very similar in configuration. The most outstanding, though, of this type of aircraft is the Lockheed SR-71 Blackbird. It can cruise at a speed of over 2000mph for over two hours at a height of 15 miles, and carries a long focus camera which can cover 125 miles of ground with one shot. It also has infrared (IR) cameras which can photograph through clouds, and sideways looking airborne radar (SLAR).

A further intelligence source lies in the field of communications and electronics. Two forms of intelligence are involved here, communications intelligence (COMINT) and electronic intelligence (ELINT). COMINT involves the monitoring of

US Nike-Hercules air defense missile.

radio nets, and much information can be picked up from them. In order to minimize this, communicators using insecure nets use special voice codes, but these can be often quickly broken. Also, voice nets down to battalion level are now usually secure. This is done by scrambling the speech as it passes through the transmitter. Nevertheless, the signal is still detectable, even though it is indecipherable, and radio direction finding (RDF) equipment can pinpoint its location. It is also possible by analysing the amount of signals traffic and knowing its location to work out what type of station it is – headquarters, logistic, artillery etc. It is not, however, only radios which give out detectable signals, but radars as well, and they can also be pinpointed. Position finding of both radios and radars is known as ELINT.

ELINT and COMINT are but one weapon in the field of electronic warfare (EW) and are known as EW Support Measures (ESM) or Passive Electronic Countermeasures (ECM). A third measure which comes under this category is deception. Here, by sending out false information over the radio, especially on a known enemy frequency or spurious signals, the object is to confuse and misinform the enemy. There is also Active ECM, which takes the form of jamming of radio nets and radars and physical destruction. Jamming is a very effective method, especially against forward radio nets in a fast moving battle or air defense radars, and the destruction of headquarters and communication centers (commcens), having located them through RDF, could be carried out by artillery fire, air strike or special forces, leaving enemy forces without effective control.

C^3 is vital to the successful conduct of the modern battle, and both sides will strive to protect their systems against attack, electronic or physical. The methods they use to do this come under the broad heading of Electronic Counter Counter Measures (ECCM). The longer the transmission the more likely the transmitter will be located. Hence, one key to successful ECCM is to keep transmissions as short as possible. This can be done to an extent through good radio discipline, but modern radio design now has potential for what is known as 'burst transmission', where the transmission is sent out as a concentrated short, sharp burst. Another technical ploy is 'frequency hopping', where each transmission makes use of a number of frequencies.

Headquarters are very vulnerable to physical destruction. Also, the higher the level of the HQ, the larger it is. Thus, while a battalion HQ consists of no more than five or six vehicles, that for a division will be ten times the size. Concealment, which is one means of protection, is therefore harder. Physical protection, in the form of making all HQ vehicles armored, also helps. Another form of this is putting the headquarters in cellars, or even building hardened bunkers in peacetime in which to house it. The other form of protection is never to stay too long in the same location. As a normal rule, HQs will move at least once every 24 hours, and always have an alternate HQ or 'step up', which can take over if the main HQ is moving or attacked.

The electronic battle is just as important as the fire fight, and the measures being employed in it are becoming ever more sophisticated.

Deterrent or threat? A nuclear weapon explosion.

NUCLEAR, CHEMICAL AND BIOLOGICAL

The most awesome aspect of World War III is the very real possibility that nuclear, chemical and even biological (NBC) weapons might be employed. These threaten the very continued existence of the human race. Yet, paradoxically, their very existence has been a major reason why World War III has not so far broken out. Indeed, their very awfulness has been and is a very effective deterrent.

NATO still holds to the doctrine of Flexible Response, which was described in the previous chapter, while the Warsaw Pact believes in the ability to win a war fought at any level. Up until now, NATO has viewed tactical nuclear weapons as a force multiplier and has believed that selective use of them would make the Russians stop and reconsider. The Soviets, however, have a different perspective. If they are to overrun Western Europe, they must also concern themselves with the strategic nuclear threat from CONUS. Furthermore, they do not believe that it is possible to fight a limited nuclear war. On the other hand, although the Soviets have made a 'no first use' declaration, it is quite possible that they might well seriously consider the use of tactical nuclear weapons if their offensive had become bogged down, or if they thought that NATO was about to use them. One of their key initial objectives, however, is the identifica-

tion and destruction of NATO tactical nuclear weapon sites, and failure to achieve this might also tempt them into a nuclear strike. Nevertheless, within NATO circles there are increasing doubts as to the relevance of the tactical nuclear weapon, and in the future, less reliance is likely to be placed on it. It is, however, very unlikely that it will vanish from the battlefield, especially as long as the Warsaw Pact possesses it, and the prospect of the nuclear battle-field remains.

There are three basic categories of nuclear weapon, although the boundaries between them are difficult to define precisely. Strategic systems, which are outside the scope of this book, refer to interconti-nental systems, land, air or sea-launched. These launch media are generally referred to as the 'nuclear triad'. They have a very high yield, and examples are the US Minuteman and Trident and the Soviet SS-18 and SS-19. The next category are known as theater nuclear weapons. These are limited by range to particular theaters of operations, ie Europe. It is over these that the current nuclear debate is focussed. When the Russians began to deploy the SS-20, a mobile rocket system with a range of almost 3000 miles, west of the Urals in the mid-Seventies, NATO became increasingly concerned. The existing Per-

shing Is had a much smaller yield in comparison and only had a range of 500 miles. The only other weapon that they had which could match it without using strategic weapons was aerial delivery, using the General Dynamics FB-111. The decision was therefore taken in 1979 to modernize the theater nuclear forces (TNF) in Europe by deploying Pershing II, with over double the range of its predecessor, and the Cruise system, a very accurate weapon with a range of 1700 miles, which is designed to fly at low level in order to avoid radar defenses. It is an ideal weapon against fixed targets, but its slow speed means that it is not suitable against mobile targets. The Soviets see this deployment as a very grave threat and, in retaliation, are now deploying theater systems in the satellite countries. An offer by the US not to deploy Cruise and Pershing if the Soviets would dismantle their SS-20s was not taken up. However, these systems are more likely to be used against strategic targets in Europe such as seats of government.

Tactical nuclear weapons are, on the other hand, very much part of the land battlefield. They are low yield with ranges limited to less than one hundred miles. NATO has two missile systems which it uses in this role, Lance and Honest John, while the Warsaw Pact equivalents are the FROG and SCUD

Far left: US FB-111 bomber launching Short Range Attack Missile (SRAM) which carries a 200KT warhead 100 miles.
Left: Soviet SCUD-B tactical nuclear missiles with a range of some 150 miles.
Below: Soviet FROG-7 with a range of 40 miles.

series. There are also nuclear shells which can be fired from conventional artillery guns, and NATO uses the M110 203mm self-propelled howitzer for this, as well as in conventional roles.

There are five major effects of nuclear weapons – heat, blast, immediate and residual radiation, and electromagnetic pulse (EMP). The core of a nuclear explosion is at a very high temperature, which can be measured in millions of degrees centigrade. Thermal radiation being emitted by the core causes a fireball around it, and this produces dazzle and heat effects. Dazzle caused by the brightness of the burst can produce temporary blindness, and a few might suffer retinal burns if their eyes were focussed directly on the explosion. The thermal effects are caused by flash and flame. Flash causes first and second degree burns to exposed skin, and will set clothing, dry grass and undergrowth alight within a certain range of the

explosion. The smaller the yield, the more likely that these effects will be felt, since the thermal radiation arrives more quickly and produces a sharper temperature rise. Blast consists of a shock wave caused by the explosion, and a wind which follows closely behind it. While the former will blow objects in its path down, and be reflected if they are solid, the wind produces a drag effect.

Radiation exists in four forms – alpha, beta, gamma and neutron. Alpha and beta particles have little penetrating power, although the former can cause damage to human tissue if inhaled or absorbed through an open wound. Neither is of much military significance. Gamma and neutron particles are, however, highly penetrative, and it is from them that most casualties are caused. They attack the body cells, and bone marrow, which produces new blood cells, and the lining of the intestine and brain and

Previous page: Multiple Launch Rocket System (MLRS) in action. This can be used to deliver chemical warheads.
Left: Setting up a SCUD launch position.
Above: SS-21 launcher vehicle. SS-21 is to replace FROG in Soviet use.

muscle cells are also particularly susceptible. The amount of damage caused to the individual is dependent on the dose received, and is measured in terms of rads. By way of example, a dose of up to 150 rads will cause no immediate effects, while between 150 and 250 rads will result in nausea and vomiting within 24 hours, but recovery within 48 hours. A 250–350 rad dose brings about nausea and vomiting within four hours, and then the patient will appear to recover. However, the symptoms will then reappear leading to some deaths within two to four weeks. 350–600 rads produces the initial symptoms within two hours and prolonged incapacity. Half of those exposed to a 450 rad dose will die within two to four weeks. Over 600 rads results in almost 100% deaths in one week, while 3000 causes total incapacitation within one hour. Neutron radiation is more complex because, unlike gamma particles which react with the electrons in the atoms of the target, it reacts with the nuclei of these atoms. It can either bounce off, thereby displacing the atom, or be absorbed by the nucleus, which will result in the emission of gamma radiation. Ionization is likely to be caused and this will effect the electrical properties of the target.

Immediate radiation is that which is emitted within one minute of the burst, and will result in neutron and gamma radiation, with the former traveling very much faster than the latter. In order to give some idea of the results of immediate radiation, an individual unprotected at 1000 yards from a 20 kiloton (KT) burst could expect to receive 3000 rads in ten seconds. Residual radiation, on the other hand, is mainly made up of gamma and beta radiation, and

is spread either through neutron induced activity (NIA) or fallout. NIA means that all material close to the burst is bombarded by neutrons which may react with the nuclei of some of the target atoms to produce radioactive isotopes, while fallout represents the radioactive material which falls to earth, and will be carried by the prevailing winds. Both types of residual radiation do decay, and as a very rough rule, what is known as the Seven and Ten Law is applied. If the time after the burst is multiplied by seven, the dose rate is divided by ten. Thus, if the dose rate is 1000 rads per hour one hour after the explosion, it will drop to 100 rads per hour seven hours later.

The electromagnetic effects of a nuclear explosion are often ignored, but are very significant. They come in two forms. Firstly, there is the emission of a pulse of electromagnetic (EMP) radiation, and then there are changes in the electromagnetic characteristics of the atmosphere due to ionizing radiation from the explosion and fallout, together with an excess of vapor. While the first can cause direct damage to electrical and radio equipment, the latter brings about a radar and radio blackout or propagation problems which can last for several hours. In particular EMP can cause insulation failures in cables, the tripping of relays and circuit breakers by excessive induced voltages, direct damage to signal equipment and items which contain magnetics can be upset by induced magnetic fields. As for the ionization aspect, it is High Frequency (HF) radios and radars which will be the most affected. Such a possible breakdown in communications and surveillance equipment could be very damaging.

The degree of these effects is dependent not only on the size of the nuclear warhead and the distance away from the explosion, but also on the height of the burst above ground. This is defined as high or low airburst, surface and subsurface burst. A high air-

Left: A US Pershing 2 being fired. Now being deployed to
Europe it can carry a 200KT warhead 1000 miles.
Above: A US 203mm M110 self-propelled howitzer which
can fire small yield nuclear and chemical warheads.

burst is ideal for 'soft' targets, like men in the open,
and will also produce the most effective disruption
of long range radio communications. A low airburst,
on the other hand, probably produces the best
balance of effects against the majority of targets likely
to be found on the battlefield, but each separate
weapon yield has its own optimum height of burst for
producing the maximum casualties and damage, and
these are laid out in tables. A surface burst, where the
fireball actually touches the ground, is known as a
'dirty' explosion because of the large amounts of fall
out which it produces. It would only be used against
very hard targets or to contaminate a very large area,
and is unlikely to be used on the battlefield. Sub
surface bursts are used in atomic demolition mines
(ADM) as a means of causing extensive demolitions,
but this form of tactical nuclear weapon is now being
phased out.

A 15 KT airburst would produce the following
approximate affects to men in certain situations
within certain radii of the burst, or what is known as
Ground Zero (GZ):

a. Men, unwarned and unprotected except by
   normal combat clothing could expect to be
   decapacitated by blast and radiation within
   1050m of GZ and suffer second degree burns
   within 1400m.
b. If they are in slit trenches with some overhead
   cover, they will not be affected by thermal
   effects, but will suffer badly from radiation
   within 800m and blast within 400m.
c. If they are in armored personnel carriers
   (APC), blast will cause casualties to them and
   their vehicles within 600m and radiation
   within 950m.
d. In main battle tanks they will survive blast
   above 500m from GZ and radiation above
   750m.

From this it will be seen that a measure of protection
against nuclear weapons is possible.

Individual protection comes from a sound knowledge of the immediate action drills and the wearing
of protective clothing. If a nuclear burst is spotted,
the immediate action is to close the eyes to protect
them from the flash and go to ground, covering all
exposed parts of the body, and to remain there until
the shock wave and wind have passed. Radiation is
guarded against by the wearing of respirators and

NBC clothing. All Warsaw Pact and NATO armies are equipped with this, and do much of their training wearing it. In terms of comfort, NATO has the edge over its potential adversary, who uses suits, overboots and gloves made of a rubberized material, which is comparatively bulky and very uncomfortable to wear for a long period, especially when the weather is hot. NATO armies have long used clothing made up of charcoal-based materials, which is much lighter than the Warsaw Pact equivalent. Nevertheless, eating, drinking and other bodily functions in a contaminated area are very difficult to carry out, and some are impossible to do without being contaminated. A more satisfactory way of enduring the nuclear battlefield is by collective protection. Almost all armored fighting vehicles (AFV) are equipped with so-called collective NBC protection, meaning creating an NBC free atmosphere within the vehicle. This is done by sealing the crew compartment, both physically and by creating an air overpressure inside, with air from the outside being passed through charcoal filters in order to decontaminate it. Another form of collective protection is the construction of shelters with sufficient overhead earth cover. Thus, a shelter with three feet of overhead earth cover will give the individuals inside more than ten times the level of protection against residual radiation that of those in a main battle tank, and two hundred times that of an unprotected man in the open.

Nevertheless, soldiers are going to have to fight on a contaminated battlefield without the advantage of collective protection, and it is most important that commanders constantly monitor individual radiation levels. For this, personal dosimeters are provided and the latest British example is worn like a watch on the wrist. The commander checks it with another instrument which gives a read out in rads, and from this he can determine the radiation status of his unit. Once a unit has reached a certain radiation level, usually 150 rads, they should be withdrawn to a decontaminated area, but must, before anything else, decontaminate themselves. This normally takes the form of hosing down with water and detergent.

It is also important to know precisely the extent of a contaminated area. After the burst, it is possible to be able to predict the rate and area of contamination by residual radiation if Ground Zero, the speed and direction of the wind, height and time of burst are known, as well as a rough idea of the yield. This will enable troops in that area to receive warning and prepare themselves. However, this must be confirmed later by radiation survey and constantly monitored.

Although neither side will be likely to use nuclear weapons at the outset of hostilities, nuclear planning

Left: German NBC clothing. Note special overboot on right foot.

36

will be carried out and is a constant process. There will be a continuous updating of information on targets. Both sides will be looking especially for concentrations of troops to make a worthwhile target, and indeed one of the commander's major problems is in trying to achieve the right balance between sufficient concentration to make a conventional attack and defend against it, and dispersing his troops so as not to make an obvious nuclear target. Target location, type, size and shape are particularly important aspects. At the same time, nuclear planning staffs must be aware of the positions of friendly troops, their radiation states and level of protection, as well as the direction of the wind. They will also need from the commander, guidance on the level of damage required, the acceptable risk to own troops and any particular limiting requirements. Knowing what nuclear weapons and warheads they have available, they can then select the most suitable system for the target and determine the required height of burst, ground zero and the time of burst, as well as predicted coverage. As a basic rule, the minimum yield available which will give adequate target coverage is selected. If nuclear release is then given, it is important to warn friendly troops in the area so that they can take precautions, but this must not be done too soon as the enemy is also likely to be warned. Once, however, the first tactical nuclear weapon has been exploded on the battlefield, it is hard to predict the course that the war will take from then onwards.

Chemical warfare first made its presence felt during World War I, and is estimated to have caused over one million immediate and delayed casualties. Such was the revulsion against it, that all the major powers signed the 1925 Geneva Protocol banning its use, but the Soviet Union and US only interpret the Protocol as banning first use, and reserve the right to use it in retaliation. Between the wars there was evidence that the Japanese employed chemical warfare in China, and the Italians used it in Ethiopia. It was, not, however, used in World War II, although both the Allies and Germans had extensive chemical stocks. Since World War II, the US employed a form of chemical warfare in their jungle defoliation operations in Vietnam, using Agent Orange, a herbicide containing a lethal compound called dioxin. There have also been accusations that the Vietnamese have used Soviet made chemicals in South East Asia, and that the Soviets have employed them in Afghanistan. These are the so called 'yellow rain' weapons. It is fact, however, that both the Soviet Union and US possess large stocks of chemical weapons. The Americans have not added to theirs since 1969, but now appear, in the face of the Soviet chemical threat, to be beginning to modernize their stocks. Furthermore, Soviet military doctrine regards chemical warfare as part of conventional war, and it is very likely that she will employ it from the outset.

Chemical agents are divided into two broad types, persistent and non-persistent, lethal and incapacitating. The main lethal agents used are known as nerve agents because they attack the nervous system. The two most well known were developed by the Germans during World War II, and are tabun and sarin, which are respectively coded GA and GB, and are known as G agents, while a postwar development, VX, which is now the most common of the nerve agents, is known as a V agent. The early symptoms of nerve agents are running nose and excess of saliva, tightness in the chest, pinpointing of the pupils, blurred vision, and muscle twitching if the agent has entered through the skin. These will grow more severe, and be joined by headaches, drooling, excessive sweating, dizziness and general weakness. Finally nausea and vomiting will be induced, along with involuntary defecation and urination, muscle twitching and jerking, and eventually breathing will stop. G agents appear in the form of a vapor and are relatively non-persistent, while V agents are non-volatile highly oily liquids, and very persistent.

Blister agents include one of the original World War I agents, mustard gas, now known as HD. While nerve agents incapacitate and cause death quickly, blister agents act much more slowly. The initial symptoms will be irritation in the eyes, burning and reddening of the skin and, if inhaled, a burning sensation in the throat, accompanied by hoarseness and fever. Blisters will then develop, causing blindness and more fatally will attack the lungs. They appear either as a heavy vapor or liquid and are fairly persistent. Blood agents cause death by attacking the enzyme in the red blood cell which is responsible for removing carbon dioxide from the body. The victim will initially feel irritation in his eyes, nose, mouth and throat, accompanied by growing dizziness, nausea, headache, difficulty in breathing and, eventually, unconsciousness leading to death. AC (hydrogen cyanide) and CK (cyanogen chloride) are examples and were again developed during World War I. They are found in the form of a non-persistent vapor. The final category of lethal agents are known as choking agents, of which phosgene (CG) is perhaps the most well known. This attacks the lungs and brings about shortness of breath, choking and coughing, as well as general weakness. Death is brought about by the lungs flooding and usually occurs within about three hours. Choking agents are non-persistent.

Incapacitating agents are designed to make personnel militarily ineffective for varying lengths of time, and are not lethal. Thus, it could be argued that they fall outside the Geneva Protocol. Certainly, the Soviet Union is known to take a great interest in them, and they are the most likely type of chemical weapon which they will initially employ in World War III. The most effective of the decapacitating agents are known as physiochemical agents which act

Above: US GIs in NBC clothing.
Below: US 203mm gun and the immediate effect of the nuclear round it has just fired.

Right: Soviet NBC survey team in action. The man in front is measuring radiation levels. Contaminated areas are usually marked on the ground.

on the brain and central nervous system. Typical symptoms are confusion, distortion of vision, hallucinations, fear and anxiety, uncontrollable laughter, inertia and apathy and schizophrenia. A typical example is the drug LSD. They cannot be detected by the senses, unlike the lethal agents, but tend to be slow acting, can be unpredictable and can cause permanent psychotic disorders. The most common type of decapacitant, and one which has been frequently used, is the Riot Control agent, of which the most well-known examples are CS and VN gas. They cause a burning feeling in the eyes, as well as streaming tears, difficulty in breathing, coughing and tightness in the chest. However, against an enemy well trained and equipped in NBC protective measures, they are unlikely to be effective, and indeed, apart from being used to quell civil disturbances, are an ideal medium for chemical warfare training.

Chemical agents can be delivered in a number of ways. During World War I the main means was the artillery gas shell, and this is still in use. Mortars and rockets, especially multi-barrelled rocket launchers are other methods, as well as chemical land mines. Chemical agents can also be delivered from aircraft, in the form of sprays, bombs or bomblets.

As protection against chemical attack, troops are likely to wear NBC suits, with their respirators close at hand from the moment that hostilities break out. They will also have detector papers attached to their suits which will change color if chemicals are present. NBC sentries will be posted, with particular instructions to look out for low flying aircraft, to be suspicious of any form of bombardment and mist and smoke. Apart from the decapacitating agents, chemical agents do have distinctive smells. Choking agents have an odour of new mown hay, while blood agents are like bitter almonds. If a chemical attack is detected, the NBC sentry will sound the alarm, which in NATO is the banging together of two metal objects. Everyone in the area would then immediately mask up, and tests would be carried out to detect the type of agent being employed. This is important, since the first aid given is different for each. Nerve agents have chemical antidotes. In the British service, troops take oxime tablets, one every six hours, if a nerve agent attack is thought likely, and if they have been affected by it, they inject themselves with atrophine sulphate, using a high speed automatic hypodermic needle, which will act through NBC clothing. Oximes, however, can have undesirable side effects, and both the US and the British are currently developing new antidotes, which are likely to be in the form of a pyridostigmine tablet, taken every eight hours. Blood agents are countered by giving artificial respiration, but this should not be done for choking agents. Blister agents, are treated by washing out the eyes, and applying dry dressings to the blisters, which should not be burst. As for

decapacitating agents, victims of psychochemical attack should be allowed to rest and sleep, but need to be under close supervision. As with nuclear radiation contamination, areas which have been subjected to chemical attack must, if a persistent agent has been used, be surveyed and marked.

In terms of chemical warfare planning, wind direction, as in nuclear planning, is an important factor, but so is the temperature gradient, which is the variation between temperatures taken just above the ground and at greater heights. Three conditions are defined – inversion, lapse and neutral. Inversion is when atmospheric conditions are stable, and temperature increases uniformly with height. With no turbulence and convection currents present, inversion produces the ideal situation for the use of chemical weapons. Lapse, on the other hand, is the least favorable condition. Here the air temperature decreases with height, and the atmospheric conditions are unstable, with no guarantee that the chemical might not blow back in the faces of friendly troops. This state normally exists on clear days with light winds. The neutral state lies in between the other two. Temperature remains roughly constant with increasing height, and it normally occurs on heavily overcast days. With meteorological information, it is, as with nuclear fallout, possible to predict chemically contaminated areas.

Chemical warfare will almost certainly be employed during World War III. Generally, non-persistent agents will be used, since contaminated areas are likely to inconvenience the user almost as much as the recipient. Furthermore, it is psychochemical agents which will be the most widespread, because of their obvious advantages.

In 1972 the major powers signed a Geneva convention prohibiting biological weapons and their stockpiling. Any party, however, may withdraw having given six months notice, and no provision was made for verification and inspection. Indeed, efforts to agree a similar ban on chemical weapons have stumbled on the last two points. A biological agent is a micro-organism which causes disease in man, plants or animals or deterioration in material. The micro-organisms themselves are grouped into fungi, protozoa, bacteria, rickettsiae and viruses. During World War II the Japanese employed biological warfare in China, and also carried out human experimentation at a research station which they set up at Harbin in Manchuria.

As far as the land battle is concerned, it is only the use of biological agents against personnel, which is relevant. There are two methods of delivery, either direct or through a vector, which is an animal or insect which transmits the disease. Thus, the mosquito is the vector for the transmission of yellow fever. On the battlefield, however, if biological agents are to be effective, they must act quickly and cause sufficient casualties, and therefore the direct method is preferred, using bomblets or sprays. The problem is that most diseases have a relatively long incubation period, which makes them unsuitable for battlefield use.

Nevertheless, advances in the field of biotechnology are growing rapidly, and the boundaries between chemical and biological agents are becoming blurred. The traditional basic difference between the two, that one is manufactured in the laboratory while the other exists naturally, is now no longer so, in that biological agents can be produced artificially, and there is the prospect of as yet unknown powerful and virulent diseases being developed.

Nuclear and chemical warfare are a very real threat in World War III, especially the latter. Biological weapons, on the other hand, are not likely to be used as a weapon of mass destruction on the battlefield, but could be used in a covert manner against small and vital targets.

Right: A Soviet soldier decontaminates a BRDM scout vehicle.
Below: Soviet troops undergoing personal decontamination. Only once their protective clothing is 'clean' will they be able to remove it.

ARMOR

The traditional cornerstone of mechanized warfare is the tank. It was the introduction of this on the battlefield in 1916 which broke the deadlock of trench warfare. Since then tanks and other armored fighting vehicles (AFVs) have helped make the land battle ever faster moving.

The Soviet Union still attaches great importance to the tank as a means of achieving a quick conventional victory, while NATO still regards it as a very effective anti-armor weapon. However, for the tank to realize its full potential, it must be committed to battle at the right place and the right time.

Ground reconnaissance will always be preceded by air and signals reconnaissance, and the information gained from these will influence the deployment of ground reconnaissance elements. The workhorse of the latter is the divisional reconnaissance battalion. In the Warsaw Pact forces this is organized as four companies. One will be equipped with six BRDM and six main battle tanks, another with 14 BRDM, the third, a motor rifle company, has ten BMP, while the fourth is a COMINT company. The BRDM scout car is the main reconnaissance vehicle, with the BRDM-1, with open turret, entering service in 1959, and the BRDM-2, with closed turret, appearing a few years later. It is a fully amphibious vehicle with 2 × 2 retractable cross-country wheels, and armed

with 12.7mm or 7.62mm machine guns for air defense and 14.5mm and 7.62mm hull/turret mounted machine guns.

The divisional reconnaissance battalion will normally operate on a frontage of 15–20km and up to 50km ahead of the main body. Its main task is to discover the extent of enemy positions, to identify gaps and weak points and bypass routes. The latter is especially important, and first echelon forces need to break through the crust of the defenses as quickly as possible. Furthermore, there is the need to find routes for the OMG to break through into the enemy's rear area. Although the divisional reconnaissance battalion has tanks and mechanized infantry, it will not fight for information unless really forced to do so.

The division is not the only level at which reconnaissance elements are found in Warsaw Pact armies. At regimental level there is a reconnaissance company of 4 BMP and 6 BRDM, whose tasks are mainly engineer and chemical reconnaissance. There are also elements found at army level, and these will be used to cover the gaps between the divisional reconnaissance battalions.

The US is currently restructuring its organizations to reflect both the Airland Battle doctrine and the arrival of new equipment, especially the M1 Abrams main battle tank, and the M2/3 Bradley infantry fighting vehicle (IFV). The new divisional organization is known as 'Division 86', and has as its reconnaissance element an armored cavalry squadron of two armored cavalry troops and two air cavalry troops. The former each consist of 16 M3 Bradleys organized into platoons, with two more at troop HQ. The air cavalry troop has six scout and four attack

Previous page: Leopard 2 main battle tanks of the Bundeswehr carry out night firing exercises.

**Left: British Army Scimitar with 30mm Rarden gun.
Below: Soviet T-62s in typical attack formation.
Bottom: T-55s show their paces in soft going.**

helicopters. The squadron also has a motorcycle platoon and NBC platoon with nine reconnaissance vehicles. The M3 Bradley is officially termed the Cavalry Fighting Vehicle (CFV) and has a five man crew. It is armed with the Hughes TOW antitank guided weapon (ATGW), with twin launcher tubes, a 25mm rapid fire cannon and a 7.62mm coaxial machine gun. Apart from integrating aerial reconnaissance with ground at divisional level, the US Army also differs from those of the Warsaw Pact in that there is a reconnaissance element at battalion level, both armor and mechanized infantry. This is

The US Army's Main Battle Tank – the M-1 Abrams.

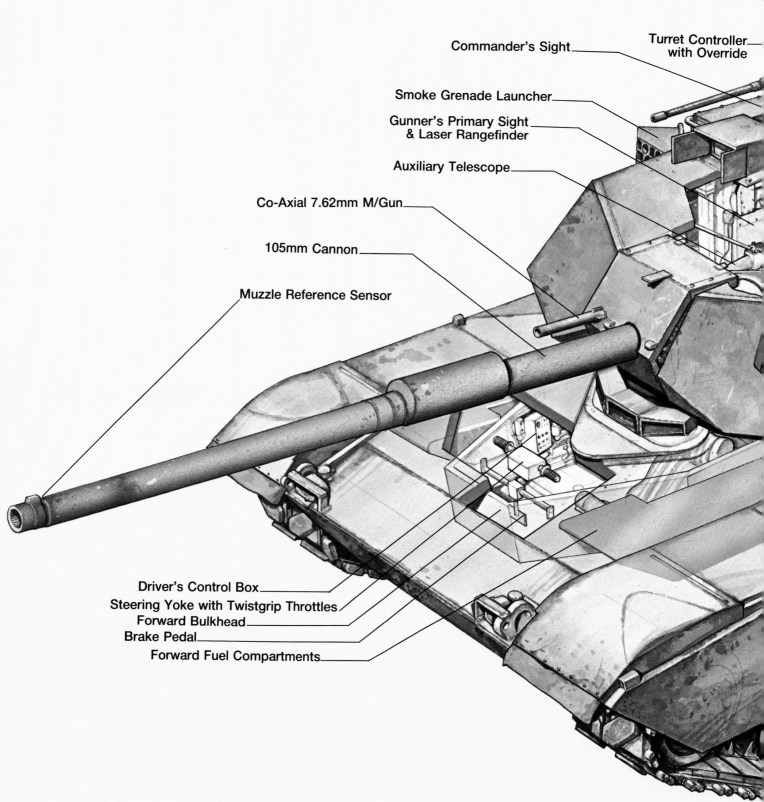

Wind Sensor

Commander's Hatch

Commander's 0.5in M/Gun

Commander's Seat

Turret Controller
with Override

Commander's Sight

Smoke Grenade Launcher

Gunner's Primary Sight
& Laser Rangefinder

Auxiliary Telescope

Co-Axial 7.62mm M/Gun

105mm Cannon

Muzzle Reference Sensor

Driver's Control Box
Steering Yoke with Twistgrip Throttles
Forward Bulkhead
Brake Pedal
Forward Fuel Compartments

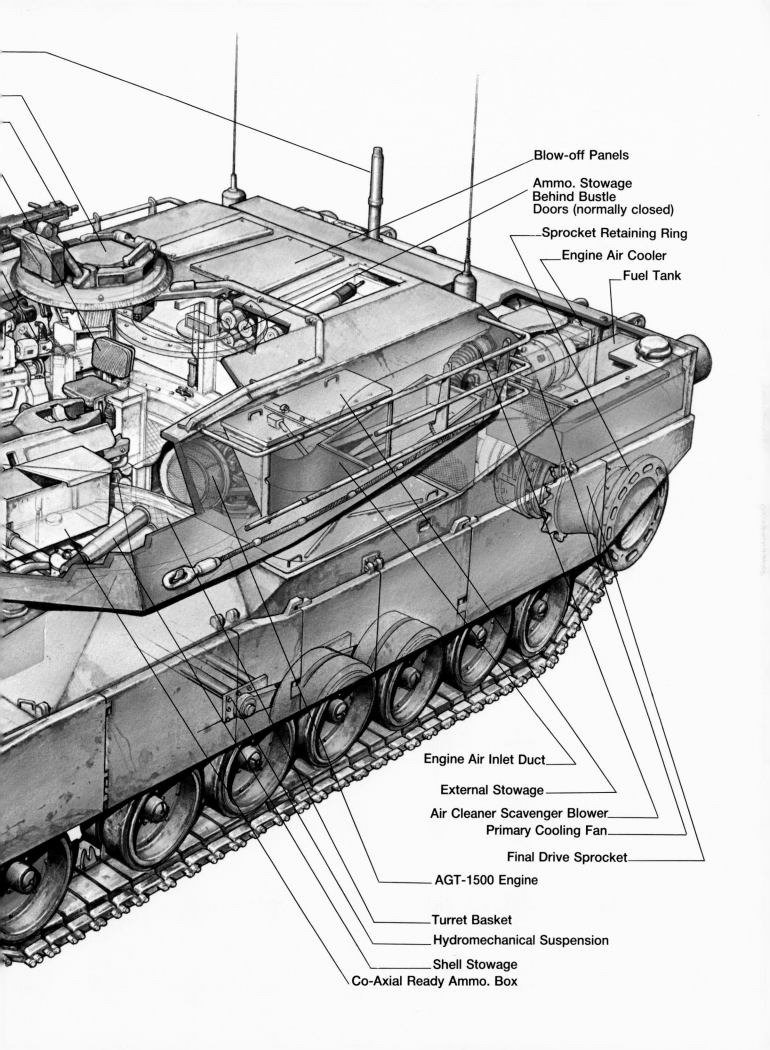

Blow-off Panels

Ammo. Stowage
Behind Bustle
Doors (normally closed)

Sprocket Retaining Ring

Engine Air Cooler

Fuel Tank

Engine Air Inlet Duct

External Stowage

Air Cleaner Scavenger Blower

Primary Cooling Fan

Final Drive Sprocket

AGT-1500 Engine

Turret Basket

Hydromechanical Suspension

Shell Stowage

Co-Axial Ready Ammo. Box

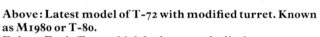

Above: Latest model of T-72 with modified turret. Known as M1980 or T-80.
Below: Basic T-72, which lacks grenade dischargers on turret front.
Right: T-64s, with which GSFG is equipped, although some at least are being replaced by the T-80.

known as the Scout Platoon and has six M3 Bradleys.

The West German reconnaissance vehicle is the SPPZ2 Luchs (Lynx). This is a large eight-wheeled vehicle, and owes its ancestry to the World War II Puma armored car. It is found at divisional reconnaissance level, and is organized into a battalion of 17 light reconnaissance patrols, each having two vehicles. The debate as to whether tracks or wheels are better for reconnaissance is a finely balanced one. Wheels mean a quieter vehicle, which is better for reconnaissance 'by stealth' and maintenance is also easier. However, tracks provide better cross-country performance. Nevertheless, with drive on all eight wheels, Luchs is highly mobile, but is rather large for this role. It is also somewhat lacking in fire power, with only a 20mm cannon and 7.62mm machine gun as armament. The Germans do not have reconnaissance elements at battalion level, but each brigade has a scout platoon, also equipped with Lynx.

The British, like the Americans, currently favor tracks for reconnaissance, although they do have some wheeled reconnaissance vehicles. The Combat Vehicle Reconnaissance (Tracked) [CVR(T)] family

provides the basis, notably the Scorpion and Scimitar, both of which performed excellently in the Falklands campaign. Each of the three armored divisions in Germany has a medium reconnaissance regiment equipped with three squadrons of Scorpion, which mounts a 76mm gun. Each squadron has four troops of four Scorpions each, and also a surveillance troop with another member of the CVR(T) family, the Spartan APC. Five of these are in the troop and equipped with the ZB298 radar. Again like the US, the British have reconnaissance platoons with their armored and mechanized infantry battalions, and here the Scimitar, with the 30mm quick firing Rarden gun is used, six being in the platoon. The Belgians also use CVR(T) and indeed produce them jointly with the British. As for wheeled reconnaissance, the British Army uses the CVR(Wheeled) Fox, which also mounts a 30mm Rarden gun, and is found in the reconnaissance regiments of the 2nd Infantry Division, which reinforces 1(BR) Corps from the UK in time of war, and is responsible for the security of the Corps rear area.

If a Warsaw Pact attack in the Central Region is

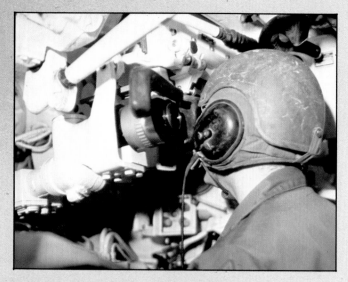

Above: US M60A3 gunner looking through his sights.
Above right: Leopard 2 with its 120mm smoothbore gun.
Right: A Bradley M2/3 IFV in action.
Below: The US M60, which will be replaced by the M1
Abrams in time.

impending, NATO divisional reconnaissance elements will deploy right forward to the border and take up a line of observation. Initially, in front of them will be the FRG Border Police, who are responsible for the borders with the GDR and Czechoslovakia in peacetime, but they will probably withdraw before the Warsaw Pact actually crosses the border. It will be the task of the reconnaissance forces to try and prevent Warsaw Pact reconnaissance elements from penetrating. As the pressure builds up in front of the line of observation, so it will gradually pull back, imposing as much delay as its limited armament will allow, although it will be supported by attack helicopters and artillery. It is vital, though, that during this period it does not lose contact with the enemy, and the information which it passes back should be sufficient, along with other intelligence sources, to enable commanders to decide where the main thrusts are likely to occur, and to plan accordingly. Once the line has almost reached the main position, it will 'break clean' and move back to the rear to refurbish.

The main characteristics of the AFV are firepower, mobility, protection and flexibility. The task of the designer is to evolve the best balance between them in order to best suit the role of the particular vehicle. Nowhere is this more difficult to achieve than with the main battle tank (MBT). Its two main tasks on the battlefield are the destruction of enemy armor and infantry support, and the tank is also used for shock action, hitting the enemy unexpectedly and catching him off balance. In definition it is a mobile gun platform and ideally needs to be hard hitting, highly mobile and well protected. While all tank producing nations agree that firepower is the most important characteristic, there is much debate over protection and mobility. The more protection in terms of armor given to a tank, the bulkier and more cumbersome it will be. Conversely, for a tank to be fast and highly mobile, it can only be lightly armored. Traditionally, the US and the Germans have always considered mobility to be the more important, while the British and Soviets prefer protection.

The tanks in service, or coming into service today, represent, in the eyes of some pundits, the last of the heavy breed. They believe, and there is much in what they say, that the ever growing multiplicity of threats to the tank and its present size make it very vulnerable on the modern battlefield, and that tanks of the future will be very much smaller. They will make use of externally mounted guns, with the crew being housed in the hull rather than a turret. Their small size and agility will make them very much better protected than now, but just as effective. This new generation, however, is unlikely to be seen much before the turn of the century, and for World War III it is the current generation which is of more concern.

The main two tanks in service with the Warsaw Pact today are the T-64 and T-72, which came into service at the beginning of the Seventies. There are, however, still a large number of older T-62s about, as well as some T-54/55s. The Soviets do not believe in discarding weapons systems unless they have to, and many of the divisions which are only at cadre strength in peacetime will be equipped with the older models in time of war. All the satellite armies are equipped with Soviet tanks. The main NATO tanks are the US M1 Abrams and M60, which will eventually be entirely replaced by the former, the German Leopard 1 and Leopard 2, and the British Chieftain and Challenger. Earlier US and British models, notably the M48 and Centurion, are still to be seen in some NATO armies.

In terms of tank guns, the NATO 105mm gun has now given way to the 120mm, while the Soviets have dispensed with the 115mm on T-62 for the 125mm on the two later models. There is also a marked move away by both sides from the traditional rifled gun to the smoothbore. In the past rifling was considered necessary in order to impart accuracy. The penalties are, however, that the barrel wears out relatively quickly. Also, the hotter the propellant charge, the higher the muzzle velocity of the round, which means improved accuracy and greater range, but also increases wear to the rifling, which degrades accuracy. A smoothbore gun, does not suffer this limitation, but accuracy has to be enhanced in another way, and this is done by using fin stabilized projectiles, which are, however, much more expensive than the conventional projectile. Nevertheless, the Soviet 125mm gun is smoothbore, as is the 120mm on Leopard 2. The US is also about to replace the rifled 105mm on the Abrams with the latter. The next French MBT, the EPC (Engin Principal de Combat) will also have a 120mm smoothbore. Only the British are staying with the rifled gun, with the Challenger 120mm, but are developing fin stabilized ammunition for it in order to get the best of both worlds.

Tank ammunition is of two main types, kinetic and chemical energy (KE, CE). The former relies on its speed combined with mass to penetrate armor, and is known as armor piercing ammunition. Being high velocity rounds, they are more accurate than CE types, and are the most favored for killing other tanks. The type used by the tanks of both sides is the armor piercing discarding sabot fin stabilized (APDSFS) round. This consists of a rodlike penetrater made of very dense material like tungsten carbide, with fins on the rear like those on a dart. It is enclosed in a sabot or pot, which brings it up to the caliber of the gun. As the projectile leaves the barrel, the pot separates and flies off, and the energy imparted to the projectile is transferred to the penetrater, which enables it to maintain its velocity and pierce the armor of the opposing tank.

Chemical energy rounds exist in two main forms. High Explosive Piercing (HEP) or, as it is known in

COMPARISON
T-72
T-64
SOVIET MEDIUM TANKS

NEW 12.7mm MACHINEGUN FIRED FROM OPEN HATCH

DIE-CAST IDLER WHEEL

T-72

IR LIGHT TO RIGHT OF MAIN GUN

SIX LARGE, DIE-CAST ROAD WHEELS

VENTS ON REAR DECK

T-62 TYPE SNORKEL CARRIED ON LEFT REAR OF TURRET

T-72

The T-64 and T-72 medium tanks are the latest additions to the Soviet armored forces. They feature increased mobility, firepower and improved armor protection over the T-62 medium tank and are a formidable foe for any free-world tank!

TURRET TURNED TO TRAVEL POSITION

T-64 · SIX SMALL, STAMPED ROAD WHEELS

12.7mm MACHINEGUN CAN BE FIRED FROM INSIDE TURRET

EXHAUST VENTS AT REAR

T-64

NEW SNORKEL CARRIED ON BACK OF TURRET

IR LIGHT TO LEFT OF MAIN GUN

T-64

T-72 Soviet Medium Tank
Main Armament: 125mm Smoothbore Gun

T-64 Soviet Medium Tank
Main Armament: 125mm Smoothbore Gun

PREPARED BY THE U.S. ARMY INTELLIGENCE AND THREAT ANALYSIS CENTER (IMAGERY INTELLIGENCE PRODUCTION DIVISION)

1027-79 UNCLASSIFIED

Europe, High Explosive Squashhead (HESH), and High Explosive Antitank (HEAT). The HESH or HEP projectile is filled with explosive, and has a soft nose and base fuse. When it strikes the target, the nose flattens and the explosive forms a 'cowpat'. The base fuse is then triggered, detonating the explosive. The resultant shock waves then pass through the armor causing a scab and particles to break off inside, and these will fly at very high velocity. As a means of causing maximum damage inside the tank, HEP is the ideal round. It is also dual purpose as it can be used as a conventional high explosive (HE) round. HEAT, on the other hand, works on an entirely different principle. This is the shaped charge or Monroe effect, named for the US engineer who first discovered it. It consist of an inverted cone with metal liner, behind which is explosive. It has a flat topped casing with a rod on top. This is important, and is there to provide the correct stand off distance without which the round would not work. When the tip of the rod hits the armor, the explosive is detonated and a thin stream of gaseous molten metal, which has very good penetrative powers, passes through the armor

Above: The visual differences between T-64 and T-72. T-72 is being widely exported abroad, unlike T-64, which has not been seen outside the Soviet Army.

penetrating everything in its path. Both these rounds are now available in fin-stabilized form, with the fins opening out once the projectile has left the muzzle.

One other general type of armor defeating ammunition exists, and this combines KE with CE. These rounds are commonly known as Armor Piercing High Explosive (APHE) or Armor Piercing Special Effects (APSE). Here the round penetrates the armor, and then explodes. It is, however, only used on light armored vehicles with smaller caliber guns, and is only effective against thinner skinned targets than MBTs. It is an ideal means of knocking out APCs.

However good the tank gun and its ammunition, they cannot be effective on their own without a good fire control system. Most tank fire control systems now incorporate computers and range finders, which usually make use of lasers. Both tank commander and gunner have their own sights, and the sequence of

drill is for the commander to acquire the target, which he indicates to the gunner by automatically lining his sight up with it. The gunner then lays onto the target and takes the range by firing his laser at it. This, and the type of ammunition to be fired are fed into the computer, which automatically puts the gun in the correct ballistic lay. The gunner is now ready to engage.

Armored protection traditionally consists of three types. Against KE attack solid armor, usually steel based, which relies on thickness and slope, has always been the most effective. However, this is not so against CE attack. Here spaced or laminated armor

are used. The former consists of two separate thicknesses, with a space in between, and the best example is the bazooka or skirting plate which is bolted on to the side of the tank. Laminated armor consists of layers of different material bonded together. In the last few years a type of this, using new forms of material, has been introduced. Known originally as Chobham armor, after the research establishment in Britain which originally developed it, it has been found to double the protection against HEAT attack, and all the new MBTs in service have adopted it in various forms.

All MBTs now use diesel engines, since this fuel

Left: The Chieftain Main Battle Tank which has been in service for nearly 20 years and is likely to remain so for many more in spite of the introduction of Challenger.
Top: Challenger, which reinforces the British belief in the rifled gun.
Above: Striker, which mounts the Swingfire ATGW and is used by the British and Belgians. It has a range of 4000m.

is less inflammable than petrol and gives better fuel consumption. Apart from the British, whose tanks have tended to have relative low top speeds, the MBTs of both sides are capable of travelling up to 45mph. One limitation on speed is the ability of the crew to stand up to high speeds when traveling cross-country. Unless suspension systems are sufficiently robust, there is the danger that the crew will be too shaken up to fight efficiently.

During World War II tanks, lacking night vision devices, apart from searchlights, were limited during the hours of darkness. Since then, with the development of infrared and image intensification, which works on the principle of concentrating the ambient light, the MBT can fight almost as well by night as by day. This does, however, put a much greater strain on the crew. Traditionally this consists of four men – commander, gunner, loader/radio operator and driver. While current Western MBTs have retained this configuration, the Soviet T-64 and T-72 have only a three-man crew. The loader/operator has been removed and an autoloader installed.

Soviet armies are either tank or infantry heavy, and vary in size and makeup. Thus the five armies of GSFG are each organized differently. While 20th Guards Army has three motor rifle divisions only, and

55

8th Guards Army has the same, but with the addition of one tank division, 2nd Guards Army is a balanced formation with two of each. The two tank heavy armies, 3rd Shock Army and 1st Guards Tank Army have three tank and one motor rifle, and four tank and one rifle divisions respectively. In essence, motor rifle formations are used for the break in operation, while the tank formations exploit it. OMGs will also be tank heavy. However, it must be stressed that the Soviets are believers in combined arms, and the tank division does contain some infantry. The basic organization is three tank and one motor rifle regiment. The former has 94 tanks, divided into three battalions each of three ten tank companies, with one motor rifle company in BMPs as the regiment's infantry element. The infantry regiment, on the other hand, has three motor rifle battalions, also equipped with BMP, and a large tank battalion of 40 tanks, broken down into three companies each of 13 tanks. The lowest tank sub-unit is the three tank platoon, and there are three of these in each tank regiment company, and four in the motor rifle regiment tank companies.

Warsaw Pact tanks normally attack in line abreast, either on their own if the opposition is considered weak, or leading motor rifle elements. The infantry may or may not dismount from their APCs, again dependent on the strength of the defenses. Supporting fire will be supplied by artillery and mortars, with the tanks also firing on the move. Ideally, the Soviets like to fight an encounter battle, catching the enemy on the move, and deploying immediately off the line of march to attack him in the flank. Against prepared defenses, however, a more deliberate attack will be mounted. For the tanks in the tank division the main task is to keep the battle moving and penetrate as fast and as deeply into the enemy's defenses as possible. The infantry with them are there to help deal with small pockets of resistance which cannot be easily bypassed.

The US armored division, of which there are two in the Central Region, 3rd Armored with V(US) Corps and 1st Armored with VII(US) Corps, is much more balanced than its Soviet equivalent and has a more flexible organization. In essence, it has six armor and five mechanized infantry battalions, and three brigade headquarters. The latter equate to the combat commands of World War II and like them do not have a standard mix of infantry and armor under command, but are tailored to suit the situation at the time. In the Division 86 organization the armor battalion is almost twice the size of its Soviet counterpart and has 58 Abrams or M60A3 tanks. These are broken down into four companies each of 14 tanks. These are further split into three platoons of four tanks each. In addition, it has a scout platoon, and a mortar platoon with six 107mm mortars mounted on the M113 APC.

The other NATO armies use the brigade as a fixed formation. The Germans, like the Americans, are in the process of a reorganization, and are slimming down their armor and mechanized infantry battalions to the same size of those of the Soviets, but are providing more of them to each brigade. Thus the new panzer brigade will have three armor battalions, each of 33 Leopard 2s, and one mechanized infantry (panzer grenadier) battalion, as opposed to the former two and one. The Panzer division has two panzer and one panzer grenadier brigades. The British armored division, of which there are three based in Germany, is also organized on a three brigade basis. The majority are 'square' brigades with two armored regiments (equivalent to the US battalion) and two mechanized infantry battalions. Some brigades are, however, armor heavy, with three armored regiments and one mechanized infantry battalion, while others have three mechanized infantry and one armored unit. The armored regiment is larger than any other NATO tank battalion, with 66 tanks, Chieftain or Challenger, on peacetime establishment, which is increased to 74 in wartime. It has four squadrons, each of four tank troops, a reconnaissance troop and an ATGW troop with Swingfire ATGW mounted on Striker, another member of the CVR(T) family. The Belgian and Dutch armored brigades are also square and use Leopard 1s, although the Dutch are now receiving the Leopard 2.

Like the Warsaw Pact, NATO doctrine stresses the concept of combined arms operations and, in terms of the anti-armor battle, the tank is viewed as but one weapon in the armory, which will combine with the others in order to destroy the enemy tanks and APCs. It is only by inflicting unacceptable losses on these will the Warsaw Pact offensive be halted. In the Sixties and early Seventies, NATO armies were forced to put the majority of their tanks in the front line in order to offset Warsaw superiority in armor. Now, with the rapid increase of other forms of anti-tank weapon available, the need is not so pressing, and NATO is able to keep more armor in reserve for counterattack and counterpenetration, which adds to the depth of the defenses.

Nevertheless, a significant proportion will be involved in the main defensive position, especially in giving anti-armor support to the infantry. Normally tanks remain in hides close to their battle positions, to which they will only deploy when an enemy attack is imminent. Fire positions are taken up ideally on reverse slopes, and one advantage that Western tanks have over their Warsaw Pact counterparts is their ability to depress their guns at a greater angle, which means that the tank presents less of a target.

When supporting infantry in the attack, NATO tanks, unlike those of the Warsaw Pact, tend to operate from a flank, shooting the infantry in, and aiming to arrive on the objective at the same time.

They also make much more use of fire and movement, with some tanks moving, while others support them from static positions. The Soviets, on the other hand, lay much more emphasis on shock action with firing on the move. All MBTs are now fitted with gun stabilizers to enable them to fire the main and secondary armament with reasonable accuracy on the move, but the chances of a hit are never as good as from a static position, although it can be very effective as suppressive fire to keep the enemy's heads down.

The NATO armor held back in depth is a vitally important component of the overall defense scheme, especially in the context of the OMG. Its flexibility in its radio communications and ability to deploy quickly from one location to another, make it a very effective counter to the OMG. It can either take up blocking positions in the path of the OMG, which is counterpenetration, or attack it from a flank. Likewise, it will use the same tactics if a major break-through takes place. One problem of movement, however, is that by day it is vulnerable to attack by aircraft and attack helicopters, and, wherever possible, all major movement will take place during the hours of darkness.

In the past NATO has always believed that the technical superiority of its tanks would considerably offset numerical inferiority. It is now clear, however, that Soviet tank design, especially with the T-72, has made significant strides forward, especially in terms of firepower and protection. However, a tank is only as good as its crew, and NATO tankers still have the edge on their Soviet counterparts. Although the latter are being allowed more initiative than hitherto, there is still a rigidity in tactics and training. Nevertheless, the Warsaw Pact armor threat is formidable, and can only be defeated if NATO armor is able to think and act more quickly.

Below: An Italian Leopard 1 fords a river.

Canadian infantry well equipped to face the tough wintry
conditions of the Northern Flank of NATO.

The task of infantry in war is to seize and hold ground, and all other arms and services exist to support the infantryman in this. The past 30 years have seen the firepower available to the infantry battalion grow at an impressive rate, both in range and concentration.

In terms of personal weapons, there is a very significant change taking place in both NATO and the Warsaw Pact armies. This is a change of the basic small arms weapon caliber from 7.62mm to 5.56mm and 5.45mm respectively. The main reason for this is that since 1945 there has been a move away from the requirement to be able to engage accurately the enemy at long ranges, towards the need to put down concentrated fire. Both the Warsaw Pact Kalashnikov AK-47 and Belgian FN rifle, which is currently used by a number of NATO armies, recognized this. Although they fired a 7.62mm round, the change from the manual bolt action rifle to semi-automatic weapon, gave a significantly higher rate of fire, but with a maximum effective range of not more than 600m. It was, however, the success of the US Armalite rifle in Vietnam which has perhaps influenced the reduction in caliber more than anything else. Although it fires a 5.56mm round, its lightness compared to 7.62mm weapons, the fact that more ammunition can be carried, and that it compares very favorably to the

Above: US M60 light machine gunner on exercise with blank ammunition.
Top right: Romanian AKM version of AK-47, recognizable by foregrip.
Right: AKM with collapsible butt, which is often used by paratroops.
Bottom right: Soviet RPK-74 5.45mm light machine gun with folding bipod.

Below: Dutch light machine gun team with Belgian FN 7.62mm MAG.

7.62mm in terms of penetration, have led to the adoption of smaller caliber weapon. The Soviets began to replace their AK-47 with the AK-74 in the early Seventies. On the surface it looks very similar, but has a much higher rate of fire, and the 30-round magazine has been replaced by a 90-round magazine.

The US Army has now been equipped with the Armalite, also known as the M16, for some years, although a few of the older M14 7.62mm rifles are still to be found among reserve units. At present a product improvement program on the M16 is taking place, and the M16 A2 will be very much more robust. Its most noticeable feature will be a three round burst capability in place of the fully automatic capability on the M16A1. This should certainly help to conserve ammunition. Looking further into the future,

development work is being undertaken on the Advanced Combat Rifle (ACR), and it is likely to include caseless ammunition and the concept of the multiple bullet as a means of controlling dispersion and thereby obtaining increased accuracy with burst fire. The British, on the other hand, are about to introduce a new system to replace their present FN family. SA80 consists of two weapons, both using the new 5.56mm standard NATO round. The first is known as the Individual Weapon (IW) and will replace both the 9mm submachine gun (SMG) and the selfloading rifle (SLR). The Light Support Weapon (LSW), on the other hand, will replace the General Purpose Machine Gun (GPMG) and the older Light Machine Gun (LMG), the Bren gun of World War II vintage. Other NATO member

Above: Canadian Special Service Force troops fire the 0.30in Browning.
Below: US M16A1 Armalite being fired in wintry conditions.
Below right: The British Army's new 5.56mm Individual Weapon.

Above right: Covered by two RPG-7s Soviet motor riflemen assault with AK-47 light machine gun and assault rifles.
Right: US airborne troops with Armalites and 105mm towed artillery.

nations are also developing similar concepts. Indeed, as its squad automatic weapon, the US Army has adopted the Belgian FN Minimi LMG and has designated it the Squad Automatic Weapon (SAW), and this will replace the M60 7.62mm machine gun. The Soviets, too, have a variant of the AK-74, known as the AKS-74, with folding bipod, which can be used as an LMG and also have the RPK-74, a variant of the PK machine gun, but rebarreled to take 5.45mm ammunition. Thus, the infantry squad of the future will have much heavier firepower and will be able to sustain itself in combat for much longer without resupply than it can do at present.

Like the tanker, the infantryman is also obtaining better and better night fighting aids, and individual weapon night sights, using image intensification, are becoming very effective. At squad level, too, the grenade plays an important part, especially the US M79 grenade launcher, which is in service with a number of NATO armies and fires a 40mm grenade. Grenades are either HE, antitank or smoke.

As far as support weapons are concerned, the mortar is particularly important. The Warsaw Pact has a wide range of calibers. They have recently replaced the 82mm mortar in the mortar platoon of the motor rifle battalion with the 120mm, which fires a bomb with over four times the weight of that of its predecessor out to a range of almost 6km, with a rate of fire of 15 bombs per minute. The Soviets also have 160mm and 240mm mortars, but these are an artillery

**Above: Soviet 30mm AGS-17 automatic grenade launcher.
Below: British 57mm mortar, found at platoon level.**

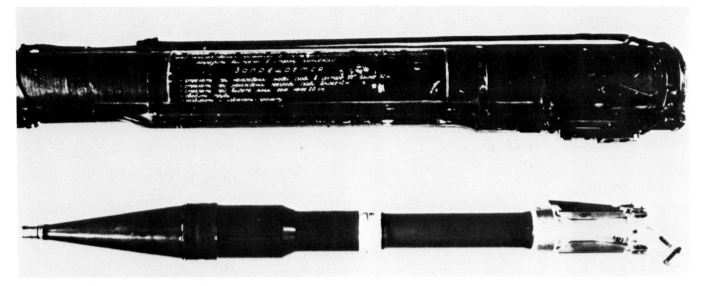

Above: The RPG-16 which is replacing the RPG-7 in Soviet service.
Left: On maneuvers, a tank hunting team surprises M60 tanks.
Below: Milan is now the most common type of NATO medium range ATGW.

responsibility. The standard NATO mortar is the 81mm with a range of almost 6km, but the 107mm (4.5in) is also used. The key to the mortar is that it is the infantry battalion's own integral artillery, and that it can bring down an impressive concentration of fire very quickly. Furthermore, being a high trajectory weapon, it is particularly effective against dug-in infantry.

What concerns the infantry most is its ability to deal with the armor threat, and the modern infantry battalion has a wide range of weapons to do this. Antitank grenades have already been mentioned, but these are only effective at ranges of 20–30m and against thinner armor. Thus they are not suitable against an MBT. The next category is the handheld weapon, which fires a HEAT warhead. Perhaps the most well known of these is the Soviet RPG-7, which is very popular among insurgent forces throughout the world. This fires an 85mm projectile, but is being replaced by the RPG-16 with a 73mm warhead. The Czechs also have the RPG P-27 with a 45mm war-

head. On the NATO side, this type of weapon comes in the form of the light antitank weapon (LAW) and medium antitank weapon (MAW), which are found at squad and platoon level respectively. The LAW is a 66mm disposable launcher found at squad level, and is ideal for tank hunting parties, or for combating armor in close country. MAW is a platoon weapon, and in many European NATO armies this is the 84mm Carl Gustav, which also fires a HEAT warhead with an effective range of 400m. The Germans, however, have replaced this with ATGW, while the US Army, which previously had the 90mm recoilless rifle, have done the same.

In terms of antitank weapons it is ATGW which has been the 'growth industry' on the battlefield during the past twenty years. No better demonstration of their effectiveness has occurred than during the opening days of the 1973 Yom Kippur War, when Soviet made Saggers in Egyptian hands put paid to the omnipotence of the Israeli tank on the battlefield. Indeed, it was this and heliborne ATGW, which

Left: The Soviet AT-3 Sagger was a success of the 1973 Yom Kippur War.
Above: The 2nd Generation Soviet AT-4 Spigot ATGW.
Below: TOW, the main ATGW at battalion level in the US Army.

Above: The US Improved TOW (TOW 2) showing initial flight stages.
Below: A Canadian M-72 66mm disposable LAW.

caused some 'instant experts' to state that ATGW had sounded the death knell for the tank. They have made the tank more wary, but have not eradicated it. Nevertheless, they are a significant threat. What its introduction has done in particular for the infantryman is to give him an armor defeating capability at twice the range of the recoilless guns which he had before.

All ATGW systems have HEAT warheads. The missile is guided onto the target using what is known as command guidance, which means that the operator has to give the missile commands. First generation ATGW normally had manual command to line of sight, which meant that the controller had to first gather the missile, and then manuever it onto the line between his eye and the target and maintain it on this line. The main problem, as the French first found in Algeria, is that the controller under the stress of battle finds this difficult to do. Consequently the second generation missiles are on semiautomatic command to line of sight (SACLOS). Here the controller merely has to keep his sight on the target and a computer gives the missile signals to enable it to fly along the line of sight. The US Army's TOW missile is a very good example of this, and has a range which has been increased over the years from 2000 to 3750m and is the infantry battalion's primary anti-armor weapon. It also has a thermal-imaging infrared night sight, which enables it to be used in darkness

and poor visibility. The European NATO nations use the Franco-German Milan system. In terms of MAW, the US also has Dragon, with a range out to 1000m.

The Soviet ATGW systems are numerous. Snapper, Swatter and Sagger belong to the first generation, but the Swatter-B and Sagger-B now have SACLOS incorporated. Spigot and Spandrel have also been introduced as second generation systems. Their ranges tend to be lower than their NATO counterparts, with none above 3000m. Again, they are either manportable or carried in vehicles. Indeed, almost every type of light armored vehicle is equipped with some form of ATGW. Unlike NATO, the Soviets still believe in the traditional towed anti-tank gun, and the latest model the 100mm T-12 has a smoothbore gun and fires APDSFS ammunition, which will penetrate 400mm of armored plate at 500m range. A battalion of these is found in every motor rifle division.

Currently, however, there is concern, in the light of improvements to tank armor, over the effectiveness of current infantry manned anti-armor weapons, especially ATGW. HEAT warhead effectiveness is very much dependent on diameter, and it is noteworthy that the US Army is now introducing TOW 2 into service with the diameter of the warhead in-

Above: The ubiquitous M113 APC with US infantry dismounting.
Right: The French AMX VTP M56 MICV, which is now being replaced by the AMX-10P.
Below right: The German Marder with 20mm cannon.

creased from four to six inches in order to successfully engage T-64 and T-72 frontal armor. Other countries are making similar improvements.

The past two decades have been the era of the mechanized infantryman with his ability to move quickly about the battlefield. Initially, his vehicle was the APC, which in NATO eyes was little more than a battlefield cab, usually armed with no more than a 7.62mm machine gun. The idea was that it carried the infantry to their deployment position, dropped them off and then retired to the rear, collecting them again when they had finished their task. Even in the attack, the normal practice was for the infantry to debuss short of their objective and make the final assault on foot. The Soviets, however, have always attached much importance to the infantry remaining mounted as much as possible in order to maintain the momentum of the assault, and it was this that caused them to introduce a new type of infantry AFV.

When the BMP-1 first made its appearance in the late Sixties it caused a considerable stir in NATO.

Armed with a 73mm smoothbore gun and Sagger ATGW launcher, it was a true armored fighting vehicle rather than merely a transport vehicle, which the infantry could actually fight from. The need to dismount would in the future be much less. The West Germans, however, were not far behind. Drawing on their World War II panzer grenadier experience, they brought Marder into service in 1972, which is armed with a 20mm cannon and 7.62 mm machine gun. Other Western nations were somewhat slower in producing Mechanized Infantry Combat Vehicles (MICV), as they are called. The British experimented with a Rarden 30mm gun mounted on top of their FV432 APC, but discarded the idea, and are now about to bring MCV-80 into service, which will also have a 30mm Rarden on the basic version. US efforts in this field have resulted in the M2 Bradley, with 25mm cannon and TOW missile launchers. At present, however, many NATO nations are still reliant on the APC, the ubiquitous M113, although the Dutch and Belgians have the US private venture FMC Armored Infantry Fighting Vehicle (AIFV).

Although the Soviets see the MICV as helping considerably in maintaining the momentum of the attack, within NATO there is still much discussion as to how it should be used in defense. On the surface it is seen as a valuable addition to the antiarmor battle, with the firepower available to knock out like vehicles, which means that tanks and ATGW can concentrate on knocking out the opposing tanks. There are two snags to this. Firstly, it is still the mechanized infantry's means of transport and, if introduced into the firing line, there is the danger of it being knocked out, which will deprive the infantry of their mobility. Then again, if the infantry are dismounted and dug in, to have MICVs operating too close to them is likely to bring down enemy artillery fire onto their positions. It is therefore very likely that a proportion will be held back out of the immediate battle in order to safeguard the mobility of the infantry, while the remainder will operate with the tanks, away from the infantry positions.

The Soviet Motor Rifle division consists of three motor rifle and one tank regiment. The tank regiment has the same organization as in the tank division, while the motor rifle regiment has a tank battalion of 40 tanks, and three motor rifle battalions, each of three companies of three platoons each. The platoon has three MICVs or APCs, with a further one at company headquarters. One of the regiments is equipped with BMP, as in the tank division, while the others have the BTR-60PB APC, which mounts 14.5mm and 7.62mm machine guns. Also found in the regiment is an ATGW company with nine

70

Below left: The US Marine Corps' amphibious LVT7A1.
Above: Soviet naval infantry with a BTR-60P.
Below: US M113 APC in Germany.
Below right: Backbone of the Soviet Motor Rifle Division is the

BTR-60PB. The latest version, the BTR-70, has a lengthened hull and larger engine compartment.

BRDM-2s mounting Spandrel. Recently, the tank strength of the motor rifle division has been increased by adding an independent tank battalion of 50 tanks to it. It also has a reconnaissance battalion, as mentioned in the last chapter, and a battalion with 18 T-12 100mm smoothbore antitank guns. In total, it has a strength of some 12,000 men with 265 tanks and over 400 MICVs/APCs.

The US Division 86 mechanized infantry division is organized very much like its armored counterpart, with three brigade headquarters under which battalions will be placed under command, dependent on the tactical situation. Currently, each of the US corps in Germany has one complete mechanized division on the ground, 8 Mech Inf Div with V(US) Corps and 3 Mech Inf Div with VII(US) Corps. Each also has a brigade of 4 and 1 Mech Divs respectively, with the balance to be deployed from CONUS when hostilities are imminent. The mechanized division has four armor battalions and six mechanized infantry battalions. The latter are very much based on the Bradley IFV, and each has four rifle companies. These are broken down into three platoons, each of three M2 Bradleys, with a further two at company headquarters. In addition, the mechanized battalion has a scout platoon with six M3 Bradley CFVs, an antitank company with twelve TOW 2s and a mortar platoon with six 107mm mortars mounted in M113s.

The German panzer grenadier division has two armored infantry brigades and one tank brigade. The former now has two tank battalions and two armored infantry battalions, each with 33 MICVs. In addition, it has a light infantry battalion mounted in light trucks or M113s, which is kept only at cadre strength in peacetime. The British mechanized battalion is organized on very similar lines to the American, with four rifle companies each of three platoons, and also had a support company with an 81mm mortar platoon and an antitank platoon with 16 Milan launcher systems. Both the Belgians and the Dutch have slimmer mechanized infantry brigades, with only two mechanized and one tank battalions. They also have TOW ATGW companies at brigade level.

There is no doubt that if there was a conflict in the Central Region, it would be the mechanized infantry of both sides who would bear the initial brunt of the fighting. While the Warsaw Pact infantry would attempt to remain mounted as long as possible, the bulk of NATO mechanized infantry will be dismounted and dug in, with at least some of their MICVs joining in the armor battle. They will try and destroy the Warsaw Pact infantry while they are still inside their vehicles, and those that do dismount will be engaged with small arms fire.

One very noticeable change to the geography of the Central Region during the past thirty years has been the rapid growth of built up areas, what is known as conurbization. This clearly favors the defender, and both sides have recently begun to pay serious attention to Fighting in Built Up Areas (FIBUA). The Soviets realize that they cannot avoid them, and that they will slow down the momentum of the advance. The specter of the fighting in the streets of Stalingrad, Budapest and Berlin during the Great Patriotic War is there to haunt. Of particular concern is the ability of the defender to throw up effective defenses in villages and use antitank weapons from them in large quantities. In the past, FIBUA was a slow business, especially in towns, and

Top left: Soviet LPO-50 flamethrower – particularly useful for fighting in built up areas.
Left: Soviet 82mm M1937 mortar.
Bottom left: An armored CCC vehicle developed for the US Army.
Above: Live firing practise.
Below: US mechanized infantry put in a dismounted attack.

meant a gradual crumbling of the enemy's defenses. Now, when attacking towns, the Soviets are planning to mount raids designed to secure key objectives in the center as a means of maintaining momentum.

The other primary role of light infantry at present is that of rear area security. In the Central Region, this is mainly the task of the German *Territorialheer*, or Territorial Command. In particular it has respon-sibility for the defense of the territory behind the frontline NATO corps, and is divided into two sub-commands for this purpose, German Territorial Northern Command (GTNC) which supports NORTHAG and German Territorial Southern Com-mand (GTSC) with CENTAG. Their main tasks are the guarding of vital supply routes, key bridges across waterways and vulnerable points like power stations, ammunition depots and communication centers. In the rear part of the national corps areas of operations, light infantry are also employed on much the same tasks, but also as quick reaction forces in the event of airborne or heliborne landings.

One other type of infantry which is also used in the Central Region is mountain infantry. The most southern of the NATO divisions, which comes under II(GE) Corps, is the German 1st Mountain Division. This is made up of one armored, one mechanized infantry and one mountain brigade, with the last named having four mountain infantry bat-talions. They are trained in mountain climbing and skiing and, although they have wheeled transport, they also use mules to a large extent. Mountain infantry is also employed by the Italians, in the form of the famous Alpini, and on the flanks of NATO. The Soviets, too, have three mountain divisions.

In spite of the ever increasing technology of the land battle, infantry still have a vital role to play, not just in ever more sophisticated AFVs, but also on their feet or dug in. Apart from seizing and holding ground, they also act as a shoulder or anchor for the mobile forces fighting around them.

'God fights on the side with the best artillery' Napoleon Bonaparte was reputed to have said, and indeed it has played a very dominant part on the 20th Century battlefield. Time and again it has been the quick and effective response of artillery which has turned the fortunes of both defender and attacker. Moreover, any soldier on the battlefield of today feels that much more confident in the knowledge that his own artillery is available to support him at a moment's notice.

Artillery is generally divided into three main types – nuclear, which has already been covered, conventional and air defense. Conventional artillery has a number of tactical roles, all tied in to the support of armor and infantry. Close support artillery is designed to give intimate support to combat units, while general support artillery gives a heavier weight of fire, which is used to reinforce close support artillery, to counter enemy artillery, long range harrassing of the enemy, and interdiction tasks. Locating artillery pinpoints enemy guns, mortars and missile systems so that they can be engaged by retaliatory fire, as well as providing a surveillance capability through the use of drones and Remotely Piloted Vehicles (RPV), and meteorological and survey data, which is essential for the guns to lay down accurate fire.

Both the Warsaw Pact and NATO recognize similar types of fire. In defense the most vital type is what is known as Defensive Fire (DF). This is fire put down on pre-agreed targets – enemy forming up places, likely approaches etc. Most crucial is, in NATO parlance, the Final Preventive Fire (FPF) target, which is usually linear and placed just in front of the defenses and is used when the enemy is poised to overrun them. In the attack the main two types are preparation fire, which is used to soften the defenses up before the attack, and covering fire, which, as it implies, keeps the enemy's heads down while the attack is going in. The Soviets subdivide covering fire into close support fire, which is that delivered during the assault, and accompaniment fire, which is fired from guns accompanying the attacking troops in to the depths of an extensive defensive position. If the attacker pauses to reorganize on the objective, he may well have to use DF in the event of an enemy counterattack. Other types of fire, which might be used in both defense and attack, are harrassing fire, which is designed to interfere with enemy movement and lower morale, counter battery (CB) fire against enemy artillery, smoke, illuminating and marking.

Fire can either be observed or predicted. The former is the more accurate, in that the guns can be visually corrected onto the target, and this is usually done by forward observers (FO), who will be with the forward tank and infantry subunits. However, certainly in NATO armies, every platoon leader and tank commander is trained to correct artillery fire,

Previous pages: British Army M109 155mm selfpropelled howitzer.
Above: The US M101 105mm towed howitzer, with excellent elevation.
Above right: US M109 155mm SP howitzer, here manned by the Bundeswehr, is used by most NATO armies.
Right: Canadian L-5 105mm towed howitzer is, like the US M101, unlikely to be used in the Central Region, but more on the flanks of NATO.

and may well have to do it when the FO cannot see or identify the target. Predicted fire to be effective requires accurate survey and current meteorological information, as well as accurate map coordinates of the target. Computers now make this possible, and can give instant readouts on the laying details for each gun. Those like the US Field Artillery Digital Computer (FADAC) can also store the details of up to 30 targets, and this is especially useful for DFs.

Left: FH70 155mm wheeled howitzer, which was
developed jointly by the British, Germans and Italians.
Below: Lance, which carries both conventional and
nuclear warheads to a range of 25 miles.

If artillery fire is to be instantaneously responsive, communications between the FO, the fire control center and the guns must be efficient. To this end, the US Army has introduced the Tacfire system at artillery battalion level and above. Using a digital message entry device, the FO can pass fire directions directly into a computer, where they are quickly checked by the fire direction officer, and passed to the guns in just a few seconds. At battery level, FADAC has now been replaced by the Battery Computer System (BCS), which is compatible with Tacfire, and this operates very much on the same principle.

The most common NATO gun is the US M109 155mm self-propelled howitzer, which has now been in service with almost all NATO armies for some 20 years. This has a range over 18,000m, which can be boosted to 24,000m with rocket assisted projectiles. The British still have the 105mm self-propelled Abbot in their close support artillery, but this will be replaced shortly by SP70, a 155mm howitzer, which has been developed jointly with the Germans and the Italians. NATO general support artillery is virtually wholly American in origin, and is made up of the M107 175mm, which has been up until now the main counter battery weapon, and the M110 203mm. The A2 version of the latter has now replaced the M110 in the US Army, and fires a rocket assisted round out to 30,000m and a conventional round to just over 24,000m. In the Central Region almost all NATO guns are self-propelled, although the German mountain division does have the FH70 155mm towed

gun. This, like SP70, was developed by the British, Germans and Italians jointly. Light infantry, too, have wheeled guns, and here the US M198 155mm howitzer is making an increasing appearance.

While Pershing is a nuclear dedicated weapon, Lance can be used with a conventional warhead as well, and the most popular version contains a large number of bomblets. Lance uses an inertial guidance system, whereby details of the launch and target positions and the desired flight path are fed into a computer carried by the missile, which ensures that the missile maintains the correct flight path.

Another general support system which is just entering the NATO armory is the Multiple-Launch Rocket System (MLRS). This consists of 12 launchers mounted on an M2 Bradley chassis, which will fire 230mm rockets to ranges in excess of 30km, either singly or in a ripple mode, which enables all 12 to be launched in less than a minute. The warhead consists of 644 M77 submunitions, which combine a shaped charge with fragmentation. The complete load of rockets can effectively cover an area of 30,000 square yards, and is particularly effective in the counterbattery role. Developed by the US, the British, French, West Germans and Italians will begin manufacturing them under licence by the end of the Eighties.

Below: Soviet M-1973 152mm SP howitzer.
Right: 122mm D-30 howitzer, which is still found in both Soviet tank and motor rifle divisions.

Up until the early Seventies Warsaw Pact artillery guns were all towed. The Soviets, however, became increasingly concerned over the growing power of the NATO defenses and the need to be able to penetrate them quickly. One way of making this possible was to have artillery much further forward than previously, but towed artillery is obviously very vulnerable. Hence, they introduced the M-1974 122mm self-propelled howitzer, with a range of 15,000m with conventional ammunition and 21,000m with rocket assisted projectiles, and the M-1973 152mm howitzer with a range of 18,500m. Nevertheless they retain much towed artillery. Most common is the 122mm D-30 gun/howitzer, which has a high rate of fire of eight rounds per minute. The 130mm M-54 and 152mm M-55 D-20 are also found. In the satellite armies, and Soviet second-line divisions,

the earlier M-38 122mm, M-43 130mm and M-37 152mm are still used. The Soviets have also recently deployed a 203mm self-propelled howitzer which matches the US M110.

The Soviet Frog and Scud series of tactical rocket launchers are, like Lance, capable of firing both conventional and nuclear warheads, as are the medium range Shaddock, Scaleboard and Shyster. Frog-7 has a range of 60km, while that of Scud-B is almost five times the distance. The medium range missiles have ranges of 1000km and beyond, and are unlikely to affect the immediate battle. Unlike NATO, which has only recently woken up to the value of MLRS, the Soviets have always considered it as an essential support fire weapon. The most common system is the BM-21, which has 40 122mm rocket launcher tubes, and can fire the full load off in 30

seconds, although it takes 10–15 minutes to reload. The BM-24 240mm 12 tube system is also in service, but both this and BM-21 are likely to be replaced by the new BM-27, which is also 240mm, but has 16 tubes. 130mm, 140mm, 200mm and 250mm systems are also found, especially among the satellite armies. All Warsaw Pact MLRS is truckborne, except for the 140mm 16 tube RPU-14 system which is towed and used by airborne troops.

The lowest level at which artillery is found in the Soviet Army is at regimental level. While the tank regiment does not have its own integral field artillery, the BMP motor rifle regiment has a battalion of eighteen M-1974 122mm guns, while its BTR60 counterpart has a battalion of 122mm towed howitzers. At divisional level, both types of division have two 122mm towed howitzer battalions and one M-1973 152mm SP howitzer battalion. In all these battalions there are three six gun batteries. Also at division is a heavy rocket launcher battalion with four Frog-4 or 7 and a rocket launcher battalion with eighteen BM-21, also divided into three batteries. At army level there is further artillery found in the form of an artillery brigade and a rocket launcher brigade. The artillery brigade includes two battalions of M-54 130mm towed howitzers and a battalion of 152mm guns. In tank armies the latter is the M-1973, while other armies have the towed M-37. Armies other than tank also have a battalion of 85mm or 100mm antitank guns. The rocket launcher brigades have three battalions each of four Scud. Even more additional artillery is found at front level, with a complete artillery division of three brigades, organized on the same lines as the army artillery brigades, as well as a heavy rocket brigade with Scud and Scaleboard. Thus, by way of example, GSFG has the 34th Artillery Division to support its five armies.

The mass of artillery available to the Soviets indicates that their traditional belief in it, especially borne of the massive barrages which they mounted on the Eastern Front during the Great Patriotic War, still holds very firm. In terms of organizing it for a particular operation, the practice is to form artillery groups, which can be at any level from regiment through division to front or army. In order to decide how much artillery is required, the Soviets have laid down artillery norms. For a start, they precisely define three levels of destruction. Neutralization is designed to cause minimum damage, but will temporarily paralyze the defense during and just after the bombardment. Suppression is defined as 25% destruction of men and equipment, while total destruction is 60% or more casualties to men and materiel, with the result that the target no longer has any military value. Against a carefully prepared defense it is calculated that 200 rounds of 122mm will be required per hectare (100 × 100m) to suppress it, but only 150 rounds if it is a hasty defense. This represents 0.7lbs of explosive on every square meter in the latter case, and almost 1lb in the former. British studies of the fighting in NW Europe during 1944–5 concluded that as little as 0.25lbs of explosive per square yard was sufficient to cause a complete breakdown of morale if fired over a short period of time, 15 minutes, and this is similar to the length of the preparatory bombardment envisaged by the Soviets. Indeed, it is not the physical destruction caused by artillery fire, but the effect on morale which causes defenses to cave in. Since NATO forward troops may have little time in which to prepare their defenses, there is much study at present into methods of constructing shellproof positions quickly so that the effects of this type of bombardment are minimized. Nevertheless, these Soviet norms are ambitious and will need a large number of guns to achieve them. The ammunition expenditure will also be high, which will require a very efficient resupply system.

NATO direct support artillery is generally organized on the basis of one battalion of eighteen guns being in direct support of each brigade. By direct support is meant that the fire of those guns is guaranteed to that brigade at all times. In turn the brigade commander will allocate the three batteries to the direct support of battalion task forces, which are a mix of armor and infantry. In order to build flexibility into the system, batteries can also be placed in support of combat units. This means that when they are not involved in giving supporting fire to the unit in which they are in direct support, they are available to other units. In the US and British corps this close support artillery is controlled at divisional level, but in other armies it is integral to the brigade organization. In the general support role at divisional level the US has one M110 battalion and will also have an MLRS battery of nine launchers. The Germans

have a four battery battalion at divisional level, two M107 and two M110. They also have a locating battalion and a rocket battalion, which has one Lance battery and two MLRS batteries. The other NATO armies keep their general support artillery pooled at Corps level, but will place elements of it in support of the divisions. Thus the British have a four battery M107 battalion and a locating battalion, as well as a Lance battalion. While the last will always be retained under corps control, the other two elements will give support to the forward divisions.

NATO artillery commanders do not strive to achieve laid down norms like their Warsaw Pact opposite numbers, and tend to do their fire planning in terms of what is available and how much ammunition they have. They also have laid down rates of fire. Thus for an M109, burst fire can either be three rounds in one minute or six rounds over three minutes. Anything above this is considered sustained fire and will be at a rate of one round per minute. On this basis targets will be engaged for set periods of time and at particular rates of fire. What is stressed very highly in NATO armies is that artillery representatives at all levels must keep physically very close to the commanders whom they are supporting so that they can react quickly as well as be able to give immediate advice on artillery matters.

The main type of artillery ammunition is the HE round. These can either be ground or air burst. Smoke rounds are also used extensively to cover movement, as well as illuminating rounds by night. Target indicating rounds, using colored smoke are employed to guide ground attack aircraft onto targets. Most artillery guns also have an anti-armor round, normally HEP or HESH for NATO and HEAT for the Warsaw Pact, and can be used in the direct fire role if necessary. Indeed, Soviet self-propelled artillery is often used this way when giving accompanying fire during an assault.

The last few years, however, have seen two developments which are about to radically affect the power of artillery. The first of these is the submunition. The US MLRS rocket warhead has already been described, but conventional artillery 155mm and 203mm rounds are also being developed by the US to release dual purpose anti-armor and anti-personnel submunitions. The 203mm round has 180 of these, while the 155mm has 88. This gives artillery much more flexibility and an ability to destroy armor at long range. The fact that the latter is attacked on its top armor, which until now has always been relatively thin as a means of saving weight, is of particular concern to tank designers.

Top: Soviet FROG-7 firing unit and its crew.
Top right: German 110mm LARS MLRS which will be replaced by the US system.
Right: Soviet BM-21 MLRS.

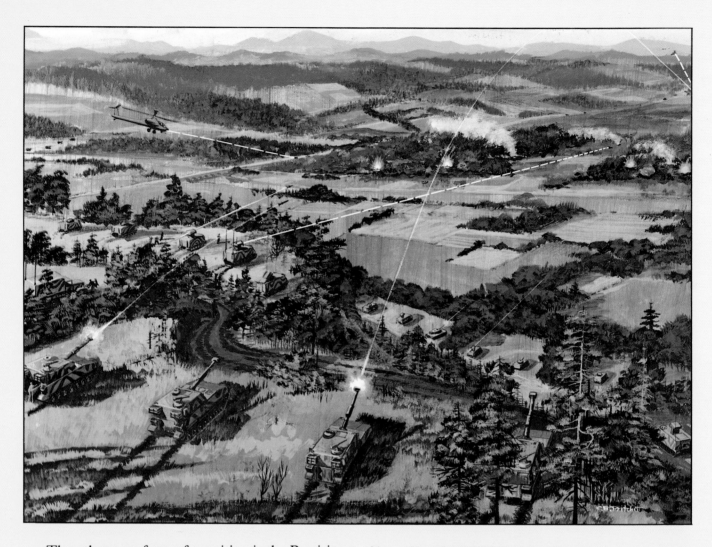

The other new form of munition is the Precision Guided Missile (PGM). In the early 1970s the US produced a new concept, that of Cannon Launched Guided Projectiles (CLGP), which became known as Copperhead. The idea is to use laser to guide an artillery round onto a precision target, and in this case it was the tank which was very much in mind. Using an observer with a laser designater to identify the target, the Copperhead round is fired and when it gets into the target area, sensors in its nose pick up the reflected laser energy and it homes in on the target. For a decade, however, Copperhead has suffered problems in that it has not been able to achieve the laid down accuracy of 90%, and was for a time canceled. Recently, the accuracy has improved, and the US Army has ordered some, but at over $50,000 per round it has become an expensive means of killing a tank. In the meantime, a more effective anti-armor precision round is being developed. Sense-and-Destroy Armor System (SADARMS) works on the principle of having a radar sensor to detect armor. The round, which is to be fired from the M110, as opposed to M109 for Copperhead, contains three antiarmor submunitions, each of which has a radar sensor in it. They are ejected from the carrier shell by time fuse. Suspended by parachute, the

Above: How Copperhead works. Targets are designated by helicopter, aircraft or MICV and then engaged by the guns in the foreground, who need to merely know the map square in which the target is in.
Top right: Soviet SA-7 GRAIL SAM, which is being replaced by STRELA-2.
Far right: British Blowpipe SAM in action in the Falklands.
Right: The highly effective ZSU-23-4.

sensor scans the ground below it and when an AFV is detected it locks on to it, and the submunition lands on top of the vehicle. This concept, and ones like it, are now being developed by the US Army and US Air Force in conjunction for use with medium range missiles and, combined with MLRS, indicates a very feasible method of offsetting Warsaw Pact numerical superiority in armor using conventional means.

The air threat is of very great concern to both sides, and air defense artillery is another vital ingredient of the land forces of both sides. Aircraft in the ground support role can have a decisive influence on the battlefield, especially if they are operating in conditions of air superiority. In particular it is their ability to inhibit movement. As friendly air forces never have enough aircraft to fully carry out all the roles assigned to them, they cannot be expected to keep the enemy's air entirely off the ground troops.

Air defense artillery comes in two types, missile and gun. In order to discuss the use of the two, it is simplest to consider them in terms of the NATO height band definitions which are:

Very Low Level – below 150m
Low Level – 150–600m
Medium Level – 600–7500m
High Level – 7500–15,000m
Very High Level – above 15,000m

At very low level, aircraft and helicopters can be engaged initially by small arms fire. Many AFVs of both sides have air defense 7.62mm machine guns mounted and these, together with cannon, can be used. However, the aircraft, and more especially the helicopter, which will be contour flying, will be only fleeting targets, and it is most unlikely that ground troops will acquire them in time to engage, let alone put up effective fire because of the speed of the target.

The problem is very much the same when dealing with low level aircraft. Here, however, the individual surface-to-air (SAM) missiles can also be used. The Soviet SAM-7 Grail has been used extensively in the Middle East and by the Vietcong and North Vietnamese with varying success. It is a heat seeking weapon using infrared guidance, which makes it a 'fire and forget' system, but also means that it is a tail chaser, which can only engage an aircraft once it has made its attack. Even then it would have to be traveling relatively slowly for the missile to catch it up. Recently the Soviets have introduced an improved version called Strela-2, which has increased velocity and range, which for SAM-7 is 3600m up to a height of 1500m. The US Redeye is very similar, but is now being replaced by the Stinger, with an improved guidance system, still infrared, which enables it to engage targets from all angles. It also has an Identification Friend-or-Foe (IFF) system and, operating in the ultraviolet, as well as infrared, is less vulnerable to countermeasures, the most usual of which is for the target aircraft to drop flares to divert the missile. Its range is also increased to some 5000m, and it can travel at Mach 2. The British Blowpipe is a manual command to line of sight (MACLOS) system, which means that it can engage a target from any angle, being non heat seeking. They are now introducing an improved version, Javelin, with SACLOS, a more powerful warhead and higher velocity.

The more sophisticated gun systems can be very effective at low level. These incorporate a radar which picks up the enemy aircraft and then passes signals which bring the weapons system automatically on target. Most famous of these is the Soviet ZSU-23-4, which has quadruple 23mm cannon mounted in a turret on a PT-76 light amphibious tank chassis. It can, using all four guns, fire 4000 rounds per minute and take on targets up to 3000m in range. It had much success during the Yom Kippur war

Top: US Vulcan system mounted on an M113 variant, M163A1.
Right: Vulcan tactically deployed in order to cover all possible air approaches.
Below right: British Tracked Rapier, now coming into service and likely to be even more responsive than the towed version.

against Israeli aircraft which had been forced to fly low because of the missile threat. The German Gepard, with two 35mm rapid fire guns, also has an impressive performance, and is used by the Dutch as well. The current US Army system is Vulcan, which works on the Gatling principle, with six revolving 20mm barrels. However, it is limited by weather and daylight, although it has a crude radar system, and is about to be replaced by the Sergeant York. This has twin Swedish Bofors 40mm, a much more effective air defense weapon than the 20mm, and is mounted on an M60 tank chassis.

At medium height another range of air defense weapons comes into play. In Warsaw Pact armies this is represented by the SAM-8 Gecko and SAM-9 Gaskin with horizontal maximum ranges of 12km and 7km respectively, and vertical ranges of 6km and 5km. While Gecko is mounted on a 6×6 truck, Gaskin uses the BRDM-2. The US equivalent is Chaparral, with a 4800m maximum horizontal range and a height of 2500m, and mounted on the M730 tracked chassis. It was the intention to replace this with the Franco-German Roland system, but this was cancelled for budgetary reasons in 1981, and improvements are now being made to make Chaparral more effective. Roland is popular with a number of Continental European NATO armies and is usually mounted on a Marder chassis. It can engage aircraft flying up to speeds of Mach 1.5 at a horizontal range of over 20km up to a height of almost 1700m. The other major system in this family is the British Rapier, which had much success in the Falklands. This has a horizontal range of 7km and can engage aircraft up to a height of 3000m. Until now it has been mounted on a wheeled trailer, but is being put on tracks to give it added mobility.

Weapons operating in the high and very high level bands are all missiles, and Warsaw Pact examples are the SA-5 Gammon and SA-6 Gainful. On the NATO side, the US is carrying out an improvement program on its Hawk missile, which has been in service since 1960. Improved Hawk has a horizontal range of 40km and can engage aircraft from heights of 30m to 12,000km. Further back is found the Nike-Hercules system, but this is now being replaced by Patriot, which is designed to counter large numbers of high speed aircraft and short range missiles at all altitudes. It was originally planned that Patriot would

Above: The Euromissile Roland SAM system which was to have been bought by the US, but is used by a number of other NATO countries.
Right: Nike-Hercules is backbone of NADGE, but is now being replaced, eventually along with Hawk, by the Patriot.

also replace Hawk, but the latter, now that it has been improved, will remain in service for some years.

Air defense weapons can be used in two ways, for area defense or point defense. The former implies the protection of a formation or unit area of operations, while the latter is for defending a specific target such as a vital bridge on a main supply route, headquarters

or nuclear missile launcher site. One of the major problems in the employment of air defense ground weapons is over IFF. While certainly on the NATO side, the large majority of systems have an IFF capability and are able to interrogate aircraft, there is always the danger that the IFF equipment is malfunctioning. It is also very vulnerable to ECM. Therefore, it is likely in the heat of battle that any aircraft or helicopter, unless positively identified as friendly, will be engaged. In order to safeguard against shooting down friendly aircraft, the NATO practice is to define three states of air defense posture. 'Weapons tight' means that targets may only be engaged on order, while 'weapons hold' indicates that fire can only be opened after positive identification. The third, which is used when the enemy has obtained overwhelming air supremacy and allows any aerial target to be engaged, is 'weapons free'.

The Soviets have an air defense company consisting of four ZSU-23-4 and four SA-9 Gaskin in each tank and motor rifle regiment. At division there is an air defense regiment of five batteries each of four SA-6 Gainful or SA-8 Gecko. At army level there is a complete air defense missile brigade with three battalions. Each has three SA-4 Ganef batteries (three launchers each) and four batteries with six ZSU-23-4 in each. Further missile elements are available at front level. In NATO armies, air defense assets in the immediate battle area tend to be controlled at divisional level. The US corps has Stinger teams down at unit level, and the division also has an air defense artillery battalion with two Sgt York batteries, with eighteen systems in each, and two Chaparral SAM batteries (12 systems per battery). The Germans also control their assets in much the same way. The British, however, split control. Blowpipe teams are controlled at divisional level, but the two Rapier regiments in 1(BR) Corps are held in the Corps Artillery Division. The six batteries are then either sent to support the division or retained to guard vital point and area targets in the rear of the corps area. The high and very high level systems are deployed back in depth in an air defense belt which represents the NATO Air Defense Ground Environment (NADGE).

Locating artillery has a variety of very important roles. Besides obtaining current data on survey and meteorology, which is vital to the accuracy of the

guns, there is also the task of locating enemy artillery and mortars. The US Army is just bringing into service the Firefinder Artillery Locating System, which consists of two advanced phase array radars, one to locate artillery guns and the other mortars. They have the ability to locate a shell or mortar bomb in flight and then backtrack down its trajectory to the fire position. This is the principle behind all locating systems, and they work closely with the counter-battery units, feeding their information through artillery intelligence.

The other area in which locating artillery is involved is battlefield surveillance through the use of RPVs and drones. Drones have been in service for some years, and are essentially missiles which contain a camera. They fly on a preset flight path and then return. Their photographs are developed and the results analyzed in terms of possible targets. With the growing awareness that the land battle is likely to be ever fast moving, there is the danger that drone information will be out of date before it can be used,

and hence the need for 'real time' intelligence. Lockheed are therefore developing an RPV for the US Army. This will have a television camera for surveillance and a laser device for range-finding and target designation, which means that it can also be used in conjunction with aerial weapons systems. It can either fly on a preset course or be controlled by an operator and on return to its base it is recovered using a special net developed by the German firm of Dornier GmbH. Each division will have an RPV unit controlled by the divisional artillery. The Israelis used RPVs very successfully to pinpoint Syrian SAM sites in the Bekaa Valley in Lebanon in 1982, and all nations, including the Soviets, are recognizing their value. A variation is the Remotely Piloted Helicopter (RPH), which is also likely to appear above the battlefield in the next few years.

With the revolutionary technological developments now taking place, artillery is likely to assume an even more dominant role on the battlefield. Indeed, especially in NATO eyes, it could prove decisive in its ability to bring down devastating fire on both hard and soft targets with almost instantaneous response.

Left: Soviet SA-9 Gaskin mounted on BRDM-2.
Below: Canadian Remotely Piloted Helicopter.

SPECIAL TO TASK

US 82nd Airborne Division arrives on the battlefield.

Special to task forces are those which are organized and dedicated for particular strategic tasks. NATO has two major forces which come witnin this context, the ACE Mobile Force, which was mentioned in the introduction, and the Rapid Deployment Force.

The ACE Mobile Force was set up in 1960 to counter threats to the flanks of NATO without being forced to the ultimate step of immediate nuclear retaliation. In many ways it reflects more than anything else the true spirit of Article 5 of the North Atlantic Treaty, which recognizes that an attack on one member nation is an attack on the Alliance as a whole and that each member will 'assist the Party or Parties so attacked by taking forthwith, individually and in concert with other parties, such action as it deems necessary, including the use of armed force, to restore and maintain the security of the North Atlantic area'. In particular, being a multinational force, the ACE Mobile Force provides a clear demonstration of NATO solidarity.

The force has two major elements, land and air. The latter, ACE Mobile Force (Air) (AMF(A)), has no permanent commander or headquarters and when activated it is placed under the control of the Allied Tactical Air Force or Regional Air Commander of the area in which the AMF is deployed. Each nation in the force is responsible for providing its own airlift, although additional assistance is given by the US Military Airlift Command (MAC). The land element, AMF(L), is a permanent standing force, with headquarters at Seckenheim in the FRG and comes directly under SACEUR.

The post of Commander AMF(L) is held in turn by each of the nations involved and is currently a Canadian major general. His headquarters is multinational and no less than seven nations contribute to the force. The Belgians have a battalion of their Parachute Commando Regiment, a 105mm howitzer battery and Milan ATGW company, while the Canadians produce a battalion from their Special Service Force, a 105mm pack howitzer battery and a flight of tactical lift helicopters. The Italian contribution is an Alpini battalion, another 105mm battery and, if required, a field hospital. The Luxembourg element is notable in that it is the whole of her small operational army, the 1st (Light) Infantry Battalion. The Germans produce a heliborne battalion and 105mm battery, hospital and signals company, while the British have an infantry battalion, 105mm battery, CVR(T) reconnaissance squadron, communication elements, and the artillery and logistic headquarters, together with four Puma helicopters. Finally, the US provides another battalion and 105mm battalion, engineer and aviation companies. All elements, apart from the US, which is based in Northern Italy, are located in peacetime on national territory, but, being on light scales the force is quickly deployable.

The most likely areas to which the AMF will be

Far left: US psychological warfare (psywar) team with portable loudspeaker system.
Above: Soviet naval infantry landing from an air cushion vehicle.
Left: US Special Forces team wading a river.
Below: Soviet mountain troops. Because most Soviet training is carried out on open steppes, they consider the closer NATO Central Region terrain as semi-mountainous.

Left: British paratroops about to board a C-130 Hercules.
Below left: Soviet paratroops attack supported by a BMD MICV.
Above: British and US paratroops prior to a drop.
Below: Canadian paratroops from the Canadian Airborne Regiment.

deployed are Norway, Denmark, Italy, Greece and Turkey. Of particular concern are the maritime choke points, which are very likely Soviet objectives. The decision to deploy the AMF in a period of tension would take place at the very highest NATO level, the North Atlantic Council. If they considered that a show of force was needed to defuse the situation, they would call on the NATO Military Committee to recommend the form it should take. Provided that the member nation under threat agreed, and it was a threat on the flanks, SACEUR would be instructed to deploy the AMF. He would then give orders to the AMF(L) commander, and alert member nations providing the AMF(A) elements, as well as the Regional Air Command involved. AMF(A) would deploy on orders of the latter, while AMF(L) would be placed under AFNORTH or AFSOUTH, who would, as likely as not, delegate operational control to the local command in which the Force was being deployed. It must be emphasized, though, that the AMF is essentially a political deterrent, and that deploying it will, it is hoped, avert war. If hostilities do break out however, it would be, in spite of its light equipment, a valuable immediate reinforcement for the host nation. Its main problem is its size. If simultaneous crises should appear on both flanks, it is currently not large enough to be deployed to both.

The Middle East oil crisis and Yom Kippur War of 1973 made Western nations realize how dependent

they were on oil supplies from the Persian Gulf. The vulnerability of them was further reinforced by the overthrow of the Shah of Iran, the seizing of the US Embassy in Teheran and the holding of many of its members as hostage, as well as by the Soviet intervention in Afghanistan. Until this time, NATO attention had been concentrated firmly on Europe, but it was the US that recognized that threats could be developed against the Alliance elsewhere. The first public announcement of US concern came in President Carter's State of the Union address in 1980 when he warned the Soviet Union and the world in general that 'an attempt by any outside force to gain control of the Persian Gulf region will be repelled by any means necessary including military force'. In order to counter this threat, the Rapid Deployment Joint Task Force (RDJTF, or RDF for short) was set up, with a US Marine Corps general to command it. Initially it was placed under the US Readiness Command and its strength was envisaged as one Marine and four Army divisions. In fact, it is made up of a Marine Amphibious Force (MAF) with its associated air wing and 7th Marine Amphibious Brigade. The Army elements are spearheaded by the only airborne division remaining in the US inventory, 82nd Airborne Division of three brigades. One of these, the Division Ready Brigade (DRB) is on permanent standby. 101st Airborne Division is now an airmobile formation, equipped with the Black Hawk helicopter, and is also assigned to the RDF. A mechanized infantry division, the 24th, is also available, along with Ranger and Special Force elements. In all the RDF has a strength of 220,000 men, excluding USAF elements.

The main problem is the quick deployment of the force to the Persian Gulf. This would be carried out by MAC's strategic airlift, and ideally men and materiel would be fed in through a friendly airfield in the area. This, however, cannot be guaranteed. Thus the base of Diego Garcia in the Indian Ocean is being used, and the Marines would land here and draw their equipment from ships already prepositioned in the Indian Ocean. Indeed a Marine Task Force is permanently positioned in the Indian Ocean, and this could act as a spearhead, especially since Diego Garcia is some 2400 nautical miles from the Straits of Hormuz at the entrance to the Gulf. The Marines therefore might well have to lead the way. The other option is for 82nd Airborne Division to carry out a drop in order to seize and secure an airfield.

The RDF is not without its problems. There has been a question mark on its response time, and the placing of it under a new command, US Central Command (USCENTCOM) has shortened the lines of communication between it and the White House. The remoteness of Diego Garcia from the RDF's potential area of operations and the massive airlift resources required to lift the RDF from CONUS

mean that it will be some time before a force in reasonable strength will be on the ground. In the meantime, Soviet forces from the Southern TMO might well have seized the Gulf oilfields. There is also concern that the force lacks the weapons to deal with a large armor threat. Although it has ATGW, armor and air support, again it will take time to deploy it, and difficulty in coping with an armored thrust.

There is also a political problem. The RDF is essentially a national US force and is not part of NATO. Its existence and role benefit NATO countries and the US would like material contributions towards it from them. However, this has so far met with a lukewarm response, especially since NATO European members are finding it difficult enough to maintain their present force levels because of budgetary difficulties. At the same time, the Reagan Administration has called for the force to be increased to over 400,000 men in order to give it more of a global capability. If this is agreed, unless NATO nations are prepared to take over some of the RDF out-of-area commitments in the Middle East or contribute more to the defense of the Central Region, the US might well be forced to withdraw troops from Europe and the gap left might be hard to fill. Another point is that the Army divisions assigned to it also have a NATO reinforcement role, and by the time the RDF begins to deploy, World War III might well have broken out elsewhere, and these formations might be already committed.

Nevertheless, like the AMF, the RDF is essentially a political instrument, designed to deter a would be aggressor by its very existence, and this might be sufficient to prevent an overture to World War III being conducted in an area far removed from NATO's main area of interest.

In terms of spearheads, one of the notable aspects of the initial Soviet operations in Czechoslovakia in 1968 and Afghanistan in 1979 was the use of airborne units. Although they were not used in the parachute role, it was they who initially secured the civil airport at Prague so that further troops could be airlanded, and they were also deployed to Kabul a month before the actual intervention took place. In both cases, the ground troops then moved across the national borders and linked up with them. The Soviets have eight airborne divisions and these are considered an elite, an indication being that they all have the 'Guards' prefix.

There are two types of airborne troops, the normal airborne divisions and brigades, and those organized for long range reconnaissance and operations with partisans. The strategic missions of the former in general war are the seizure of centers of government and disruption of attempts to organize resistance, attacks on key ports and airfields which the enemy might use to pass reinforcements through, disruption of major logistic centers and to spearhead major assaults. At the operational and tactical levels they would be used to destroy NBC delivery means and attack reinforcements and headquarters, and in seizing key demolitions and bridges and other points which would facilitate the advance of the ground forces. Soviet airborne divisions are organized on a triangular basis with three airborne infantry regiments, each of three battalions of approximately 450 men each. The Soviets claim to be able to drop a complete airborne division in the space of 30 minutes and, if this is so, it would be an ideal way of seizing control of a vital area such as the Skagerrak or Dardanelles at the outset of war. Certainly with the weaponry which they have, they could hold for some time until reinforcements arrived.

Apart from the airborne divisions themselves, the Soviets have also introduced air assault brigades, which are made up of two light infantry battalions and two BMD battalions and are equipped with helicopters. They are likely to be placed under command of a front headquarters for a particular operation, the most likely being in conjunction with an OMG. In this case they would be used to seize and hold vital ground such as bridges over a major water obstacle, and the OMG would then link up with them. It is known that GSFG has an air assault brigade.

NATO places very much less emphasis on airborne forces than the Warsaw Pact. As has been described already, the US has one division, but this is very much part of the RDF, although it could be deployed to Europe. The British airborne element is retained in 5th Airborne Brigade based in the UK, but this is dedicated specifically to out-of-area operations. The Germans have three airborne brigades, but they are being used more and more for airmobile operations with helicopters. Indeed, the airmobile concept which was developed by the French in Algeria and the US in Vietnam is now considered to have very much more relevance to the Central Region than airborne operations, which would, in any event, be difficult to mount in a hostile air environment. Heliborne troops can react very much more quickly and hence are very much more effective in defense.

Another Soviet combat force which must be taken into account is the Naval Infantry, equivalent to the Marines. Here the threat is specifically on the flanks. The Soviet Baltic Fleet has two Naval Infantry brigades, the Northern Fleet and Black Sea Fleet a further two each, while a seventh is with the Pacific Fleet. These are trained in amphibious operations and although their equipment is generally obsolescent, the PT-76 amphibious tank and BTR-60PB being their main vehicles, and are on light scales, they nevertheless do provide a threat. An amphibious assault behind the forward defenses in Norway, the seizure of the Danish islands, or even a diversionary attack on the German or Dutch coast well in the rear of the Central Region would cause NATO problems.

Below: RDF Hueycobras over the Pyramids.

ENGINEERS

US Corps of Engineers bridging boat.

The overall role of the combat engineers in war is to improve the mobility of their own troops, while impeding that of the enemy's. Their tasks are therefore neatly divided into mobility and countermobility.

Mobility tasks are mainly concerned with the improvement of routes which combat troops wish to use. They cover improvements to roads and tracks, the overcoming of natural obstacles such as rivers and streams, the clearing of artificial obstacles, including minefields, and the construction, maintenance and repair of airlanding facilities for fixed and rotary wing aircraft. Countermobility, on the other hand, includes route denial to the enemy by demolition, mining and cratering, the preparation of obstacles, artificial and the enhancement of natural obstacles and the destruction of logistic installations to prevent them falling into enemy hands. In order to carry out these tasks a wide range of equipment is needed.

In order to put these tasks in their proper context, it is simplest to describe the role of the engineer as the battle unfolds. Once NATO has made the decision to deploy its troops in the Central Region, the engineers will be especially busy. Because detailed plans are already drawn up, they will be well aware of their tasks and engineer units will have been allocated to them. Almost all NATO armies have an

engineer battalion in each division, with further support at corps level, and Warsaw Pact forces have a similar organization, except that each tank and motor rifle regiment also has an engineer company. The first task of NATO engineers will be to put the barrier plan into effect. This is the overall construction plan for obstacles which each corps has.

First and foremost is the laying of minefields. There are five different kinds. Protective minefields are those laid close to a defensive position, normally just out of grenade range, and are often put down by the unit itself. Nuisance minefields are self-explanatory, and are scattered groups of mines laid to disrupt the enemy. Ideal sites are approaches to bridges, around roadblocks, ferry sites and fords. Defensive minefields are more extensive and are laid as part of the overall tactical plan in order to disorganize and delay the enemy by breaking up his attacks. They are always covered by direct and indirect fire weapons. Barrier minefields are usually the largest and are placed to deny the enemy entry into a particular piece of terrain. They are often combined with a natural obstacle and again covered by fire. The final type is the phoney minefield, which is marked as a minefield, but has no mines laid.

Mines are either antitank or antipersonnel and minefields normally consist of a mixture of both. The basic type of antitank mine is the heavy handlaid

Left: A British Barmine layer towed by an FV432 APC.
Above: The oblong Barmines are fed into the chute of the
layer enabling an antitank minefield to be rapidly laid.

type which relies on blast to destroy the tracks and
suspension of the tank, and is represented by the
US M15 antitank mine, the Soviet TM-46 and the
British Mk 7. They are usually fitted with antihandling devices. A heavier version is the US M21
heavy antitank mine which has a shaped charge
effect, producing a self-forging fragment and this is
known as the Misznay-Schardin effect. These are all
metallic mines and can be easily detected. In order
to make them more difficult to locate all-plastic mines
have now been introduced including the US M19
Antitank mine. Another type of antiarmor device is
the Off-Route Antitank Mine (ORATM). Here a
pressure tape is placed across the route and when an
AFV crosses over it, a hollow charge projectile is
launched from the side of the road, hitting the vehicle
in the side. The US uses the M24 and the British,
the French MIACAH (Mine Antichar à Action
Horizontale) system. The US is also developing a
new system which replaces the tell-tale tape with an
acoustic sensor and infrared fuse. A further type of
antitank mine is the British Barmine, with an unconventional oblong shape, which has been designed
this way for speed of laying.

The main antipersonnel mine used by NATO
armies is the US Claymore mine. It was originally
developed by the US as a defensive weapon against
enemy infiltration and mass attack and consists of a
container with 700 steel balls, which, when detonated
using a trip wire or electrical impulse, fires the balls
over a 60° arc. They are lethal up to 50m range. The
Soviet OZM3 works on a similar principle. The
Soviets also still use a number of wooden mines, both
antitank and antipersonnel, which, although hard to
detect and cheap to produce, cannot be laid using
mechanical means.

The manual laying of minefields is a time consuming business, and several mechanical laying
systems are now in service. The Soviet PMR-3 is a
two-wheel trailer with plough incorporated, and is
normally towed behind a modified BTR-152 wheeled
APC and can lay mines at a rate of 4–6km per hour.
The US Ground-Emplaced Mine-Scattering Systems
(GEMSS) lays 4lb antitank surface mines and is a
trailer, like the PMR-3, and can lay a 2500m minefield,
which will consist of several rows, in much less time
than the 50 hours using M15 and M21 mines.
The mine itself has a magnetic influence and can be
set for deactivation after a certain period so that
friendly troops can move across the area. The British
and Germans also use the Barmine layer, again
similar to PMR-3 and GEMSS. While GEMSS also

lays antipersonnel mines, the British and Germans use the Ranger for this type. This is a multibarrel projector system normally mounted on an APC. It has 72 disposable tubes, each with 18 antipersonnel mines, which have been specially designed for the system. A tube is launched every second, and the 18 mines in it are randomly distributed up to a range of 100m, being automatically armed 20 seconds after launch. When laying a minefield the Barmine layer and Ranger will operate together.

Both the US and Soviets also lay mines using helicopters, but the latest development in mine warfare is the remotely delivered mine (RDM), fired by artillery or MRLS. The US Army has combined GEMSS with its Family of Scatterable Mines (FASCAM) program. This is designed to lay down hasty minefields in order to canalize the enemy into areas where he will present a good target. While conventional minefields have the disadvantage that they can impede the defender's mobility as well as that of the attacker, FASCAM has much more flexibility and fits in much better with the highly mobile battle which the US Army expects to fight in the future.

Defensive minefields will be laid with clear lanes running through them so that the covering forces in front of them are able to get back through when the

time for withdrawal comes. NATO doctrine considers the control of these and key bridges which have been set for demolition as very important. Indeed, history is littered with examples of bridges being blown too early, thus trapping friendly forces on the wrong side of the river, or too late, enabling the enemy to capture it intact. A classic example of the latter was the Remagen Bridge over the Rhine, which the US 9th Armored Division captured in March 1945 and cost the life of the German officer in charge in front of a firing squad. The basic principles of reserved demolitions are that control over them is kept at the highest level for as long as possible and that there must be sufficient force to defend them against enemy surprise attack. It is also necessary for all concerned to have accurate information on the troops likely to pass back through the reserve demolition and monitor their progress. As the battle gets closer, so the power to authorize the firing of the demolition is passed down the chain of command and normally ends up with the demolition guard commander, who will give the engineer firing party the order. Special forms are used so that there can be no confusion over the instructions, and these are standard throughout all NATO armies.

The Soviets are faced with a mine clearance problem before they even cross the border since they

must clear lanes through the minefields which run the length of the IGB and Czech-German borders. In order not to sacrifice surprise, these mines will be removed some time before hostilities break out. Indeed, some mines were lifted by East German border guards in 1983. Once across the border, however, the problem becomes much more severe. The simplest form of detection device is the probe which, in view of the non-metallic mine, is still widely used. For metallic mines, metal detectors are used. Often, though, it will only be when the first vehicle has blown up that the unit will know that it has come across mines.

The basic method of minefield clearance is by hand, but it is very time consuming, especially in dealing with mines equipped with antihandling devices. Since, for the Soviets, speed is of the essence, this method will be seldom used. Instead they will attempt to 'storm' the minefield with engineers leading the attack, while artillery and armor attempt to suppress the enemy fire. Smoke will also be used to provide cover. As a quick way of blowing lanes, the Soviets use hose charges. These are in 500m rigid lengths and are either winched over the minefield or pushed by tanks. The former is either done by means

Far left: British Combat Engineer Tractor towing the Giant Viper minefield clearance device.
Left: British entrenching machine.
Below: Soviet BTM Trencher. It can remove 600–800m³ of earth per hour.

of a pulley or by means of a rocket propelled grapnel. Another method is to lay it across the minefield with an explosive charge. A better and more effective method is to use a flexible hose, which comes coiled in a box and can be fired from a tank or APC. Both the US and British have similar systems in the M-1 and Giant Viper. The main drawbacks are that the hose is much shorter than the rigid one and the rocket propulsion system is not totally reliable. Indeed, there have been incidents where the hose has wrapped itself round the turret of the tank detonating it and blown it off. The other method, especially when there is not sufficient covering fire available, is to use tanks equipped with ploughs or plough-roller combinations, but this still requires engineers to follow them up as they can only clear an imperfect lane, often missing some mines. Interestingly, the British and US developed many such systems in World War II, which were generally ignored afterwards. The mine threat in Vietnam forced the US Army to reintroduce them, and the US formations in Germany are now equipped with

AFV mine clearance devices.

There are other types of barrier or obstacle which can and will be constructed. One of the more traditional ones is the antitank ditch. This can be constructed using explosives and plant equipment. The Soviets also have a trench digging and ditching system. An antitank ditch can be surmounted in a number of ways. One is by dropping fascines made up of pieces of wood bound together in a large roll, an old method which the British developed for use with the early tanks crossing trench lines in World War I. If time permits, plant equipment, or dozer blades mounted on tanks can push the spoil back into the ditch. Both NATO and the Warsaw Pact have dozer blade attachments for tanks and they are also very useful in enhancing AFV fire positions. The third method is using a bridgelayer tank, and some of these will accompany the leading engineers in a Soviet advance, along with mine plough and dozer tanks. There are three basic types. There is the straight forward bridge for short gaps – the Soviet MTU-1 with a span of 12m and mounted on a T-54 chassis. The cantilever bridge, which is carried with the two end sections folded on top of the middle, is represented by the Soviet MTU-20, which is on a T-55 chassis and has a 20m span. Finally, there is the scissors bridge for wider gaps, and this is the most popular with both alliances. The US M60 Armored Vehicle

Left: British sappers prepare a makeshift landing strip.
Below left: British Combat Engineer Tractor carrying trackway, often vitally important for maintaining bank entry and exit trafficability during river crossings.
Below: Launching a pontoon section of a Soviet PMP floating bridge.

Above left: Soviet TMM 60 ton scissors bridge. A bridge set is four spans and can cover a 40m gap.
Below left: Soviet GSP ferry with a T-55 tank. Only four minutes are needed to put it into operation.
Above: Canadian Leopard bridgelayer.
Below: US Engineers construct a Ribbon Bridge.

Launched Bridge (AVLB) has a span of just over 18m, while the British Chieftain AVLB can cover 23m. The Warsaw Pact armies rely on the East German BLG-60 (T-55 chassis, 21.6m span) and the Czech MT-55 (T-55 chassis, 18m span). In all cases the bridge is laid hydraulically and takes 2–5 minutes to place in position. The tank will then retire behind cover and wait until it can retrieve the bridge again.

Other types of artificial obstacle include chopping down trees onto forest rides, the cratering of roads and blowing down houses in urban areas. If time permits, natural obstacles can be enhanced. Slopes can be made steeper so that AFVs cannot climb up them, and the banks of rivers and canals made steeper so that amphibious vehicles cannot enter or exit. In places it is possible to cause flooding. However, unless some of these measures can, where acceptable to the local population, be carried out in peacetime, it is most unlikely that NATO engineers will have sufficient time to carry out more than local route denial. What, however, is important is that minefields, demolitions and other obstacles are properly recorded. Unless friendly troops know of their location, they will suffer both mobility problems and casualties, apart from the problems of clearing minefields after the war is over.

The Central Region is crisscrossed by numerous rivers, streams and canals. These provide ideal natural obstacles, and are of particular concern to the Soviets. Their first thought would be to try and seize bridges still intact over the river, before they reach it. This would be a typical objective for a heliborne or even, if the obstacle was a formidable one, the air assault brigade, airborne troops or the OMG. If they were unable to do this or it was not considered feasible, the next option would be to try a 'bounce crossing' off the line of march, and finally a deliberate crossing. In all this, the most important role is that of the engineers. The first task is reconnaissance. Although they will have detailed technical information about the river and likely crossing places, the engineers will still need to confirm the state of the river, new obstacles and defenses, including mines. Using BRDMs, they will carry out a detailed technical reconnaissance, not just in the area where the crossing is to be made, but over a long stretch of the river in order not to indicate the likely crossing places to the enemy. A Division will usually require four crossing points.

In terms of actually crossing the river, the first stage is to secure a lodgement on the far bank. This will usually be done by motor rifle elements swimming their vehicles across under the cover of both direct and indirect fire and smoke. It may be, however, that the entry and/or exit banks are unsuitable for this, in which case they will be transported across on special amphibious load carrying vehicles – the PTS-M and the older and smaller K-61. Once the bridgehead is established ferries, usually the GSP, will bring across tanks to give added support to the bridgehead and, in conjunction with additional motor rifle elements and self-propelled artillery, to continue the advance.

Finally, floating bridges will be put in.

The main floating bridge employed by the Soviets is the PMP, which was first seen in operational use by the West during the Egyptian crossing of the Suez Canal in 1973. It is made up of a number of pontoons, which are each transported folded on a KrAZ-255B truck. They are offloaded into the river, unfolded and then married up together, with the assistance of power boats. A complete bridge set consists of 32 river and four shore pontoons, but is normally used in a halfset and manned by a pontoon company. A halfset can be laid in some thirty minutes and will span 110m, giving a weight capacity of 60 tonnes. The older TMM bridge is also still in service, and airborne forces use the PVD-20, which is air droppable and will take loads up to 8 tonnes. NATO floating bridges have an advantage over their Pact rivals in that the vehicles which transport the pontoon sections are themselves amphibious and make up the floating supports for the bridge, which can be

Left: A Chinook delivers plant equipment to British Royal Engineers.
Below: US M577 armored command vehicle crossing a Dutch pontoon bridge.
Bottom: Soviet 110 ton ferry constructed from PMP equipment.

assembled and dismantled in a faster time.

Because of the vulnerability of bridges to air attack, the normal practise on both sides is to assemble them at last light and dismantle them again before first light. Thus a crossing might well take place over two or even more nights. Vehicles waiting to cross will remain in hides until called forward, and this needs an efficient control system. In the Soviet Army this is done by the engineers themselves, but NATO armies prefer to use other units for this task, which is often given to reconnaissance units. Another aspect which has to be carefully watched is the state of the approaches to the bridge on either side, and trackway will often be used to prevent the ground from becoming too churned up, resulting in bogged vehicles. By the same token, the means to recover vehicles which have broken down close to the bridge need to be readily available. A final point is that, although the ability of Soviet tanks to deep ford using schnorkelling kit has been much publicized in the past, it is very dangerous and there have been numerous accidents. Hence the Soviets are very unlikely to employ this crossing method unless nothing else is available. Even then, it will only be attempted after a very careful inspection of both the banks and river bottom by frogmen.

Up until recently, NATO engineers have suffered from a shortage of modern equipment and have found it ever more difficult to carry out their tasks effectively. One of the main problems is that they have had to be reliant on ordinary APCs for much of their work, and these have proved very unsatisfactory. As a result a number of light armored vehicles have been especially designed for the combat engineer, and including dozer, winch and crane devices. Typical of this new type of vehicle is the British Combat Engineer Tractor (CET) and the US M9 armored dozer, which is just entering service with the US Army. The Germans, too, are developing a specialist engineer vehicle based on the Leopard 2 chassis. The Soviets also have the IMR Combat Engineer Vehicle (CEV), which is on a T-55 chassis.

Another valuable engineer role is that of assisting the forward troops in constructing field defenses, especially in the construction of weapons positions and dugouts. Cratering kits, like the US M180, which can create a hole 2m deep by 9m across in 30 minutes, enable effective defenses to be prepared very much more quickly than hitherto, and the introduction of prefabricated devices to enhance protection is going some way to counter the ever increasing weight of fire which can be brought down on field defenses. The engineers of both sides also advise on camouflage, and the Soviets have special camouflage companies at army level who can also construct dummy trenches and vehicles. Other tasks include water supply and purification and the construction of Petrol, Oil and Lubricants (POL) pipelines and storage facilities.

LOGISTICS

Air resupply – C-130 Hercules delivers palletized supplies using the Low Altitude Parachute Extraction System (LAPES).

Admiral Ernest J King, the US Naval Chief of Naval Operations during World War II, who masterminded the war at sea against Japan, once remarked, 'I don't know what the hell this "logistics" is that Marshall (Chairman US Joint Chiefs of Staff) is always talking about, but I want some of it'. In a nutshell, it is the supplying and maintaining of forces in the field. Although it is widely considered as the 'unglamorous' side of war, without an efficient logistics system an army will 'wither on the vine', as Admiral King recognized.

Logistics embraces a wide range of subjects from vehicle repair, the supply of clothing and the provision of radio batteries to the treatment of wounded and prisoners of war, mail and the supply of reinforcements. They can, however, be broken down into two broad categories – equipment and personnel.

In terms of supplies, the three essential items that any army needs are ammunition, POL (Petrol/gas, Oil, Lubricants) and food. Ammunition expenditure, especially by artillery, is likely to be very high in World War III. Since the average self-propelled gun seldom has a carrying capacity of more than fifty rounds and is likely to move frequently, much of an artillery unit's immediate reserves of ammunition has to be kept on wheels. One problem with this is the vulnerability of soft skinned vehicles in the battle area, and the US Army is solving this by means of the field artillery ammunition support vehicle (FAASV). This is an armored vehicle which can carry 93 rounds of 155mm or 48 rounds of 203mm. Using an automatic

stacker and hydraulic conveyor, the rounds can be passed to the gun without the crews of either vehicle having to get out and expose themselves to enemy fire.

If the war is to be as mobile as both sides envisage, consumption of POL is going to be very high. Both sides will construct pipelines as far forward as possible, but fuel will have to be transported by truck to the forward troops. In the past, fuel was normally put in jerricans. The major advantage of these was the ability for POL to be manhandled to forward positions. However, replenishment with them takes time. Instead, almost all armies now use bowsers, which can refuel as many as four vehicles simultaneously, and what is called 'running' replenishment is carried out. The POL vehicles travel to a prearranged rendezvous, and the unit to be replenished passes through, taking on fuel and ammunition as it does so. Because of the air threat, replenishment of forward units is almost invariably done by night.

With high combat vehicle attrition rates, recovery and repair is vital. The armies of both sides have mechanics at company level in their mechanized units. Their main tasks are vehicle recovery and minor repairs which are beyond the limitations of the crews. Both the Germans in North Africa and the Russians on the Eastern Front during World War II recognized the importance of recovering vehicle casualties from the battlefield in order to maintain strength in armor. Often it was found that relatively simple repairs were all that was needed to make AFVs

Left: Soviet ZIL-131 6 × 6 truck.
Above: US 8 × 8 M985 cargo truck.

fit again, but also, as the Soviets recognize, where spare parts are difficult to obtain, vehicle casualties can often be cannabilized in order to repair other vehicles. All NATO and Warsaw Pact armies use the armored recovery vehicle (ARV), which is normally a tank chassis with a winch and sometimes a crane for lifting major assemblies. Casualties, if they cannot be repaired by the unit, will normally be backloaded for second line repair.

Logistic vehicles operating in the forward area need to be highly mobile, especially as they might well have to travel across country. Although all military trucks have drive to all wheels, which enables them to move off roads, they can only travel slowly cross-country. The answer to this is the High Mobility Load Carrier (HMLC), designed specifically for movement off the road. The British were the first to enter this field when they introduced the Stalwart in the mid Sixties. The Soviets have the ZIL-135, which was originally designed for transporting the Shaddock and Frog-7 missiles. The best of this type of vehicle in the Warsaw Pact is, however, the Czech 8 tonne 8 X 8 Tatra 813. The West Germans now have the Transportpanzer Fuchs, a multirole armored vehicle, which uses many of the Luchs reconnaissance vehicle components. The US Army has developed the Hummer, which will replace most of its jeeps and Gama Goat trucks, and is introducing an entirely new truck fleet.

Turning to personnel, casualty treatment and evacuation is perhaps the most important aspect. Even if World War III remains conventional, casualties are likely to be very high on both sides. They will not occur just from gunshot wounds, mines, shrapnel, burns and blast, but also from chemical attack. Furthermore, shell shock or battle fatigue casualties are likely to be high in view of the concentration of fire to which front line troops will be subjected. Thus the medical services of both sides will be very stretched, and should the fighting turn nuclear, the situation will be even worse. At the very lowest level, as the British learnt in the Falklands, much can be done if every man is well trained in First Aid. Normally, there is at company level a medic with an armored ambulance, and the first task is to recover the casualty and give him immediate First Aid. He is then taken back to battalion, where there is a medical officer. Every man usually carries a field dressing and a morphine syrette, and if he has been given the latter, this must be noted – it is normally written on his forehead. The medical officer will diagnose his injuries and redress his wounds. The next stage is then to get him back to a collecting station in the rear. This will be done by armored ambulance or ideally, if available, helicopter. At the collecting station, casualties will be sorted into categories and those requiring surgery are taken to what, in US Army terms, is called a Mobile Army Surgical Hospital (MASH), which is situated in the divisional rear area. From then on, the patient is taken back by

stages to a base hospital. This is the outline system used by NATO armies, and the Soviet system is roughly similar, although it is questionable whether the Warsaw Pact soldier will receive the same standard of treatment and attention.

Prisoner of War (PW) handling is also likely to be a problem in a fast moving battle. On initial capture, PWs are searched and interrogated. The latter can result in valuable intelligence, since the PW is likely to be in a state of shock and may well volunteer information without realizing that he has done so. This is even though the Geneva Convention allows a man only to give his name, rank, number and religion. It is then important to pass PWs back as quickly as possible.

Refugees may severely restrict the movement of troops unless they are properly controlled. During the campaign in France and the Low Countries in May 1940, the sheer mass of people fleeing from the Germans often forced military units off the roads. In the Central Region, the civil population will be encouraged as much as possible to stay put in their houses, but it is unlikely that this will be more than partially heeded, especially by those living near the border with the East.

As for those routes required specifically for military purposes, these are designated, in NATO parlance, Main Supply Routes (MSR). As their name suggests, these will be the main logistic arteries for the forward troops, and it is important that they are kept open the whole time. One of the enemy's tasks will be to disrupt them, and hence they

Top: Soviet BMP company refueling. Bowsers will be used in forward areas.
Above: T-62 climbs aboard a MAZ-537 tank transporter.
Above right: A Soviet field hospital.
Right: In order to save track wear, tanks will, where possible, use tank transporters or railroad for long moves in rear areas. These are M60A1s.

will need to be guarded by mobile patrols and static guards at vulnerable points such as bridges. Engineer support will have to be readily available in case they are blocked by damage, and diversions put into effect while they are being repaired.

Both NATO and the Warsaw Pact have large static logistic installations well to the rear, where are held what is known in NATO as the War Maintenance Reserve (WMR). These contain everything required to fight the war and, while probably not more than seven days worth is held with corps or Warsaw Pact armies, the balance is held in these depots. The NATO depots, which each member nation has, are either in national territory or, in the case of overseas countries, as the USA, UK and Canada are in the Central Region, within theater. The Warsaw Pact has a very large depot at Grossborn in Poland, with subsidiaries in the GDR, Czechoslovakia and Hungary. When these stores are outloaded they will be moved by rail, water or road forward to the corps area and then broken down into divisional slices in corps dumps. The Warsaw Pact is especially reliant on railroads, which are not as dense as those in Western Europe and hence make obvious targets for air attack. They will run right up to the armies, and each of the latter will have a railhead, where the supplies are then crossloaded onto trucks. One significant point is that, although Eastern European railroads are a wider gauge than in the West, the Soviets keep stocks of conversion kits close to the borders. In this way they can, once the advance has penetrated deep enough take advantage of the FRG railroad system.

The initial NATO priority for reinforcements will be those earmarked to bring front line divisions up to strength. These can either be individual or unit reinforcements. The former are for units and formations already in place and are normally additional staff officers or specialists. As for the latter, USAREUR's prime concern will be the bringing across from CONUS of the two brigades each for 3rd and 4th Mechanized Infantry Divisions. The Germans will be mobilizing their Territorial Command, while the British bring across the reinforcing infantry battalions for their three armored divisions and deploy 2nd Infantry Division from UK. The Dutch and Belgians will be bringing the elements of their corps which are stationed on national territory up to strength and moving them into the corps areas. In terms of the calling up of reserves, the conscript armies have an advantage over those which are volunteer in that they have a larger pool of trained manpower to call upon. Thus the Dutch, for example, retain their conscripts for two years on the reserve after they have completed their active duty, and have them already organized into units, which carry out a period of training each year. The US Army has recently evolved the concept of the Total Army. This is aimed at binding the National Guard and

Army Reserve more closely to the Regular Army, with much more integration than hitherto. In general, National Guard units are organized into combat divisions and brigades, while the Army Reserve provides individual reinforcements and units to strengthen regular formations. Most of the latter are in the combat support, combat service support and general support roles, although there are some combat units. The British Regular Army reserves are earmarked as individual reinforcements, while the Territorial Army provides formed units and brigades and indeed makes up the greater part of 2nd Infantry Division. The Canadians will look to the Militia.

Reinforcements from CONUS will come initially by air, flying in MAC's C-5 Galaxies, C-130 Hercules and C-141 Starlifters. Civil airliners will also be commandeered for use as well. For those regular units which are permanently earmarked for the Central Region, which include III (US) Corps, made up of 1st Cavalry Division, 2nd Armored Division, 1st, 4th and 5th Mechanized Infantry Divisions, 6th Cavalry (Air Combat) Brigade and 3rd Armored Cavalry Regiment, their vehicles and equipment are already in theater. Under a new system, Prepositioned Material Configured to Unit Sets (POMCUS), which operates on the same principle as the US Marine Corps prepositioned ships in the Indian Ocean, units arriving in the Central Region from CONUS draw up complete sets of vehicles and equipment, thus very significantly reducing the time needed to prepare them. CONUS formations have the opportunity to confirm POMCUS during the annual *Reforger* maneuvers which involve airlifting units from CONUS to Europe. Although the airlift is vital for speedy reinforcement, the majority of National Guard and Army Reserve units will come by sea, along with their equipment, and will begin embarking about thirty days after mobilization has been called. Indeed, 90% of the total lift across the Atlantic will be by sea.

Apart from reinforcements to strengthen the order of battle, there is also the need to cater for vehicle and personnel replacements for those who have become casualties. In the Warsaw Pact, the echelon system, whereby divisions continue in action until they have suffered 50% casualties or more, means that replacements take the form of formations rather than individual replacements. Thus, once the 1st echelon divisions have become exhausted, the 2nd echelon will take over, while the remains of the 1st will be refitted and requipped over a period of time. NATO, having fewer divisions available, will try and keep them topped up with replacements.

Right: The Japanese Maritime Self Defence Force has built a series of light escorts of the *Chikugo* class, of which the *Iwase*(DE.219) is a unit.

FIGHTING SHIPS
OF THE WORLD

SUB-LAUNCHED MISSILES

HMS _Revenge_, one of the four British Polaris nuclear-powered ballistic missile submarines. Built in the late 1960s, they will be replaced by four Trident boats in the late 1980s.

Until the 1950s navies were undoubtedly outranked by armies and in particular air forces, because not even the United States Navy could boast of a long range ballistic missile. All that changed when in 1956 the US Navy was given permission to develop a solid-fuel intermediate range ballistic missile (IRBM), code-named Polaris.

The technical problems were formidable. Not only must the missile travel accurately along a ballistic trajectory to a target a thousand miles away, it must also be fired underwater and rise from the water before the main rocket motor ignites. Given that a whole range of new technologies had to be developed, the period of four years from the 1956 decision to the moment on 20 July 1960 when the submarine *George Washington* fired two operational UGM-27A Polaris A1s was remarkably short. By comparison the Soviets were able to deploy the SS-N-4 Sark IRBM in the *Golf* and *Hotel* class submarines by roughly the same time (1960–61) although the Sark had a range of only 300 miles and could not be launched underwater. Even the substitution of the SS-N-5 Serb missile, with a range of 700 miles only marginally increased their chance of surviving Western antisubmarine measures, and by 1967 the United States had moved on to the Polaris A3, with a range of 2880 miles.

The original Polaris and its nuclear-propelled submarine delivery platforms were virtually immune to a preemptive strike, primarily because Soviet anti-submarine forces could not operate in the areas in which the American, British and French nuclear ballistic submarines (SSBNs) would launch their missiles. So sure was the US Navy in its assurance of the SSBN's invulnerability that the successor to Polaris, the UGM-73A Poseidon was given the same range, and merely used its increased size to double the payload and provide greater accuracy and penetration aids ('penaids') to beat Soviet defenses.

All this changed when the Soviets developed the SS-N-8. When it was first deployed in 1973 Western Intelligence was deeply worried to learn that it had a range of 4800 miles, as against 2880 miles for Polaris A3 and Poseidon. It was also credited with a circular error probable (CEP) of about 1300ft, similar to the American land-based Minuteman. Unlike the Sark and Serb the SS-N-8 could be launched underwater, and the Delta type submarines had a configuration similar to Western SSBNs, for the first time. To add to Western fears, the SS-N-8 proved that it could outrange the successor to Poseidon, the as yet untried Trident; whereas Trident I was planned to have a range of 4350 miles the SS-N-8 showed that it could reach out to 5700 miles – making it a submarine-launched ICBM rather than an IRBM.

As Polaris had been originally conceived as a survivable system, which could retaliate if US land-based strategic forces were by some mischance to be destroyed, this Soviet development was unwelcome

news. US strategic planners had previously assumed that any Soviet 'first strike' would be on a massive scale, so that the Polaris submarines would have to launch their 'second strike' promptly. All that was needed to ensure the 'survivability' of Polaris was the issue of the necessary commands to the SSBNs at sea to fire. However, by the late 1960s it was becoming clear that a much bigger risk was the 'escalating' conventional war which culminates in a nuclear exchange – possibly even a limited one such as Sir John Hackett envisages in his book *The Third World War*, with Minsk and Birmingham (UK) wiped out but no other nuclear weapons used.

If such a sequence of events happens (and many believe that it fits more closely with Soviet thinking than the original idea of an immediate all-out exchange) a high-priority target for Soviet missiles would be US submarine bases and the Polaris, Poseidon and Trident command and control centers. As all the available SSBNs would have been sent to sea (including those already on station) they would now be running short of food and water, and equipment would be needing maintenance. They would also have been attacked by Soviet antisubmarine forces, and it must be assumed that some would have been located and destroyed – perhaps as many as half their number might be sunk or out of action.

Above: The USS *Ethan Allen* (SSBN.608) is one of a number of Polaris and Poseidon boats being replaced by Trident subs.
Below left: Soviet Yankee class submarines carry 16 SS-N-6 missiles.

Since the mid-1960s the Soviet Navy has undergone a subtle change in its makeup. As the strategic threat posed by the attack carriers' twin-engined bombers began to recede (or at least to appear less dangerous) the threat to the Russian heartland from Polaris missiles became more believable. And yet, how could the Polaris submarine be attacked, when they were operating in Western-dominated waters?

The answer was to push antisubmarine warfare (ASW) forces further out into those traditional 'friendly' seas, where they could quite legitimately track and identify Western submarines, so that on the outbreak of war they could be quickly attacked and sunk. Evidence for this change in tactics lies in the building of large numbers of powerful antisubmarine ships, culminating in the helicopter carriers *Leningrad* and *Moskva* and the hybrid cruiser carriers *Kiev* and *Minsk*. Even the development of weapons and tactics clearly intended to attack the US Navy's aircraft carriers reinforces the argument, for the Soviets know that the 'sanctuary' provided by carrier air power in the Mediterranean, for example, prevents their ASW forces from tracking SSBNs.

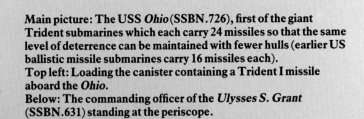

Main picture: The USS *Ohio* (SSBN.726), first of the giant
Trident submarines which each carry 24 missiles so that the same
level of deterrence can be maintained with fewer hulls (earlier US
ballistic missile submarines carry 16 missiles each).
Top left: Loading the canister containing a Trident I missile
aboard the *Ohio*.
Below: The commanding officer of the *Ulysses S. Grant*
(SSBN.631) standing at the periscope.

One of the most powerful arguments, therefore, for developing a longer-ranged Submarine-Launched Ballistic Missile (SLBM) is the need to get the SSBNs further away from hostile ASW forces – for the Americans this means closer to the Atlantic and Pacific seaboards, and for the Russians it means the Arctic and the Black Sea, where friendly aircraft and ships can provide cover. In other words, the SSBN becomes no more than a mobile vehicle for getting the SLBMs out of harbor and beneath the waves.

There were other unrelated reasons for the US Navy to reorganize its SSBN fleet of 41 Polaris and Poseidon submarines, the need to streamline maintenance and to enable each SSBN to spend a greater proportion of its service life 'on station'. This feature, combined with the Undersea Long-range Missile System (ULMS) proposed in 1967, promised a more efficient and cost effective underwater deterrent for the 1980s and 1990s, but it was not until the end of 1972 that Lockheed received the development contract for the C4 Trident. Initial plans were to retrofit 10 (later 12) of the *Lafayette* and *Benjamin Franklin* classes of SSBN with 16 Trident missiles, and to replace the remaining 31 SSBNs with 16 new *Ohio* class, carrying 24 Tridents each.

With a submerged displacement of 18,700 tons the *Ohio*'s were the largest submarines ever designed, although subsequently eclipsed in size by the Soviet *Typhoon* type (30,000 tons). Apart from their massive length of 560ft overall they are similar to the earlier SSBNs, with the Trident missiles launched from a double row of vertical tubes abaft the sail. Although SSBNs are not intended to take offensive action against surface ships or other submarines, for self-defense they are armed with four 21-inch torpedo tubes, angled out to port and starboard, ahead of the sail, and they have a big BQQ-6 spherical sonar in the bow compartment.

The first of the US Navy's Trident submarines, the USS *Ohio* (SSBN-726) went to sea at the end of 1981, and her sisters *Michigan*, *Florida*, *Georgia*, *Rhode Island* and *Alabama* are in varying stages of construction. Another ten, numbered SSBN.732-741 are authorized, and the cost of the latest is running at more than $350 million. Backing them up are ten earlier SSBNs, converted from Poseidon to Trident in 1978–82, starting with the *Francis Scott Key* and ending with the *Casimir Pulaski* in 1982. Ten older boats, the *Ethan Allen* and *George Washington* classes were reclassified as attack submarines (SSNs) in 1980, which involved cutting them into three sections,

removing the 16 missile tubes and then re-welding the forward and after sections together. This elaborate procedure was necessary to comply with the terms of the first Strategic Arms Limitation Treaty (SALT 1), which limited the number of nuclear warheads each side could deploy.

The Soviet equivalent to the American SSBNs was the 9300-ton Yankee class, which, unlike the earlier boats, had SS-N-6 missiles with a range of 1100–1600 miles. In all 34 of these submarines were built before production switched to the 10,000-ton Delta I, which had 12 tubes carrying the long range SS-N-8. After 18 were built a slightly larger type, the 11,400-ton Delta II, was built, with 16 missiles. In 1979 the Delta III appeared, its higher casing over the missile tubes indicating a longer missile; this was codenamed SS-N-18 by NATO, and it is believed to be a 4000-mile range missile with no fewer than seven warheads in one version.

The impact of the SS-N-8 on Western planning has already been mentioned, but this was nothing compared to the psychological shock when in 1981 the Pentagon revealed the existence of the *Typhoon* class, displacing 30,000 tons and 600ft long, and armed with a missile tentatively identified as SS-NX-20 (the 'X' signifying experimental). It was no use commentators pointing out that SSBNs are not intended to fight one another, and that sheer size is not a measure of fighting power (almost certainly the greater size of Soviet missiles is largely a reflection of their designers' inability to design smaller rocket motors). As far as public opinion was concerned, the Soviets had out-flanked the West.

The reality was that American technology was still ahead, and that the cruise missile would more than redress the balance in strategic forces. As we have seen, the main aim of the Russian naval effort is directed towards tracking the big American carriers and their battle groups. To achieve that objective the Soviets have carefully built up an elaborate world-wide surveillance system, using ships' radars, submarines' sonars, maritime patrol aircraft and reconnaissance satellites to provide hour-by-hour information on the whereabouts of US Navy and NATO surface units. Known as the Soviet Ocean Surveillance System (SOSS), it is operated by 'snoopers' of all kinds, even down to radar-equipped trawlers known as AGIs, which appear with monotonous regularity whenever Western warships carry out exercises. Although at first sight SOSS seems foolproof it has the basic weakness of being vulnerable to saturation and deception; if too much information is fed into SOSS the Soviets have to guess where the real threat is located.

The cruise missile lends itself to such deception, for it is in reality only a weapon-carrying pilotless aircraft, which can fly long distances on preprogrammed flight paths, using electronic 'maps' stored

The Soviet Delta class of SSBNs falls into three distinct categories. The Delta I (bottom) carries 12 SS-N-8 missiles with over 5000 miles range. Delta II (center) increased the number of SS-N-8 missiles to 16 but the Delta III (top) has the much larger SS-N-18 missile which can carry up to seven warheads. The extra height of this missile accounts for the more prominent 'hump' abaft the sail.

Above: The 6000-ton attack submarine USS *Phoenix*, being launched, is dwarfed by the first two Trident boats *Ohio* and *Michigan*.
Left: 'Sherwood Forest' – the massive missile tubes on the lower deck of the *Ohio*.
Opposite: The French SSBN *l'Indomptable* under construction at Cherbourg. Construction of deep-diving nuclear submarines requires special steel and heavy shielding for the reactor.

The question of whether a Tomahawk cruise missile (the naval variant) is better at penetrating Soviet defenses becomes irrelevant, for the deployment of a comparatively small number of missiles among all the other anti-submarine, antiaircraft and antiship weapons already at sea in Western warships would complicate Russian problems immensely. SOSS would have to track every NATO warship which could *in theory* be armed with strategic cruise missiles. In the words of one distinguished commentator, a few sea-based strategic cruise missiles seem a low price to pay for what may be a major dilution of SOSS effectiveness. It poses to the Russians the same sort of Hydra-headed threat that the SS-20 poses to NATO's land forces.

Current plans are to launch Tomahawk from torpedo tubes, in the same way as Sub-Harpoon and Subroc missiles are, an option which limits the number of rounds which can be carried. Another solution is to insert vertical launching tubes at either end of the pressure hull of attack submarines. Two basic variants of Tomahawk have been designed, a

in its computer memory. It can be fired from the deck of a warship or from the torpedo tubes of a submarine, and so can form part of a 'mix' of other weapons. Its warhead can be high explosive or nuclear, and its payload can even be used to put airfields out of action.

131

tactical type with a range of some 300nm (nautical miles) and a strategic type with a range of 1500nm. The tactical variant has a conventional blast warhead based on that of the Bullpup-B, while the strategic variant carries a weight of nuclear explosive equal in weight to 1000 pounds of high explosive.

Although the cruise missile has been termed the 'Doomsday Doodlebug' it is nothing new. The German V-1 of 1944–45 was a land-launched cruise missile, while in the 1950s US submarines were armed with the air-breathing Regulus I and Regulus II nuclear cruise missiles. What has changed is the technology; the Tomahawk uses inertial guidance and a terrain-matching radar known as TERCOM to fly at low level and to keep it on course. All that is needed to make the system effective is the provision of accurate radar-altitude maps of potential target areas. Unfortunately for the United States and its allies considerable opposition to cruise missiles has been whipped up, and President Carter seemed willing to consider a three-year protocol to the Salt II Treaty (negotiated but still unsigned), under which cruise missiles with a range of more than 375 miles would have been banned for three years.

No such inhibitions were attached to the 'stretched' version of Trident, the D5 Trident II. The need for a longer range had been foreseen, but the need to be able to update the Poseidon-armed SSBNs had forced designers to design the first ULMS with a 72-inch body which could fit into Poseidon tubes. The *Ohio* class submarines could be built with larger-diameter (82inch) tubes, which were then given liners to take the Trident I until such time as Trident II was ready. Trident I (UGM-93A) now weighs 70,000 pounds and can carry up to 24 multiple independently targeted reentry vehicles (MIRVs); the D5 Trident II will have a range of 6000 miles, but it is still under development, and will not come into service until 1987.

The introduction of the *Ohio* class SSBNs is

bedeviled by the rapidity with which the original Polaris program was implemented; block obsolesence means that the first SSBNs reached the end of their useful life in 1980, and even the later *Lafayette* and *Benjamin Franklin* classes, whose hull-lives are five years longer, will have to be scrapped by the later 1980s and early 1990s. Putting 24 Tridents into each *Ohio* was just a way of avoiding the staggering cost of replacing all 41 SSBNs (in Fiscal Year 1981 the cost for one *Ohio* was $1.5 billion).

The biggest drawback to the submarine-based nuclear deterrent is the difficulty of communicating with a submerged submarine. The US Navy's current Very Low Frequency (VLF) radio can penetrate water to a very limited degree, and that means that SSBNs must come close to the surface at prearranged times to receive messages. Transmitting causes fewer problems, as security demands that SSBNs should not broadcast except in the gravest emergency. At present the US Navy maintains a force of 12 EC-130

TACAMO (TAke Command And Move Out) aircraft to provide an airborne link. The next development may be an Extra Low Frequency (ELF) system which can transmit through the earth's crust, and after that blue-green lasers may provide the answer, but that technology is not likely to be around until the next century.

As the *Ohio* class come into commission they are sent to a new base at Bangor, Washington if assigned to the Pacific Fleet, where they join the remaining 10 Polaris boats. Atlantic Fleet submarines are currently forward-based at Holy Loch on the Firth of Clyde in Scotland (the Pacific counterpart is Guam), but the Trident boats will be based at King's Bay in Georgia. The reason for this redisposition is not simply because of the additional range of Trident but to provide a new level of support and maintenance.

European fears of being abandoned to Soviet aggression led to the creation of parallel nuclear forces by France and the United Kingdom. Until 1963 the British relied solely on air-launched nuclear weapons,

HMS *Resolution* in the Gareloch, home base of the British Polaris submarine force.

Right: The commanding officer of the British SSBN *Repulse* at the periscope. Modern periscopes have such refinements as thermal imagers, film cameras and laser rangefinders.
Far right: Artist's impression of the massive new Soviet Typhoon class which differs from all previous SSBNs in having the missile compartment ahead of the sail.
Below: A Sea King helicopter winches a crewman off the after casing of the British SSBN HMS *Resolution*.

but their hopes of buying a replacement for their Vulcan bomber were dashed when the US Air Force canceled the Skybolt air-launched ballistic missile. Instead the British were offered Polaris, and the momentous decision was made to build five (later cut to four) SSBNs for the Royal Navy. The hull and reactor was to be British in design, but the missile compartment and fire control system were provided by the US Navy.

The keel of the first SSBN, HMS *Resolution* was laid early in 1964, and she went to sea in October 1967. The last, HMS *Revenge* was laid down only 15 months later, and went to sea at the end of 1969. It was a remarkable achievement, for the first British nuclear submarine, HMS *Dreadnought* had only been commissioned ten months before the *Resolution* was laid down, and yet the entire project was on time and within budget.

The British SSBN force is based at the Gareloch, not far from the American SSBNs at Holy Loch. Many observers have commented on the vulnerability of both bases to mining, but in fact they were deliberately chosen because they are hard to block. Although called 'sea lochs', they are similar to Norwegian fjords in having very deep water, so deep that in an emergency an SSBN could leave harbor submerged. In peacetime a tug accompanies each SSBN as she leaves, to reduce any risk of collision with merchant shipping in the Clyde, but this is to provide public reassurance. Another important reason for basing SSBNs on the Clyde is the high noise-level from shipping, which makes it very hard for Russian submarines to maintain a listening watch.

As the most forward Polaris bases, Holy Loch and the Gareloch are kept under constant surveillance by the Soviet Navy, who are believed to keep a submarine on a 24-hour watch in the Clyde Approaches. For some years this has been countered by keeping a sonar-equipped guard ship in the area, tracking 'Ivan' and giving British and American submarines timely warning of his movements. The British have permanent base facilities at HMS *Neptune* but the Americans use a submarine tender moored in Holy Loch.

The biggest difficulty encountered by the British strategic deterrent force is caused by the cancellation of the fifth submarine. In 1964 the incoming Labour Government was forced to retreat from its pledge to scrap the Polaris submarines, but the new Defence Minister Denis Healey made a gesture of appeasement to the party's left wing by canceling the fifth submarine. This ill-judged economy puts a heavy strain on the men who man the submarines and the civilians who have to maintain them. To maintain the nuclear deterrent it is essential that one submarine is always at sea, and although this has caused great difficulties at times, the SSBN force has always remained operational. Like the US Navy's Blue and Gold manning system, the Royal Navy operates Port and Starboard crews, who do a rapid exchange at the end of each mission and immediately take the submarine back to sea for another three month patrol.

Life on board Polaris submarines is not particularly arduous, apart from the strain of maintaining strict radio silence and not surfacing for three months. The biggest problems are to keep fit and mentally alert while living in comparatively cramped quarters, with no sunshine. Boredom is the great enemy, and every effort is made to keep officers and men occupied. Apart from the high rates of pay, the biggest inducement is the long leave and the ability to plan time with families according to a predictable cycle of time at sea.

It had been hoped that France and Great Britain could share responsibility for a joint European submarine deterrent but a rift between France and the

United States exacerbated Anglo-French suspicion. It was said at the time that discussions between the Royal Navy and the *Marine Nationale* had only reached the subject of what to eat for breakfast before breaking down irrevocably. But for the French there was to be no purchase of American missiles, for the United States refused to sell the Polaris system· to France.

Determined to achieve her goal of self-sufficiency in defense France went ahead with the development of her own SLBM, the Mer-Sol Ballistique Systeme (MSBS or Sea-to-Surface Ballistic System). The M-1 version of the missile was installed for trials in the experimental submarine *Gymnote* and then became operational in the SSBN *le Redoutable* in 1971. The next development, the 1300-mile M-2, went to sea in the third SSBN *le Foudroyant* in 1976 and was retrofitted to the *Redoutable* and her sister *le Terrible*. The M-2 missile was followed by the M-20, and from 1987 *le Tonnant*, *l'Indomptable* and the earlier boats will receive the M-4.

A sixth SSBN of enlarged design, *l'Inflexible* was authorized in 1978, followed by a second unnamed unit a year later. The reason is officially that a constant patrol cannot be maintained with only five *Redoutable* class, but the more likely reason is simply the need to replace the first of that class, which will have been in commission for 20 years in 1991; by the end of the century even the others will be 20–27 years old. The M-4 missile will be a great improvement over the earlier missiles, having a range of 2500–3000 miles and six 150-kiloton MIRV warheads, but these improvements will not match even Trident I's performance.

For the British the problem of updating their deterrent was more acute, for unlike the French they had not had control over the development of their own SLBMs. Nor had they taken the opportunity to replace the A3 Polaris with Poseidon, and as all four *Resolution* class SSBNs were completed in 1967–69 they would become obsolete by the end of the 1980s. In the late 1970s a program codenamed Chevaline was initiated to update the A3 Polaris warhead by giving it

a partial MIRV capability, but in 1980 the Government announced that it would buy Trident I missiles and build a new class of SSBNs for them. However, this time the entire cost was to be put on the naval budget, whereas the cost of Polaris had been spread over the whole defense budget.

The need to find £1000 million out of the Royal Navy's slender budget from 1985 to 1995 provoked a furious discussion but even though the more expensive D5 Trident II is to be bought and the cost is therefore to be even greater than first thought, at the time of writing the Royal Navy still plans to build four *Vanguard* class Trident SSBNs. There has been discussion inside the Royal Navy about buying Tomahawk missiles instead and using them to arm the nuclear hunter-killer submarines, but the Government remains firmly committed to Trident, while the Labour Party, as before, has pledged itself to cancel the program.

The only other country to possess nuclear ballistic missile submarines is the People's Republic of China, but until recently progress has been slow as China's

SSBNs do not operate together but on one occasion it proved possible to photograph France's first three SSBNs Redoutable, Terrible and Foudroyant off Brest.

resources have been dedicated to other more urgent projects. In 1964 a single diesel-electric ballistic missile-firing submarine similar to the Soviet Golf class was completed at Luda in Manchuria. No sisters followed, and it was assumed by Western commentators that she was merely an experimental prototype. Not until 1980 was the launch of an SSBN reported. Though earlier land-based missiles were liquid-fueled, the Chinese have seemingly overcome the technical problems involved in making solid rocket fuel, the only obstacle to developing some sort of equivalent to the Western and Soviet SSBNs and their missiles.

It has always been assumed that the role of the SSBN would terminate on the outbreak of war, as her function was thought to be limited to 'second strike'. However as we have seen, they could easily find themselves in a protracted naval war, in which they would still play an important role. Like the King in a chess game they would have to be kept out of trouble and would be able to do little to win the war, but would be an absolutely crucial element in deciding the outcome. It is this paradox that leads some commentators to treat SSBNs as somehow different from 'normal' fighting ships, but they are just as much a part of modern naval warfare as any other type of warship.

The *City of Corpus Christi* (SSN.705), one of the US Navy's *Los Angeles* class attack submarines. They are being built in large numbers as the standard SSN for the 1990s.

UNDERWATER WARFARE

More than any other single warship-type, the submarine has transformed naval warfare in recent years. The dream that had eluded designers in two world wars, the creation of a 'true submarine' independent of atmospheric oxygen, came to fruition in 1955. In January the USS *Nautilus* signaled 'underway on nuclear power', signifying that she could now travel submerged without having to use her snorkel to recharge batteries. While it was true that her crewmen still needed to eat and breathe, and that these two needs imposed some finite limit on the time that the *Nautilus* could spend submerged, she was no longer *forced* to come up for air at intervals, and therefore had much greater tactical freedom than ever before. With the steam generated by her nuclear heat-exchanger the *Nautilus* could also run for long periods at maximum power, down below the turbulence of wind and waves.

Within the year the US Navy had ordered more nuclear 'hunter-killer' or attack submarines, and by 1959 it was confirmed that no more 'conventional' diesel-electric submarines would be built for the US Navy. This was as much a reflection of the enormous cost of nuclear submarines (SSNs) as their outstanding qualities. Not only does each reactor demand a large capital investment but each submarine requires more highly trained engineers and technicians than a conventional 'boat' or SSK (hunter-killer submarine).

Under Stalin the Soviet Navy had built very large numbers of conventional submarines in the 1950s, nearly 300 of the Whiskey and Zulu classes. The intention was apparently to exploit captured German expertise, but all plans were thrown back in the melting pot with the advent of nuclear propulsion, and by the end of 1959 the first Russian-built SSN, a 4500-ton boat dubbed the November type by NATO, was at sea. By 1965 the total built was 14, and production had switched to the more successful Victor I and Victor II types.

As we saw in the previous chapter the logical follow-on from nuclear submarine propulsion was the submarine launched ballistic missile and the SSBN was the result. But there remained a need for the nuclear attack submarine, or SSN. She offered the only realistic countermeasure against the SSBN, for she could outrun the clumsier and heavier SSBN; she could also screen surface forces against attack, or take the offensive against enemy forces.

The SSN resembles earlier submarines in layout, with accommodation forward and propulsion aft, but because the ideal hull form for high underwater speed and maneuverability demands a single large propeller aft, the traditional after torpedo tubes have disappeared, and modern SSNs have only bow tubes. The latest US Navy submarines have a big spherical sonar in the bow compartment, and so the torpedo tubes have been moved further aft, angled outwards.

The standard weapon is still the torpedo, but sup-

Above right: Soviet Type 641 boats, more commonly known by their NATO Foxtrot designation, in their base.

plemented by longer range guided missiles for surface attack. The US Navy uses primarily the Mk 48 torpedo, which employs a sophisticated guidance system to 'home' itself onto a target, just like a guided missile. However, it differs in one important respect from atmospheric missiles: guidance is by means of a thin wire trailed out from a spool inside the torpedo. Two-way signals are passed down this wire, from the submarine's sonar to the torpedo's guidance system, and back from sensors in the torpedo's homing head to the main fire control system.

The reason for such complexity is that water is a comparatively opaque medium. Sound travels great distances underwater but it is very easily distorted by

layers of differing temperature (called thermal layers), and even of differing salinity. Water is even more opaque to radio waves, so a submerged submarine is not able to communicate freely with other submarines or friendly surface warships. Surface warships enjoy the benefits of radio, radar and even visual signaling, but the submarine has to come to periscope depth to put up an aerial or from a slightly greater depth can unwind a trailing aerial before she can transmit. Extra

The wire used for guiding torpedoes is similar to piano wire, and as it is light it hangs in the water, rather than sinking. There is a risk that if the submarine continues to close with her target she may overrun her own wire, and that it might entangle itself around the propeller, or that she might cut the wire. The reason why such an eventuality is not taken too

seriously is that the engagement time is quite short; the torpedo may be traveling at a speed of 50 knots for 20,000 yards, which means that it will take only 12 minutes to reach maximum range. If the torpedo has failed to detonate the empty wire spool in the torpedo tube is ejected, and if the guidance wire is cut the torpedo's own control system automatically switches to an 'autonomous' mode, in which it functions like an ordinary homing weapon. As the torpedo has its own active or passive acoustic sensor in its homing head, it can be used to send back information to the main fire control computer, and this means that in poor sonar conditions the torpedo itself can provide information about the target.

The virtue of the wire-guided torpedo is that it remains under positive control throughout its run, and

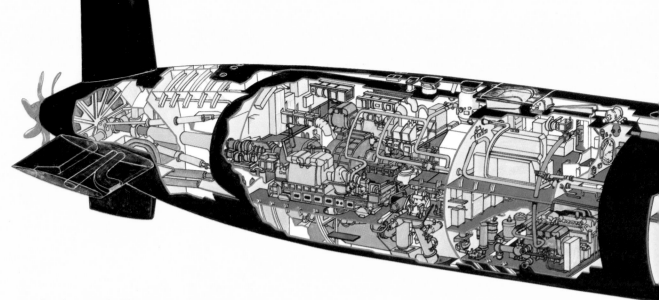

so it cannot be jammed. However there are still a number of free-running torpedoes. In the war between Great Britain and Argentina in 1982 the nuclear submarine *Conqueror* used a pair of Mark 8 unguided compressed air torpedoes to sink the Argentinian cruiser *General Belgrano*, in spite of carrying a number of electrically driven wire-guided Tigerfish torpedoes. The anti-ship version now in service has a dual surface/sub-surface capability.

Supplementing the torpedo rather than replacing it, is the submarine-launched antiship missile. The United States has developed a version of the Harpoon, designated UGM-84, capable of being launched from a torpedo tube. The missile is packed in a canister resembling a torpedo; when the canister is fired from the tube it rises to the surface slowly, being set at the correct angle by small actuating fins. As soon as the tip of the canister 'broaches' or breaks the surface of the water the cap blows off and the missile fires itself out of the canister as it would in the ordinary way. Target data, particularly the bearing relative to the submarine, have already been entered in the missile's computer, so that it can fly the intervening 60 miles on inertial guidance. Only when it is within the lethal radius of its target does the missile turn on its radar seeker, and it then enters its terminal or homing phase.

The French SM-39 version of the Exocet missile is similar, but with a shorter range. It has only recently become operational in the *Agosta* class diesel-electric submarines, and will equip the *Rubis* class SSNs.

The Soviet Navy produced its first Charlie class submarine in 1968, and Western intelligence sources were startled to note eight horizontal hatches on the forward casing. They turned out to contain a 30-mile range antiship missile designated the SS-N-7, and since then more Charlie IIs and the bigger Papa class have been built.

The US Navy is introducing an antiship variant of the Tomahawk cruise missile, with a range of 350 miles.

The practical problem of deploying such long

range missiles is the difficulty of providing midcourse guidance. Without an aircraft, helicopter or warship closer to the target, the submarine launching a Tomahawk missile 200 miles away will have very little idea of the target's course and speed. There is another drawback; even the largest submarines have a limited amount of space in which reload missiles and torpedoes can be stowed. The mission of each submarine will therefore have to be closely examined, to decide how many of each type must be embarked.

Very few countries can afford the luxury of nuclear submarines. The Royal Navy started work on its prototype, HMS *Dreadnought* in 1959, using an American Westinghouse S5W reactor similar to those in the US *Skipjack* class. She commissioned in 1963, and three years later HMS *Valiant* followed, the first to have a British-designed reactor. The Netherlands Navy considered the idea for a while but dropped it, leaving the French as the only other European Navy to adopt nuclear propulsion. The first French efforts were directed at establishing their SSBN force, and

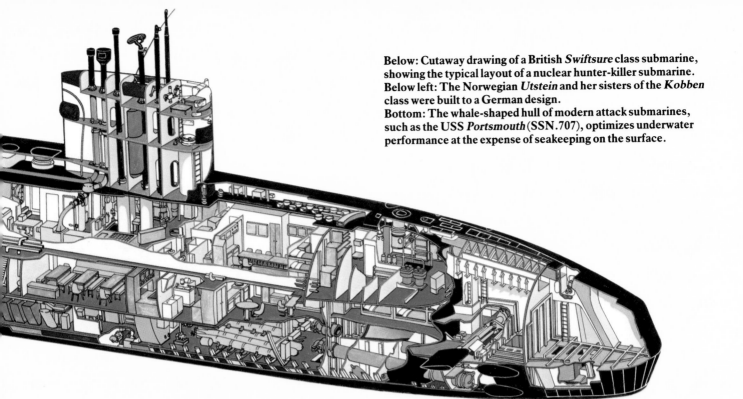

Below: Cutaway drawing of a British *Swiftsure* class submarine, showing the typical layout of a nuclear hunter-killer submarine.
Below left: The Norwegian *Utstein* and her sisters of the *Kobben* class were built to a German design.
Bottom: The whale-shaped hull of modern attack submarines, such as the USS *Portsmouth* (SSN.707), optimizes underwater performance at the expense of seakeeping on the surface.

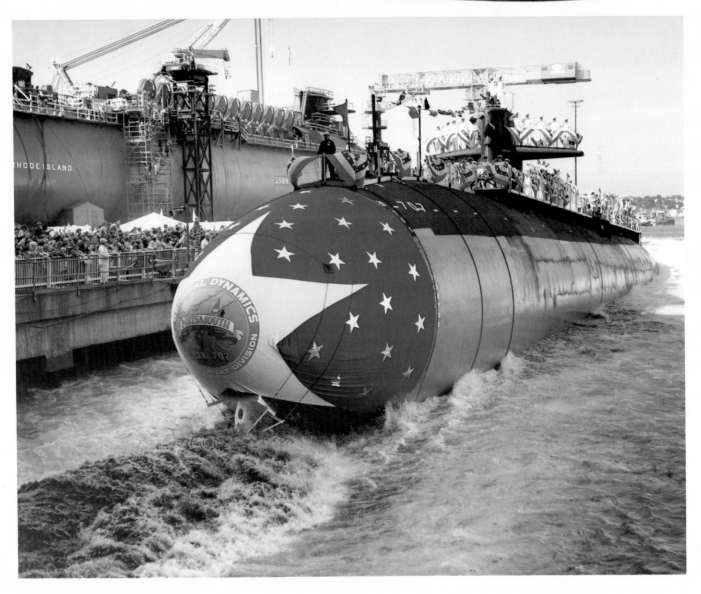

Above: The swans on the casing of *U.18* (left) and *U.17* show how small the German Type 206 submarines are.

the first SSN was not laid down until 1972. Today the lead boat *Rubis* is in service and four more are in various stages of construction.

The Chinese have taken their time in building up a nuclear capability, but in 1974 it was reported that the first of a class known as the *Han* had come into service. The existence of a second boat is doubtful, and trials of the first were reported to be very lengthy, suggesting an experimental prototype. Given the reluctance of the Chinese to sit back while potential enemies open the gap in technology still further, we can expect to see some sort of SSN and SSBN program before long.

From all this it might be assumed that there is no future for the diesel-electric submarine, but this is far from the case. Despite its awesome advantages of performance, the 'nuke' has certain limitations. Apart from the difficulties of communication already mentioned, she is a big sonar target and her bulk prevents her from venturing into coastal waters. She is inherently noisy, for her steam turbine machinery needs a gearbox to transmit power to the single shaft, and the reactor needs cooling pumps. Great efforts have been made in recent years to silence the machinery of nuclear submarines, primarily by isolating the machinery from the hull by putting it on a 'raft'. These expedients push up cost, of course, and also

size; it has been admitted by the US Navy that silencing measures account for the fact that the *Los Angeles* class SSNs are over 2000 tons bigger than their predecessors, the *Sturgeon* class.

Some of the attempts to reduce noise have resulted in unorthodox solutions. In 1957 the USS *Seawolf* went to sea with her S2G reactor cooled by liquid sodium, the idea being to eliminate cooling pumps. It was not a success, and two years later the reactor was replaced by a pressurized water type similar to that in the *Nautilus*. The smaller SSN *Tullibee*, commissioned in 1960, used turbo-electric drive for the same reason, while the *Jack*, a member of the *Sturgeon* class was given contrarotating propellers and turbines. The newest British SSNs, the *Trafalgar* class, have a single pump-jet unit instead of the normal seven-bladed propeller; it reduces noise considerably, but at the cost of one or two knots' speed. Another aid to silent running is to cover the hull in anechoic tiling, which absorbs noise.

It was only a matter of time before Germany returned to the business of designing and building submarines. Once NATO agreed to the recreation of West German military forces the way was clear to develop a new generation of U-Boats, starting with three rehabilitated World War II hulls. A dozen Type 205 boats (*U.1-12*) were built by 1968. They were unusual in layout, with eight 21inch torpedo tubes forward, but on a surface displacement of only 370 tons they were so cramped that the torpedoes had to be loaded externally. The crew of 22 officers and men was made up entirely of specialists, who embarked only for the mission, much like aircrew. Apart from meals, little attention is paid to habitability; in harbor the crewmen are accommodated on board a tender.

Some of the Type 205 U-Boats have since been scrapped, and the class was superseded by the 18 Type 206 (*U.13-30*), built in 1969–74. An increase in displacement of about 100 tons permitted a number of improvements, particularly another eight reload torpedoes. The design is particularly suited to the shallow, restricted waters of the Baltic, and similar submarines were built for Denmark and Norway, while a larger variant, the Type 209, has been sold to many countries. In the fighting around the Falklands the Argentine Navy's two Type 209 boats, the *Salta* and *San Luis* were reported to have made several attacks on the British Task Force. Reports suggest that one of the two submarines got near the British ships, but fired only three torpedoes at too great a range to be effective.

France has maintained a strong submarine force since the 1950s, when the losses of World War II were replaced. With a long Atlantic coastline to patrol there was a need for something larger than the German Baltic types, but the ten *Daphné* class of 1955–70 displaced only 700 tons on the surface, whereas the older *Narval* class displaced 1320 tons. The *Daphné* has proved popular with other navies, having been built for South Africa, Portugal, Spain and Pakistan, although it has also had its share of bad luck, with one lost by accident. The Pakistani *Hangor* is also one of the few modern submarines to see action when she torpedoed the Indian frigate *Khukri* in 1971.

The latest diesel-electric submarines built in France are the four *Agosta* class, 1230-tonners armed with four 21.7-inch (550mm) torpedo tubes. The first export customer was South Africa, which ordered two in 1975, the *Adventurous* and *Astrant*, but when France enforced a United Nations embargo the two became the Pakistani *Hurmat* and *Hashmat*. Another four have been built in Spain by the same yard which built four *Daphnés*

The Royal Netherlands Navy has built on the excellent reputation earned by its submarines and submariners in World War II. In 1949 Dutch designers produced an unusual triple-hulled design known as the *Potvis* class, in which the crew and torpedo tubes were housed in the uppermost cylinder, while batteries and propulsion were housed in two lower parallel cylinders. Four submarines were built to this design in 1954–66 but the novel arrangement was not repeated; although successful in providing extra diving depth it made for extremely complicated internal arrangements. The submarines most recently commissioned are the two *Zwaardvis* class, 2370-tonners armed with a combination of 20 Mk 48 torpedoes and Sub-Harpoon missiles. The US Navy provided some technical assistance, particularly by making the plans of the *Barbel* class available.

The *Zwaardvis* design has been developed further, into the 2300-ton *Walrus* and *Zeeleeuw*, which come into service in 1987–88. They differ mainly in being able to dive deeper, and in saving 18 men by a greater degree of automation. When the third and fourth of the class are completed in the early 1990s the last of the *Potvis* and *Dolfijn* classes will be scrapped.

The Italians relied for some years on a quartet of 535-ton boats, the *Enrico Toti* class, and four elderly ex-American 'Guppy' Type submarines, but in 1974 the first of a new class of four, the *Nazario Sauro* was laid down. Like the Dutch boats they have benefited from American experience with the *Barbel* class, but are armed with Italian A-184 torpedoes.

The British, faced with the cost of maintaining a comparatively large force of SSNs and SSBNs (17 by 1984) had made up their minds that the 13 *Oberon* and three remaining *Porpoise* class diesel-electric boats would not be replaced when they wore out in the 1980s. However the growing difficulties of manning SSNs and the realization that SSNs could not provide sufficiently accurate inshore surveillance led to a new Naval Staff Requirement (NSR) for an SSK or *Oberon* Replacement in the mid-1980s. This has now been ordered as the *Upholder* class, and the prototype is expected to join the Fleet in 1988.

The *Upholder* class derives many of its design features, particularly the hull form, from the most recent SSNs, although it is of course, much smaller. The emphasis is on weapons and fire control, rather than maximum range and performance; they are designed for 20 knots on the surface and submerged, and carry 18 Spearfish torpedoes or Sub-Harpoon missiles (six in the tubes and 12 reloads). The 21-inch Spearfish is the replacement for the Mk 24 Tigerfish, and because it is intended to match the latest Russian SSNs has been designed to dive down to 3000 feet and run at 55 knots. To achieve such remarkable performance the designers abandoned electric batteries in favor of a compact Sundstrand turbine running on enriched Otto fuel, and on trials one of the test vehicles is reported to have exceeded 72 knots while running on the surface (the extra margin is necessary to guarantee 55 knots at maximum depth).

The weapons ranged against submarines are formidable. To match the long detection ranges achieved by modern sonars the antisubmarine weapons have had to extend their range. Against the ships which launch such weapons the submarine can fire a torpedo or antiship missile, but against its most numerous and persistent enemy, the helicopter with a dipping sonar and lightweight torpedoes, there is no easy response. Some years ago a British company produced a solution known as the Submarine Launched Airflight Missile or SLAM, using four small Blowpipe missiles in a special launcher which retracted into the fin, like a periscope or snorkel mast. Guidance was by a TV

link, with the operator guiding the missile from a monitor down below in the control room. SLAM worked, and the Israeli Navy even went so far as to fit their submarines for it but it had one great disadvantage; no submarine commander is happy about loitering at periscope depth when he knows that helicopters are in the vicinity. Helicopters are such a threat to submarines that it can only be a matter of time before a countermeasure is developed, but for the moment the main defense is to avoid them, and this is usually done by tracking the emissions from their radars and sonars. All modern submarines have an Electronic Support Measures (ESM) mast fitted with receiving aerials to measure and analyze signals above water; as ESM is passive a submarine can put up a mast before surfacing, to make sure that there is no threat nearby.

The Soviet Navy, as we have already seen, embraced the idea of the nuclear hunter-killer sub-

marine, building the Tango class to follow the Novembers and Victors, but what caused more alarm in Western navies was the appearance of attack submarines armed with cruise missiles. The earliest were somewhat crude, the diesel-electric Juliett class in the early 1960s, which could fire SS-N-3 missiles on the surface. Much more potent, however, was the Charlie class SSN with its ability to hit surface warships such as aircraft carriers with their SS-N-7 missiles from a range of 30 miles. The risk is that a submarine with such a missile can close within the antisubmarine screen, so that the missile 'pops up' well inside the screen around the carrier. Such an attack stands a good chance of overwhelming the normal defenses in depth, leaving the target nothing but last ditch defenses against the missile.

Clearly the Soviet Navy found the idea of an SSGN (nuclear submarine, guided missile) attractive; the Charlie II is believed to have eight SS-N-9

Main picture: HMS *Otter*, one of the British *Oberon* class submarines which have been sold to foreign navies. The 13 in service with the RN will eventually be replaced by the *Upholder* class.
Top left: The French nuclear attack submarine *Saphir*, second of the *Rubis* class, ready for launch at Cherbourg. These are the first SSNs built for the French Navy and a class of six is planned.

missiles, with possibly double the range of the SS-N-7. Two more SSGN classes have been reported, a single Papa class and the Oscar class.

Soviet naval planners are believed to favor a 'high-low mix' of capability, and in line with a policy of building high-value SSNs they have continued to build SSKs in large numbers. The majority of the diesel-electric boats of the 1950s have been scrapped, put into reserve or relegated to training, but 20 Romeo class were completed in 1958–61, to complement the 60 Foxtrot type completed in the late 1950s. The 2000-ton Foxtrot is seen all around the world and has been supplied to a number of foreign countries as a replacement for obsolete Whiskey boats. A total of 74 Romeos was built in China to Soviet plans, and a derivative, the Ming class, is reported. In October 1981 one of the dwindling number of Whiskey class, *No. 137*, achieved notoriety by running ashore in the approaches to the Swedish Navy's main base at Karlskrona. The luckless captain claimed that a faulty echo sounder had led him astray, following a navigation error which put him somewhere off the coast of Poland! Subsequently the Swedes claimed that they had detected radiation, and suggested that *No. 137* was armed with nuclear torpedoes, something which is hard to reconcile with the great age of the Whiskey.

Clearly in wartime both nuclear and conventional submarines have important roles to play in Soviet strategy. The SSNs and SSGNs would have the primary task of attacking the West's Sea Lanes of Communications (SLOCs), to prevent the United States and its allies from deploying their military power at will. Neutralization of the Carrier Battle Groups and Surface Action Groups would be another priority, using both torpedoes and missiles. The longer ranged missiles might well be supplied with target data from long range maritime patrol aircraft or surface ships. The North Atlantic SLOCs are likely to be the main objective, for through these crowded shipping lanes would have to pass the vital convoys of war materiel, ammunition and fuel to resupply Europe.

Fortunately for the NATO alliance geography still constrains the Russians in the same way that it did France and Germany in previous wars. The shallow waters of the Baltic have only one narrow exit to the open sea, and that is securely guarded by the naval and air forces of Norway, West Germany and Denmark. This leaves the burden of attack to the Northern Fleet, based on Murmansk, and from there all Soviet forces must run the gauntlet of surveillance by NATO forces long before they reach the North Atlantic hunting grounds. Even then the exit to the Atlantic is blocked by Iceland and the British Isles, for submarines could not hope to transit the English Channel or the Irish Sea. Hence the vital importance of the Greenland–Iceland–UK Gap (usually abbreviated to the GIUK Gap). It is a 'choke point' through

Above: *U.24* (S.173), one of the 18 Type 206 submarines built for the Federal German Navy in the 1960s.
Below: No Soviet submarine had caused quite as much alarm in Western naval circles as the Alfa with its reputed 45-knot underwater speed.

which Soviet submarines *must* pass if they are to fulfil their main missions, and therefore NATO concentrates its ASW forces in that area.

The major problem in hunting submarines is to narrow down the area of search, in order to eliminate the largely futile effort of spreading ships, aircraft and hunter-killer submarines over a wide area. This was done in the 1960s by laying a series of antisubmarine barriers in the GIUK Gap. This is a series of passive sensors on the bed of the ocean which are linked by cable to shore stations in Iceland, Northern Ireland, England and Scotland. The system, which is constantly being refined, is known as the SOund SUrveillance System or SOSUS, and its existence was a well-kept secret until the mid-1970s. Briefly its passive sensors record the passage of any surface ship or submarine within audible range, and relay it to a shore station; there computers rapidly triangulate the submarine's position from the various bearings, classify the submarine as 'friendly' or 'hostile', and direct friendly forces to the location.

What makes SOSUS effective is the rapidity of modern electronics; within microseconds the 'library' of individual propeller noises is scanned, to identify the submarine by nationality, class, and even in some cases, down to an individual boat. Equally quickly the forces in the GIUK Gap are alerted to the presence of, say, a third November class SSN.

There are many SOSUS barriers, all at strategic positions, where the right combinations of topography force hostile submarines through a predictable channel. Special weapons have been developed for these barriers, particularly the Captor mine; in essence it is a canister containing an acoustic homing torpedo such as the Mk 46, which is launched automatically on 'hearing' the noise of an approaching submarine. Captor is intended to catch submarines diving deep to avoid detection by the sonars and sonobuoys of ships and aircraft above.

Clearly the existence of such barriers imposes severe limits on Soviet plans to use their submarines decisively, and almost certainly the Alfa class nuclear submarine was one such solution. In 1980 reports began to filter through to the Western press, suggesting that a new type of Soviet submarine could make 40 knots and dive to well over 2000ft. According to 'well-informed sources' American and British submarines had tailed these new SSNs and had lost them at an estimated 40 knots. Known as the Alfa by NATO, the new craft is an SSN, credited with a surface displacement of 2600 tons and an armament of six 21-inch torpedo tubes firing a 'mix' of six long range torpedoes, 10 short range antisubmarine torpedoes, two nuclear-tipped torpedoes, two nuclear antisubmarine missiles and two conventional antisubmarine missiles.

Such a heavy armament is by no means unusual, and conforms to the Soviet tendency towards maximum weapon-load, but it leaves some questions unanswered. At maximum depth weapon launching would be so dangerous as to be almost impossible, and sonars and homing heads would have great difficulty in identifying targets on the surface. The Alfa must therefore be assumed to require its immense speed to pass through SOSUS barriers at maximum depth, in effect outflanking the defending forces. If this theory is right, her armament would only be used at a later stage, when she had reached her patrol area.

Some observers ask how the size of the Alfa has come *down* from the 4000 tons of the Charlie class and yet must have doubled the power output to increase speed from 30 knots. One explanation may be that the Soviet designers have simply chosen to ignore the normal safety limits on reactor output in order to achieve a decisive margin of speed. There are persistent rumors that the Alfa prototype had to be scrapped after the reactor had suffered a 'melt-down' – with the loss of her entire crew. The resistance of the hull to pressure at maximum depth is apparently the result of using a double titanium hull – an immensely expensive way to build a submarine, but understandable as titanium is much lighter than steel. Certainly the double hull would make the Alfa resistant to a hit from a typical Western light torpedo such as the Mk 46, which has only 75 pounds of explosive, designed to knock off a propeller. The next generation of NATO submarine torpedoes have a heavy warhead to ensure a 'first-time kill' – something which is absolutely necessary when attacking an SSBN. It is easy to imagine the captain of an SSBN realizing that his boat had been crippled, and giving the order to fire his deadly load of missiles as a last act of defiance.

The underwater battlefield will be one of the most crucial, even decisive. It will be a campaign of ambush and sudden catastrophe, with a clear-cut distinction between survivors and non-survivors.

The USS *John F. Kennedy*'s air group practically obscures her flight deck. US aircraft carriers cannot accommodate their entire aircraft complement in the hangar.

150

SURFACE COMBAT

In the final analysis surface warfare is the most important element of naval conflict, at least for those navies with an interest in 'power-projection'. Put at its simplest, men and some equipment can be flown rapidly from one continent to another, but heavy materials must go by sea; if they cannot cross that sea because of enemy action they cannot influence the outcome of any events away from their homeland. From this simple fact stems the concept of 'Sea Control' as against 'Sea Denial'; sea control is needed to move not only military equipment but vital raw materials, aid to allies, etc, and an enemy who lacks such control can only attempt to deny the use of the sea.

The outcome of two world wars hinged on sea control, for in 1917 and 1942–43 the United States was very nearly prevented from supporting its ally Great Britain because Anglo-American sea control was threatened by German sea denial forces in the form of U-Boats. Since 1945 the United States and its allies have enjoyed undisputed control of the sea, but the growing Soviet Navy created under the leadership of Admiral Gorshkov poses a very real threat of sea denial. Added to that is an enormous increase in the potential of the submarine and the aircraft, to the point where some commentators question the ability of the surface fleet to survive at all.

The US Navy's response is to state categorically that it intends to retain control of the sea, and that it will pay the higher price of sea power. It can very easily be forgotten that the West currently has only two means of taking the offensive at sea: with attack submarines or carrier air strikes, so any abdication from surface warfare would free powerful Russian forces to act against Western sea communications.

Today the defense of a surface fleet against air-flight weapons, whether launched from aircraft, ships or submarines has to be in 'layers'. The outermost layer is provided by fleet interceptor aircraft, using their own radars and those of the carrier battle group to provide a complete picture of the area and to make accurate interceptions. Ideally these interceptors will be able to destroy hostile aircraft before they can launch their antiship missiles, using air-to-air missiles or guns. The next layer of defense is provided by the fleet's missiles, which provide 'area defense'; they can shoot down the larger and slower antiship missiles as well as the launching aircraft. Any aircraft which 'leak' past these two layers are to be dealt with by the so-called 'point defense' systems mounted in individual ships.

The concept of layered defense was developed in the later 1950s to cope with bomber-launched

missiles and the early Soviet long range cruise missiles such as the SS-N-3 and the later SS-N-12, in open waters. In narrow waters, however there is always the risk that the long range defenses can be bypassed, by fast strike craft firing SS-N-2 Styx or SS-N-9 missiles. A further complication was the appearance of the Charlie class submarine firing SS-N-7 missiles from underwater. This missile could, for example, 'pop up' from a submerged submarine only 25 miles from its target. Traveling at one-and-a-half times the speed of sound an SS-N-7 would cover that distance in about 90 seconds, giving the target ship's defenses very little time to react. Nor can the missile be allowed to approach too close, for even if the guidance system is destroyed by hits on the nose cone there is a risk that the missile will 'go ballistic' and hit the ship. Even if the warhead fails to detonate, the impact of a ton or more of missile body will inflict massive damage on the superstructure of a warship and will knock out her radars, so the only valid defense is to prevent missiles from getting close.

The current family of US Navy missiles are descendants of the 'Bumblebee Project' of 1944, when the Applied Physics Laboratory of Johns Hopkins University started the development of stand-off defenses agsinst the early German antiship missiles such as Fx-1400. Out of this came the 'Three-T' surface-to-air missiles, Talos, Terrier and Tartar. The very long range Talos (70 miles) has now been retired, but Terrier proved to be the basis for continuing development, and is still in service. An attempt in the mid-1950s to produce an ultra-long range defense system, Typhon, foundered when size and cost ran out of control, but experience gained helped to get the current Aegis program under way.

The close range guns of World War II were inadequate to cope with fast aircraft, even in 1945, and so they disappeared. However missiles were found to have minimum ranges as well as maximum, and as data-handling has improved radically since the 1950s guns are back in favor as short range defensive systems.

The Soviet Navy differs from the US Navy in concentrating its air element on land, rather than in aircraft carriers. The central philosophy of tying the airborne striking forces to bases in the Soviet Union may change, but for the moment the Soviet Navy lacks the ability to project power on a large scale, and so it remains committed to a role of sea denial. The evidence that this philosophy is undergoing change is the building of what is believed to be a 60,000-ton carrier, probably nuclear-powered, but one carrier will not be a match for the US Navy, and the real question must be, how far will the Soviet Navy go down this new path?

The importance attached by Soviet leaders to the Strategic Rocket Forces has in the past hampered a coherent development of naval strategy. The first heavy cruise missile, the SS-N-3, was developed originally for strategic attack, but was retailored to permit attacks against US carriers.

Even the construction of strategic missile-firing submarines was suspended at one time, to avoid any suggestion that the Soviet Navy might be overlapping the mission of the Strategic Rocket Forces. Only after the downfall of Nikita Krushchev, the most fervent admirer of the SRF, and the advent of Polaris did the Navy begin to win back some ground in the battle for funds.

By 1973 the voice of Admiral Gorshkov could be heard, delineating the new power projection role for the Navy. In his book *Sea Power of the State* he suggested that in the future only a powerful and balanced Navy would be able to guarantee Soviet influence in the Third World. While dismissing the role of sea power in World War II (the standard Soviet line is that their land forces alone defeated Nazi Germany, and that the war in the Pacific was irrelevant) Gorshkov predicted that missiles and nuclear weapons were altering the very nature of naval warfare.

The new policy took several forms. The new Backfire bomber began to appear in numbers, and a steady series of classes of 'rocket cruisers' began to join the Fleet. In 1976 the *Kiev* appeared, an unusual hybrid cruiser/carrier capable of operating the Yak-36 Forger vertical takeoff strike aircraft. With her sisters *Minsk* and later *Novorossiisk*, as well as two earlier helicopter carriers, it seemed as if the Soviet Navy was rapidly expanding its anticarrier capability, and the appearance of a 22,000-ton 'battlecruiser', the *Kirov*, was taken to herald the imminent appearance of carrier battle groups in hitherto sacrosanct NATO areas. The carrier is still under production and is not expected to be ready until the early 1990s.

The four Kynda class were the first purpose-built guided missile ships, although previously the somewhat primitive SS-N-1 Scrubber missile had been added to existing destroyer designs, the Kildin and Krupny classes. With a long forecastle, two large funnels and massive radar arrays, the Kynda class made a great impression on Western and Third World observers, but in particular their eight massive launch tubes containing SS-N-3 Shaddock missiles marked them as powerful surface combatants. Unlike contemporary Western warships the Kyndas were bristling with weapons, a further eight Shaddock reloads, a twin launcher for SA-N-1 Goa antiaircraft missiles, two twin 76mm guns and two sets of triple torpedo tubes. All this, and an estimated speed of 35 knots achieved on a full load displacement calculated at 5700 tons, suggested to Western observers that the Soviets were more skilful at designing warships.

The perspective of nearly 25 years (the first Kynda appeared as long ago as 1961) suggests a different view. The sea trials almost certainly revealed significant defects, which were mitigated by reconstruction to reduce topweight, but the ships were still sent to the Black Sea and Pacific squadrons, where they faced less demanding weather. Even more significant, the class was cut from 12 to four units, and the next class mounted a smaller number of missiles. This was the so called Kresta I class, the first of which appeared in 1967, six years after the first Kynda.

Although hailed at the time as another leap ahead for the Soviet fleet, sober opinion now sees the Kresta I as a worthy attempt to correct the deficiencies of the Kynda. The number of SS-N-3 Shaddock missiles was cut from 16 to 4, a reduction of 75 percent, and a helicopter was included to provide mid-course guidance for the 170-mile Shaddock. A second twin launcher was provided for the SA-N-1 area defense missiles and a long range air surveillance radar were provided. Once again, however, only four were built before another major shift in policy supervened. Fortunately for the Russians the basic Kresta hull could be adapted, and so in 1970 a Kresta II appeared.

What distinguished the cruiser *Kronshtadt* from her earlier sisters was the redesigned central tower superstructure to accommodate a three dimensional radar, linked to the new SA-N-3 Goblet area defense missile system, of which two systems were provided. Another important change was to replace the two twin Shaddock missile tubes with two quadruple launchers for a new type of large missile. For seven years Western intelligence maintained that these were a new long range cruise missile designated SS-N-10, but finally it was revealed to be a comparatively short range antisubmarine missile designated SS-N-14 – in effect a pilotless delivery vehicle for a homing torpedo. This squared more believably with the Russians' own designation of the ships as Large Anti Submarine Ships but it also implied a drastic revision of Soviet ideas on fleet distribution, for these big ships (7500 tons full load) have no gun bigger than 57mm and no antiship missile, apparently.

The Kresta II does, however, appear to meet Soviet needs, for no fewer than ten were built between 1970 and 1978, and they have been seen around the world. While they were still under construction yet another type of missile cruiser appeared, the 9000-ton Kara. Although bearing a superficial likeness to the Kresta II, they complemented them rather than replaced them, and the *rationale* seems to be a wish to exploit higher technology in propulsion and weapons, but without interrupting the flow of ships from the Black Sea shipyards.

The big difference is the adoption of gas turbines for the Kara, most probably four 'marinized' versions of the NK-144 turbines which powered the Tu-144 'Concordski' supersonic airliner. This allowed the

Right: A stern view of the guided missile cruiser USS *Leahy* (CG.9) shows her after missile launcher and two radar trackers.

designers to use a big square upright funnel set well back, in place of the complex 'mack' used in both Kresta types. Although the armament remains similar to the Kresta II, eight SS-N-14 missiles forward and twin SA-N-3 Goblet SAMs forward and aft, a new point defense system is installed amidships, the twin SA-N-4 missile. These are housed to port and starboard in twin 'pop-up' launchers to protect them from spray. Also mounted on either side amidships are a pair of twin 76mm guns and four six-barreled 23mm 'Gatling' guns for close range defense against aircraft and missiles.

If the succession of Kyndas, Krestas and Karas from Soviet shipyards provoked unease it was nothing compared to the explosion of analytical comment set off by the appearance of the cruiser/carrier *Kiev* in 1976. It was partly her massive size, 40,000 tons full load, but in particular her port-side angled flight deck and general aircraft carrier characteristics which provoked disquiet. Immediately specters were raised of *Kiev* and her sisters combining with the helicopter carriers *Moskva* and *Leningrad* to form a powerful task force in the Arabian Sea ready to threaten the West's vital oil supplies.

In fact the *Kiev*, *Minsk* and *Novorossiisk* (plus a fourth sister *Kharkov*, believed to be ready for sea in 1985) bear only a superficial resemblance to the US Navy's carriers. They have very few of their capabilities, lacking specific airborne early warning (AEW) or electronic warfare (EW) functions. The air group is particularly weak: 18–24 Ka-25 Hormone antisubmarine helicopters and some 10–12 Yak-36 Forger VTOL strike aircraft. The Hormone-A is a small elderly helicopter with half the range of the Western Sea King, and much less than the S-3 Viking ASW aircraft. The Yak-36 Forger squadron, should it try to attack an American carrier battle group, would face three attack and two interceptor squadrons of vastly superior performance. Nor, without AEW, could the Forgers be vectored out in time to fight off a determined air strike, and it seems they would be restricted to shooting down reconnaissance aircraft or dealing with small strike craft.

Nor can it be said that the hybrid cruiser/carrier hull contributes much to efficiency as a carrier. Only 50 percent of the ship is dedicated to air capability, for the entire forward part of the hull and much of the island superstructure is dedicated to the various cruiser functions. The armament duplicates that of the Kara, and in addition to at least eight long range SS-N-12 antiship missiles, the island superstructure is cluttered with sensors and weapons as well as fire

Above left: Yak-36 Forger VTOL aircraft on the flight deck of the Soviet cruiser-carrier *Minsk*.
Left: The *Kiev* was the first of a class of four ships originally thought to be attack carriers but Western observers now assess them as hybrids, with cruiser armament, antisubmarine helicopters and a small group of Forgers for the strike role.

control to handle the various weapon systems, making it quite clear that the 'cruiser' part of the design ranks equal to the 'carrier' function.

Current thinking is that the *Kiev* class is only a logical step in the evolution of Soviet naval doctrine. Great stress is laid on the role of long range reconnaissance bombers, the Blinders, Badgers and Bears, acting in concert with surface units and submarines. Their task is to provide data for a central bank of information about Western naval movements known as the Soviet Ocean Surveillance System (SOSS). The Bear-D is one of the key elements in this set-up, and it is intended to act as a relay station for long range missiles such as the SS-N-3. Ideally the Bear-D will locate a hostile task force, call down fire from any available air strike squadrons and surface ships, and take over midcourse guidance of the missiles to direct them onto their targets. Hormone-B helicopters can provide mid-course guidance for anti-ship missiles.

Until the advent of Polaris in the early 1960s the major function of Soviet forces in mid-ocean was to force the US carrier task forces out to a range at which their nuclear strike aircraft could not hit targets in the USSR. The existence of Polaris changed all this, for the Soviet Navy now had to try to hunt SSBNs out to new ranges, 1500 miles for A-2, and then to 2500 miles when the A-3 replaced the A-2 Polaris. This fact alone accounts for the profusion of antisubmarine weapons in the Kresta II, Kara and *Kiev* classes, and the increased number of 'blue water' combatants, for these antisubmarine forces would be operating much closer to hostile forces. What was also noticeable was a shift in the emphasis on the four Soviet fleets. Western SSBNs were to be covered by stronger ASW forces in the Northern Atlantic and the Mediterranean, and to build up the strength of the Northern and Black Sea Fleets the Baltic and Pacific Fleets were weakened.

The need to push antisubmarine forces further and further into the oceans has put great pressure on the Soviet Navy to produce a series of cruisers capable of defending themselves from heavy attack. Each class of cruiser has been larger and more powerful than the last, but apart from the Kynda, Kresta I and *Kiev* classes, the emphasis has been on ASW weapons at the expense of antiship weapons. Nor could helicopters and single bombers offer much chance of being allowed to loiter around an American carrier battle group broadcasting target data. Clearly what was needed was a large surface combatant capable of challenging NATO and the Americans in the open waters of the North Atlantic and the Norwegian Sea.

The solution was the 22,000-ton 'battlecruiser' *Kirov*, which appeared in 1981. However, even on such a large platform the designers have had difficulty in providing a massive increase in offensive power, for the defenses of the ship had to be increased as well.

Thus the *Kirov* mounts only four more antiship missiles than the Kynda (20 as against 16); the rest of the 247-meter hull is taken up with stowage for as many as 60 SA-N-6 antiaircraft missiles, SS-N-14 antisubmarine missiles, SA-N-4 point defense missiles, 30mm 'Gatlings' and a large number of fire control sets, surveillance radars and the comprehensive outfit of ECM gear necessary for survival. What is unusual is the choice of vertical launching for both the SS-N-19 and the SA-N-6 missiles – a concept long discussed in the West but slow in appearing because of the technical difficulties.

The most controversial aspect of the *Kirov*'s design was her propulsion, and it must be confessed that Western Intelligence did not show up well by predicting that she was driven by a nuclear powerplant. The sight of what was clearly a massive combined mast/funnel or 'mack' emitting smoke was airily dismissed by some intelligence sources as a

Above: Artist's impression of the nuclear-powered cruiser *Kirov*. Apart from aircraft carriers the *Kirov* is the largest warship to be built since the battleships of World War II.
Left: The *Kirov* heels to port during a high speed turn. The *Kirov* may have a top speed as high as 35 knots.
Right: Detail of the forward parts of the *Kirov* showing the oblique launch tubes for the SS-N-19 missiles (shown below) and the vertical tubes for the SA-N-6 (above). Forward of these is the twin SS-N-14 equipment.
Below: Missile hatches on the foredeck of the *Kirov*. Also shown are four of the ship's eight 30mm Gatling-type guns and (left) the tops of the retractable SA-N-4 mountings.

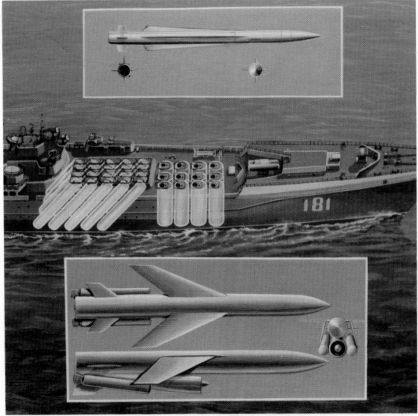

dummy, or else an exhaust trunk for auxiliary generators. Gradually, however, everyone came to accept that the likeliest explanation is that *Kirov* uses nuclear power for cruising, with oil-fired boilers providing boost power for rapid acceleration and top speed. In fact this CONAS (Combined Nuclear And Steam) had previously been proposed for US surface combatants as a way to solve the sluggish acceleration of nuclear plants, and it is easy to understand why it has been chosen by the Russian ship designers. A slightly modified sister, the *Frunze*, appeared in 1984, but there is no report of any more of this class.

Although the *Kirov* incorporates many ideas new to Soviet warships she represents in one sense the final attempt to build a surface combatant capable of autonomous operation in hostile waters – autonomous in the sense of not relying on air support. The hazards of making a 2000-mile voyage from Murmansk down to the Denmark Strait are considerable, and it is unlikely that a ship making that passage would go completely undetected by modern surveillance systems. Should she attempt to make it the *Kirov* will need every defensive system she has to survive, and that knowledge is likely to have assisted the Soviet Navy in reaching the conclusion that it needs the protection of carrier air power.

Against this array of ships is ranged the might of the US Navy's surface fleet, assisted by the rest of the NATO allies' navies. However the US Navy's 14 large strike carriers provide all the 'muscle', as all other surface combatants are primarily designed to work with and protect the carriers. The carriers changed their designation from 'attack' (CVA) to CV some years ago, in recognition of the growing need to embark antisubmarine helicopters and aircraft, but the major element in the carriers' air groups is still strike and interceptor aircraft.

The oldest US carriers are the 63,600-ton *Midway* and *Coral Sea*, completed shortly after World War II but massively modernized since then. Although in

1949 the US Navy lost its fight to build a new carrier to be called the *United States*, experience in the Korean War led to the decision being reversed, and in 1956–59 four 'super carriers' of the *Forrestal* class joined the Fleet. These giant carriers displace 78,700 tons fully loaded, and they have proved so successful that the basis of US carrier design has remained largely constant since then. Four more improved versions followed, the *Kitty Hawk* class, but to explore the possibilities of nuclear propulsion the 82,000-ton *Enterprise* was built in 1958–61.

The use of nuclear propulsion in an attack carrier opened up new possibilities in surface warfare. Not only does the carrier have much greater endurance, but also greater fuel capacity for air operations, as her internal volume is not given up to 2–3000 tons of oil fuel. In fact all subsequent improvements to US carriers have gone on extending the time that the air group can keep flying, and enhancing the air group's efficiency.

Congress tried to keep the cost of naval aviation down by blocking funds for more nuclear carriers but each time the logic of the argument won through, and in 1968 the first of three more nuclear carriers was laid down. The *Nimitz* (CVN.68), *Dwight D Eisenhower* (CVN.69) and *Carl Vinson* (CVN.70) are now in service, with three more under construction, the *Theodore Roosevelt* (CVN.71), *Abraham Lincoln* (CVN.72) and *George Washington* (CVN.73) to permit 15 Carrier Battle Groups to be maintained. Loaded displacement has risen to 93,400 tons but improvements in nuclear technology mean that they can make 35 knots with only two reactors, as against eight in the *Enterprise*. The age of the *Forrestals* has been a cause of concern but they have been earmarked for a Service Life Extension Program which will add 10–15 years to their lives. This involves major overhauls of the hull and machinery, rather than an update of their electronics and hardware, for the hulls are now 30 years old.

A typical NATO escort group, showing (left to right) a Norwegian *Oslo* class destroyer escort, a Dutch *Leander* class frigate, the American DDG *Luce*, a British *Leander*, and a Canadian destroyer escort.

Composition of a Typical Carrier Air Group

Two interceptor squadrons, each with F-14 Tomcats	24 aircraft
Three attack squadrons, each with A-7 Corsairs or A-6 Intruders	36 aircraft
One recce detachment, with RF-14 Tomcats	3 aircraft
One AEW detachment, with E-2 Hawkeyes	4 aircraft
One ECM squadron, with EA-6 Prowlers	4 aircraft
One tanker detachment, with KA-6 Intruders	4 aircraft
Two ASW squadrons, one with S-3 Vikings, one with SH-3 Sea King helicopters	10 aircraft 6 helicopters
Total	91 aircraft

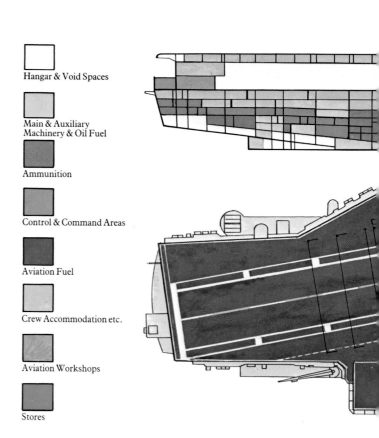

☐ Hangar & Void Spaces

▨ Main & Auxiliary
Machinery & Oil Fuel

■ Ammunition

■ Control & Command Areas

■ Aviation Fuel

☐ Crew Accommodation etc.

▨ Aviation Workshops

■ Stores

Below: The *Forrestal* class carrier *Ranger* makes a high-speed turn.
Bottom right: An A-7E Corsair II attack aircraft in flight over the *Kitty Hawk* class carrier *America*.

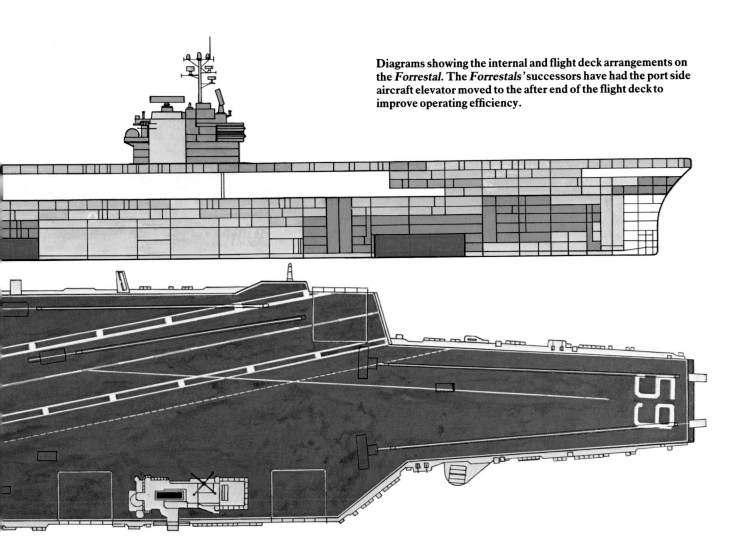

Diagrams showing the internal and flight deck arrangements on the *Forrestal*. The *Forrestals'* successors have had the port side aircraft elevator moved to the after end of the flight deck to improve operating efficiency.

Modern carriers carry very little in the way of defensive armament, usually point defense missile launchers or the new 20mm Phalanx 'Gatling' gun, capable of firing 3000 rounds per minute against missiles. Defense at any greater distance is left to escorts, and of course the carrier's own aircraft. The all-important second layer of air defense is provided by guided missile armed destroyers (DDGs) and cruisers (CGs), armed with area defense weapons. The backbone of the carrier escort force is the *Charles F Adams* class of 23 DDGs, armed with the Standard medium range missile. They were built in 1959–63 and have proved very successful in service. They are good general purpose escorts as well, for in addition to their Standard missile systems they can fire Asroc antisubmarine missiles and Harpoon antiship missiles. When built they had two single 5-inch Mk 42 dual-purpose guns but one of these has been removed during modernization.

Similar to the *Adams* class in configuration are the ten DDGs of the *Coontz* class, but they displace 1300 tons more. They were built in 1957–61 as missile-armed destroyer leaders (DLGs) but were later downgraded to destroyers. Apart from size they differ from the DDGs principally in being armed with the Terrier missile, which is being replaced by the Standard (Extended Range) missile. They have their missile launchers and fire control aft, and the Asroc anti-submarine missile system forward.

Despite being guided by radar, antiaircraft missiles have blind arcs, like other weapons, and the successors to the *Coontz* class DLGs were intended to be 'double-enders', with missile systems forward and aft to cure this problem. Two somewhat similar classes were built in 1959–67, nine *Leahy* class and nine *Belknaps*. They were also armed with Terrier SAMs and Asroc, but in recent years they have been given Harpoon antiship missiles as well, and are receiving Standard (ER) missiles in place of Terrier.

Although the nuclear-powered *Enterprise* was a great success she imposed a great strain on her 'fossil-fueled' escorts, as they had to refuel frequently. The

answer was to build a series of nuclear-powered escorts, capable of keeping pace with her. The cruiser *Long Beach* was completed in 1961, a 17,350-ton ship armed with a twin Talos launcher and two twin Terrier launchers.

The *Long Beach* was followed by two more nuclear 'frigates' or DLGs built between 1962 and 1967, the *Bainbridge* and *Truxtun*, both armed with Terrier and Asroc missiles. They were experimental ships, basically enlarged versions of the *Leahy* and *Belknap* classes, and in 1975 they were all upgraded to guided missile cruisers (CGs and CGNs). The decision to build more nuclear carriers inevitably led to the construction of more CGNs, starting with the two *California* class and leading on to the four *Virginia* class. These 11,000-ton ships appear underarmed for their size, with only two twin Standard (MR) missile-launchers and two lightweight 5-inch guns but they are formidable fighting ships, well equipped with sensors and data handling. The Mk 26 missile launchers can fire more rapidly than older launchers.

The Combat Information Centre (CIC) of a typical surface warfare combatant is located in the forward superstructure, just behind the bridge. In the *Belknap* class, for example, it is a vast area divided into spaces for the different functions. The central section of the CIC forms the command area, with positions for the Commanding Officer or Tactical Weapons Officer, the Ship's Weapons Coordinator (SWC) and the Surface/Subsurface Coordinator (SSSC).

In addition to the Standard missiles the SWC has responsibility for the eight Harpoon missiles. As they are a recent addition an extra console has been added to the left of the SWC console. Positions and tracks of friendly and hostile units are monitored on 'table-top' displays and vertical screens. Close to the command space, at the forward end of the CIC, is a 'flag space' where an admiral and his staff (if embarked) can follow progress of the battle on their own horizontal and vertical displays.

The SSSC supervises the ASW operations, iso-

The newly-commissioned support carrier HMS *Illustrious* leaves for the Falklands on 2 August 1982. She relieved her sister *Invincible* and took over part of her air group. Note the Phalanx gun system fitted on the starboard stern corner of the flight deck.

Above: The nuclear-powered missile cruiser *Bainbridge* (CGN.25) at sea in 1979.
Left: HMS *Glamorgan*, a County class DLG was partially rearmed with Exocet antiship missiles in the 1970s. She survived a hit from an Exocet in the closing stages of the Falklands campaign in June 1982.

lated as much as possible from noise to allow the sonar operators to concentrate on the difficult task of following a contact. Alongside the Anti Submarine Warfare Officer (ASWO) supervises the hunting of underwater contacts. On his left, the Anti Submarine Air Controller (ASAC) directs the ship's helicopter toward a contact to allow it to drop depth charges or homing torpedoes.

The air-intercept and air-engagement consoles are located on the right hand side of the CIC. From a group of three the Fire Control System Coordinator (FCSC) and the Engagement Controller can direct the fire of the Mk 10 missile-launcher and the 5-inch gun.

The next generation of control systems makes current systems look very simple and old fashioned. The Aegis Fleet Defense System is designed to protect surface combatants, particularly the carriers, from the saturation attacks favored by the Russians. As far back as 1958 work had started on the ill-fated Typhon system; this was canceled but out of it came a study for an Advanced Surface Missile System (ASMS), later named Aegis after the shield of Zeus. At the heart of Aegis is a unique hexagonal planar (flat) radar array, the SPY-1A, which contains more than 4000 radiating elements. Instead of a rotating antenna, SPY-1A's four plane faces at the corners of

the superstructure provide all-round and azimuth radar cover around the ship. The four electronically scanning arrays provide data to a bank of computers which automatically grade incoming threats in order of priority and provide fire control data. Air targets are engaged by Standard SM-2 missiles, and the rapid fire Mk 26 launchers put a number of missiles into the air to provide rounds for the Aegis system to allocate as it chooses. As many as 18 Standard missiles can be tracked in the air, allowing the four SPG-62 illuminating radars to illuminate each target in turn and direct the missiles to the point where their own tracker head can home them to impact. By comparison a conventional 'double-ended' CG or CGN can engage four targets simultaneously, using the SM-1 missile.

There were long arguments about platforms for Aegis, but finally approval was given to modify the hull of the new *Spruance* class destroyer to accommodate Aegis. This resulted in the *DDG.47* design, later redesignated *CG.47* in recognition of the vastly improved performance of Aegis. The lead ship, named *Ticonderoga*, went to sea in May 1982 and the *Yorktown* and *Vincennes* are at sea. More of the class are under construction, and by the early 1990s it will be unusual for a carrier battle group to be unaccompanied by at least one of these ships.

Like all high technology the cost of Aegis has delayed its introduction into service, but now that the development phase is over, cost and complexity of manufacture are coming down. A lighter and more compact form of SPY-1A will be installed in the new *Arleigh Burke* (DDG.51) class destroyers and four

Above: Two Turya class torpedo-armed hydrofoils en route to Cuba as deck cargo on a Soviet merchant ship.

improved *Virginia* class nuclear cruisers (CGN.42-46) were planned to receive Aegis as well.

The US Navy is also modernizing its armory of antiship weapons. Although it was originally hoped that area defense SAMs like Tartar and Standard would have a limited surface capability this flexibility has always been suspect. After the Soviet SS-N-2 Styx missile had shown its deadliness by sinking the Israeli destroyer *Eilat* in 1967 the US Navy released funds for the development of a 60-mile range antiship missile. The Harpoon has been in service since the early 1970s, and exists in ship-launched, submarine-launched and air-launched variants. It is also widely deployed among friendly navies.

Harpoon follows a preset flight path under inertial guidance, and when it is close to the target it switches on its radar seeker and executes a 'pop up' maneuver to allow it to dive onto the target for maximum destructive effect. Later Harpoons have been modified to allow the missile to follow a 'sea-skimming' path, making them much harder to detect.

Other navies have adopted antiship missiles to counter the threat from the Soviet Styx. France developed its MM-38 Exocet, but unlike the Harpoon, the designers made it a sea-skimmer right from the start. Like Harpoon it is a 'fire and forget' weapon which needs only initial identification and fixing of the target before being launched, but the MM-38 version has only horizon range. Later variants include the longer-range MM-40, the air-launched AM-39 and the submarine-launched SM-39. Italy produced the Otomat,

a much larger missile using an air breathing engine to gain longer range, and it has been sold widely. Israel became the first Western navy to fire antiship missiles in anger when in 1973 its fast missile boats won a convincing victory with its home developed Gabriel missiles over Styx-equipped Syrian and Egyptian FPBs. The Norwegians also developed a small missile, the Penguin, to take advantage of the numerous islands and fjords along their coast. Unlike the others it homes on infrared emissions from the target. This allows the use of passive sensors, making the launching patrol boat harder to detect.

Although cruise missiles are not new (the German V1 was nothing more than a strategic cruise missile, and several derivatives were operational in the 1950s) new technology has made them more reliable and accurate. The new BGM-109 Tomahawk is the naval cruise missile, and it exists in two versions, a 350-mile tactical missile, and a 1600-mile strategic missile. The heart of the Tomahawk and its land- and air-launched equivalents is a Terrain Contour Matching Radar (TERCOM) which forms part of TAINS (Tercom-Aided Inertial Navigation System). In simple terms, TAINS allows the missile to fly at 15–100 meters' height, following ground contours by comparing them with a 'radar map' stored in the computer memory.

From the Navy's point of view Tomahawk has the advantage of flexibility, as it can be used to attack surface ships or to threaten important land targets as part of the nuclear deterrent. This means, for example, that nuclear attack submarines and surface warships can be armed with both types of weapon, whereas a Trident or Poseidon submarine has only one function.

To exploit the potential of the Tomahawk missile

the US Navy plans to build up four Surface Action Groups (SAGs) based on the four *Iowa* class battleships. The *New Jersey* (BB.62) saw action in Vietnam in 1966–69, then joined her sisters *Iowa* (BB.61), *Missouri* (BB.63) and *Wisconsin* (BB.64) in mothballs and is now at sea again. Under President Reagan's plans to expand the US Navy, plans were announced to recommission all four and to rearm them with a mix of Harpoons and Tomahawks, as the core element of the new SAGs. The rationale is that four large missile platforms will pose such a potent threat to the Soviet Navy that significant forces will have to be allocated to defend against them, thereby tying down forces that would otherwise be free to operate offensively against US and allied forces. The four battleships have not seen much service, and so despite being 40 years old are in good condition; to build new hulls would cost billions of dollars and would take at least five years.

The SAGs have been criticized on the grounds that they would be excessively vulnerable, but the US Navy points out that modern electronic aids and close-in weapons can be mounted in profusion on such large hulls. The SAGs would be protected by the Carrier Battle Groups, and in any case the sheer size of the 48,000-ton hulls gives them the power to absorb a number of missile hits. The *New Jersey* recommissioned in December 1982 with an interim armament of 32 Harpoon missiles in quadruple canisters, and a defensive armament of six 20mm Phalanx 'Gatlings' added. The *Iowa* is receiving a more elaborate conversion, with Tomahawk missiles in armored box launchers. She joined the Fleet in 1984 and, after the conversion of *Missouri* and *Wisconsin* the *New Jersey* will be brought up to a similar standard. If funds are available it is even hoped to give the battleships a limited air capability, with helicopters or even AV-8 Harrier V/STOL aircraft operating from a flight deck aft, but the cost of removing a triple 16-inch gun turret makes such a conversion extremely expensive.

Tomahawk missiles will, of course, arm smaller surface combatants. The new *Arleigh Burke* class (DDG.51) destroyers will carry a total of 90 missiles in vertical launchers, including SM-2 SAMs, Tomahawks and Asroc ASW missiles. What is certain is that after years of neglect surface warfare is once again a primary naval task, for it has at last been recognized that if ships cannot safely cross the water, control of that sea has been lost.

So far we have looked only at major combatants, but there is a whole field of surface warfare in which major warships play little or no part. The defense of coastal waters is entrusted to small strike craft, sometimes called FACs or Fast Attack Craft. They are the lineal descendants of the *Schnellboote*, R-Boats, MTBs, MGBs and PT-Boats which fought so many desperate actions in World War II, but modern technology has given them much greater punch.

Whereas most Western navies had run down their light forces after World War II the Soviet Navy kept large numbers of strike craft in commission, mainly with the intention of frustrating what they imagined to be the Western aim of invading the Russian landmass. Under Stalin the Navy was entrusted with protecting Mother Russia's flanks, and from 1952 some 500 P-4 and P-6 type motor torpedo boats were built. In 1959–61 a number of P-6 hulls were converted to launch the SS-N-2 Styx surface-to-surface missile.

These Komar type boats were tiny, only 85ft long, but their two missiles had a range of about 25 miles. The Komar was only an interim conversion, and shortly afterward a proper missile boat, the Osa type appeared. The hull was 131ft long, allowing four Styx missiles as well as twin 30mm guns and fire control and search radars to be fitted.

The Western world made no attempt to copy the Komar and Osa, apart from fitting some fast patrol boats with SS-11 short range wire-guided missiles, and indeed largely ignored the large number of missile boats transferred to pro-Soviet nations, until 21 October 1967, that is, when they suddenly leapt into prominence.

The event which transformed naval warfare was the sinking of the Israeli destroyer *Eilat* off Port Said by a pair of Komars lying behind the breakwater. No matter that the *Eilat* was 20 years old and lacked any modern defenses, or that she had been maintaining a fixed patrol line for days, inviting some sort of counterstroke from the Egyptians. What mattered was that two 75-ton boats had sunk a 1700-ton destroyer, with three out of four missiles.

What can only be described as a 'Styx Panic' swept through Western navies, and no fewer than five missile-programs received their first impetus from the *Eilat* sinking. The US Navy went ahead with its Harpoon program, the French immediately funded the MM-38 Exocet and the Italians started work in conjunction with the French on Otomat. Not surprisingly, the Israelis speeded up their own program, called Gabriel, and a not dissimilar weapon called Penguin went forward in Norway. The Royal Swedish Navy already possessed an antiship missile of its own, the Rb05, but this was not regarded as an unqualified success, and it was never seen as a serious competitor for the other weapons.

The Royal Navy, needing a weapon quickly, signified its intention to buy Exocet as soon as it was seen to be progressing well, and by 1974 the first British warship, the DLG *Norfolk* was carrying out firing trials in the Mediterranean. The adoption of Exocet by a leading NATO navy improved its chances, and the Federal German Navy also chose to instal it in a new type of fast patrol boat. This was the French *Combattante II* design, actually a French 47-meter modification of a German 45-meter design

Above: The F-14 Tomcat is the standard US Navy carrier interceptor aircraft. The Tomcat shown is armed with Phoenix missiles capable of destroying targets at 60 miles range.
Left: The French patrol boat *La Combattante* was used to test the Exocet antiship missile.
Below: FRS.1 Sea Harriers seen in the light gray camouflage scheme introduced shortly before the Falklands campaign.

(a ruse to allow Germany to sell FPBs to Israel without ruffling Arab feelings). No fewer than 20 *Combattantes* were built for the Federal German Navy, which wished to use them to block the exit from the Baltic, using the small islands off Denmark as cover.

Only the Israeli and Russian-designed missile boats have been tested in action, and the results give some idea of what future battles will be like. The tactics needed to defeat the Soviet SS-N-2 Styx missile were complicated by the fact that the Gabriel Mk 1 had a range of 21,000 meters, as against 40–50,000 meters for the Styx. The solution devised by the Israelis was to use evasive maneuvering and electronic warfare (jamming, decoys and analysis of radar and radio signals) to get their missile boats within range without being hit. We may never know the full story but we can judge how effective the Israeli plans were by the fact that 13 *Reshef* and *Sa'ar* class boats, mounting between them 63 Gabriels, suffered no losses in defeating 27 Syrian and Egyptian Osa and Komar craft, mounting between them 85 Styxes of roughly twice the range.

Partly as a result of these actions but also because the small missile boat seems a better investment for a small navy, the building of missile boats has steadily

Above: The Swedish patrol boat *Piteå* is the test ship for the new RBS.15 antiship missile.
Below: The Soviet *Komar* Class were the world's first missile-armed strike craft.

increased. The Russians have put missiles into hydrofoils, and have steadily developed designs. NATO tried to get a similar trend under way, with plans for the United States, Italy and West Germany to collaborate in a NATO Hydrofoil program, but it failed when costs ran out of control. The Americans were left to go it alone with a planned class of six Patrol Missile Hydrofoils or PHMs, and after many changes of heart the PHM Squadron is now in operation at Key West, Florida.

Although the Italian Navy dropped out of the NATO Hydrofoil venture there was still great enthusiasm for the new technology. A smaller, cheaper Boeing prototype hydrofoil called *Tucumcari* was chosen as the basis, rather than the US Navy's PHM, and out of this came the *Sparviero*, 22.95 meters long and displacing only 64.5 tons. Like the *Pegasus* she is armed with a 76mm gun forward, but aft she has only two Otomat missiles. The *Sparviero* proved a great success and six more have been built, the *Nibbio* class. The only other armed hydrofoils in the West are the Israeli *Shimrit* class, which came into service in 1981–82. These two craft were built to a Grumman design, one in Florida and the second at Haifa. They are 70-tonners armed with a twin 30mm antiaircraft gun forward, two Gabriel missiles amidships and four Harpoon missiles aft.

The Western world looks to the Israelis as acknowledged experts in the design and operation of strike craft, so it is worthwhile looking at their latest fast patrol boat. The 500-ton *Aliyah* class have grown to 61.7 meters in length and are armed with eight Harpoon missiles, four Gabriels, a single 40mm gun, a new design of twin 30mm AA gun and a twin 20mm as well as four machine guns. But they also find space for a hangar and flight deck to operate a Bell Kiowa helicopter. Apart from providing valuable reconnaissance the helicopter can also provide over-the-horizon data to permit the Harpoon missiles to exploit their full 60-mile range. However the provision of a helicopter on such a small hull may prove too ambitious and there are reports that the rest of the class will have a 76mm gun and four more Gabriels instead of the hangar and flight deck. However, the *Aliyah* class demonstrate the trend for strike craft to cope with the problem of providing better command and control, as the range of weapons gets greater.

Nothing has been said so far about the Chinese Navy. More correctly designated the People's Liberation Army (PLA) Navy, it is still a force largely dedicated to surface warfare. Like the Soviet Navy of the 1950s and early 1960s its main role is to defend mainland China against invasion, and has little or no preoccupation with power-projection at any distance from the home base.

Notwithstanding its modest aims, the most impressive feature of the PLA Navy is its sheer size. At the beginning of 1982 the strength stood at 100 submarines, 11 destroyers, 22 frigates, some 200 missile boats, nearly 300 torpedo boats, nearly 1000 patrol craft and minesweepers, and 500 amphibious warfare craft. Many of these are either Russian-built or based on Soviet technology, but since the breach with the Soviet Union efforts have been made to develop indigenous designs and weapons. Despite this understandable desire for self-reliance the Chinese make no secret of their wish to import Western technology for the modernization of their navy.

The main strength of the surface fleet comprises a class of destroyers known as the Luda class, because they were built at the Luda Shipyard in Manchuria. Although based on the Soviet Kotlin design they differ in several respects. Amidships they have two sets of triple antiship missiles; the missile is reported to be a development of the SS-N-2 Styx.

The remainder of the destroyer force is made up of four Russian-built Gordy class, 1700-ton ships which have been rearmed with four SS-N-2C missiles. They are now over 40 years old, and it seems highly probable that they will be replaced when more Ludas are commissioned.

The next class of surface escorts is the modern Jianghu class, which are capable of $25\frac{1}{2}$ knots on a displacement of 1900 tons full load. The remaining armament is light; two single 100mm guns, four twin 37mm AA guns and two ASW rocket launchers. On the same hull, the Jiangdong class mount surface-to-air missiles, but reports from intelligence sources suggest that the system is not yet operational.

In 1954–57 four of the Soviet Riga class frigates or light escorts were built at Shanghai, followed by five similar Jiangnan class. The first four have been rearmed with missiles, a triple group of SS-N-2Cs on a rotating turntable, as in the Luda class, whereas the Jiangnan class have three 100mm guns of obsolete design, four twin 37mm AA guns and ASW rockets.

Apart from some very ancient veterans of World War II the remainder of the PLA Navy's surface strength is concentrated in strike craft and patrol boats. There are approximately a hundred locally-built versions of the Soviet Osa type, and a steel-hulled variant of the smaller Komar, known as the Hoku type.

Like their erstwhile Soviet allies the Chinese showed a keen interest in hydrofoils, and some of their numerous Huchuan type torpedo boats built in the late 1960s have been exported. There is also a hydrofoil version of the Hoku missile boat, known to Western Intelligence as the Homa. The remainder of the torpedo boat force is made up of Russian-built P.4 and P.6 types. The best-known local patrol craft are the Shanghai IIs, sturdy diesel-engined craft armed with two twin 37mm guns, machine guns and depth charges. In all as many as 350 of these craft may have been constructed, and they have been followed by the Hainan class, armed with 57mm guns.

AIR DEFENSE

The guided missile cruiser (formerly destroyer leader) USS *Leahy* (CG.16) and her sisters were the first 'double ended' missile ships.

Ever since World War II, when Japanese torpedo- and dive-bombers devastated the US Pacific Fleet at Pearl Harbor and sank the British capital ships *Prince of Wales* and *Repulse* off Malaya, defense against the air threat has been paramount. The bloody operations off Okinawa added a new element, the suicide attack, in which a human brain functioned as a terminal guidance system to turn the aircraft into a missile, rather than a delivery vehicle.

The answer, as we have seen, was to design anti-aircraft missiles which could be guided by radar to the point of impact. In theory at least, such missiles could guarantee the destruction of an attacking aircraft, whereas gunfire, even with proximity-fuzed shells, could only predict a percentage of hits in the area of the aircraft.

The first missiles were bulky, and so cruisers had to be converted to accommodate the tracker radars and the magazines. In all 11 US Navy cruisers were converted to act as antiaircraft screening ships for the fast carrier task forces, and the nuclear *Long Beach* was built for the same purpose. However by the 1960s it was clear that smaller destroyer-sized hulls could accommodate the same type of firepower, even if they lacked the same magazine stowage and could not accommodate an admiral and his staff.

The first missile-armed fleet escorts designed for the task were planned as 'frigates' or Destroyer Leaders (DLGs). The *Farragut* (DLG.6) class was the result of recommendations made by the Schindler Committee as long ago as 1954, making the case for specialized Fast Task Force Escorts equipped for Anti Aircraft Warfare (AAW). The initial design substituted a twin launcher for Terrier missiles in place of two single 5inch guns aft. After some hesitation all ten ships of the program (DLG.6-15) were built with missiles, but in response to the growing threat from submarines the antisubmarine armament was strengthened.

The Terrier missile had started life as a supersonic test vehicle for the long range Talos missile, but preceded it into service as work was accelerated by the outbreak of the Korean War in 1950. Like other missiles of that era it was something of a disappointment, being difficult to maintain and erratic in performance. Although Operational Evaluation (OPEVAL) did not begin until 1955, a Terrier Improvement Program had already been running for two years. The method of guidance was changed from beam-riding to semiactive homing, and the original range of 10 miles was doubled, and then redoubled by 1964 to 40 miles. Today it is no longer in production, but Terrier-armed ships are being rearmed with the Standard (Extended Range) RIM-67A, which has a similar airframe but new electronics.

At 4167 tons (light) the *Farraguts* were big and costly, and there was clearly a need for a smaller destroyer (DDG) for fleet screening. The solution

was to design a single-stage version of the Terrier which could go into a 3000-ton or smaller ship. Tartar was intended to be effective between 2000 and 15,000 yards and at an altitude of 50,000 feet. Subsequently these figures were raised to 25,000 yards and 65,000 feet respectively, and development was advanced as rapidly as possible. Unfortunately the weapon system did not live up to its early promise, and when OPEVAL began in the *Charles F Adams* (DDG.2) in 1961 there were many red faces. Maintenance problems, particularly in the fire control system, proved almost insurmountable and OPEVAL had to be terminated in November 1961 without the system being passed as serviceable.

Despite these disappointments the Tartar-armed destroyers of the *Charles F Adams* class were successful. In all 23 ships were commissioned between 1960 and 1964, and they are still highly regarded; three were built for the Federal German Navy (the *Lütjens* class) and three for the Royal Australian Navy (the *Perth* class). From the *Berkeley* (DDG.15) onward the twin-arm launcher was replaced by the single-arm Mk 13, which was more reliable and capable of firing the same number of missiles. The later ships (DDG. 15-24) have undergone an AAW modernization since 1981; this involves replacing Tartar with the Standard (Medium Range) RIM-66A and improved electronics.

By the late 1950s the missile was taking over completely from the gun in air defense, and the successors to the *Farragut* class, the nine *Leahy* (DLG.16) class marked a new departure. They were made 'double-ended', with twin Terrier launchers forward and aft. Instead of the conventional profile of the *Farraguts* they were given two 'macks' or combined mast/stacks to save deck space. Each twin-arm launcher is served by a 40-round magazine and two large AN/SPG-55 trackers. At 5146 tons (light) they were another 1000 tons bigger than the previous DLGs, and the three-quarter length forecastle deck enhanced their appearance.

The size and cost of the *Leahy* class horrified Congress, and there was pressure on the US Navy to build a successor to the *Charles F Adams* class, but more austere. Even by cutting the number of missiles to 12, the requirement to push endurance up by 1500 miles to 6000nm and the inclusion of the new AN/SQS-26 sonar resulted in a ship which was far more expensive than the *Adams* class. Then the planners decided that Terrier was a better missile for a large ship, and to save further trouble the hull of the *Leahy* was adapted. The nine *Belknap* (DLG.26) class were built in 1964–67, and they have been followed by two nuclear equivalents, the *Bainbridge* (DLGN.25) and *Truxtun* (DLGN.35), and the *California* and *Virginia* class nuclear cruisers.

Other navies wanted to build missile ships to protect their major fleet units against air attack. The British started development of a beam-riding missile

Below: Three modified versions of the *Charles F. Adams* class DDGs were built for the Federal German Navy in the 1970s as the *Lütjens* class. The *Molders* is shown here.

Bottom: The French DDG *Suffren* is armed with the French Masurca SAM aft, the Malafon antisubmarine missile amidships and 100mm guns forward.

Above: The USS *Horne* (CG.30), a unit of the *Belknap* class.
Above left: The USS *Cochrane* and the rest of the *Charles F. Adams* class are the mainstay of US fleet air defense forces.
Below left: The new Aegis missile cruiser *Ticonderoga*.

immediately after the war, and the Staff Requirement was issued in 1946. The first test vehicle flew five years later, enabling the dimensions of the airframe to be fixed. Unfortunately large booster rockets could not be manufactured in Britain at the time, and so four $\frac{1}{4}$-ton boosters were adopted, wrapped around the body of the missile. This resulted in a very bulky missile known as Seaslug, which in turn had a serious impact on the design of the ships which were to use them. Thus, instead of the vertical loading system used in the first Terrier-armed cruisers, the County class DLGs had a huge tunnel through the superstructure. The missiles travel from the forward magazine back through the ship, having the wings put on, circuits checked etc, before being run out on the launcher.

Two Seaslug ships took part in the fighting around the Falklands in 1982, and although the beam-riding guidance system is not suited to attacking modern high speed aircraft HMS *Antrim* was able to break up formations of Mirages by firing Seaslug as a barrage weapon, using a simple alteration to the fuzing to give a time-delay burst. Her sister *Glamorgan* put Seaslug to an even less orthodox purpose by firing it at Argentine artillery positions. It was reasoned that, as the missiles are to be withdrawn for scrapping, they

should at least be fired to destruction if the opportunity arose. In fact the scrap value of guided missiles being negligible the normal method of disposal is to fire them live during exercises. Old missiles can also be used as target vehicles for more modern missiles.

The eight County class DLGs were completed in 1962–70. In the year that the first ship commissioned work started on a missile to follow the Seaslug. Named Sea Dart, it was driven by a ramjet and used semi-active homing. Its effective range is about 25 miles, and one of its advantages is good performance against low-level targets. During the Falklands fighting the DDG *Exeter* shot down two Argentine A-4 Skyhawks in quick succession, and is credited with a 'kill' below 50 feet.

The first ships designed for Sea Dart were a quartet of DLGs intended to screen a pair of aircraft carriers planned in 1966. In the event the carriers were canceled and only one of the DLGs, HMS *Bristol* was built. A class of small DDGs was started in 1970, the *Sheffield* class, but on 3500 tons they proved too small, and the design had to be stretched by adding 30ft more. The ten *Sheffield* class (Type 42) and the four stretched *Manchester* class were designed without allowance for a close range defensive armament, although after the sinking of HMS *Sheffield* by an air-launched Exocet missile and the loss of her sister *Coventry* to a conventional glide-bombing attack by A-4 Skyhawks the rest of the class were hurriedly given twin 30mm guns amidships as a close range defense.

The *Sheffield* was in fact sunk by a combination of human errors. Hostile air activity had been reported but the ship was not brought to Action Stations, and the main radar was closed down to permit a message to be transmitted via the satellite link. The Exocet was launched from one of a pair of Super Etendards some 25 miles away, and was apparently undetected, although it seems likely that an electronic warning was received but ignored. The missile struck on the starboard side, above the waterline and went through both engine rooms before hitting the after engine room bulkhead without exploding. Even so the friction of the missile body and unspent fuel in the rocket motor was sufficient to set the fuel alight, and within seconds the central part of the ship was filled with choking black smoke. Even though damage control parties were able to get power supplies working, smoke made it impossible for firefighters to reach the flames, and after five hours the ship was abandoned after the crew had been taken off. Six days later the gutted hulk was cut loose and allowed to sink in deep water.

The *Coventry*, in contrast, achieved considerable success, lying to the north of Falkland Sound in company with the frigate *Broadsword*, tracking hostile aircraft on her long range air surveillance radar, and directing Sea Harrier aircraft to attack them. In fact she had been performing that task from 1 May, the day in which the Task Force entered the Total Exclusion Zone around the Falklands.

On the first day the air battle went well, with seven Argentinian aircraft shot down by the Sea Harriers of the carriers *Invincible* and *Hermes*. The first engagement with Sea Dart took place when *Coventry* fired a single Sea Dart to destroy two Skyhawks at a range of 25 miles, and a few hours later a second missile destroyed a troop-carrying helicopter at 13 miles' range. On 24 May the *Coventry*'s coordination of air defense off Falkland Sound vectored the Sea Harriers onto three 'kills', and the following day she shot down three aircraft with missiles. But at about 6 pm four aircraft made a determined low-level attack. The frigate *Broadsword*, following astern, was about to fire Sea Wolf short range missiles at the attackers when the *Coventry* swung across her bows while taking avoiding action, and in the confusion a solitary Skyhawk was able to get through and hit with three out of four 1000 pound bombs.

Those in the *Coventry*'s Operations Room remembered only a flash of searing flame, followed by dense clouds of black smoke. Those who were still alive were badly burned, and even their clothing was alight. All power and communications were destroyed and the ship began to list to port. Within 15 minutes she was lying on her side, and then she slowly rolled over. Surprisingly, only 19 men were killed by the explosion, and some 280 officers and ratings escaped.

The Task Force had left Britain with only three

Main picture: The Italian DDG *Ardito* has the US Standard missile system and associated radars aft but the rest of her armament is of Italian design comprising two 5-inch guns, four 3-inch guns and six antisubmarine torpedo tubes

air defense ships, and had now lost all three, for in addition to the *Sheffield* and *Coventry*, their sister *Glasgow* had been disabled by a bomb early in the fighting. Luckily reinforcements which had arrived a few days earlier included the DLG *Bristol* and the DDGs *Exeter* and *Cardiff*. The *Exeter* had a newer air warning radar than the earlier ships of the class, and as already mentioned, this helped her to achieve missile 'kills' against low flying aircraft. Her moment of fame came on 30 May, when the Super Etendards made an attempt to sink the carrier *Invincible*, using their last Exocet missile; two of the six accompanying Skyhawks were destroyed by Sea Dart missiles from the *Exeter*, persuading the survivors to head for home.

The most important lesson learned by the British in the air defense of the Task Force was that older surveillance radars were not good enough to cope with low level attacks. With no airborne early warning to guide defending Sea Harriers, all depended on the radars in the DDGs and the carriers, but the ships were not equipped with the sort of '3-D' radars which the US Navy insists on for its air defense ships. A three-dimensional radar is, in simple terms, one which combines a height-finding radar with the conventional type capable of giving range and bearing of targets. The objection to a 3-D radar is that height-

181

Main picture: The nuclear powered guided missile cruiser USS *Truxtun* (CGN.35) like her predecessor the *Bainbridge* was designed to screen nuclear-powered aircraft carriers.
Left: The nuclear missile cruiser *Arkansas* (CGN.41) is the last of a series of six fast carrier escorts. Experience has shown that the nuclear carriers do indeed need escorts with equally high endurance.

finding is generally less accurate than the ranging and bearing indication, but this is comparatively unimportant, so long as the defending aircraft are correctly vectored to an altitude where their own radars can take over.

The Type 965 long range air warning radar was designed in the 1950s to track comparatively high flying Soviet bombers, and does not provide data at a fast enough rate to cope with fast targets. Even worse, it is intended to work with a target-indicating radar, the Type 992Q, which has difficulty in identifying targets against the 'clutter' of land or the surface of the sea. The need for a new Surveillance and Target-Indicating Radar (known as STIR for short) was recognized, and the Type 1022 fitted in the *Exeter* and later DDGs is regarded as an interim STIR. Ironically, a year before the Falklands, development of a new STIR radar had been canceled, but a new staff requirement has since been drawn up for a cheaper commercial equivalent.

The French Navy also decided to go its own way on missile development, but found the cost of developing area defense weapons a great strain on its resources. Even with American technical assistance the Masurca missile (roughly equivalent to the US Navy's Terrier) had a lengthy period of trials and development before it became operational. To gain practical experience the decision was taken to convert five large destroyers of the *Surcouf* class (T47 type) to DDGs, using American radars and missiles. Between 1962 and 1965 the *Dupetit-Thouars*, *Kersaint*, *Bouvet* and *du Chayla* were rebuilt with a single-arm Mk 13 launcher for Tartar missiles and two SPG-51 trackers in place of the after pair of 127mm gun mountings, and an SPS-39A '3-D' radar antenna on the mainmast.

The first Masurca-armed ships were the 'frigates' *Suffren* and *Duquesne*, built in 1962–70. When they first appeared they set new standards in appearance, with a single tall 'mack' amidships and a vast 'golf ball' dome protecting the big DRBI-23 surveillance radar. In the 1970s the armament was further increased by the addition of four MM-38 Exocet antiship missiles. In the interim Masurca underwent the same sort of updating as Terrier, being converted from beam-riding to semi-active homing.

Only one more ship was destined to receive Masurca. In 1970–72 the 8500-ton cruiser *Colbert* underwent a major reconstruction, during which her after 127mm and 57mm guns were replaced by a twin-arm launcher and two DRBR-51 trackers. When the time came to order an air-defense version of the new C70 type antisubmarine 'corvettes' or destroyers, the missile chosen was the American Standard SM-1 instead of the Masurca. The electronics, however, are French: a new DRBJ-11 phased-array radar and a SENIT 6 action-information system.

The Dutch and Italian Navies have been content to buy American missiles for installation in their own

ships. The cruiser *de Zeven Provincien* was given a Terrier system aft, replacing two twin 6-inch gun turrets, while the large DDGs *Tromp* and *de Ruyter* completed in 1975–76 had Standard SM-1 systems. The last two of 12 'Standard' or *Kortenaer* class frigates built since 1975 are being built to a modified air-defense design, also with Standard SM-1 missiles.

Typically the Italians went for a most elaborate conversion of the old 6-inch gunned cruiser *Giuseppe Garibaldi*, dating from the 1930s. Between 1957 and 1962 she was completely gutted and rebuilt with a new bridge, upperworks and single funnel. The former 'A' and 'B' 6-inch guns were replaced by twin 135mm (5.3-inch) guns, eight 76mm guns were sited amidships, and a Terrier system was installed aft. There was talk at the time of creating a multinational NATO surface deterrent fleet, and to demonstrate its feasibility the *Garibaldi* was given four Polaris launch tubes below the quarterdeck. Test vehicles were fired from these tubes, but the idea of deploying Polaris in surface ships went out of fashion and the *Garibaldi* never embarked them operationally.

In their next class of missile ships the Italian designers achieved a remarkable blend of air-defense and antisubmarine capabilities. A twin-arm Terrier launcher was installed forward, while the after part of the ship was devoted to a flight deck and hangar capable of housing three Sea King helicopters. The idea was overambitious, for on 5000 tons it proved impossible to carry the big helicopters, and four smaller types had to be embarked. The *Andrea Doria* and *Caio Duilio* pointed the way to other hybrid helicopter cruisers, but the next ship, the *Vittorio Veneto* was made considerably larger to improve the helicopter handling. She is much more successful in many ways, not least because the Terrier launcher was modified to permit Asroc antisubmarine missiles to be launched from the same magazines.

Only two more classes of air-defense ships have been built for the Italian Navy, but they are more conventional DDGs armed with Tartar SAMs, rather than hybrid helicopter-cruisers, the *Impavido*, *Intrepido*, *Audace* and *Ardito*.

The Japanese built their first missile-armed ship in 1962–65, the 3000-ton *Amatsukaze*. Unlike the European ships she was armed with Tartar missiles, but these have since been replaced by Standard SM-1. She has been followed by the three *Tachikaze* class, completed 1976–82, and a new class of gas turbine-driven DDGs is currently building. They will be armed with Standard SAMs and eight Harpoon missiles, as well as 5-inch guns, Asroc missiles and antisubmarine torpedoes. The *Hatakaze* (DDG.171) is also the first warship to be driven by the Rolls-Royce SM1A Spey gas turbine.

At this point it is time to turn to the Soviet Navy, for the Russians could hardly ignore the trend toward area-defense SAMs in Western ships, particularly as

their surface warships could expect to be attacked by Western carrier aircraft. In 1961–62 two six year old Kotlin class destroyers were taken in hand for conversion to operate the SA-N-1 Goa, following trials with a land missile, codenamed Guideline, in the cruiser *Dzerzhinski*. Apparently the Guideline was unsuitable, for it very soon gave way to the Goa, which has since been installed in other classes.

In all eight Kotlin class destroyers were reconstructed as DDGs, starting with the *Bravy*. One, the *Spravedlivy*, was transferred to Poland in 1970 and renamed *Warszawa*. In 1963 the first of a new class codenamed Kashin appeared. She was the first major warship driven entirely by gas turbines and also the first Soviet purpose-built DDG, with twin-arm Goa launchers forward and aft, backed up by two twin 76mm dual-purpose gun mountings and a set of quintuple torpedo tubes. The silhouette was unique – two widely separated pairs of split uptakes. No fewer than 20 Kashins were built for the Soviet Navy and three more for India, the *Rajput*, *Rana* and *Ranjit*.

The Kashins have proved successful, and have appeared around the world. However one, the *Otvazhny*, was lost in the Black Sea in September 1974. She suffered some sort of internal explosion and caught fire, burning for five hours. According to various sources, including the Russians themselves, combustible materials such as plastics generated large

quantities of smoke, and casualties are believed to have been nearly 300 dead.

Because the Soviet Navy has no aircraft carriers as such, the air defense role is not yet of prime importance, although of course individual major warships are equipped to defend themselves. Thus the Kynda and Kresta I type cruisers carry Goa missiles, while the Kresta II and Kara types carry the later Goblet missile. Since then the big nuclear cruiser *Kirov* has appeared with a new missile codenamed SA-N-6 by NATO. What makes it unusual is that it is vertically launched from 12 forward positions, although clearly more than 12 missiles are carried. The successor to the Kara class, the 8000-ton *Sovremennyy*, has been to sea without weapons, and although a new pattern of 130mm gun has since been added, along with anti-submarine SS-N-14 missiles, the new SAM has not been identified. Western intelligence sources credit the SA-N-6 missile with a ceiling of about 100,000ft, a slant range of 40 miles, a 200 pound warhead and a speed of Mach 6. This should be taken as the 'worst case', but it shows how missiles have been improved.

So far the air defense systems talked about have been long and medium range area defense systems. By their nature these missile systems are not good at coping with targets which fly low, and inevitably a defense has had to be found against aircraft and missiles which 'leak' through the outer layers of protection. This was formerly left to fast-firing guns, but the growing dominance of guided weapons in the 1960s and 1970s resulted in guns disappearing from NATO warships. As early as the 1950s the British had

Above: The Sparrow air-to-air missile was adapted to provide US Navy ships with the Sea Sparrow short range air defense system. Left: The Norwegian destroyer escort *Bergen* fires a Penguin anti ship missile from its quarterdeck canister.

investigated the idea of adapting air-to-air missiles to defend ships, in a project called 'Hot Shot', but it was the Americans who persevered with it. The Sparrow missile was adapted to be launched from an 8-cell box mounted on top of a 3inch gun pedestal, and christened the Basic Point Defense System. 'Point defense' is the modern term for close range defense, as opposed to area defense. From this concept other developments followed, notably Improved Point Defense Missile System (IPDMS) and NATO Sea Sparrow, and today a number of navies use variants of these.

The Italians, who manufacture Sea Sparrow launchers for NATO, decided to redevelop the Sparrow, and within the same airframe provided improved electronics for a family of three missiles, all known as Aspide. With only minor changes Aspide is used as an air-to-air weapon, a ship-mounted point defense weapon and a land-based air defense weapon.

In its naval version the Aspide missile is fired from an Albatros system, and it is compatible with the original NATO Sea Sparrow, requiring only minor modifications to convert from one type of missile to the other.

The British, after abandoning their 'Hot Shot' program, decided in 1951 to develop a simple missile defense for ships. The range was to be 5000 yards, outside the range to which aircraft had to close before launching their weapons, and for simplicity visual Command to Line of sight was chosen as the method of guidance. Under the codename 'Green Light' test vehicles flew in 1955, and a contract was signed in 1958. The system, known as Seacat, went to sea in the destroyer HMS *Decoy* in 1960, and in July 1962 became operational in the destroyer *Barrosa*.

Seacat was designed to cope with targets having a slow crossing rate, and although this remained adequate for some years the Royal Navy knew that the new generation of aircraft targets would require something better. Furthermore the Soviet Navy was known to be introducing new types of antiship missile. In 1964 a Naval Staff Target for the Seacat replacement was drawn up. Known as Confessor, the project was undertaken by Hawker Siddeley Dynamics and British Aircraft Corporation, and full development by BAC began in mid-1968. In 1969 six vertically launched test vehicles (quaintly codenamed 'Sinner') were fired from the old frigate *Loch Fada*, but the decision was made to use a more conventional 6-cell above-deck launcher. The new weapon, now known as Sea Wolf or GWS.25, went to sea in the frigate HMS *Penelope* in 1976, and the first operational warship to receive the new system was the frigate *Broadsword* in 1979. Sea Wolf used many ideas developed for the land-based Rapier system, principally the concept of a 'hittile', a small missile agile enough to guarantee a very high probability of hitting its target, rather than relying on a proximity burst. In fact Sea Wolf was given a proximity fuze to increase its effectiveness, but it retains the original Rapier qualities of ultra-fast acceleration off the launcher and a spectacular agility against rapidly maneuvering targets.

The performance of the missile would be needed, for in 1968, the year in which development began, the Soviet Gorky shipyard delivered the first Charlie class attack submarine. Western intelligence observers noted with interest the eight hatches in the forward casing, which concealed a new antiship cruise missile capable of being launched underwater. Here was an alarming new dimension to the surface threat, a missile which could be fired from well inside the normal range of air defenses. In theory a Charlie could slip inside a task force's screen, and the first the defenses would know would be when the SS-N-7 missile popped out of the water and headed straight for the largest object detected by its radar seeker.

The electronics of Sea Wolf could be made capable of handling the data sufficiently fast to allow a rapid response to a 'pop-up' missile, but it would take no fewer than five computers. Two radars were provided, the D-Band pulse-doppler Type 967 capable of detecting targets up to 75 degrees, and the E-Band monopulse Type 968 capable of detecting low level targets. To speed up the data-rate the radars are mounted back-to-back, and rotate 30 times per minute. In theory the GWS.25 system is ready only 5–6 seconds after the 967/968 radars detect a target, and unless the operator countermands the order, a missile will be fired automatically. As it accelerates to Mach 2 it is 'gathered' into the beam of the Type 910 I/J-Band tracker, which is tracking both the missile and its target. Commands to the missile are sent through a microwave link, and two missiles can be handled by the tracker simultaneously. In cases of extreme sea clutter or jamming control can be handed over to a TV camera boresighted to the 910 tracker.

To provide the sort of reaction time needed the Sea Wolf system has been made automatic, but as a safety device the control system will only generate an automatic response to a target behaving like a missile flying toward the ship, ie a small diameter, high speed target on a collision course. This means that the system is programmed to ignore passing aircraft and helicopters.

Unlike other point defense systems, Sea Wolf has

been tested in action, having been fired by both the *Broadsword* and her sister *Brilliant* in the fierce air-sea battles around the Falklands in 1982. One alarming discovery was made in the engagement which resulted in the sinking of HMS *Coventry*; the computer program had not allowed for two air targets weaving and crossing over, and a firing solution was delayed as a result. Fortunately modern computer software is comparatively easy to alter, and discovery of such a shortcoming does not invalidate the whole system.

The drawback to the Mk 1 version of Sea Wolf is that the weight of the tracker and below-decks equipment restricts its use to large warships. The *Broadsword* class frigates displace over 4000 tons, and have a 'double-headed' system with two launchers and two trackers; the smaller *Leander* class and the new Type 23 could only take one launcher and tracker, as well as the masthead radars. A Mk 2 version has a lighter equipment, and the vertical launch GWS.26 Sea Wolf will be lighter still.

The Russian point defense system is known to NATO as SA-N-4, and it differs in having a twin-arm launcher which pops up from inside a cylindrical weatherproof housing set in the deck. Photographs of the SA-N-4 out of its housing are rare, but it is believed that the missile reloads are stowed around the inside of the cylinder. It first appeared in the Kara class cruisers and the Nanuchka class missile corvettes, but has since been fitted in a wide variety of

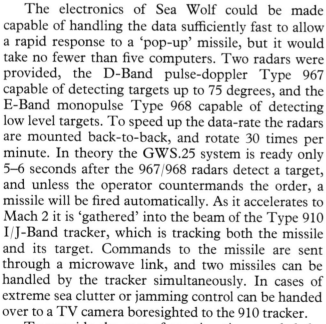

Above: Soviet Kanin class destroyers are modifications of the Krupnyi class with SA-N-1 Goa missiles.
Above left: The US Navy's standard medium caliber gun for the 1980s is the 5-inch Mark 45.

ships. Its successor may already be in service in the latest classes, in a vertically-launched configuration.

The attraction of vertical launch is that it dispenses with bulky loading systems and launchers, all of which are as complex as any gun mounting and therefore constitute an additional drain on manpower, both to operate and maintain. If a missile can be embarked as a 'wooden' round in a sealed container, and simply dropped into a hole in the deck it will always be ready to fire. There are, of course, drawbacks to vertical launching, which is why it has taken so long to be perfected. For one thing, it had to wait until the design of the missiles themselves and their electronics had progressed to a point where they could be left unattended in a sealed container for months on end. Another difficulty was the stress on the missile exerted when it swings through as much as 90 degrees from its launch-trajectory to its flight path. Modern thrust-vector control has overcome the problem, but it has proved necessary to provide extra boost to make up for the loss of range in 'gathering' the missile back into the guidance beam. The US Navy has now adopted vertical launch for the Standard missile, and

the later *Ticonderoga* class cruisers and the *Arleigh Burke* class destroyers will dispense with the twin-arm Mk 26 launchers.

The French Navy has developed its own point defense missile, a 'navalized' version of the land-based Crotale. This uses an 8-cell launcher with its own on-board radar tracker. Crotale Navale is now operational in the *Georges Leygues* class 'corvettes' and is being retrofitted to older surface ships. Like the British Sea Wolf it is a bulky system, and the designers have drawn up plans for lightweight versions. Although not claimed as an antimissile system when introduced, the Mk 2 version has been upgraded to allow it to engage sea-skimming missiles.

The final form of point defense is the gun. Once regarded as virtually useless, it has made a remarkable comeback, and the reason is not hard to find. The cost of missiles is so high that even practice firing has to be restricted, whereas gun ammunition is comparatively cheap. What has also changed is the accuracy of fire control; guns can derive the same benefit from computers and modern electronics as any missile system. The gun has therefore returned to warships in recent years, not as a medium range weapon but as a 'close-in' defense against missiles and aircraft which have evaded the outer layers of defense. To put it bluntly, the morale of sailors demands something capable of shooting at close range targets, rather than mere reliance on chaff launchers and jamming.

Above: A Soviet Kynda class missile cruiser 'riding herd' on the USS *John F. Kennedy* and her escorts.
Above left: The Soviet Kanin class DDGs are designed to provide air defense for task groups. Like their US equivalents they are 'double enders' with separate missile systems fore and aft.
Below: The British DDG HMS *Sheffield* on builder's trials in 1975. She was sunk by an Argentinian ASM early in the Falklands conflict.

There are several solutions to the problem. One school of thought favors a 'wall of lead' simply interposing sufficient metal to penetrate the warhead, guidance system or rocket motor of a missile to disable it. The other approach is to use larger projectiles with proximity fuzes to detonate close to the missile. Both methods rely on getting sufficient hits on the sensitive parts of the missile, 'splashing' it into the sea or detonating the sensitive warhead. The risk is always that large fragments of the missile will 'go ballistic' and continue on the same course to crash into the ship, but supporters of gun systems claim that the hail of metal will almost certainly destroy such large pieces of wreckage.

The best known close-in gun system is the Phalanx, a naval version of the 20mm Vulcan 'Gatling' or revolving aircraft cannon which first saw action in Vietnam. The Phalanx is an autonomous system which is bolted to the deck, and merely requires an external power source. A radar on the mounting tracks not only the incoming target but the stream of 20mm rounds (fired at a rate of 3000 per minute), and by 'closed loop spotting' fires the gun when the target reaches a predetermined spot some 3000 yards away. The Phalanx has shown its capabilities by shooting down a Walleye laser-guided bomb, and it is now being fitted in all US Navy surface combatants. During the Falklands fighting five Phalanx mountings were supplied in great haste to the Royal Navy, one for shore training and two each for the carriers *Invincible* and *Illustrious*. It is also used by the Japanese Maritime Self Defense Force and other navies. A new 4-barreled 30mm version is under development.

The Russians have also adopted a 'Gatling' type of point defense gun, a 30mm mounting which can be seen in most large combatants; it has replaced an earlier 23mm 'Gatling', presumably to give greater stopping power. The number varies from eight mounted in the *Kiev* and *Minsk*, down to one in the Grisha class light escorts. Unlike the Phalanx they have a separate fire control system, known to NATO as Drum Tilt.

Also in the 30mm range are such weapons as the Oerlikon twin 30mm, which is also made in Britain by their subsidiary B-MARC. As already mentioned, the heavy air attacks by Argentine aircraft led to the hurried installation of twin B-MARC 30mm guns as well as single 20mm. The only limiting factor was the restricted space available in the DDGs, which had to sacrifice their boats to make way for the guns amidships.

The Italian company Breda Meccanica Bresciana came up with a different solution. In conjunction with the Selenia and Elsag companies they produced the Dardo point defense system, using a twin 40mm Bofors gun mounting controlled by a low-level fire control system. The guns are in fact license-built versions of the original Swedish 40mm L/70 and they

Above: The *Sovremennyy* is the lead ship of a new Soviet class of 'large antisubmarine ship'.

192

fire specially designed proximity-fuzed and pre-fragmented ammunition designed to riddle a missile with tungsten balls. What Breda has done is to provide a very advanced feed system, which allows the guns to fire 300 rounds a minute from each barrel. Such a rate of fire has to be seen to be believed, and firing trials against simulated sea-skimmer targets show a remarkably high rate of 'kills'.

For those customers who adhere to the 'wall of lead' philosophy Breda has produced a similar mounting with twin Mauser 30mm guns. The Dutch company Signaal has developed a system known as 'Goalkeeper', originally with four 30mm Mauser guns but later with a General Electric GAU-8A revolving 30mm gun. It resembles the Phalanx in having its own radar on the mounting. Goalkeeper is undergoing trials before delivery to the Royal Netherlands Navy, and is under consideration by the Royal Navy and the Federal German Navy.

The latest and in many ways the most advanced system is the multi-national Sea Guard. Oerlikon-Buhrle provided a quadruple 25mm mounting with an unusual skewed trunnion to permit shooting close to 90 degrees overhead, while Contraves provided the tracker, Siemens the processing and Plessey the C-Band missile-detecting radar. Testing of the individual components was complete in 1982, and the first fully engineered system started trials in 1984. As a genuine example of international cooperation Sea Guard could be a great success, and the Royal Navy is known to be looking at it as a successor to the Phalanx. An alternative is Sea Dragon using the GAU-8A 30mm 'Gatling', a Sea Wolf tracker, a Swedish C-Band radar and a Vickers gun mounting.

A totally different approach is offered by the Ram system, a joint American-German development for the defense of fast patrol boats. Using the Phalanx mounting General Dynamics provided a Rolling Airframe Missile (RAM), while various German companies developed subsystems. The advantage of the rolling airframe is that it provides accurate response to commands with only a single guidance channel. The missile homes passively on the radar seeker of an incoming missile, and when detection is achieved it switches to infrared homing. The appeal of Ram is that it can cope with multiple attacks, and because of its simplicity and the use of many off-the-shelf components its price is considerably cheaper than most point defense systems.

The great conflict between the sea-skimming missile and the various point defense systems remains nothing more than a war of words so far. Neither side is prepared to submit to a 'shoot-out', for a decisive result would be a public relations disaster for one or other. However the success of Exocet in the Falklands must push the leading navies into the expense of a full-scale trial sooner or later, to establish whether there is a credible defense.

Below: The West German *Bremen* class frigates (*Bremen* is shown) have the same hull as the Dutch *Kortenaer* class but different propulsion and electronics.

Below: Three of the US Navy's missile frigates, *Oliver Hazard Perry* (FFG.7), *Antrim* (FFG.20) and *Jack Williams* (FFG.24).

ANTI-SUBMARINE OPERATIONS

The growing power of the submarine has inevitably led to a great increase in the amount of money spent on antisubmarine warfare. ASW, as it is known, has changed little in basic principles from the techniques by which the Allies defeated the German U-Boats in 1943–44; close escort for formations of merchant ships or warships, distant escort to bring support where it is needed, long range maritime patrol aircraft, and above all, integral air support for the close escort. What have changed beyond all recognition are the techniques.

In both World Wars there was a divergence of opinion about the basic strategy for fighting submarines. The 'offensive' school wished to pursue submarines wherever they might be, a strategy which is described today as wide area hunting.

In April 1917 the strategy changed to one of convoying shipping, and the change seemed truly miraculous. Losses fell while sinkings of U-Boats climbed rapidly. From near-defeat in April 1917 the Allies reached a point in October 1918 where the U-Boats were suffering 40 percent losses. The reasons were twofold: the U-Boats were forced to come to the convoys, where they faced well-armed escorts, but equally important was the fact that a U-Boat would only have one chance to fire torpedoes before taking evasive action.

When World War II started the British had no reservations about convoy, but in the United States

Navy the offensive strategy had many supporters. The six months after Pearl Harbor came as a rude awakening, therefore, when U-Boats inflicted enormous casualties on American shipping off the East coast. Once again convoy provided the solution, and thereafter the US Navy put its massive resources into developing ASW escort forces. The major difference from World War I was the important part played by aircraft.

There was another element in antisubmarine warfare. In World War I the British had been able to read radio messages to the U-Boats and to pinpoint positions by direction-finding, but until the advent of convoy the methods of counterattack were too crude to achieve worthwhile results. In World War II, however, a similar cryptographic 'break-in' yielded immense benefits, once sufficient hunting groups and maritime patrol aircraft were available.

It was one thing to know of the whereabouts of a U-Boat, but quite another to sink it. In 1914–18 all ASW was hampered by the lack of an underwater sensor; a crude hydrophone helped to redress the balance, but nothing much would be achieved until the British perfected their Asdic, the precursor of modern sonars.

The first effective ASW weapon was the depth charge, a canister of high explosive detonated at a preset depth by a hydrostatic valve. At first depth charges were dropped over the stern of an escort but

Above: A US P-3 Orion maritime patrol aircraft drops the new Mark 50 lightweight torpedo during development trials.
Left: The Danish destroyer *Peder Skram* has been modernized with eight Harpoon missiles in B position and NATO Sea Sparrow SAMs aft.

in World War II 'throwers' were used to form patterns of charges around the target. The next innovation was to drop them from aircraft. In 1943 the first homing torpedoes appeared, using passive receivers to steer the torpedo toward the noise of a U-Boat's propellers.

In the past 20 years modern technology has enabled ASW forces to develop a wide-area strategy. It is called the SOund SUrveillance System (SOSUS), and comprises a network of hydrophones or passive receivers laid on the seabed. By positioning the SOSUS arrays near 'chokepoints' through which hostile submarines must pass to reach their hunting grounds it is possible to reduce the area in which hunting forces, whether aircraft, ships or friendly submarines must operate. Any noises detected by the hydrophones are transmitted by cable to a shore station, where computer processing calculates the position, course, speed and even type of submarine. Within seconds the information is radioed back to the ships and aircraft acting as 'pouncers' inside the SOSUS barrier.

A maritime patrol aircraft receiving such a signal would begin a hunt for the target, using sonobuoys to localize the submarine still further. Sonobuoys vary in type, but broadly they are miniature receivers (some are active) which are parachuted into the water over a wide area, in the hope that two or more will give a 'fix' on the submarine. Their information is signaled back to the aircraft, whose processing equipment translates the signals into a plotted position. There are other methods of detecting a submarine from the air; magnetic anomaly detectors (MAD) can identify the distortion in the earth's magnetic field made by the steel hull of a submarine, and the Autolycus 'sniffer' can detect the diesel fumes of a snorkeling submarine from their infrared content.

Having detected its target the maritime patrol aircraft (known as an MPA for short) would normally drop a homing torpedo, retarded by parachute to make sure that it enters the water at the most favorable angle. The torpedo immediately enters a preset pattern, usually a descending spiral, until the passive sensor in its homing head detects propeller noise. It then tracks the target's noise and steers itself to impact. The previous generation of acoustic homing torpedoes, notably the American Mk 37, Mk 44 and Mk 46, have small warheads designed merely to blow off a submarine's propeller. Nowadays, however, it is reckoned that a missile-firing submarine might well launch its deadly strategic missiles as a last gesture of defiance before sinking. The latest 'lightweight' (air-dropped) torpedoes are therefore designed with a heavy warhead capable of sinking the submarine with a single shot. The British Stingray takes the process further by being programmed to hit the submarine amidships, and uses a special shaped charge to penetrate the titanium outer skin of the latest Russian submarines. Its American equivalent, the Mk 50 Advanced Light Weight Torpedo (ALWT) will presumably use similar techniques to enhance its killing power.

The majority of Western homing torpedoes are built with some degree of interoperability; the Mk 44, Mk 46, Stingray and Italian A.244 all have a diameter of 324mm (12.75 inches) to enable them to be fired from the standard Mk 32 triple launcher used aboard ships, as well as being dropped by aircraft.

Torpedoes are mainly used against submarines operating down to medium depth (down to 1500ft), but something more potent is needed against modern deep-diving submarines, which can exceed the 2000ft mark, and are even credited with a diving depth of 3000ft in some cases. The first weapon designed to function at maximum depth was the fearsome nuclear depth charge codenamed 'Betty', introduced in the 1950s. With an all-up weight of 1243lbs 'Betty' was too big to be lifted by most naval aircraft, and even the Grumman S-2F Tracker had its bomb bay enlarged to house it. The next generation was 'Lulu', otherwise known as the Mk 101 depth charge, which could be lifted by a helicopter. Advancing techniques of manufacture led to the Mk 105, christened 'Little Lulu', which is currently in service.

The workhorse among Western maritime patrol aircraft is the P-3 Orion, a four-engined derivative of the Electra turboprop airliner which entered service in 1958. It serves widely throughout the West, and has gone through many variants. The latest is the Canadian CP-140 Aurora, which uses the same airframe to accommodate more modern sensors and equipment. In addition to the US Navy, Orions are in service with Australia, Canada, Iran, New Zealand, Norway and Spain.

The Dassault-Breguet Atlantic was built to meet a NATO requirement for the Neptune successor, but only Germany backed the French in joint production as other nations insisted on their own design. However the Dutch and the Italians finally came into the program, and a New Generation Atlantic is coming forward, capable of carrying more payload and having more modern detection equipment.

In going their own way the British ended up with a very expensive but efficient maritime patrol aircraft. The MR.1 Nimrod was adapted from the Comet IV airliner, and is unique among shore-based aircraft of this type in having turbofan engines – four Rolls-Royce Speys. Like other ASW aircraft the Nimrod

An RAF Nimrod MR Mk 2 maritime patrol aircraft (top) circles its base at Kinloss in Scotland. The Soviet Il-38 May ASW patrol aircraft is pictured in flight over the Indian Ocean.

has been modernized to take advantage of new technology, and the airframe has been adapted as an Airborne Early Warning radar platform. The 50ft bomb bay of an ASW Nimrod can carry a wide range of stores, including Mk 46 or Stingray torpedoes, mines, 'Lulu' nuclear depth charges, conventional bombs and fuel tanks. Two or four underwing pylons also carry air-to-surface missiles such as Martel.

The US Navy uses twin-engined antisubmarine aircraft from its big carriers (CVs). For many years the standard ASW airframe has been the Grumman S-2 Tracker, a remarkable aircraft capable of providing radar search as well as strike functions in one. Its replacement is the S-3 Viking, which like the Nimrod, uses turbofan jet engines to provide power for rapid transits, but without excessive fuel consumption. So comprehensive is its outfit of sensors and processing equipment that their total cost is more than double that of the airframe.

The Russian equivalent of the P-3 Orion is the Ilyushin Il-38, known to NATO as the May, but it compares poorly with its Western counterpart, and has not been developed further. This is largely because of a differing Soviet philosophy, which concentrates more resources on reconnaissance aircraft, to provide data for coastal units.

The 'pouncer' ships operating behind the SOSUS barriers are equipped with antisubmarine helicopters. The concept dates from World War II, when attempts were made to spot U-Boats with helicopters operating from freighters, but exploitation of the helicopter had to wait until the machines themselves had advanced in design. The British developed the MATCH system in the 1950s, using a light helicopter from a flight deck on the stern of a 2000-ton frigate to deliver torpedoes. The Canadians, however, were more ambitious and put a bigger HSS-1 helicopter onto a frigate, allowing the use of a 'dunking' sonar to search for submarine contacts well away from the ship. The US Navy tried to compromise between these extremes, using a remote-control drone called DASH to deliver torpedoes to the point of sonar contact.

The debate today is not whether or not a helicopter is necessary, but whether to have one or two. Helicopter facilities in a frigate-sized ship place a great burden on the design, for a hangar must be provided to protect the delicate machine from weather damage.

The first helicopter designed for operating from small flight decks was the remarkable Westland Wasp. Weighing only 3232lbs empty (5500lbs fully loaded) it is not a great weightlifter, but it can carry two Mk 44 homing torpedoes or rockets, machine guns or wire-guided antitank missiles. This allows the Wasp to be used either as a weapon-delivery vehicle in conjunction with the ship's sonar, or as a support aircraft for troops ashore. The best example of the ground support role was in the Falklands, when the British recaptured the island of South Georgia from Argen-

199

tine forces. Two Wasps from the Antarctic patrol ship HMS *Endurance* used their antitank missiles to disable the submarine *Santa Fe* off Grytviken. The AS-12 missiles are guided by an optical sight.

The Wasp was intended for small frigates, but for larger ships the Wessex (derived from the American S-58) could lift more payload. The 150 HAS.3 ASW versions built were given a radar capable of tracking submarine snorkel masts; others were configured to lift assault troops or simply as air-sea rescue machines. Its successor is the Sea King, which used the US Navy's S-61 airframe as a basis for development.

The HAS.1 version of the Sea King incorporated not only the weapons (four homing torpedoes or an equivalent weight of depth charges) but also a 'dunking' sonar, doppler navigation radar (to permit accurate navigation away from the carrier or the shore), a search radar, autopilot and automatic hovering system. In addition the helicopter has a small tactical center in which the sonar and radar operators can exchange information and plot target data.

Both the Wasp and the Sea King are due for replacement, the Wasp having become operational as long ago as 1962 and the Sea King seven years after that. The Wasp replacement, the Anglo-French Lynx, has already proved itself to be an outstanding machine, but the Anglo-German-Italian Sea King replacement, designated EH.101 is still under development. The Westland/Aerospatiale Lynx is equipped with a Seaspray radar which enables it to use Sea Skua antiship missiles as an alternative weapon-fit to depth charges or torpedoes. During the Falklands fighting two Lynxes fired the then untested Sea Skua (preproduction rounds had been hurried into service) against three Argentine ships.

The US Navy, having been let down by DASH, was understandably nervous about asking for funds for another ASW helicopter, and the first LAMPS (Light Airborne Multi-Purpose System) did not appear until 1970. The helicopter, the SH-2 Seasprite, is regarded one of the world's best-designed and neatest solutions to the problem, and the SH-2D carries more than two tons of equipment, including a powerful 'chin-mounted' radar, sonobuoys, MAD gear, electronic warfare receivers and jammers, and a variety of weapons, including depth charges and torpedoes.

A proposal to build a LAMPS II came to nothing, and the US Navy has gone straight onto LAMPS III, the Sikorsky SH-60B SeaHawk. This big machine is closer to the British idea of an airborne autonomous ASW platform, rather than a mere weapon-carrier, for it carries a comprehensive outfit of sensors and weapons. Unlike the British and other European navies, however, the American ASW philosophy maintains that the processing of sonar, MAD, sonobuoy and radar returns is better carried out aboard the parent ship. The SeaHawk accordingly transmits its data back to the ship, and receives instructions about prosecuting contacts, rather than operating independently.

Although the Soviet Navy has an impressive record in helicopter developments the current generation of Russian naval helicopters does not bear comparison with Western counterparts. The Kamov Ka-25 Hormone-A in payload or performance lags behind the Seasprite, for example, and has been in service since 1965. A replacement, the Ka-27 Helix, was first seen in Exercise Zapad '81 held in September 1981, aboard the new *Bolshoy Protivolodochny Korabl* (large antisubmarine ship) *Udaloy*.

Although all US Navy escorts are capable of detecting and attacking submarines, the primary ASW platforms are the frigates of the *Knox* and *Oliver Hazard Perry* classes and the *Spruance* class destroyers. The 46 *Knox* (FF.1052) class were built in 1965–74, the largest single group of surface combatants since the Russian Skory class destroyers in the 1960s. They are attractive ships, with a big single 'mack' amidships; the main armament is an 8-cell Asroc missile-launcher, from which Harpoon antiship missiles can also be fired. Mk 32 torpedo-launchers in the superstructure provide a quick reaction against submarines, and the SH-2D/F helicopter is an extension of the ASW systems, exploiting the long range of the bow-mounted SQS-26CX sonar. The ship also carries a single 5inch gun and a Sea Sparrow system.

The *Perry* (FFG.7) class were intended to meet criticism that the *Knox* class lacked armament, and were accordingly given a mix of ASW and AAW systems. They carry a single-arm Standard SAM launcher forward (like the Asroc launcher it can also launch Harpoon SSMs). Instead of Asroc they carry two SeaHawk helicopters (the later ships), and in addition to the SQS-56 sonar in the bow they have the new TACTASS (TACtical Towed Array Sonar System). This new type of sonar, which can be operated by submarines as well as surface ships, provides the first big advance in submarine detection since the advent of medium range active sonars after World War II. In simple terms it is a line of low-frequency hydrophones mounted in a flexible tube towed at a considerable distance behind the ship. This distance enables the array to be kept clear of the noise of the towing ship's propellers.

A towed array can be up to several hundred meters long, and it provides a series of detection 'funnels' or 'beams' capable of detecting the low-frequency noise made by submarines. The biggest advantage of towed arrays is the phenomenal distance at which submarines can be detected, but they impose new operational and tactical restrictions on ASW ships. In the

Above right: An SH-2F Seasprite landing on the flight deck of the USS *William V. Pratt* (DDG.44).
Right: The new Soviet naval helicopter, the Helix, on the flight deck of the *Udaloy*.

200

Above: A French Navy Lynx dropping a Mark 46 acoustic homing torpedo. The braking parachute has just started to open and the retaining straps are falling clear.
Left: A Westland Sea King helicopter winching up its Type 195 dipping sonar.

1970s a typical escort force might have been composed of maritime patrol aircraft in close support at about 30 miles' range, helicopters operating their 'dunking' sonars at about 15 miles, and frigates forming a close screen at about five miles. Today the same aircraft, using the new directional sonobuoys and processors as capable as those in the surface ships, are more likely to be 100 miles out or more. The towed array ships will take up a new mid-field distance of about 50 miles, leaving a small number of escorts to handle the close range screen against any submarines which sneak through the outer and middle layers of protection.

When announced the *Spruance* class destroyers provoked bitter criticism for their apparent lack of armament. On a length of 563ft and a displacement of 7800 tons full load, the critics could not understand why the ship carried only two single 5inch Mk 45 guns, an Asroc missile-launcher and two triple torpedo tubes. What they ignored was the careful attention paid to quietness, efficiency as a helicopter platform, and above all, room for the installation of future equipment without the need for drastic reconstruction. Since completion the ships have received Sea Sparrow short range missiles aft and Harpoon antiship missiles, and there are plans to fit them with Tomahawk cruise missiles and Phalanx close-in weapons.

The most advanced feature of the *Spruance* design is their gas turbine propulsion, with four General Electric LM-2500 gas turbines driving two shafts. Great attention is paid to quiet running, with special mountings to reduce radiated noise, a Prairie-Masker device to reduce cavitation noise from the propellers, and sound-absorbent material around the bow sonar dome. The big beamy hull is very seaworthy, allowing sonar contacts to be pursued in rough weather and facilitating helicopter operations. When they first went to sea from 1975 onwards the ships operated a single SH-3 Sea King, then two SH-2 Seasprites, but in due course they will receive two SeaHawks.

The British *Broadsword* class frigates are designed to much the same philosophy. Although smaller than the *Spruances* their 4500-ton hulls emphasise seakeeping and steadiness as helicopter-platforms. As with the American ships they encountered bitter criticism from within and outside the Service, and as recently as mid-1981 it was openly advocated that the class should be cut short at seven units. Two years later, after experience in the Falklands seven more were on order. They are intended to work with the three *Invincible* class ASW carriers in mid-Atlantic, acting as 'pouncers' behind the SOSUS barriers in the GIUK Gap. For that purpose they are equipped with the Type 2031 towed array sonar, a hull-mounted Type 2016 low-frequency passive sonar and two Lynx helicopters armed with Stingray torpedoes. To defend themselves against surface-, air- or submarine-launched missiles the first eight ships have MM-38 Exocet antiship missiles, and a double-headed Sea Wolf short-range missile system.

The Royal Navy hoped to retrofit Type 2031 and

203

Above: The Soviet fleet oiler *Boris Chilikin* refueling the helicopter carrier *Moskva* (right).
Right: The new Soviet destroyer *Udaloy* strongly resembles the US *Spruance* type not only in layout but also in design philosophy, with some weapons sacrificed to improve seakeeping and habitability.

Type 2016 sonars to ten of the *Leander* class frigates, but as explained previously, the essence of towed array operations is the elimination of ship noise, and after the first four conversions it was realized that silencing their steam turbines was far too expensive. The decision was then made to cut back the conversion program, and to build instead a new class of frigate, the Type 23, suitably silenced at the design stage. To achieve the degree of silencing required the designers chose three Rolls-Royce Spey gas turbines for main drive, with a separate diesel-electric unit for quiet running while operating the towed array.

The Dutch *Kortenaer* and *Van Speijk* class frigates will also operate towed arrays, but will use the American SQR-18 set. The French, who have for a long time used a combination of bow sonar and variable-depth sonar from the stern, hope to have their own towed array, the ETBF at sea in the fifth and sixth *Georges Leygues* class destroyers, which are planned to go to sea in 1985–86. These 4000-ton ships are very similar in general configuration to the British *Broadsword* class, being armed with four MM-38 Exocet missiles, two Lynx helicopters and a point-defense missile system.

The standard US Navy ASW weapon is the RUR-5 Asroc, which uses a solid-fuel rocket motor to lift it into a ballistic trajectory out to six miles. The payload is either a Mk 17 nuclear depth charge or, more usually a Mk 46 torpedo which is released to parachute into the water shortly before impact. Its submarine counterpart is Subroc, which is fired from a torpedo tube in a canister, fires itself from the canister when it broaches the surface and follows a ballistic path some 30–40 miles to the target. There it functions like Asroc, releasing a nuclear depth charge (a torpedo-carrying variant never materialized). To-day Subroc is obsolescent, and is being phased out in favor of the Mk 48 heavyweight torpedo, but a replacement, the Stand-Off Weapon (SOW) is under development.

Mention has been made of homing torpedoes, and for many years the US Navy's Mk 44 and Mk 46 weapons have been standard among Western navies. Two countries, Britain and Italy, have developed new homing systems compatible with the dimensions of the American torpedoes, the Stingray and the A.244, which means that they can still use the standard triple Mk 32 launching tubes. Other countries like Sweden and France continue to develop their own torpedoes.

The British also use a stand-off weapon to make use of increased sonar ranges. The Ikara was developed jointly with the Australians, and is basically a

small pilotless delta-wing aircraft, carrying beneath it a Mk 44 or Mk 46 torpedo. Like Asroc it suffers from having too little range to work effectively with modern sonars, and plans to boost its range were not pursued. However it remains a potent weapon, and is mounted forward in the DLG HMS *Bristol* and many of the *Leander* class frigates. The three Australian DDGs *Perth*, *Brisbane* and *Hobart* have two Ikara launchers amidships, and their 'River' class destroyer escorts mount a single launcher on the starboard side aft.

The French equivalent, named Malafon, uses a rocket to launch the missile, which then glides to the point of detection before releasing its homing torpedo.

Many navies still use the Bofors 375mm rocket-propelled depth charge, either from twin launchers or from multiple launchers. The French built their own six-barreled launcher to fire these rockets, and the Norwegians developed the Terne system for their destroyer escorts. The old standard depth charge rolled off the stern has now virtually disappeared from warships, if only because sonars are now sufficiently precise to make such crude methods unnecessary.

It is interesting at this point to contrast the Soviet approach to ASW. For some years Western observers concentrated on the Soviet Navy's anticarrier forces, failing to notice a significant shift toward antisubmarine warfare. With hindsight the reason is not hard to understand; as the threat of nuclear attack from carrier-borne bombers receded the threat from SSBNs was becoming more credible. By 1964, with ten Polaris SSBNs at sea and a new class of 31 boats under construction, the Soviets had reason to think that the Americans had transferred their nuclear strike effort from carriers to SSBNs. It can hardly be a coincidence that in 1963 two antisubmarine cruisers (*Protivolodochny Kreyser*) were laid down. The ships, named *Leningrad* and *Moskva* are clearly intended to take a large number of ASW helicopters to sea, as their half-length flight deck and hangar allow a total of 15 to 18 Kamov Ka-25 Hormone-As. In this they were only following the precedent set by the French with the *Jeanne d'Arc* and the Italian *Andrea Doria* class and the *Vittorio Veneto*.

The forward part of the hull is devoted to armament, being separated from the flight deck by a massive centerline superstructure. A heavy defensive armament of 44 SA-N-3 Goblet SAMs is mounted, with two twin-arm launchers, backed up by two twin 57mm gun mountings, one on either side of the superstructure. The antisubmarine armament includes a hull-mounted low-frequency sonar and a medium-frequency variable-depth set streamed from a well under the quarterdeck. For close range defense against submarines two pairs of 12-barreled rocket launchers are mounted forward. Originally two sets of quintuple torpedo tubes were mounted low down in the hull amidships but these were removed in the late 1970s, probably because they were flooded out in heavy weather. These tubes were almost certainly for antiship torpedoes, rather than homing types, as the main offensive ASW weapon is the FRAS-1 (Free Rocket Anti Submarine, or SUW-N-1 in its NATO designation) rocket launcher.

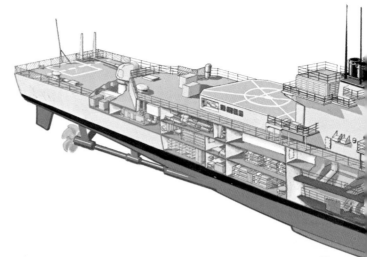

The next step in the evolution of Soviet ASW was the adaptation of the Kresta cruiser design to the antisubmarine mission. The *Kronshtadt*, first of a new class designated Kresta II in the West, differed in having a new long range antisubmarine missile in place of antiship weapons. Muddled perception of Soviet intentions led Western intelligence sources to spend seven years trying to identify a new long range cruise missile known as SS-N-10, but finally the quadruple launch tubes on either side of the Kresta II's superstructure were admitted to be holding an Ikara equivalent designated SS-N-14.

Although also rated as a large antisubmarine ship, the Krivak class which followed a year after the first Kresta II was a smaller and simpler ASW escort. The Soviets are not alone in wanting to find cheaper alternatives to first rate ships, but unlike the major Western navies they deliberately aim for a 'hi-lo' mix, using second rate or utility ships to eke out the small numbers of first rate ships. Confusion over the SS-N-10/SS-N-14 missiles caused the Krivak to be greatly overrated in the West, but finally Western sources agree that it is an austere ASW escort armed with four SS-N-14 missiles and driven by two gas turbines at a speed of 30–31 knots. Apart from two sets of quadruple torpedo tubes put in for traditional reasons rather than to meet any serious tactical requirement, the remaining armament is defensive: two twin 76mm AA guns, and two SA-N-4 point defense missile systems. The Krivak II, which appeared in 1976, substitutes single 100mm guns for the twin 76mm, and updated fire control, but otherwise differs little. Twenty of the Krivak Is were built in three shipyards, followed by 11 Krivak IIs; a Krivak III, *sans* SS-N-14 missiles, has also appeared.

The next class of large warships was the Kara class, an expansion of the Kresta II, but driven by gas turbines instead of steam. There is visible evidence of an improved outfit of sensors, notably a variable-depth sonar, like the one in the *Leningrad* and *Moskva*, and the Krivaks, and the seven Karas seen so far represent a great improvement in appearance, at least when compared with the two Kresta classes. Like the Kresta II they have eight SS-N-14 missiles in two quadruple banks disposed on both sides of the bridge.

The appearance in 1976 of what appeared to be an aircraft carrier caused consternation among Western navies, and many observers believed that the Soviets had at long last built an attack carrier. But the *Kiev* and her sisters *Minsk* and *Novorossiisk* turn out on close examination to be yet another permutation in the Russian battle to master Western SSBNs.

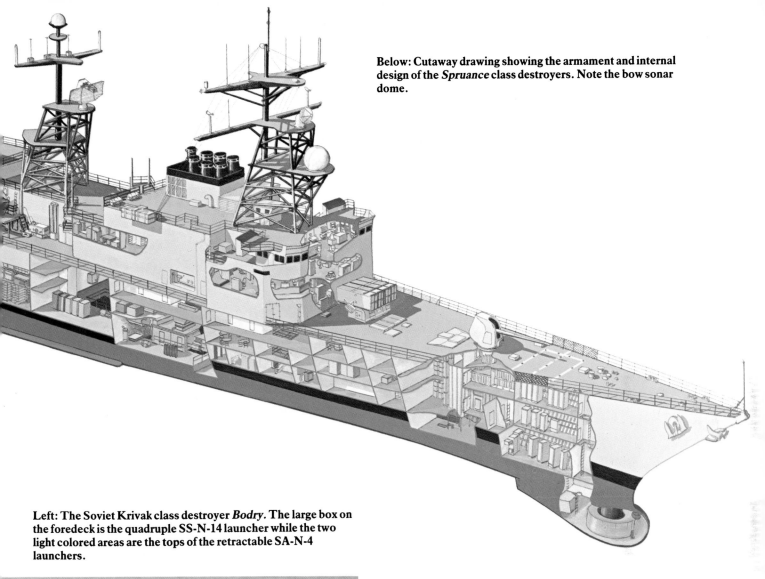

Below: Cutaway drawing showing the armament and internal design of the *Spruance* class destroyers. Note the bow sonar dome.

Left: The Soviet Krivak class destroyer *Bodry*. The large box on the foredeck is the quadruple SS-N-14 launcher while the two light colored areas are the tops of the retractable SA-N-4 launchers.

Left and below: Two of the *Spruance* class destroyers. Left, the *Spruance* herself and below the *Caron*. By early 1984 there were 31 *Spruance* class ships (DD.963-92 and DD.997) in service with the US Navy.

The Italian cruiser *Vittorio Veneto* has a twin Terrier/Asroc missile system forward and a large helicopter hangar and flight deck aft. She normally operates four AB.202 antisubmarine helicopters.

The *Kiev* design is a hybrid cruiser/support carrier, equipped primarily to operate Ka-25 Hormone-A antisubmarine helicopters, but with a flight of Yak-36 Forger vertical takeoff strike aircraft to provide local air superiority and to force hostile surface forces to keep their distance. An interceptor/strike aircraft would permit a Soviet ASW group to operate in hostile waters, beyond the range of land-based fighters. The most likely area of operations is the North Atlantic, where any Soviet surface group trying to clear NATO forces from, say, the GIUK Gap and its SOSUS barriers, would come under attack from US carrier battle groups and shore-based strikes.

The latest major antisubmarine unit in the Soviet inventory is the new destroyer named *Udaloy*. First seen in 1981, the *Udaloy* is radically different from previous Soviet designs. In fact she bears a strong resemblance to the US Navy's *Spruance* class, in having a big hull with comparatively few weapons (by Soviet standards), and enhancing the antisubmarine warfare at the expense of other roles. It is ironic that the Soviet designers appear to have grasped the necessity to build seaworthiness into ships rather than merely packing weapons into a hull, just as a rising tide of largely ill-informed criticism in the West demands more weaponry 'like the Russians'.

Top: The *Philips van Almonde*, one of ten *Kortenaer* class frigates built for the Royal Netherlands Navy. Their main role is antisubmarine escort but they also carry a powerful antiship armament of eight Harpoon missiles.
Above: A Soviet Krivak class frigate refueling from an oil tanker. This is one of the 20 Krivak I type with twin 76mm guns.

The Federal German Navy's inshore minesweeper *Hertha* enters the British port of Harwich. The sweep gear aft is painted yellow to aid recovery.

As naval warfare becomes embroiled in an upward spiral of mounting costs it is hardly surprising that navies have turned back to one of the oldest and most cost effective weapons – the mine. What is surprising, on the other hand, is that until recently only the Russians appeared to show any great interest in mine warfare.

Mines were used as long ago as 1776, when David Bushnell's primitive keg mines were used on the Delaware River to deter the redcoats. It went down in history as the 'Battle of the Kegs' and 80 years later the Russians laid chemically-fuzed mines in the Baltic. They were cast-iron conical mines, and a small field laid in the approaches to Kronstadt damaged the British sloop *Merlin* in 1855. Only six years later in the Civil War the hard-pressed Confederacy tried to match Northern naval strength with a series of inge-

nious mines, known at the time as 'moored torpedoes'. Admiral Farragut may have said 'Damn the Torpedoes', but these primitive devices sank the monitor *Tecumseh*.

Mine warfare came of age in the 20th Century, when both the Japanese and the Russians used them with deadly effect in 1904. The two World Wars saw an enormous increase in not only numbers but efficiency of mines. The statistics were staggering; in World War II the British alone laid nearly 80,000 offensive mines which sank or damaged 1917 Axis ships. Overall one mine in 40 was effective, but in some areas efficiency rose to one in five; mines laid by aircraft proved seven times as effective as bombing, torpedoes or any other form of air attack. In Germany 60 percent of seagoing naval personnel were employed on minesweeping, close escort or harbor duty. The

British started the war with 70 minesweepers, and by increasing this to more than 1500 by 1944 succeeded in holding losses down to 500 merchantmen and 281 warships.

The most frightening aspect of mine warfare today is that the successes of World War II were achieved by relatively simple mines, whereas today's mines are many times more deadly and harder to sweep. Then the moored mine could be swept by cutting its mooring wire and letting it float to the surface. Trawlers could be commandeered from the fishing fleet and converted quickly. Then came the magnetic mine, first used by the British in the last months of 1918, but used in

The British minesweeper support ship *Abdiel* is intended to support a squadron of mine countermeasures craft but she can also lay mines for exercise purposes.

large numbers from 1939 onwards. Then, shortly after, came the acoustic mine, set off by the noise of a ship's propeller. Both types of 'influence' mine could be dealt with, one by sending a strong electromagnetic pulse through a towed cable, the other by towing a noise maker. This was not the case, however, with the 'oyster' or pressure actuated mine, which responds to the pressure wave set up as a ship passes through the water. No completely suitable way of simulating this pressure wave has ever been found, but fortunately, like the other influence mines, its use was restricted to shallow waters. Today most influence mines combine all three types of influence fuze, making the task of mine countermeasures yet more complex.

In spite of the problems posed by German ingenuity in design of mines and antisweeping devices, the Allies finished World War II with a convincing margin of superiority over the mine; hundreds of wooden minesweepers had been built, the residual magnetism of steel ships' hulls could be reduced by 'degaussing', and apart from pressure mines in very shallow waters, the threat was under control. The first shock came in the Korean War, when the Russians supplied North Korea with magnetic influence mines of such sensitivity that even the World War II wooden-hulled sweepers could set them off – the actuator was sensitive enough to pick up the magnetism of the diesel engine and metal fastenings in the hull, for example. The big amphibious landing at Wonsan was held up for days by 3000 of these mines, and a startled US Navy reluctantly woke up to the fact that the Russians had lost none of their cunning in mine warfare.

The result was a panic program to build non-magnetic minesweepers in the early 1950s. On both sides of the Atlantic a new generation of wooden minesweepers was built, using non-magnetic metals such as phosphor bronze for anchors and other fittings. The ships of that program proved a great success and many are still in service 30 years later.

The biggest advance of the 1950s was the development of new techniques to cope with pressure mines and other influence types. The minehunter is a ship fitted with a high-definition sonar capable of detecting mines on the seabed in relatively shallow waters (60 meters or less), where influence mines are most effective. She steams slowly until she detects an object on the seabed, and then sends down a diver to investigate the contact. It may, of course, turn out not to be a mine, but a biscuit tin or similar piece of debris, but if it is a mine the diver lays a charge to be detonated alongside it, once he is clear of the scene.

Clearly the use of clearance divers involves an element of risk, and the diver is increasingly being replaced by a remotely piloted vehicle. This is similar to a tiny submarine, fitted with powerful lighting, a TV camera and a jettisonable demolition charge; it is

Above: The PAP.104 remote controlled mine disposal system is used by the French, British, Dutch and German navies.
Right: A US Navy MH-53E Super Stallion helicopter towing a minesweeping sled.
Far right, bottom: The French *Eridan* is the lead ship of the tripartite French, Dutch and Belgian mine hunter program.

maneuvered from the ship alongside the suspicious object, allowing the TV camera to photograph all around, and giving the specialists time to make an assessment. If the contact is finally classified as a mine, the remotely piloted vehicle is instructed to drop its explosive charge before returning to the ship.

The French Navy was the first to introduce such a vehicle, known as the Poisson Auto-Propulsé, the PAP-104, and it is now in service in the Royal Navy, the Royal Netherlands Navy, the Federal German Navy and several others. The Italians have developed the Min, which works on similar lines, the German Pinguin is a competitor, and the US Navy is developing its own, and within a few years the mine clearance diver will be a thing of the past.

The problem about such equipment is that it can no longer be fitted easily into the older minesweepers, for they also have to accommodate new electrical sweeps, towed noise generators and other bulky items. Instead it must be accommodated in specially designed and expensive hulls constructed out of non-magnetic material. However, minehunting remains a lengthy and maddeningly tedious business. The hunter must be prepared to spend at least 20 minutes on each sonar contact, whether it be a mine or a

biscuit tin. As any skin diver knows, the seabed is littered with such objects.

There is an alternative to minehunting, the use of helicopters. The US Navy for many years put its faith in the large helicopter towing a 'sled' containing a noise maker or a turbine-powered magnetic sweep. This method was used to sweep the Suez Canal, and to clear the approaches to Haiphong at the end of the Vietnam War, but it has two big disadvantages. The helicopter is very vulnerable to the blast of a mine detonating underneath it; the machine is flying close to stalling speed, and the plume of water can strike the rotor blades, flipping the helicopter over, and in wartime there are not likely to be sufficient big helicopters available for large-scale sweeping. It is of course supremely flexible, in that helicopters and their equipment can be moved rapidly from one place to another, but it has so far provided no answer to the pressure mine. For that minehunting remains the only solution. Helicopters can also be used to hunt for mines, and the French have developed a suitable high-definition 'dunking' sonar, but the problem remains that helicopters are so valuable for other tasks that none may be spared in wartime for mine countermeasures.

The one remaining method not discussed is the

hovercraft. Experiments show that the hovercraft is virtually immune to mine detonations, as the blast is vented outwards from under the rubber skirt. It has virtually no pressure, magnetic or acoustic signature, and so can cross minefields with little risk. Trials in Britain show that a big hovercraft can carry all the sweep gear, dipping sonar and plotting equipment needed for minehunting, and also sweep along a fixed line without any trouble. It is widely recognized that a minehunting hovercraft or MCH is not only feasible, but desirable as well, and all that prevents it from becoming reality is a shortage of money. However several hovercraft have been used to support mine countermeasures ships, and it is the next step.

The only inexpensive way of coping with widespread mining by a potential enemy is still the construction of minehunters, but 'inexpensive' is a relative term. The need to eliminate magnetism almost totally has meant a switch to glass-reinforced plastic (GRP), non-magnetic machinery, and even plastic knives and forks, a process which makes GRP minehunters the most expensive warships in the world, ton-for-ton. The numbers which can be built are therefore small; Britain is completing 12 *Brecon* class GRP ships, and is following them with a cheaper but less effective design. France, Holland and Belgium are building 25 'Tripartite' minehunters between them, and Italy is building 10 *Lerici* class. The US Navy is caught in a similar dilemma, having allowed its mine

countermeasures forces to dwindle to 23 wooden ocean sweepers. Current plans allow for 14 *Avenger* class MCMs for long-distance work and 12 MSHs for coastal minehunting. They will be wooden-hulled with GRP superstructures (the MCMs) and GRP-hulled (the MSHs).

The British, always acutely aware of their vulnerability to mining of their harbors and estuaries, took the lead in developing the new type of craft. HMS *Brecon*, launched in 1978, displaces 725 tons, making her and her sisters the world's largest GRP warships. They are known as Mine CounterMeasures Vessels (MCMVs) to underline the fact that they undertake both conventional sweeping and minehunting. The propulsion plant includes two Deltic non-magnetic diesels for main drive at a maximum speed of 17 knots, and two hydraulic units for maneuvering at a maximum speed of 8 knots. The 60-meter hull is deliberately capacious, not only to accommodate the full range of equipment, but to provide adequate crew comfort on long voyages; an ability to make an ocean voyage was a prime feature of the Staff Requirement.

The size of the *Brecon* class led to considerable criticism until the Falklands, when the *Brecon* and *Ledbury* proved capable of making the 8000-mile voyage to the South Atlantic to sweep mines in Port Stanley. It was known that the Argentine Navy had a large inventory of modern mines, and two minefields were in fact laid in the harbor. In spite of adverse weather conditions and poor sonar conditions the two MCMVs had no difficulty in sweeping the mines. What came as a great surprise was that the only mines laid were Argentina-made copies of a German World War II moored contact mine – as always, the threat of mines is just as potent as their presence.

The Royal Navy intends to order 12 of the *Brecon* class, but their high unit cost and complexity of manufacture makes it necessary to build a 37-meter GRP 'single role' minehunter, without the extra size and lacking the ability to sweep for mines. They are to be known as the Gem class, and at least 12 are planned.

A word of explanation about sweeping is needed. Although the modern mine is always laid on the seabed, there is, as we have seen, a large number of conventional mines still in existence, and these may well be actuated by magnetic or acoustic influence. There is also the problem of the Continental Shelf Mine and the deep-laid antisubmarine mine. The Captor mine already exists, an encapsulated homing torpedo which is fired when a hostile submarine's propeller noise is detected. It can be laid by maritime patrol aircraft, and its chief role is to protect barriers such as SOSUS by denying choke points to hostile submarines.

The Intelligent Hunter Mine is an extension of the Captor concept, a torpedo (note how the words 'torpedo' and 'mine' are becoming interchangeable, as they were a century earlier) which can track a target some thousands of yards away. To dispose of such mines it is necessary to use a wire sweep, kept down to low-level by special apparatus. The mine is laid too deep for any actuator to be set off by magnetic or acoustic influence, so a steel hull may be used instead. At the end of 1978 the Royal Navy took over two commercial trawlers, the *Suffolk Monarch* and *Suffolk Harvester*, and converted them to Extra Deep Armed Team Sweep ships (EDATS). Under their new names, *St David* and *Venturer* they have been successfully operated by Royal Naval Reserve crews, providing a fresh source of trained manpower. A new class of 12 steel-hulled fleet minesweepers, the *Waveney* or 'River' class, are being built. They will replace the ageing wooden coastal minesweepers and minehunters operated by the Royal Navy Reserve.

The French, Belgians and Dutch face the same mine threat as the British, but they chose to build their own design. The resulting tripartite program apportioned the work between all three countries, guaranteeing commonality of spares but at the same time ensuring that each country's industries are supported. The French naval design bureau, Direction Technique Constructions Naval had responsibility for overall design and French industry provided the minehunting sonar; the Dutch build the diesel engines and the Belgians manufacture the electrical equipment.

The lead ship, the *Eridan*, was built in an ex-German U-Boat pen at Lorient on the coast of Brittany. She joined the Fleet in 1982, followed shortly afterwards by the first Dutch ship, the *Alkmaar*, but difficulties with the consortium chosen to build the Belgian ships prevented the first order being placed until 1982. GRP construction requires a mold, and ships are normally built in pairs at intervals of up to a year. When the program is complete in 1988–89 a number of the older wooden minesweepers will be well beyond the age limit, and many will have been scrapped.

The Italians, like their European allies, favor GRP construction, and produced their own design. The ten *Lerici* class are 49.98 meters in length and displace 500 tons, making them slightly bigger than the tripartite design. They also differ from the British and tripartite ships in using a minehunting sonar of American origin, the SQQ-14, nicknamed the 'Squeaky Fourteen'. It is lowered on a chain through an aperture in the keel, whereas the British Type 193M and 2093, and the French DUBM-20A and DUBM-21A are hull-mounted.

The Federal German Navy has hitherto used a British sonar, the Plessey Type 193M in wooden coastal minesweepers built in the 1950s, but has now adopted a radically different 'Troika' system. This uses unmanned vessels under control from a parent ship, in order to avoid injury and loss of life. The principal component of the 'Troika', so called because three unmanned hulls are used, is a pressure-resistant conventional steel hull, whose diesel engine, controls, and power supply are on shockproof mountings. The magnetic clearance field is generated by two coils, which are positioned at each end of the hull. Acoustic mines are exploded at a safe distance by a pair of medium frequency noise makers in the bow section and an additional towed noise maker.

The FGN intends to follow the Troika mine countermeasures craft (although not capable of mine-hunting, they do carry wire sweeps) with ten Type 343 combined minelayer/minehunters to replace the existing *Castor* and *Schutze* class minehunters, which were commissioned in the early 1960s. What is even more intriguing is a plan for a Type 355 sweeper capable of sweeping pressure mines. If successful, these will be the first sweepers capable of dealing with the 'unsweepable' pressure mine.

On the opposite side of the world, the Japanese Maritime Self Defence Force is often overlooked as a powerful navy. The Japanese have not forgotten how the American mine offensive in 1943–44 virtually cut them off from raw materials and food imports. The *Hatsushima* and *Takami* class minehunters are equipped with a license-built variant of the British Type 193M minehunting sonar, designated ZQS-2, but differ from the latest European craft in being wooden hulled. The *Hatsushima* class, which have been coming into service since 1979, are equipped with Type 54 remotely piloted vehicles, similar to the PAP-104.

As already mentioned, the US Navy has only recently started the construction of minehunters, and the keel of the *Avenger* (MCM.1) was not laid until June 1983. She and her planned 13 sisters will be 64.9 meters long and will displace 1032 tons, making them the largest mine countermeasures craft for 30 years. They will have an SQQ-30 dipping sonar, which is an improved version of the SQQ-14, and a new Mine Neutralization Vehicle (MNV) is under development. Like other minehunters the *Avenger* class and their small counterparts will be propelled by specially redesigned non-magnetic diesels, but the MCMs have a wooden hull; only the superstructure is made of GRP. One of the reasons for European shipbuilders switching to GRP as the alternative to wood for non-magnetic hulls is, sadly, that timber of the right quality from South-East Asia is likely to contain pieces of steel shrapnel. Wooden construction also brings in its train a substantial problem of maintenance, as even the most water-resistant timber will eventually succumb to rot.

From 1947 to 1957 the Soviets built well over 200 seagoing minesweepers or *Morskoy Tral'shchik* of the T.43 type, 58-meter steel hulled 570-tonners. Most have been transferred to satellite navies, but others have been converted to radar pickets, tenders or handed over to the KGB Border Guard. They were succeeded by some 50 Yurka class, slightly smaller and built with an aluminum alloy hull. The Natya class (all names are code names assigned by NATO,

not Soviet class names) are similar, but large enough to serve as coastal antisubmarine escorts as well. Since 1970 some 35 have been built, and they will presumably continue in production for some time.

From 1961–1973 seventy Vanya class coastal minesweepers, wooden hulled 39.9-meter craft rated as *Basovyy Tral'shchik* or base minesweepers, were built. Between 1967 and 1972 the two Zhenya class GRP sweeper/hunters appeared, but Western intelligence sources suspect that they were not a success as the larger wooden hulled Sonya went into quantity pro-

The *Enoshima*, one of the Japanese Maritime Self Defense Force's current *Hatsushima* class coastal minesweepers.

218

duction instead. The first of these, named *Komsomolets Kirgiziy*, came into service in 1973, and at least 30 more have been built since then. In parallel a number of inshore minesweepers have been built, *Reydovy Tral'shchik* or roadstead sweepers, whereas the equivalent in Western navies, the inshore minesweepers built in the 1950s, were found to be too small to accommodate the necessary influence sweep gear.

The subject of minelaying has been left to last, for there is less variety in the methods used. In fact minelaying can be relatively unsophisticated, as mines can be laid from almost any platform. During World War II converted train ferries were used to lay defensive minefields, and destroyers and motor torpedo boats frequently laid mines off enemy coasts under cover of darkness. Before World War II special submarine minelayers had been built, but during the war mines were redesigned for laying through the standard 21inch torpedo tube. But the aircraft proved by far the best minelayer, able to sow large numbers of mines over a large area, and today it can be assumed that any widespread use of offensive minelaying would be done by aircraft.

The benefits of offensive minelaying demonstrate the effectiveness of this mode of warfare. When in 1972 US aircraft mined the approaches to Haiphong to prevent Warsaw Pact military supplies from reaching North Vietnam over a quarter of the Russian and Polish merchant ships sailed immediately. The mines were apparently activated on a time-delay, for none of

the ships was sunk, but 26 ships which did not get out in time remained bottled up for a year. What is even more noteworthy is that the North Vietnamese Navy apparently lacked the knowledge to sweep the mines, and had to leave the task to the Americans. It is no coincidence that the US Navy has since shown such interest in mine countermeasures, for it is widely believed that the Americans themselves had great difficulty in neutralizing their latest marks of mine.

The threat from mines is so potent that the mere threat of mining can be sufficient to close a waterway. In 1974 the Suez Canal was reported to be blocked by mines and sunken ships, following the Yom Kippur War the previous year. In response to international demands to reopen the Canal Egypt permitted an international force, including American, British and Russian units, to undertake clearance. After a long and costly operation it was confirmed that the only explosive ordnance found was a miscellany of unexploded mortar bombs and other munitions dumped in the Canal by Israeli and Egyptian soldiers. Yet, to all intents and purposes, the Suez Canal had been closed to shipping, as if real mines had been laid.

Great secrecy surrounds the types of mines in service today, each side wishing to keep quiet about how much it knows about the other's mines. At least ten types of mine are listed in the inventory of the US Navy, and the development of new types is being pursued. The Mk 52 is a ground mine weighing 568kg, and capable of being laid by B-52D and B-52H bombers as well as Navy aircraft of various types. The various models have combinations of influence actuators. The Mk 55 is similar, but weighs 989kg and

carries a heavier weight of HBX explosive. Both these are restricted to less than 50 meters' depth of water, whereas the Mk 56 has a more sensitive actuator, allowing it to be laid down to 350 meters. The Mk 57 is a 1012kg submarine-laid mine carrying 935lbs of HBX-3 explosive, and can be laid in 250 meters of water.

The Mk 60 Captor mine, already mentioned, has been under development since 1961 and is known to have encountered teething troubles in the early days. It uses a Mk 46 Mod 4 torpedo, and weighs 908kg. It is 3.66 meters long and is moored, in order to be laid at varying depths, being primarily an antisubmarine weapon. Its maximum depth is reported to be over 600 meters. The Mk 67 Submarine-Launched Mobile Mine is another advanced type of mine under development. It is apparently a converted Mk 37 Mod 0 torpedo which is fired from a submarine. Its purpose is to allow the submarine to lie off an enemy harbor at a safe distance, and to project mines into the harbor. It weighs 754kg and clearly any combination of actuators can be programmed to respond to the sort of targets which are to be attacked.

Some years ago work was in hand on a device known as the Propelled Rocket Ascent Mine (PRAM);

the explosive charge was to be propelled upwards once the mine was actuated, bringing it into range of the target. Since then it has been succeeded by the Intermediate Water Depth Mine (IWDM), a moored mine capable of being laid out to the edge of the Continental Shelf to sink both surface ships and submarines. After many setbacks and cost overruns, NATO has given the British responsibility for developing a workable IWDM, and three companies have submitted proposals.

To replenish its long-neglected armory of mines the US Navy initiated the Quickstrike program, adapting the large numbers of 'iron' bombs left over after the Vietnam War. Three models of Quickstrike mine are known to exist: DST-36, converted from 500lb Mk 82 bombs, DST-40 converted from 1000lb Mk 83 bombs, and DST-41, converted from 2000lb Mk 84 bombs. All are fitted with magnetic actuators, while the DST-41 may also have a seismic actuator.

No US Navy surface warships are now fitted to lay mines, as the task is entrusted entirely to submarines and aircraft. In addition to 80 US Air Force B-52 bombers earmarked for minelaying the Navy's P-3 Orion, S-3 Viking, A-6 Intruder and A-7 Corsair aircraft are all capable of laying mines.

If the British public announcements are to be believed they possess no mines whatsoever, but it is known that several varieties of ground mine are in the inventory, and several more are under development including the Stonefish and the Sea Urchin. Both France and Italy are also active in the development of mines, and various models are exported to other countries. One of the mysteries of the Falklands Campaign was why Argentina made no use of the sophisticated British, French and Italian mines known to be in her possession. The only rational explanation is that they were being held in reserve in case of hostilities against Chile.

Mines, whether moored or bottom-laid, can be laid by any surface warship with sufficient clear deck-space. The Baltic NATO navies, the Danish and Federal German, provide their destroyers, escorts and strike craft with mine rails to allow rapid conversion to the minelaying role. Normally a gun is removed to compensate for the additional weight, and the mines are simply hoisted aboard, the length of time depending on the size of ship and the number of mines to be embarked. Small ground mines can be rolled over the side, but the bigger types and moored mines (which include a heavy sinker) must be winched aft along the rails, and so the winch gear has to be installed as well. It is noticeable that all varieties of Soviet warship, from 15,000-ton cruisers down to minesweepers, are fitted with mine rails, an indication of the priority given to minelaying.

The capacity of the Soviet Union to wage offensive mine warfare remains a matter of conjecture, but it is unlikely that such a cheap and deadly method of harassing Western forces is being neglected. Western intelligence sources claim that 100,000 mines are kept in reserve, but clearly a large percentage of these stocks must be earmarked for defense. Even so, allowing for 75 percent allocated to the defense of harbors and key coastal points, 25,000 mines could be available for use against Western ports – a third of the total laid by the Royal Navy in five years of war, and eight times the number needed to stop a massive American landing at Wonsan in 1950. On the World War II basis of one mine in 40 being effective, such a total could, if cleverly used, sink or disable some 600 Western ships. Against that sort of arithmetic NATO's tardy program of mine countermeasures seems pitifully small.

HMS *Brecon* lead ship of a class of mine countermeasures vessels. These are the largest glass fiber warships in the world and can sweep as well as hunt mines.

AMPHIBIOUS WARFARE

The amphibious assault landing craft (AALC) known as JEFF-B, one of two prototypes built to develop an air cushion assault vessel for the US Navy.

Above: HMS *Fearless*, one of two LPDs operated by the Royal Navy.

Left: Soviet amphibious forces make widespread use of assault hovercraft. Three classes, Gus, Lebed and Aist, are in service.

The history of amphibious warfare ought to be as old as naval warfare itself, but surprisingly the need for it has been questioned in every generation. It has often been neglected, only to reassert its demands, and the relearning of its lessons has usually been both painful and expensive.

What military planners often overlook is the inescapable fact that a battle on the oceans by itself decides nothing. 'Command of the Sea' is a ringing term which all too often ignores the fact the sea is only a bridge between two land masses; without armies, a country cannot get to the enemy's heartland to bring the campaign to a conclusion. Extreme supporters of air power have tried to ignore both land power and sea power, claiming that 'Command of the Air' will be sufficient but as always, physical occupation of the objective is the only decisive outcome of a military campaign.

The development of amphibious warfare was a laborious process of trial and error, starting with a requirement from Winston Churchill that the British armed forces should hit back at Occupied Europe, to keep the German Army on the defensive, if for no better reason.

Although prototype vehicle landing craft had been built in small numbers the first tank landing craft were ordered just after the evacuation from Dunkirk in the summer of 1940. Two years later there was a sophisticated array of specialized craft available in sufficient numbers to permit the Dieppe Raid. That was a failure but it led the way to successful landings in North Africa, Sicily and mainland Italy. By June 1944 the Allies were ready for a gigantic operation, the Normandy Landings, during which 5000 ships and a million men would be deployed. Statistics become meaningless, but suffice it to say that some 130,000 men went ashore in the first 16 hours of the landings.

The use of amphibious techniques in the Pacific was even more dramatic. There the Japanese island garrisons were bypassed in a series of 'island-hopping' raids. Any island which appeared too tough a nut to crack was simply outflanked and left to wither on the vine. Even so, the dogged determination of the individual Japanese fighting man meant that each landing was enormously expensive in lives. The brunt of these operations was borne by the Marines, whose prewar exercises gave them at least the basis of a tactical doctrine for the task.

For the major Western navies and the US Navy in particular the clearest lesson from World War II was not only that amphibious warfare worked but that it was the *only* alternative to costly land fighting against the overwhelming numbers of the Soviet Army. Despite those exponents of air power and nuclear weapons, and even some jealousy from Army officers who resented the elite status of the Marine Corps, the US Navy maintained a strong amphibious element. Korea proved its need, when the Inchon landing enabled the UN forces to outflank the North Koreans and throw them back on the defensive. During the 1950s and 1960s the role of the US Navy became increasingly one of crisis management, and for that purpose the amphibious element was absolutely essential.

The amphibious transports and specialized landing ships left over from World War II were replaced in the 1960s by a large modern assault force comprising a range of special units, each designed for specific missions. There were five groups of ships, of which the most flexible were the seven Amphibious Assault Ships (LPH) of the *Iwo Jima* class built in 1959–70. They are basically small helicopter carriers built to mercantile standards. Their task is to use their

Above left: The *Ivan Rogov*, first of a new Soviet class of large assault ship equipped with a docking well aft as well as a conventional bow ramp.
Left: The USS *Spiegel Grove* admits an LCU to her docking well.
Above: The unique extending ramp of the US Navy's *Newport* class LST allows a normal bow form when retracted for higher speed.

20 large helicopters to land 2000 Marines, but since the introduction of the AV-8A Harrier ground support aircraft they have also been able to provide ground support when required. In appearance they are carriers, with small starboard islands, but they lack catapults and arrester wires.

The direct descendants of the wartime Dock Landing Ships were 14 Amphibious Transport Docks (LPDs) of the *Austin* and *Raleigh* classes, built between 1960 and 1971. They are capable of landing some 900 marines with their amphibious vehicles and landing craft, using a large floodable well-deck in the after part of the ship. They are in fact mobile floating docks, capable of closing the stern gate and pumping out the well for a normal sea passage. The benefit of having a docking well is that landing craft can be loaded in comparative safety, whereas landing craft alongside a conventional transport are at the mercy of the weather. Very similar to the LPDs are the five Dock Landing Ships (LSDs) of the *Anchorage* class, built in 1969–72. They carry more landing craft but at the expense of carrying only 400 marines.

Five Amphibious Cargo Ships (AKAs) of the *Charleston* class were built in 1966–70 to replace World War II conversions. They carry heavy equipment and supplies for an amphibious assault, as well as nine Landing Craft, Mechanized (LCMs) to get this material ashore. They are backed up by 20 Tank Landing Ships (LSTs) of the *Newport* class, built in 1966–72. Unlike World War II LSTs, the *Newport* and her sisters do not discharge their tanks and vehicles through bow doors. To meet a requirement for a speed of 20 knots they had to be given a conventional ship-shape forward, and so they discharge vehicles over a large hinged ramp.

To coordinate the diverse activities of these amphibious warfare ships two new Amphibious Command Ships (LCC) were built in 1967–71. Using the same hull as the *Iwo Jima* class LPH, the *Blue Ridge* and *Mount Whitney* provide command and communications facilities for the naval Commander Amphibious Task Group (CATG) and the Marine Landing Force Commander (LFC) and for their respective staffs.

In peacetime, replacement of amphibious ships comes quite low in priority, but ten *Whidbey Island* (LSD.41) class Dock Landing Ships are under construction. They would have been virtually repeats of the *Anchorage* class but the design was modified to embark two Air Cushion Landing Craft (LCACs). These are based on a prototype called JEFF-B, and an ultimate total of over 100 units is planned for completion during the next five years. Four each will be carried aboard the *Whidbey Island* class, and one aboard each of the *Tarawa* class assault ships.

The amphibious warfare ships described usually

operate in amphibious task forces built around the basic amphibious squadron, known as a PhibRon. Four of these PhibRons are normally assigned to the Pacific Fleet (two on forward deployment in the Western Pacific), and four to the Atlantic Fleet (one deployed forward in the Mediterranean). Their composition varies according to the Marine Amphibious Unit (MAU) embarked in each PhibRon, and according to the specific mission, so there can be no set size or standard list of equipment for a MAU. Typical figures, however, are 1600–2500 marines with tanks, amphibious tracked personnel carriers, artillery and lighter weapons, supported by 20–25 helicopters. A typical PhibRon is made up of an LPH, LPD, LSD and two LSTs, supported on forward deployments by an AKA, and they are all 20-knot ships.

This impressive group of ships is without equal in the world, but inevitably the US Marine Corps decided in the early 1970s that greater cost-effectiveness could be achieved by combining the functions of the various units of the PhibRon in a single hull. Of course the function of the LSTs could not be absorbed, for they must be able to beach, but it did prove possible to combine the functions of the LPH, LPD, LSD and AKA in a single LHA or amphibious assault ship. The technical problems were daunting, for the designers had to combine vertical and horizontal movement of troops, as well as the flow of vehicles and supplies but the ships which resulted are impressive by any standard.

They combine a welldeck big enough to take the large utility landing craft with a full-length hangar high enough to take the biggest Marine Corps helicopters. They also stow and handle the heavy cargo of an AKA but without conventional mercantile holds and heavy-lift booms, and handle troops as efficiently as the specially-tailored LPD and LSD.

To fit a hangar above a large welldeck without excessive topweight called for a very big hull. The five *Tarawa* (LHA.1) class are 250 meters long, with a beam of 32.3 meters (just enough to get through the Panama Canal). At 39,300 tons full load they approximate to the Soviet cruiser/carrier *Kiev*, but whereas the Russian ship has a freeboard of 13 meters the *Tarawa*s have 18 meters. The difficulty of handling heavy cargo inside a part-carrier/part-floating dock hull required an ingenious application of mercantile containerization. This results in a unique ability to move cargo vertically by helicopter or horizontally by landing craft, and at the same time leave the flow of troops undisturbed.

The most visible feature of the *Tarawa* class is the flight deck, island and hangar, which gives the ships a superficial resemblance to carriers. The 65m × 30m × 8.5m hangar occupies the after part of the ship and is served by a side lift and a centerline lift right aft. The standard assault helicopter is the Boeing-Vertol CH-47 Sea Knight, which can carry 17–25 fully armed marines or 1350kg of cargo. In addition there are Sikorsky CH-53D Sea Stallions, capable of carrying 37 marines or 3600kg of cargo. It is currently being replaced by the bigger CH-53E Super Stallion, with a third engine; they can lift 14,600kg of cargo or 56 marines.

These heavy assault helicopters are backed up by the Bell AH-1 SeaCobra and the UH-1 Huey. The AH-1J version of the SeaCobra operates in the escort and defense suppression role, with a three-barreled 20mm gun, and the AH-1T can carry the TOW anti-tank missile. The 'Huey' is a utility helicopter used for command and control, or for casualty evacuation, in which role it can lift six stretcher patients and a medical orderly. The third element in the LHAs' air group is the AV-8A Harrier ground support aircraft, which is normally carried as a detachment of four, but sometimes expanded to as many as 22, if required.

The maximum stowage in the hangar is 30 helicopters, and the sight of a fully embarked air group in an LHA is a reminder that the figure of 30 is indeed a maximum. In peacetime the normal complement would be something like 12 Sea Knights, six Sea Stallions, four SeaCobras and two Hueys. Such an air group would have a lift capacity of 400–500 marines.

Underneath the hangar is the massive welldeck, 82 meters by 24 meters, divided lengthwise by a guide slip for the landing craft. Four big 41-meter *LCU.1610* class can be carried, each capable of lifting three M48 or M60 tanks. There are also two 22-meter LCM(6) landing craft, which can lift 80 troops or 34 tons of cargo; they are normally stowed on the flight deck and lifted into the water by crane. The LCUs can be loaded while the ship is underway, and when ready to disembark the dock is flooded, the ship keeping steady by using her bow-thruster.

Vehicles and tanks are parked in a huge 'multistory car park' containing 200 trucks, jeeps, tanks and LVTP-7 Amtrac armored personnel carriers. As the Amtracs are amphibious they swim out of the welldeck like the landing craft, and eight of them can be launched simultaneously. More than half the Marine Battalion can be landed by the Amtracs, as each one carries 25 marines.

Five LHAs were built in 1971–80, but the contract for the last four of the program was canceled in 1971 in spite of loud protests from the Marines. The cancellation has been felt keenly since then, especially as the five LHAs have proved an outstanding success. Their crews are proud of the versatility, and refer to the LHA as the 'ship that has everything'. Belated recognition of the error in not building all nine is implicit in the decision in 1982 to order a new class of LHD or helicopter/dock landing ships. The *Wasp* class will have a similar hull to the LHA, but will emphasize more of the qualities of the LPD, by embarking a dozen LCM(6) and two LCACs, and 1800 marines.

It is interesting to contrast the Soviet Navy's

Above: Small navies use tank landing ships for rapid movement of troops. This is the Nigerian *Ambe*, built in Germany.

approach to amphibious warfare, for although the Soviets have never achieved such a dazzling height of competence their Naval Infantry have a proud record of fighting on land, in contrast to a by and large dismal performance by the Navy during the Great Patriotic War. The later stages of that war saw considerable use of raids behind the German lines by small parties of troops, using small naval units to get in and out.

There was little incentive to develop highly specialized techniques of amphibious warfare, for unlike the US Navy which had to fight its way across the Pacific, the Russian Navy had to guard the flanks of the Red Army, either by evacuating cut-off detachments or using commando-style raids to secure bridgeheads during an advance. Amphibious forces were seen merely as adjuncts of land power, and despite its heroic record, the Naval Infantry was disbanded after the war. Not until the 1960s, when the Soviets had seen numerous plans frustrated by British and American use of their amphibious forces, was the Naval Infantry reactivated. Since then several battalions have been allocated to each of the four fleets, with a Brigade HQ in each fleet. Current strength of the Naval Infantry is estimated at between 15,000 and 18,000 troops.

Several classes of small landing craft were built in the 1950s, but not until the following decade were specialized amphibious forces deployed in large numbers. From 1965 the Polish Stocznia Polnocny shipyard at Gdansk began to turn out a new type of LST, the Polnocny class. About 100 units were delivered, of which 65 were incorporated into the Soviet Navy, the remainder going to the Polish Navy and other friendly navies. They were a competent design, but hardly a match for their Western equivalents; they are roughly half the size of LSTs built in 1944–45.

About a year after the first Polnocny, a larger LST codenamed Alligator, appeared from a Russian ship-yard. These 4000-ton LSTs are credited with lifting 20–25 vehicles and tanks and some 350–400 troops, and their high freeboard and diesel engines give them the ability to undertake long voyages. They have been seen off the coast of Africa and the Indian Ocean, and clearly gave the Soviet Navy a new capability for independent operations. The next LST to appear, the Ropucha class of 1975, seemed, however, to be an enlargement of the Polnocny design. Commentators see them as useful for 'local' amphibious operations in such areas as the Baltic, rather than in power-projection in support of foreign policy. All three classes carry a heavy defensive armament, 57mm guns in the Ropucha and Alligator classes and 30mm guns in the Polnocny class.

Surprisingly the Naval Infantry have not been given modern fighting vehicles, and the Soviet amphibious lift capability is correspondingly weak. The elderly T-54/55 tank is used, but it lacks the ability to 'swim' ashore. The PT-76 lightweight amphibious tank is capable of 'swimming' at a speed of 11 knots on its waterjets, but it has limited fighting value. The other standard fighting vehicle is the BTR-60 armored personnel carrier, which has better performance in water but poor land performance. It is being replaced by the BMP-1 Mechanized Infantry Combat Vehicle (MICV), which was introduced in 1967. It is better armored than the BTR-60 and is armed with a bigger gun as well as wire-guided anti-tank missiles, but carries fewer troops.

The next sign that Soviet ideas on amphibious warfare were becoming more ambitious was the appearance of a new LPD called *Ivan Rogov* in 1978. She is more than twice the displacement of any previous Russian amphibious ship, and is the first to have a docking well and a flight deck for helicopters. She displaces about 13,000 tons full load, is 158 meters long and has a bow door as well as a docking well in the stern. She is therefore built along traditional LST lines, with a continuous tank deck, unlike American and British LPDs.

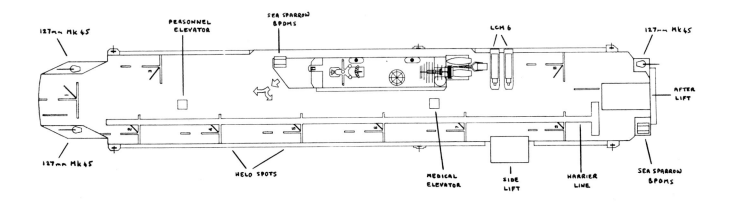

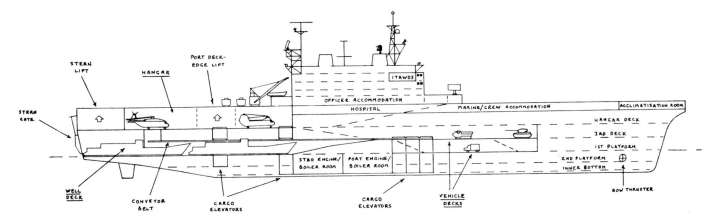

Above and left: The assault landing ships of the *Tarawa* class have an impressive multi-role capability with full-length flight decks and a docking well. At 40,000 tons they are as large as the Soviet *Kiev* class. *Tarawa* is shown at left.

Like previous amphibious warfare ships she is heavily armed, not only for self-defense but for shore bombardment. A twin 76mm gun mounting is sited on the forecastle, well positioned to support a landing as well as to defend the beachhead from air attack. Two pairs of 23mm 'Gatling' guns provide for close range defense, but there are also two SA-N-4 short range missile systems. For shore bombardment there is also a BM-21 artillery rocket launcher, similar to a system mounted in the Alligator class.

Authorities argue over the lift capacity of the ship. Some sources suggest two Gus type hovercraft, others say three Lebed type. A total of 700 troops seems very high, and is apparently based on the theory that it can embark two 350-man Naval Infantry battalions; the figure of 400 seems more reasonable if we are talking about the number of troops embarked for any length of time. Not even the Soviets, whose ideas on accommodation and personal comfort are perhaps less generous than Western navies', can expect to keep fighting men efficient by cooping them up in very cramped quarters.

The *Ivan Rogov* is clearly designed to operate her own helicopters, with a hangar built into the after superstructure. As many as six Kamov Ka-25 Hormone-A helicopters could be carried in this large hangar, but normally four are embarked. The Hormone can accommodate 12 soldiers on folding seats in the cabin, and if all six were embarked a total of 72 men could be lifted in a single sortie, but it may equally be possible that the ship is intended to act as a staging post for helicopters operated by other ships. What is certain is that the helicopter facilities are elaborate for such a small group – two separate flight decks, each with its own flying control position, plus large hangar doors and a ramp.

It seems likely that the *Ivan Rogov* is being evaluated to see just how she can fit into future amphibious warfare plans. The fact that she participated in a Baltic exercise before proceeding to the Far East on her first deployment lends support to this view. Subsequently exercises took place off East Africa, suggesting that no single role has been chosen, but she and a second ship which has not yet appeared are clearly intended to succeed the Alligator class in the furtherance of foreign policy. What should not be taken for granted, however, is that they are the spearhead of a massive incursion into the realm of offensive amphibious warfare. There are good reasons for thinking that the Soviet Navy is still tied to single-ship operations, and it is likely that the LPDs will not form part of a large amphibious warfare squadron. They are not particularly well equipped to provide command and control, by comparison with US Navy ships of similar type. They are on the large side for beaching, and carry no LCUs to take advantage of the docking

Above: Two LCUs from HMS *Fearless* on her return from the Falklands. They carry Scorpion and Scimitar armored vehicles. Left: Soviet APCs and assault infantry coming ashore.

well. On the other hand, the docking well is very small, and this restricts the number and type of air cushion vehicles and landing craft which can be embarked. Like the LHA, they are an attempt to combine a number of functions in one hull, but on only a third of the size, clearly the designers had to make compromises which have limited each function severely.

Most of the NATO and other Western navies operate small landing craft, but mainly for short range local operations. The only European navies to maintain a full amphibious capability are France and Great Britain. Each navy built two LPDs in the 1960s and a number of LSTs. The French *Orage* and *Ouragan* displace 8500 tons full load, whereas the British *Fearless* and *Intrepid* are about 50 percent larger, but both types lift about 350–400 troops. The French have built two medium-sized LSTs, the *Champlain* and *Francis Garnier*, known as the Batral type, and two more are under construction. To meet a similar peacetime need to move men, vehicles and supplies in peacetime the British Ministry of Transport in 1963 ordered six Logistic Landing Ships (LSLs) for the Army, 5600-ton ships resembling LSTs, with a bow and stern ramps for speedy movement of vehicles. In 1970 they were transferred to the Royal Fleet Auxiliary, the civilian-manned service which provides logistic support for the Royal Navy.

Named after Knights of the Round Table, the *Sir Bedivere* class were built in 1965–67.

From 1966 it had been a cardinal principle of British defense policy that there would never be an occasion for British forces acting alone to make an opposed landing. It is therefore hardly surprising that apart from the Royal Marines, who kept the doctrine of 'amphibiosity' alive, British experience of beach assault has until recently been limited to a few days' exercising each year. The 'infrastructure', the civilian agencies in the dockyards, the ordnance depots and other departments which in the US Navy exist to support the PhibRons, had little or no opportunity to practise procedures. Certainly when Argentine forces invaded the Falkland Islands on Friday 2 April 1982 there was no blueprint for a campaign to be waged 8000 miles away from the United Kingdom.

Despite these inherent weaknesses, within a week of receiving mobilization orders the Reinforced 3rd Commando Brigade had sailed with sufficient of its War Materiel Reserve (WMR) for 30 days' land operations, as well as 60 days' specialist stores, and an additional 26 days' WMR to be kept in ships for resupply. In all 5000 tons of ammunition, rations and consumable stores, everything from missiles to clothing, was loaded into various LSLs and Royal Fleet Auxiliary supply ships, within 72 hours of the order to embark. By midday on Monday 5 April the ships were loaded and they sailed within 24 hours.

As there are only 30 miles of good roads in the Falklands the decision was made to leave all wheeled

vehicles behind. The risk was also foreseen that the small number of helicopters available might be immobilized by peat bogs if too many stores were sent ashore; the answer was to hold a floating reserve of stores.

To strengthen the hand of British diplomacy it was essential to get the amphibious force to sea as soon as possible. The Commodore Amphibious Warfare embarked in the LPD *Fearless*, while her sister *Intrepid* was hurriedly recommissioned. The flagship embarked both the Commodore's and the Marine Brigade's staffs, the Brigade's HQ and Signals Company, and some helicopter controllers.

The landings at San Carlos on 21 May, seven weeks after the Argentine seizure followed a standard pattern: two LSLs supporting each assault, while helicopters lifted artillery and missiles ashore in the third phase. The simplicity of the plan was severely disrupted by the severe Argentine air raids; important ships had to be withdrawn. As the Brigadier had foreseen, air attacks disrupted movements of supplies, and helicopters supplying forward areas risked being shot down by Pucará ground-support aircraft. Not until the Navy Sea Harriers had begun to establish air superiority over the beachead and the Army's Rapier ground-to-air missile batteries were established ashore could the troops begin the break-out.

An example of how the loss of a key ship can prejudice an amphibious operation was the *Atlantic Conveyor*. This 15,000-ton roll on/roll off container ship was hit by two Exocet antiship missiles in an attack by two Argentine Navy Super Etendard strike aircraft on 25 May. She had taken RAF Harriers and Chinook heavy-lift helicopters down to the Falklands, as well as some 4000 tons of vital stores, including a portable airstrip, refueling gear and aircraft bombs.

Left: The tank landing ship *Fairfax County* in company with the amphibious assault ship USS *Inchon*. The capabilities of both these ship types, as well as of the LPDs, are combined in one hull in the *Tarawa* class.
Right: The amphibious transport dock USS *Dubuque* (LPD.8), one of the US Navy's *Austin* class.
Main picture: A Sikorsky Sea Stallion heavy assault helicopter refuels from a KC-130 Hercules tanker. The US Marines have six Sea Stallion squadrons for their amphibious assault role.

Above: Mil Mi-8 Hip assault helicopters flying over fast strike craft of the Soviet Baltic Fleet during large-scale amphibious maneuvers.

She had previously flown off the Harriers but three of the four Chinooks were lost, along with a Lynx, and six Wessex helicopters. The Chinooks, each capable of lifting 12 tons (four times the load of a Sea King) were sorely missed ashore. As a direct result, the LSLs had to shoulder a greater burden, resupplying forward units of the land forces.

The six LSLs proved invaluable, but could not be risked freely as they were so lightly defended. Just how vulnerable they were was proved dramatically on 8 June, when Argentine aircraft caught the LSLs *Sir Galahad* and *Sir Tristram* in Bluff Cove, to the South East of East Falkland. Both ships were quickly set on fire, and as a large number of troops were still on board the casualties were comparatively high – 43 Welsh Guards killed and many badly burned. It was

Before the Falklands Campaign the Royal Navy had been under strong pressure to abandon its amphibious capability. The LPDs were to be scrapped (HMS *Intrepid* had even been offered to Argentina), the LSLs were to go, and there was even talk of disbanding the Royal Marines. Since 1982 the scene looks different; two roll on/roll off ships have been chartered to replace the LSLs (*Sir Galahad* was

scuttled but *Sir Tristram* was salvaged and taken back to the United Kingdom). To resupply the Falklands garrison a North Sea ferry has been bought, and is now in service as the troop transport HMS *Keren*. The future of British amphibious forces is not clear, but what has been demonstrated is that without even the limited capability possessed in 1982 the Falklands operation could not have been contemplated.

If a government needs to project power beyond its shores, there is very little alternative. With only a short runway at Port Stanley it was not possible to fly in reinforcements, so the small garrison was overwhelmed. Even if a long runway capable of taking large military transport aircraft had existed, a surprise attack could capture it before reinforcements arrived. Once hostile forces were in occupation there remained only one option to the British, an amphibious assault. The other option, an attack on mainland Argentina was simply not feasible. What applied in the South Atlantic applies elsewhere; despite the advances in air transport heavy equipment has to be moved by sea, and heavily armed troops have to be put ashore from ships. But, even more important is the fact that the complexities of amphibious warfare have to be entrusted to specially trained soldiers, such as the US Marines and the Royal Marines – amphibiosity is certainly not a doctrine which can be hurriedly imbibed.

Previous page: The Tornado air defense variant carries four Skyflash air-to-air missiles beneath the fuselage.
Right: The USAF's new intercontinental-range bomber, the Rockwell B-1B, is to become fully operational with Strategic Air Command in 1987. A B-1A prototype is pictured during a test flight in 1975.

238

STRATEGIC FORCES

Delivery systems for strategic nuclear weapons fall into three main categories: land-based missiles, submarine-launched missiles and bomber aircraft (which can carry air-launched missiles). The manned bomber concept is of course the oldest of the nuclear delivery systems. It cannot compete with the land-based missile in speed of delivery combined with accuracy. Nor at present does it compare with the submarine-launched ballistic missile, which has a near invulnerability, because of the difficulties of detecting the launching craft. It is therefore tempting to dismiss the bomber as an anachronism, which owes its survival to military conservatism and the tendency of defense planners to over-insure.

The United States is nonetheless committed to maintaining the 'triad' of land-based ICBMs (intercontinental ballistic missiles), SLBMs (submarine-launched ballistic missiles) and strategic bombers. The Soviet Union likewise divides its nuclear delivery systems between ICBMs, SLBMs and bombers and both the Superpowers are seeking to modernize their strategic bomber forces.

One of the reasons for retaining the bomber force is the fear that silo-based ICBMs may become vulnerable to attack from enemy ICBMs. Similar concern is voiced about possible developments in ballistic missile defense technology, which could neutralize both land and submarine-based missile systems. It is therefore prudent to maintain a strategic nuclear delivery system which will be unaffected by such developments.

Bombers have other positive virtues when compared with missile systems. They can be dispersed from their bases, or put on airborne alert, thus warning the enemy, in time of crisis, of one's resolution to act and also denying him the option of a pre-emptive strike against the bomber force. A single bomber can carry a heavy load of free-fall or stand-off weapons, enabling it to attack a variety of targets in the same mission. It can be diverted after takeoff to a new target of greater importance than its original objective and it can be recalled if the order to attack proves to be a miscalculation. The bomber's crew can avoid wasting warheads on a target already devastated and they are able to make some assessment of the effectiveness of their attack. All of this represents a flexibility which is unobtainable from an all-missile force. Finally bombers oblige the enemy to devote valuable resources to his air defenses.

In the United States both the ICBM force and the bomber wings are controlled by the USAF's Strategic Air Command (SAC). With its headquarters at Offutt Air Force Base (AFB) Nebraska, this command operates from more than 50 bases and controls approximately 120,000 personnel. The ballistic-missile-armed submarines (SSBNs) are the responsibility of the US Navy. The Navy's aircraft carriers also have a measure of strategic capability by virtue of their nuclear-capable attack aircraft, although these are primarily tactical weapons.

The mainstay of SAC's bomber force at present is

the Boeing B-52 Stratofortress. This giant eight-engined bomber first entered service in 1955, but only the last two production variants (the B-52G and B-52H) now serve in the strategic role.

A total of 295 B-52Gs and B-52Hs was built (193 Gs and 102 Hs), with the last delivered in June 1962, and 269 remain in service with 14 SAC bombardment wings. The B-52G has a span of 185 feet, a length of 160ft 11in and maximum all-up weight is 488,000 pounds. It is powered by eight 13,750lbs thrust Pratt & Whitney J57-P-43WB turbojets. Fuel capacity is almost 48,000 gallons, which gives the B-52G an unrefueled range of 8400 miles. The B-52H, with the same fuel capacity, has an unrefueled range of 10,130 miles, because of the greater efficiency of its Pratt & Whitney TF33 turbofan engines. Its maximum speed of 545 knots is some five knots below that of the B-52G.

The normal crew complement of the Stratofortress is six, comprising pilot, co-pilot, navigator, radar navigator, electronic warfare officer and tail gunner. The radar navigator directs the bomb run and prepares the weapons for release. The tail gunner is located in the forward crew compartment and operates his turret by remote control. The B-52G has four 0.5in machine guns in the tail, whereas the B-52H mounts a 20mm Vulcan rotary cannon, capable of firing 4000 rounds per minute. The gun turret may seem out of place in the age of the air-to-air missile, but many Soviet warplanes are so armed, and the B-52's tail guns accounted for two MiG-21 interceptors during the Vietnam War.

The B-52Gs and Hs can carry a warload of up to eight nuclear free-fall bombs. They can also be armed with up to 20 SRAM (short-range attack missile) rounds, eight carried internally in a revolving cylinder in the bomb bay, with the remainder on wing pylons. The SRAM has a nuclear warhead of some 200 kilotons (kt) yield and has a range of between 35 and 105 miles, depending on the altitude of the launch aircraft and the preprogrammed maneuvers of the missile. In practice B-52s are likely to be armed with a combination of free-fall weapons and SRAMs. The latest addition to the Stratofortress' armory is the Boeing AGM-86B air-launched cruise missile (ALCM), with a range of 1500 miles and a 200 kt warhead.

As originally conceived, the B-52 was to rely on its high-altitude performance to penetrate enemy defenses, as the name Stratofortress implies. Yet by 1959 it was recognized that developments in surface-to-air missile (SAM) technology (later paralleled by improvements in manned interceptors) had made such tactics unworkable. The problem was compounded by the massive bomber's conspicuous radar 'signature'.

The solution was to switch to low-level penetration at high subsonic speed. However, the B-52 was ill-suited to such tactics. Its large, high-aspect-ratio wing is ideal for the still air conditions of high-altitude flight, but badly adapted to cope with the turbulence met at low level. This results in excessive loads on the airframe

A Boeing B-52G lifts off from Seymour-Johnson AFB, NC, home of the 68th Bomb Wing, during SAC's world-wide readiness exercise Global Shield in July 1979.

and control difficulties. Consequently a series of expensive modifications has been carried out to improve the aircraft's structural integrity and to prolong airframe life.

Flying at low level is not by itself enough to ensure the B-52's survival in hostile airspace. Electronic countermeasures (ECM) have an important part to play in neutralizing enemy defenses and are continually being upgraded to meet new threats. The latest ECM update (Phase VI) for the B-52G and H was begun in 1974 at a cost of $362,500,000. A separate modification program warns of enemy attack through the ALQ-153 tail warning radar, which can detect SAMs, interceptors and air-to-air missiles (AAMs).

Forward visibility at low level was found to be a problem and to supplement the terrain avoidance radar the B-52Gs and Hs have been fitted with an electro-optical viewing system (EVS). This comprises a steerable low-light television (LLTV) and a forward-looking infra-red (FLIR) mounted in blisters under the bomber's nose. The view from either sensor can be shown on displays on the flight deck, warning of such hazards as radio masts. The EVS is also useful for picking up navigational waypoints, or targets and for making a post-attack assessment.

The basic aircraft operating unit within SAC is the bombardment wing (BW). B-52 wings comprise one or sometimes two squadrons flying the bombers and one or two air refueling squadrons operating Boeing KC-135A tanker aircraft. The strategic bombers rely on air refueling to execute their mission and the importance of this support is emphasized by the inclusion of air refueling squadrons within each bombardment wing.

A proportion of the B-52 force is always on ground alert. This would typically involve six bombers and three tankers in a wing, ready to take off at a moment's notice. The B-52s are parked on hardstandings positioned off a central taxiway, which leads onto the main runway. They are armed and fueled, have been inspected by their crews and prepared for a quick engine start. Each is fitted with individual cartridge starters on all eight engines to speed up this process.

When the SAC bomber force has been launched on its mission, the aircraft fly to a predetermined point on their track to the target. There they must fly a holding pattern until they receive further orders to proceed or to return to base. Coded orders to execute the attack can only come from the National Command Authorities, the President or those authorized to act on his behalf. Thus positive control of the bomber force is ensured and the procedure can be regarded as 'fail-safe', because if no further orders are received the bombers will abandon the mission. Communications are therefore of vital importance to SAC and since 1979 the B-52 force has been fitted with AFSATCOM, the USAF's satellite communications system, which provides high-

241

priority communications anywhere in the world.

The performance of SAC's air and maintenance crews and the effectiveness of the operating procedures are constantly monitored and evaluated by an exhaustive series of inspections. Practice alerts are held to test reaction times and may be terminated once the engines have been started or the first bomber has reached the runway. An aircraft's first sortie after ground alert is an important check on the standard of maintenance during its time on the ground. The crew is also assessed during training flights, which include simulated bombing attacks.

The demanding low-level bombing mission is practiced over specially selected routes in the USA. The B-52s are flown at heights of between 1000 and 2000ft, until the defense penetration phase of the exercise, lasting for perhaps an hour, when the bombers descend to between 500 and 300ft. The routes are varied to give the crews experience over unfamiliar terrain and navigation is often an exacting task, with little information available from radar returns. Simulated attacks are made on radar bomb-scoring sites, which are maintained by the 1st Combat Evaluation Group. This unit also monitors the accuracy of the bombers' and tankers' navigation throughout the exercise. Bomb release is simulated by the attacking aircraft transmitting a 'bomb tone', which is cut off at the point of release. The radar bomb scoring site can then compute the point of impact. Several such targets are often attacked on one training mission.

Not all of SAC's training takes place in the air, however. In common with other air forces, the USAF

has been affected by the energy crisis and this means that the service is looking for substantial fuel economies. Flight simulators are one answer and have the added advantages that they conserve airframe hours and enable emergency procedures to be practiced in complete safety. The latest B-52 simulator offers the flight deck crew six-axis motion, computer generated image visual displays and simulated control force feel. The radar navigator can receive simulated radar returns and can practice weapons release procedures. Numerous simulated 'threats' can exercise the electronic warfare officer in the use of ECM equipment. Yet despite this sophistication, simulators do not offer an entirely satisfactory substitute.

Another way of saving fuel is to carry out a part of the training program in a less 'thirsty' aircraft than the B-52. It has been proposed that SAC buy about 60 business-jet aircraft, in which the bomber crews (less the gunner) could fly 25 percent of the training sorties now undertaken by the B-52. The annual fuel savings of this measure are estimated as 100,000,000 US gallons. At present B-52 flights for co-pilot proficiency training are being reduced by using T-37 and T-38 trainers for this purpose.

Since 1948 SAC has held an annual bombing competition in which every wing takes part. As with much of SAC's peacetime activity, the object of the competition, code-named 'Giant Voice', is to test efficiency and readiness of bomber units and the tanker force. The B-52-equipped wings are the primary contenders, but SAC's two FB-111 wings also take part, as do tanker squadrons from the regular air force, the Air Force Reserve (AFRES) and Air National Guard (ANG). Among the skills tested are high and low-level bombing accuracy, use of ECM, evasion of fighter interception, navigation, air refueling and SRAM launches.

Exercise 'Global Shield' is a command-wide, no-notice readiness exercise, which involves all SAC units – including missile wings and strategic reconnaissance wings – in a simulated thermonuclear war. 'Global Shield 80' held in June 1980 involved 100,000 SAC personnel and 44 bases in an exercise lasting nine days. It began with an all-out effort to place additional crews

and aircraft on alert to participate in the exercise, as of course SAC's actual alert forces could not be used. As would happen in a real period of prewar crisis, a proportion of SAC's bombers and tankers was dispersed to other military airfields or to civil airports. In addition to making the enemy's target planning more difficult, this provides SAC with more runways and so eases the problem of getting the force off at short notice after an attack warning.

The next stage was an airborne alert and aircraft were required to await positive instructions before carrying out simulated war sorties. This aspect of the exercise differed only in scale from the normal wing ORI. On return from their mission, some aircraft acted as battle damaged bombers which would require special maintenance attention at forward operating locations before they were able to return to base.

If low-level flying presents problems for the B-52, then by contrast it is the normal operating environment for SAC's other strategic bomber, the General Dynamics FB-111A. This aircraft is a supersonic, variable-geometry-wing, medium range bomber, derived from the F-111 tactical strike fighter. As originally conceived the FB-111 was to have replaced the Convair B-58 Hustler (SAC's first supersonic bomber) and early model B-52s. A total of 263 bombers was planned, but escalating costs and early technical problems with the F-111 led to a severe curtailment.

In spite of its inauspicious beginnings, the FB-111A has proved to be a worthwhile addition to the US strategic armory, largely because of its effectiveness at

Above left: A B-52's awesome bomb load explodes on a Viet Cong base camp in South Vietnam.
Left: A B-52G crew board their aircraft during a practise alert.
Below: A SRAM missile nestles in the weapons bay of an FB-111.

The Tu-20's stablemate in Long Range Aviation is the turbojet powered M-4 Bison long-range bomber (above). The Tu-16 Badger (above right) has been the mainstay of the Soviet medium-range bomber force since the 1950s. Its intended successor, the Tu-22 Blinder (below) was only produced in limited numbers.

high speed and low level. The FB-111A-equipped bombardment wings are assigned to targets on the periphery of Soviet territory because the bomber's unrefueled range of 3400 nautical miles classes it as a medium rather than a heavy bomber. Crew fatigue is also a limiting factor, as the FB-111A carries only a pilot and a navigator, compared with the six crewmembers aboard a B-52. However, the bomber is equipped for inflight refueling and tanker squadrons are assigned to the FB-111A wings.

The FB-111A is powered by two Pratt & Whitney TF30-P-7 turbofans with afterburning, each giving 20,350lbs of thrust and maximum speed at altitude is more than Mach 2. The variable-sweep wings endow the FB-111A with excellent handling qualities throughout its speed range. The wings are positioned fully forward, giving a wing span of 70ft, for takeoff, landing and economical cruise. In the fully-swept position, which is selected for high-speed flight, the span is reduced to 33ft 9in. Overall length is 73ft 5in and height is 17ft, thus the FB-111A presents a much smaller target to enemy interceptor pilots and radars than its massive stablemate the B-52. Normal gross weight of the FB-111A is 80,000lbs, which can increase to 110,000lbs maximum gross weight. Weapons carried include the SRAM missile, which can be mounted on the underwing pylons and in the internal weapons bay, which also houses free-fall nuclear weapons. Auxiliary fuel tanks can also be carried on the wing pylons.

The key to the FB-111A's impressive low-altitude performance is the aircraft's complex avionics systems. A terrain-following radar and radar altimeter enable the FB-111A to fly 200ft above the ground, following the contours of the terrain. The system is duplicated and if one should fail the second takes over automatically. In the event of a double failure the aircraft is pulled into a steep climb. Terrain following can be automatic or controlled by the pilot, following cockpit radar displays.

The main navigational aid is an inertial navigation system, which is completely independent of external sources of information and is therefore unjammable. All that is required is that the co-ordinates of the aircraft's starting point are fed into the system's computer. This is so accurate that each aircraft's parking space has been individually surveyed and marked with the exact latitude and longitude. It is claimed that the system could direct a bomber from its hardstanding to the end of the runway even in dense fog. A speed-sensing doppler radar can also be used for navigation and an attack radar is used to acquire the target during the bomb run.

The FB-111A's high speed, low altitude capability provides its best safeguard against enemy defenses. However, the aircraft also carries a range of ECM equipment. This includes a radar homing and warning system (which alerts the crew when their aircraft has been picked up by the enemy), jamming transmitters to interfere with radars and communications, chaff to blot out radar returns and flares to decoy infra-red guided missiles away from the bomber's engine exhausts.

One reason for the delay in finding a successor to the B-52 was the change from high to low level target penetration tactics, necessitated by improvements in Soviet air defenses. This led to the cancellation of the North American B-70 in 1964. The B-70 was designed to operate at altitudes of 70-80,000ft at speeds up to Mach 3. It was considered too vulnerable to Soviet missiles and in fact the MiG-25 Foxbat is believed to have been developed specifically to counter the projected B-70 force.

The long-awaited replacement for the B-52 seemed within sight in 1970, when North American Rockwell (later Rockwell International) was awarded a contract to build five test examples of the B-1A bomber to meet the USAF's Advanced Manned Strategic Aircraft requirement. The important characteristic of the new bomber was the ability to fly the target penetration phase of its mission at low altitude and high subsonic speed (Mach 0.85 at 200ft).

In 1977 it seemed that the B-1 was to go the same way as the B-70 Valkyrie, when President Carter cancelled the 240-aircraft production program. However flight testing of the four completed prototypes went on, the ECM systems continued to be developed for use on late model B-52s and work continued on the F-101 engine which could also be used to power advanced fighter aircraft. Thus when the Reagan administration came into office with a commitment to rejuvenate American defenses the reinstatement of the B-1 bomber was one option that was available to strengthen the strategic forces. In October 1981 an order for 100 B-1s was announced as part of an ambitious program to modernize the US nuclear arsenal.

The B-1B, which is expected to become fully operational in 1987, differs in several important respects from the earlier B-1A. The gross weight is some 40 tons greater, allowing it to fly a transatlantic mission with full warload and return without inflight refueling. However a more typical mission would be similar to that outlined for the B-1A. Maximum speed is reduced to Mach 1.2, the B-1A's elaborate variable-geometry engine inlets being replaced by simpler fixed inlets. A great advance over the original B-1 model is the reduction of the aircraft's radar signature by a factor of ten, giving it a signature one hundredth that of the B-52.

The B-1B can carry a variety of weapons in three internal bays and on external hard points. Loads of 20-38 free-fall nuclear bombs can be carried, or up to 38 SRAMs, although a mixture of the two is more typical. Looking ahead to the time when the B-1B supplants the B-52 as a cruise missile carrier and conventional bomber, 22 ALCMs can be carried, eight of them in an internal rotary launcher, and up to 128 500lb Mk 82 high explosive bombs can be lifted.

The B-1B's attack and terrain-following radar is based on the F-16 fighter's APG-66 radar. The defensive ECM system, designated ALQ-161, will automatically pick up hostile radar emissions, assign them a priority and initiate jamming or deception against those that appear the greatest threat. As the B-1B will be flying fast and low, the ECM system is an additional insurance against enemy interception and missile defenses, which together with the reduced radar signature should ensure its effectiveness well into the 1990s. By this time the new Stealth bomber should be in service and the B-1B will take on the role of cruise-missile carrier and conventional bomber.

By the end of the present decade it is predicted that the Soviet air defenses will begin to introduce advanced new systems capable of detecting, tracking and intercepting low-flying strategic bombers. The key to this enhanced capability is the computer-controlled pulse-doppler radar, able to pick-out low flying aircraft from the ground clutter which hides these from a conventional radar.

The same technology gives a missile-armed interceptor a 'lookdown/shootdown' capability and then the immunity of the low flying bomber disappears. The USAF's answer to this anticipated threat is the Advanced Technology Bomber, which makes use of 'Stealth' technology to hide from enemy radars. These techniques have been applied to the B-1B to reduce its radar signature, but when incorporated from the outset into the new bomber design they are so effective as virtually to eliminate any radar return. The bomber's infra-red signature is also reduced. Indeed it has been claimed that the introduction of the Stealth bomber will make Soviet air defenses obsolete overnight.

The techniques employed to achieve the elimination of an aircraft's radar return are highly classified. Nevertheless a certain amount of general information is available. The starting point of Stealth technology must be the basic design of the airframe. If those parts which act as radar reflectors, such as angular engine intakes and vertical tail surfaces, can be eliminated or reduced in size, then other techniques can suppress the residual reflectivity. It is significant that the contractor for the Advanced Technology Bomber is Northrop, a company with unrivalled experience in 'flying wing' designs, because this configuration comes close to meeting the airframe requirements of a Stealth bomber. If carbonfiber composites replace metals in an aircraft's structure and skinning, they will not reflect radar pulses to the same degree and they also have the incidental advantages of strength and lightness. Finally radar absorbent material can be applied to the remaining surfaces on the aircraft.

It is anticipated that the B-1B will find it increasingly difficult to cope with Soviet air defenses in the 1990s. It is therefore likely that the Stealth bomber will become operational early in the decade, with some 100 being procured. This assumes that such an ambitious program does not run into serious technical problems.

SAC's long-range bomber force, equipped with elderly B-52s, is to be rejuvenated with the introduction of the B-1 (top). Its Soviet counterpart, Long Range Aviation, at present relies on the 1950s-vintage Tu-20 Bear (right), which is equipped with a tail-mounted gun armament for self-defense. Its turret (above) houses two 23mm cannon.

As the improved Soviet defenses will first be deployed around high priority targets and the B-1B is not entirely defenseless against new air defense systems, it is likely that the Stealth bomber will not completely supplant it in the penetration role until the mid-1990s.

The Soviet strategic forces are divided between three armed services. The air force controls the manned bombers, the navy is responsible for submarine-launched systems and land-based missiles are the province of the Strategic Rocket Forces. This last organization is a service in its own right, quite distinct from the air force, and indeed it ranks above the other four services (Army, Air Defense Forces, Air Force and Navy) in seniority. Thus in contrast to American practice, land-based strategic bombers and missiles fall under two separate commands.

There can be no doubt that, as presently constituted, the Soviet air force's manned bomber arm is the least effective component of the strategic forces. This is due to the lack of a modern bomber of true intercontinental range to replace the 1950s-vintage Tupolev Tu-20 Bear. This type has not had the development potential of the B-52 and is now long overdue for retirement in the demanding role of deep penetration sorties over the continental USA.

Long Range Aviation (LRA) is better equipped for deep penetration missions over such target areas as Western Europe, China, Japan and possibly the periphery of the USA. Its medium range bombers, carrying either nuclear or conventional weapons, could attack such vital military targets as headquarters and supply depots. They could also be targeted against industrial complexes or centers of population. It seems most likely though that these forces would be used to extend Frontal Aviation's interdiction campaign deep into enemy territory. Therefore the primary targets of Long Range Aviation's medium bomber force are likely to be airfields, ports, and other communications and supply centers. Secondary roles for LRA aircraft include intelligence-gathering and bolstering the Naval Air Force in supporting operations at sea.

Long Range Aviation's greatest contribution to the Soviet strategic armory at present is therefore as part of its theater nuclear forces, rather than as a supplement to the ICBM and SLBM forces targeted against the USA. Nevertheless a proportion of the bomber force could be employed on follow-up strikes over North America after an ICBM attack to pick out those targets missed by the missiles. It is significant that, despite the problems of operating a force largely composed of elderly bombers, the Soviet Union thinks it worthwhile to maintain LRA in its present form. The current

The Soviet Union's Tu-26 Backfire medium-range bomber (left) poses a serious threat to US and allied forces in the European and Far Eastern theaters. Two designs competed to meet the USAF's Air Launched Cruise Missile requirement, the Boeing AGM-86 (upper and lower) beating the AGM-109 Tomahawk (center).

Union sees it as a cadre which can be expanded into an effective strategic bomber force once a modern inter-continental bomber becomes available.

Long Range Aviation is a subordinate command of the Soviet Air Force, equivalent in status to Frontal Aviation and Transport Aviation. It is commanded by a Colonel General of Aviation and enjoys a fair measure of operational independence. The basic operational unit of the force is the bomber regiment and these are assigned to three major commands. In the western Soviet Union, facing the NATO powers, are the Northwest and Southwest Bomber Corps, while the Far East Bomber Corps is deployed against China and Japan. The units of Long Range Aviation make use of air bases throughout the Soviet Union, including air-fields in the Arctic region.

The current aircraft strength of LRA comprises some 800 aircraft, of which about 120 carry out the supporting roles of reconnaissance and inflight refuel-ing. Inter-continental range bombing missions are assigned to some 100 Tu-20 Bear bombers and 45 Myasishchev M-4 Bisons, while the remainder of the force consists of medium range bombers. The most formidable of these is the Tu-26 Backfire, with some 120 in service in early 1985 (plus as many with the Naval Air Force). This aircraft, although not a true inter-continental bomber, is able to attack targets in the USA on a one-way mission, landing at bases in Cuba. There are approximately 140 Tu-22 Blinders in service and the remainder of the medium bomber force consists

missions of LRA could be as effectively performed by transferring its modern equipment to Frontal Aviation and the Naval Air Force. The Soviet Union has tradi-tionally shown itself reluctant to retire any obsolete weaponry which has some remaining usefulness (this tendency can be seen throughout the Soviet armed forces). Yet even taking this into account the continued existence of LRA makes little sense unless the Soviet

SAC operates a number of command and control and reconnaissance aircraft to support the strategic mission. The Boeing E-4 (below) may become the US President's airborne headquarters in time of crisis. The Boeing EC-135P (bottom left) is a less lavishly equipped airborne command post. Strategic reconnaissance is the task of the RC-135 (bottom right).

of elderly Tu-16 Badgers.

The introduction of the Tu-20 Bear into Soviet service in 1955 followed by the M-4 Bison, resulted in a dramatic expansion of the US air defenses. By the end of the 1950s USAF Air Defense Command controlled 40 regular fighter interceptor squadrons, in addition to ANG squadrons and an extensive radar network. In retrospect this hardly seems justified by a force of only some 200 Bisons and Bears, albeit nuclear armed.

Today seven USAF regular interceptor squadrons guard against a slightly smaller force of Soviet long range bombers. The Tu-20 is the largest Soviet bomber, spanning 167ft 8in and with a length of 155ft 10in. It is a swept-wing aircraft, powered by four massive Kuznetsov NK-12MV turboprops, each delivering 15,000shp (shaft horsepower). Top speed is 540mph and service ceiling 41,000ft. Its maximum range is 11,000 miles, which can be further extended by inflight refueling. Carrying a 26,500lb payload, the Bear's range is more than 7000 miles. In addition to free-fall bombs, the AS-3 Kangaroo stand-off weapon with a range of 400 miles, can be carried by some variants. A defensive armament of paired 23mm cannon is carried in dorsal and ventral remotely controlled barbettes and in a manned tail turret. Unlike the B-52, the Tu-20 does not appear to have been modified for the low level role and although a most impressive aircraft in its day, the Tu-20 would present few problems to the present-day Western air defense system.

The Bear's stablemate is the swept-wing, turbojet-powered M-4 Bison, which serves both as a bomber and tanker aircraft with LRA. Powered by four 28,500lb thrust Soloviev D-15s, the M-4 attains a maximum speed of Mach 0.95 at 10,000ft and its service ceiling is 56,000ft. It can carry a 12,000lb payload to a range of 5000 miles and this can be extended by inflight refueling. Its warload consists of free-fall bombs only, as air-to-surface missiles (ASM) are not carried. The tanker version carries a drogue and hose unit on a reel fitted in the bomb bay. As with the Bear, the Bison's ability to penetrate modern air defenses is minimal and most of LRA's surviving M-4s may now be used as tankers.

The most recent reports suggest that current Soviet strategic bomber development is following three lines. Firstly there are reports of a supersonic, variable-geometry bomber in the same class as the USAF's B-1. This would carry stand-off weapons and be equipped with a comprehensive range of ECM devices. The second reported development is of a subsonic, very long range multi-role aircraft, which could replace the Tu-20 Bear in its maritime roles, as well as providing a launch platform for stand-off weapons aimed at peripheral targets in North America. It is probably wrong to regard this aircraft as a cruise-missile carrier in the same class as the late-model B-52s. Although it is known to be developing such weapons, the Soviet Union is unlikely to produce an ALCM comparable with the American AGM-86B for some time. However, when a cruise missile capable of being launched outside the range of enemy air defenses does appear in the Soviet armory, it is likely that this new aircraft will be its carrier. Finally, the Soviet Union is believed to be working on an enhanced-range version of Backfire. If Backfire can be developed to attain an unrefueled range of 6000 miles, then it will be capable of true strategic missions against the United States.

The provision of a new tanker aircraft, while not presenting any of the formidable technical problems associated with the new strategic bomber, is also proceeding slowly. At present LRA relies on modified versions of the Bison and Badger for this necessary extension to the reach of its bomber force. Western sources believe that a tanker aircraft based on the Ilyushin Il-76 Candid transport is under development, but that its introduction has been delayed because of the pressing need for the military transport version. The wide-bodied Ilyushin Il-86 airliner has also been suggested as a possible basis for a tanker aircraft, on the lines of the McDonnell-Douglas KC-10 Extender version of the commercial DC-10. Whatever the future may hold for LRA, it is its medium range bomber force which at present represents the command's major contribution to Soviet military power. The spearpoint of this threat to Western Europe and the Far East is the Tu-26 Backfire bomber.

The capabilities of Backfire have been somewhat distorted by the United States' understandable wish to have it classed as an inter-continental system during the SALT process. It is true that if the Soviet Union wished to employ Backfire on strategic missions against the United States this could be accomplished, although at high risk. With inflight refueling and making use of Arctic staging bases Backfire could attack many targets in the eastern and central USA and land afterward at airfields in Cuba.

The exact extent of its coverage of United States targets would depend on how much of the mission was flown at high altitude, where fuel consumption would be most economical but the risk of interception very high. It is also doubtful whether bases in Cuba would remain immune from attack by the United States in the event of war with the Soviet Union.

The threat of Backfire to the rear areas of NATO and to the vital Atlantic re-supply route is so great that Soviet commanders may well regard its use against US targets as wasteful. Backfire is the only modern Soviet warplane that can cover all of the United Kingdom, operating at low level throughout the mission (a lo-lo-lo-profile) from bases in East Germany. Flying from bases farther east, it could execute the same mission, using a hi-lo-hi profile, with the high level points of the flight over low-risk areas. It can also range over much of the North Atlantic from bases in the Murmansk region, and it could pose as great a threat to NATO shipping as the Soviet attack submarines. The initial deployment of

Above: Supplanting the Minuteman II's single unit, the Minuteman III boasted three 165kt warheads.

Backfires supports this argument, in that deliveries have been divided equally between Long Range Aviation and the Naval Air Force. If Backfire was regarded as primarily a long-range strategic bomber, then deliveries to LRA would almost certainly have been given priority.

Span is 113ft with the wings unswept, reducing to 86ft in the fully-swept position and length is 132ft. Power is provided by two Kuznetsov NK-144 afterburning turbofans, giving 45,000lbs thrust each, and maximum takeoff weight is some 245,000lbs. Maximum speed varies from Mach 1.8 at 40,000ft to Mach 0.9 at sea level and range is some 5000 miles. Backfire is believed to carry a crew of four and has a defensive armament of two radar-directed 23mm cannon mounted in the tail. Its payload over a 5000 mile range is some 12,000lbs and weapons carried can include nuclear and conventional free-fall bombs, or stand-off missiles. Backfire has been photographed carrying one AS-4 Kitchen air-to-surface missile, but United States' intelligence sources credit it with the ability to carry two of these weapons, or two of the more advanced AS-6 Kingfish ASMs. A 745 mile range cruise missile reportedly under development by the Soviet Union would presumably be carried by Backfire.

As originally conceived the Tupolev Tu-22 Blinder was to replace the Tu-16 with LRA, but only about 170 were produced for the command. The Tu-22 was a victim of changing operational conditions, rather than a failure in its intended role. It was designed to operate at high altitude and have a supersonic dash capability to defeat the NATO interceptors and SAMs of the late 1950s. However, by the time the Tu-22 reached the bomber regiments it was clear that speed and altitude were no protection against contemporary air defense systems. Consequently production was curtailed and the Tu-16 has soldiered on with LRA until well past its allotted lifespan.

The Tu-22 is primarily armed with the AS-4 Kitchen stand-off weapon, although it also carries free-fall nuclear and conventional bombs. Its operating radius in the strike role is about 1750 miles. Crew comprises the pilot and two other members seated in tandem behind him. Defensive armament consists of a radar-directed 23mm cannon in the tail. The Blinder is a large aircraft for its class, its swept wing spanning 94ft 6in, overall length is 136ft 9in and maximum takeoff weight some 190,000lbs. Its maximum speed is Mach 1.5 at 36,000ft and service ceiling is 60,000ft. The engines, unusually mounted side-by-side high on the rear fuselage, are believed to be 31,000lbs thrust Kolesov VD-7 turbojets with afterburning. The ability of the Tu-22 to penetrate modern air defenses to any depth is extremely doubtful, but the bomber could be assigned to peripheral targets in Europe and it would fare much better over the People's Republic of China.

The mainstay of Long Range Aviation's theater nuclear capability (in terms of numbers of aircraft at least) remains the Tu-16 Badger. Although the type first flew 30 years ago, it still serves in its original medium-bomber role and also undertakes such tasks as inflight refueling, reconnaissance and electronic warfare. The Tu-16 can carry an 8000lb bomb load over a range of 3000 miles. The Badger-G variant carries two AS-5 Kelt ASMs over a 2000 mile range. Power is provided by two 19,200lb Mikulin AM-3M turbojets, giving the Tu-16 a maximum speed of 620mph, while service ceiling is 46,000ft. The Tu-16 carries a heavy defensive armament, comprising a fixed, forward-firing 23mm cannon in the nose, with paired weapons of the same caliber in a manned tail-turret and remotely-controlled ventral and dorsal barbettes. Dimensions of the Tu-16 include a span of 113ft 3in and a length of 120ft and maximum takeoff weight is 158,000lbs. Although such an elderly bomber is obviously not capable of surviving for long in the high-threat environment created by modern air defense systems, it is likely to soldier on in less dangerous operational areas for some time to come.

Although the two Superpowers hold a virtual monopoly of strategic nuclear forces, a number of second rank powers have a measure of nuclear capability. Britain has opted for a force of ballistic missile armed submarines at present armed with the American Polaris missile fitted with British nuclear warheads. This is to be replaced by the American Trident missile.

Until the early 1980s, the submarine force could be supported by six squadrons of Vulcan B Mk 2 bombers, which were part of Britain's strategic V-bomber force until superseded by Polaris in 1969. The Vulcans were thereafter retained in the strike/attack role, but by virtue of their long-range (some 4000 miles unrefueled at low level) and their ability to carry free-fall nuclear weapons, they are able to carry out theater strategic missions. With the introduction of the Panavia Tornado into front-line service with the RAF in 1982, the Vulcan squadrons were rapidly run down. The Tornado GR Mk 1 is primarily an interdictor/strike aircraft, but like its predecessor it can carry free-fall nuclear weapons and has the range to cover targets in the western part of the Soviet Union.

France's nuclear forces are divided between land and submarine based missiles and manned bombers. The bomber element of the Forces Aériennes Stratégiques comprises nearly 50 Mirages IVs, supported by eleven C-135F tanker aircraft. The bombers currently serve with the 91e Escadre de Bombardement with headquarters at Mont-de-Marsan and the 94e Escadre de Bombardement at Avord. Other bases are used by the component *escadrons* (of four aircraft each) to provide a degree of dispersal for the bombers. The C-135F tankers belong to the 93e Escadre de Ravitaillement en Vol with headquarters at Istres. Training is carried out by the Centre d'Instruction des Forces Aériennes Stratégiques No 328 at Merignac, which also carries out strategic reconnaissance with four Mirage IVAs fitted with CT-52 reconnaissance pods. The first production Mirage IVA first flew in December 1963 and delivery of 62 aircraft was completed in March 1968. A tail-less delta, like the smaller Mirage III fighter, the Mirage IVA spans 38ft 10in and length is 77ft 1in. Power is provided by a pair of SNECMA Atar 09K-50 turbojets, each delivering 15,400lbs thrust with afterburning. Maximum speed is Mach 2.2 at 60,000ft and service ceiling 65,000ft. Unrefueled range is 2500 nautical miles. The crew of two, pilot and navigator, are seated in tandem. In the strategic role a 60 kiloton free-fall nuclear weapon is carried semi-recessed in the underside of the fuselage. A conventional bomb load of 16,000lbs can be carried, or four AS37 Martel anti-radiation missiles, which operate by homing on enemy radar emissions.

Originally conceived as a high-level penetration bomber, the Mirage IVA has been modified to undertake low-level sorties. The importance of the manned bomber in the deterrent role has diminished with the build-up of the Navy's missile-armed submarine fleet. However the ASMP (air-sol moyenne portée) stand-off nuclear missile to be fitted to the aircraft from 1986 will extend its useful life into the 1990s. The ASMP's 60-mile range eases the task of target penetration and provides an interim theater nuclear system until the introduction of the Mirage IVA's successor. This is apparently not to be another manned bomber, despite

jammed or deceived by electronic countermeasures. Flares can be released to decoy heat-seeking infra-red missiles away from the bomber's jetpipes and radar-guided missiles can be similarly foiled by clouds of chaff. At one time SAC's B-52s carried the ADM-20 Quail, a miniature decoy aircraft that could be released from the bomber and present enemy radars with the same return signals as its parent. Ground based defense systems can be directly attacked by SRAM missiles and interceptors can be engaged by the bomber's defensive gun armament.

The stand-off weapon, or ASM, is one of the most effective means of attacking a heavily defended target area, as the attacking aircraft does not have to overfly its objective. Among the Soviet ASMs in service with LRA is the elderly AS-3 Kangaroo, which is carried by the Tu-20 Bear. This large missile, with a span of about

A Minuteman ICBM (above left) is loaded into its launch silo by crane. Operational missiles are carried to their silos in special transporters.

the suitability of the privately-developed Mirage 4000 for this role. The favored solution is a French-developed long-range cruise missile, or alternatively a mobile IRBM (intermediate range ballistic missile) with multiple warheads similar to the Soviet SS-20.

The People's Republic of China exploded its first nuclear weapon in 1964 and various strategic delivery systems have been developed. These include land-based ICBMs, IRBMs and MRBMs (medium range) and a submarine-launched system also. The primary manned bomber system is the B-6, a Chinese version of the Tu-16. Some 60-80 of these are believed to be in service and the type may still be in production.

A major factor affecting the design of strategic bombers and the development of their tactics is the need to evade hostile air defenses to reach the target. This requirement led to the introduction of low-level penetration tactics when medium and high altitude SAMs and interceptors made any other flight level unsafe for the bomber. The radars and communications which direct enemy interceptors and missiles can be

29ft and a length of 49ft, is in effect an unmanned, swept-wing fighter aircraft powered by a turbojet and guided by autopilot. It carries a nuclear warhead and has a range of some 400 miles. Accuracy is doubtful against all but the largest targets and the AS-3's cruising speed of Mach 2 would not provide immunity from interception.

The AS-4 Kitchen is a more advanced ASM, which arms the Tu-22 Blinder and Tu-26 Backfire. It is believed to be powered by a liquid rocket motor and cruises at Mach 2 over a range of about 200 miles. Guidance is believed to be inertial and a nuclear warhead is probably fitted. Information on the later AS-6 Kingfish is even more sparse, but it is thought to have a considerably improved performance and accuracy over the AS-4. It is inertially guided to its target and may have a terminal homing system. Cruising speed is Mach

3 over a range of up to 400 miles. The warhead yield is thought to be 200 kilotons.

The Boeing AGM-69A SRAM was the only stand-off weapon in service with SAC until late 1982. It is primarily intended as a defense suppression missile, punching a hole in the enemy air defenses which can then be penetrated by the bomber carrying its free-fall weapons. It carries a 200kt thermonuclear warhead, is powered by a solid-propellant rocket motor and has inertial guidance. SRAM is an agile and versatile missile – it can be programmed to follow a semi-ballistic flight path to its target, it can follow the terrain at low-level, or pull up from behind shielding terrain to dive onto its target. Its range depends on the way it is employed, but the maximum is a little over 100 miles. Speed is over Mach 3. Typical targets for SRAM would be Soviet air defense airfields, early-warning radar

A liquid-fueled Titan II blasts from its launch silo at Vandenberg AFB, California, where all USAF missile test firings take place.

255

sites, control centers and SAM batteries. It could also be employed against primary strategic targets.

A longer-ranging stand-off weapon than SRAM is now entering the strategic lists, after the Boeing AGM-86B ALCM entered service with the USAF's 416th BW at Griffiss AFB, NY during 1982. The cruise missile is by no means a new concept, as it can trace its ancestry back to the VI (Fieseler Fi 103) of World War II. During the 1950s the same idea produced such weapons as the US Navy's Regulus and the USAF's Matador, Mace and Snark, none of which was very successful.

There are three main reasons for the reappearance of the cruise missile, not only in its air-launched version, but also as a ground launched weapon and submarine and surface ship armament. The first is the development of TERCOM (*terrain contour matching*) an advanced navigational system, accurate over long distances. Second is the advance in powerplant technology, which makes a small light turbofan with economical fuel consumption a practical proposition. Finally there is the work of the nuclear physicists, who have produced a miniature nuclear warhead of high yield (200 kilotons). Soviet progress in these fields lags behind that of the United States and a Soviet equivalent to ALCM is some way off.

The Boeing AGM-86B ALCM is shaped like a miniature swept-wing aeroplane, spanning 12ft and with a length of 20ft 9in. It is powered by a 600lbs thrust William Research Corp F-107 turbofan, which gives a cruising speed of more than 500mph. The triangular-section fuselage houses the guidance system

and warhead in the forward section, with the powerplant to the rear and the fuel tank occupying much of the space between. The low-mounted 25 degree swept wing folds under the fuselage when the ALCM is mounted on its parent aircraft.

During its initial operational deployment the ALCM will be carried on the B-52G's wing pylons only. This gives a maximum load of 12, which will be increased by eight missiles when ALCM is carried by the internal rotary launcher. The B-1B's load of ALCMs is 14 carried externally and eight mounted in the weapons bay rotary launcher. A constraining factor in the original ALCM program was the need to accommodate the missile within the length of the B-1A's internal weapons bay. This restricted the size of the missile and consequently its range. However, with the cancellation of the B-1A this limitation was removed and the AGM-86A was superseded by the longer-ranging AGM-86B. With a range of some 1500 miles, this ALCM can attack some 85 percent of strategic targets in the Soviet Union when launched from a point beyond the effective coverage of the Soviet air defense umbrella. The need to cover the remaining 15 percent of strategic targets, and therefore for the launch aircraft to be capable of penetrating Soviet air defenses, has resulted in a cruise missile armament for the revived B-1B. The problem of accommodating the larger ALCMs in the bomber's weapons bays has been met by inserting a removeable bulkhead between the two forward bays, allowing them to be converted into a single bay long enough to house the AGM-86B.

The cruise missile depends on a combination of its small size (and therefore inconspicuous radar signature, which can be yet further reduced by Stealth techniques) and low operating altitude to evade enemy defenses. Unlike the manned bomber, it does not make use of ECM to degrade enemy air defense systems, although developments in automation and miniaturization may make this possible in the future. However, even if the Soviet Union develops radar and missiles with sufficiently accurate lookdown/shootdown characteristic to cope with these small targets, the defenses will be in danger of becoming swamped by sheer numbers. The cruise missile requirement for the B-52 force alone is estimated at 3400 rounds.

At the time of the B-1A's cancellation, the cruise missile was presented as a wonder weapon in comparison with the manned bomber which it would replace. The penetration capability of the latter was considered dubious whereas the cruise missile's ability to avoid interception was unquestioned. Wiser counsels have since prevailed and, with the rediscovery of the bomber's virtues, has come a recognition of the ALCM's limitations. As with ballistic missiles, they lack flexibility and cannot be retargeted after launch. Furthermore they will be unable to recognize and respond to threats from air defense systems. They do not have the speed of the ICBM (a flight time of under 30 minutes, compared with eight hours or more for ALCM), nor can they carry the large weapons load of a bomber. This is not to suggest that the advantages of the ALCM are illusory, but rather that it is a complement to existing systems; certainly not a weapon against which there is no defense.

After its launch at a distance of some 200 miles from the outer edge of the enemy air defense zone, the ALCM will cruise at an altitude of 5-10,000ft before descending to a terrain-following height of around 150ft. Guidance is by means of an inertial system, which is accurate over a short flight but will develop unacceptable errors during a typical ALCM mission. It is therefore periodically corrected by means of the TERCOM technique. This compares the terrain over which the missile flies with stored data, enabling course corrections to be made to bring the ALCM back to its precomputed flight path. Thus the ALCM can be guided to its target with great precision, as the degree of accuracy can be increased at every update of the navigational information. The final phase of the ALCM's flight is assisted by a scene-matching area correlator (SMAC). This carries information on the geography of the immediate target area, which is compared with that picked up by the ALCM's sensor and necessary last-minute corrections are made to the missile's flight path. Accuracy of the ALCM is such that CEP (circular error probable) is measured in tens of feet.

Before considering the land-based ballistic missiles which form such an important part of the strategic armory, airborne command, control and communications (C^3) deserve some mention. Essentially airborne command posts are back-up systems for SAC's land-based installations, which may be knocked out by missile attack. The aircraft used for this duty are EC-135 variants of the KC-135 tanker. Since 1961 a relay of EC-135 airborne command post aircraft has been continuously in the air carrying a battle staff under the command of a general officer. Named Project Looking Glass, this airborne command center is in communication with all the important national headquarters and with SAC bomber and missile forces. It can take over the control of strategic forces and order them into action, indeed Minuteman missiles can even be fired by controllers aboard the aircraft. EC-135s can also provide the basis for a Post Attack Command and Control System for forces surviving a nuclear attack. Similar aircraft also provide command posts for the Joint Chiefs of Staff, C-in-C Europe, C-in-C Atlantic and C-in-C Pacific.

A system of greater capacity is the E-4B national emergency airborne command post, which may carry the President of the United States. The E-4 airframe is essentially that of the Boeing 747 airliner, but it is fitted with an extensive array of equipment to suit it for the demanding role. This ranges from super-high frequency communications with satellites to very low frequency (VLF) radio links to submerged submarines. The E-4B can remain in the air for up to 72 hours, assuming that inflight refueling is available. Two complete flight crews will be carried and the command staff can number as many as 50 people. Four of these aircraft are now based at Andrews Air Force Base, Maryland, close to Washington DC.

The US Navy makes use of specially modified Lockheed Hercules (EC-130G and EC-130Q variants) as communications relays to its SLBM-armed submarine fleets. These aircraft carry the Collins TACAMO (take command and move out) VLF radio systems, which can relay orders to submerged submarines. This is essentially a back-up system for shore installations, but it is considered sufficiently important to justify having at least one aircraft continually available. The EC-130Q is operated by Navy squadron VQ-3 based at Agana, Guam, in the Pacific. The Atlantic is covered by VQ-4, which flies EC-130Gs and EC-130Qs from Patuxent River, Maryland.

The firmest leg of the US strategic triad has long been considered to be the land-based ICBM. This weapon has enjoyed several important advantages over the SLBM and the bomber/cruise missile. It is more accurate than present SLBMs and does not have the same problems of C^3. Its flight time is considerably less than that of the bomber and its effectiveness should not be dependent on advanced warning of enemy attack. Furthermore present missile systems are very reliable,

with few vehicles unavailable because of unscheduled maintenance requirements. However, with the long-delayed deployment of MX (scheduled to be fully deployed by 1989) a 'window of vulnerability' has been judged to have opened over the US ICBM force. This is because the Soviet Strategic Rocket Forces are claimed to be fast developing the capability of knocking-out the US missile force in a pre-emptive first strike.

SAC's current ICBM force comprises 1000 Boeing LGM-30 Minuteman missiles and 53 elderly Martin LGM-25C Titan II missiles.

The present Minuteman force is made up of two models. The LGM-30F Minuteman II carries a single thermo-nuclear warhead, whereas the LGM-30G Minuteman III has three multiple, independently-targeted re-entry vehicles (MIRVs). There are 450 Minuteman IIs in service and 550 Minuteman IIIs, but the latter force may be reduced as MX comes into service to keep within the warhead limits imposed by SALT.

Both models of Minuteman stand 59ft 10in high and have a maximum diameter of 6ft. Minuteman II weighs 70,000lbs at launch, and Minuteman III is 6000lbs heavier. Both are three-stage missiles, with solid propellant rocket fuel. However Minuteman III has a larger third-stage and its post-boost guidance system associated with the MIRV is powered by a liquid-fueled rocket. Range of Minuteman II is 7000 miles and Minuteman III's range is 8000 miles. Minuteman II's warhead has a yield of between one and two megatons and Minuteman III's warheads yield 165 kilotons each. Minuteman II became operational in 1965 and was joined by Minuteman III five years later.

Minuteman silos, 80ft deep, are clustered in groups of ten, which are controlled from a single center crewed by two officers. A separation of at least three miles is needed between each silo and also the launch control center. A number of improvements to the missile system are designed to enhance survivability and improve accuracy.

The modernization plans for SAC's ICBM force have proved to be a matter of considerable controversy. The Reagan administration intends to procure 200 MGM-118A Peacekeeper missiles. Each Peacekeeper is fitted with ten independently targetable warheads of 350 kiloton yield. However, the preferred basing mode for the missile, the closely-spaced basing system, failed to win Congressional approval. This system involved the emplacing of the missiles in superhardened silos, each 1800 ft from its neighbor, to create a missile field 14 miles long and one mile across. It was calculated that this arrangement would ensure the survival of eighty percent of the Peacekeepers, because the first Soviet warheads to detonate on target would destroy the following warheads, or at any rate knock them off course (a phenomenon known as 'fratricide'). Each silo would have to be individually targeted to ensure its destruction and the precision

needed to ensure simultaneous detonation of 100 warheads on target was considered to be beyond Soviet capabilities. However, the theory of 'fratricide' was not universally accepted by informed opinion.

As funding could not be obtained from Congress for the MX program as originally proposed, President Reagan appointed a commission under the Chairmanship of General Scowcroft to report on the question of ICBM survivability. The commission's recommendations, accepted by the President in 1983, were that deployment of 100 MX missiles should go ahead in the near future in superhardened silos, but not closely spaced. The commission did not believe that the threat to silo-based missiles would become serious for some years and that at any rate the other two legs of the strategic Triad would survive a first strike. However, it proposed that this threat should be countered by developing and deploying a small and mobile, single-warhead ICBM. Officially known as the SICBM (small intercontinental ballistic missile), but more often referred to as the Midgetman, the new missile should become operational by 1993. Its weight should be about 30,000 lb, but a heavier missile may be produced if guidance accuracy is poorer than anticipated and a heavier warhead needed. Current plans call for a force of 1000 Midgetmen to be deployed in the early 1990s.

Left: The USAF's new Peacemaker missile, scheduled to enter service in the late 1980s.
Below: A Soviet ICBM is pictured in its launch silo.

The USSR, like the USA, regards its ICBM force as the most important weapon in its strategic armory. Much effort has been expended on building up the ICBM force, both qualitatively and in numbers and by the early 1980s it was generally agreed that the Soviet Union had achieved strategic parity with the United States.

Soviet Union had in the mid 1980s deployed a total of about 1500 ICBMs, of which over half were modern, fourth-generation missiles (SS-17s, SS-18s and SS-19s), the remainder being the older, third-generation SS-11s and SS-13s.

The SS-11 Sego (these identifications are NATO reporting names not Soviet designations) has been in service since 1966 and was deployed in large numbers during the 1970s. A program is underway to convert SS-11 silos to accommodate the SS-19 Mod 3, but it is likely to take several years to complete. SS-11 is a two-stage missile fueled with storable liquid propellant. It has a launch weight of some 106,000lbs and its range is an estimated 6500 miles. The original version could carry a single warhead, either of 500 kiloton yield or alternatively in the 20-25 megaton range. The later SS-11 Mod 3 carried a multiple re-entry vehicle (MRV) with three 300 kiloton warheads, although these were not independently targetable but fell in a pre-determined pattern.

The SS-13 Savage is believed to be the first Soviet ICBM to have solid-fuel rocket motors. It is a three-stage missile with a launch weight of some 77,000lbs. Range is around 5000 miles and a single warhead of one megaton yield is carried. SS-13 entered service in 1968 and a successor, the SS-16 was developed but never deployed.

Together with the SS-19, the SS-17 ICBM is a successor to the SS-11 and has been mounted in former SS-11 silos. It has a launch weight of some 143,000lbs and a range of more than 6000 miles. It is a two-stage liquid fueled rocket which is 'cold launched', which means that the missile is ejected from its silo by compressed gas and the rocket motor ignited above ground. This technique minimizes damage to the silo during launch and enables it to be rapidly reloaded with a second missile. The SS-17 Mod 1 carries four MIRV warheads, but most deployed missiles are SS-17 Mod 2s with a single high yield warhead. This suggests that SS-17 has sufficient accuracy to be used in a counter-force role against US ICBM silos.

The largest missile in the world, SS-18 combines a high payload with a greater accuracy than earlier Soviet missiles. It is a two-stage, cold launched missile, with a launch weight of around 485,000lbs and a range of 7500 miles. Four variants have been identified, Mod 1 having a single warhead of 24 megaton yield and a CEP of 1300ft. Mod 2 has eight to ten MIRVs and CEP is the

The US Army's Pershing I battlefield nuclear delivery system is now due for replacement by longer-range Pershing IIs and Ground Launched Cruise Missiles.

same as Mod 1. Mod 3 has a greater range than earlier SS-18s and improved accuracy (CEP is 1250ft). Mod 4 shows a further improvement in range, carries ten 500 kiloton MIRVs and has a CEP of 850ft.

SS-19 is reckoned to be the most effective of the fourth-generation Soviet ICBMs. It is a two-stage liquid-fueled rocket with a launch weight of 172,000lbs and a range of more than 6000 miles. Three versions have appeared in service, but the Mod 3 appears to be definitive and earlier missiles are being modified to this configuration. Little is known of the Mod 3's warhead, except that it is made up of MIRVs. The earlier Mod 1 carries six 550 kiloton MIRVs and the Mod 2 a single warhead. Two new Soviet ICBMs are reported to be approaching the flight test stage and could be deployed by the mid-1980s. One is an SS-17-class missile to be deployed in super-hardened silos. The other is mobile and of similar size to MX. Both use solid fuel. A third development is believed to be a large liquid-fueled ICBM in the same class as the SS-18.

One of the lesser nuclear powers, China, has developed ICBMs. However, their operational status is doubtful, but the limited range (3500 nautical miles) CSS-3 is believed to be in an advanced state of development and some sources claim a few are now in service. The later CSS-4 is a true ICBM with 6000 mile range and a five megaton yield warhead. The CSS-4 can reach targets throughout the USA and some may be operational. Yet the Soviet Union is China's chief potential antagonist and the CSS-3 has sufficient range to cover any Soviet target.

Another element in the strategic equation which is sometimes overlooked is those parts of the theater nuclear forces which are theater strategic rather than tactical nuclear systems. However the distinction is not a clearcut one and many weapons can operate in both roles. For example the Soviet SS-4, SS-5 and SS-20 IRBMs and Tu-16, Tu-22 and Tu-26 bombers fall into this category. Similar NATO weapons include Ground Launched Cruise Missile (GLCM) and Pershing II, both now deployed in Europe, and F-111, Tornado and Jaguar strike aircraft.

SS-20 is a formidable mobile missile, which carries three MIRVs and can cover any NATO target in Western Europe. More than 260 had been deployed by the beginning of 1982 according to US official sources. The following year, NATO deployed the Pershing II and GLCM in Britain and Europe. It was feared the Soviet Union was gaining a superiority in theater nuclear forces which would deter NATO commanders from using their tactical nuclear weapons to blunt a Soviet attack for fear of Soviet retaliation in kind against strategic targets in Europe. The modernization of NATO's theater nuclear forces should restore the nuclear balance within the European theater and remove the unacceptable constraints on NATO's defensive plans which a Soviet superiority in 'Euro-strategic' weapons could create.

An A-10A Thunderbolt II of the UK-based 81st TFW tests his 'decelerons' before flying a sortie from one of the Wing's forward operating locations in West Germany. Decelerons are ailerons which also hinge upwards as shown to act as aerodynamic brakes.

TACTICAL COMBAT

The ability of aircraft to intervene in the land battle constitutes one of the most important roles in air warfare and a large proportion of the NATO and Warsaw Pact air forces are assigned to this task. Air forces by virtue of their speed and flexibility can help to blunt a Soviet blitzkrieg-style attack on NATO's Central Front while ground forces are still deploying to their defensive positions. The Soviet assault will likewise be accompanied by air attacks on NATO front-line forces and their rear areas. Both sides will attempt to control the air space over the battlefield to facilitate their own ground and air operations and to deny enemy aircraft the opportunity of influencing the land battle. Interdiction missions will be flown deep into enemy territory in an attempt to isolate the battlefield from reinforcement and resupply.

The operations of tactical air forces can be classified into three main areas of activity. Interdiction and tactical nuclear strike are carried out by long range attack aircraft with the ability to penetrate deep into the enemy's rear areas. The targets for interdiction aircraft will include transport systems, supply dumps and military formations moving to the battle area. Nuclear strike will be a last ditch defense, when conventional means have failed. Counter-air and air superiority missions will be directed against the enemy air forces, either on their own airfields or in the air. Similarly ground-based air defense systems including SAMs, AA artillery and their associated radars and support equipment will be attacked by specialized defense suppression aircraft, or alternatively they will be neutralized by ECM equipment. Finally the troops in contact with the enemy can call on direct close air support from ground-attack aircraft and they will be further assisted by battlefield interdiction sorties farther to the rear.

The USAF maintains a large tactical fighter force, which is assigned to Tactical Air Command (TAC) based in the United States, with additional reinforcement available from units of the Air National Guard (ANG) and Air Force Reserve (AFRES). Tactical fighter wings also serve with US Air Force in Europe (USAFE) and Pacific Air Forces (PACAF). These forces may be deployed anywhere in the world at short notice and consequently all tactical fighters are equipped for inflight refueling. Their supporting tanker aircraft are drawn from SAC assets, but TAC does control its own tactical reconnaissance, forward air control (FAC) and airborne warning and control aircraft and special operations units are also assigned.

According to the US Joint Chiefs of Staff military posture statement in 1982 the strength of the tactical fighter force was equivalent to 24 active wings and 12 reserve wings (in fact the strength on paper appears to be greater). The main aircraft types in service were the F-111 all-weather interdiction aircraft (240 on strength), F-15 Eagle air superiority fighter (396), F-16 Fighting Falcon multirole fighter (276), F-4 Phantom

A pair of F-15 Eagle air superiority fighters of TAC's 1st TFW (above) fly from their base at Langley, Va. The F-16 (inset) comes from the 388th TFW, Hill AFB, Utah.

II multirole fighter (792), A-10 Thunderbolt II attack aircraft (444) and A-7 Corsair II attack aircraft (324). Tactical air power in Europe will be augmented by some 3000 tactical aircraft of NATO Allied nations.

The Soviet equivalent of TAC is Frontal Aviation, the largest command within the Soviet air force with a front-line strength of some 4800 combat aircraft plus transports and helicopters. Soviet doctrine emphasises the co-ordination of all arms as the key to success in modern warfare and this is reflected in close links between Frontal Aviation and the ground forces it supports. Frontal Aviation is composed of 16 air armies, which are attached to the 12 military districts of the USSR and to the Soviet forces in Czechoslovakia, East Germany, Hungary and Poland. The air armies are made up of divisions, each of which fulfills a specific role such as close air support. The regiment is the basic operational unit and each flies a single aircraft type. There are usually three regiments to a division and the

regiment is made up of three squadrons each with some 18 aircraft. Air armies can vary widely in strength, with the 16th Army attached to the Group of Soviet Forces in Germany fielding 1000 aircraft in contrast to the 5th Army's strength of only 100 in the Kiev Military District. The heaviest concentration is of course on the central sector of the European theater.

The 1970s saw the transformation of Frontal Aviation from a force equipped for defensive counter-air missions, with a secondary close support role, to a more balanced tactical air force with greatly increased offensive capabilities. The numerical and qualitative improvements to Frontal Aviation's forces, together with an increasing emphasis on offensive missions against NATO ground and air forces, represent an enhancement of the Soviet Union's military capability which is every bit as significant as the far more publicized expansion of the Soviet Navy.

The key to Frontal Aviation's greatly expanded capabilities has been provided by two significant new combat aircraft – the MiG-23/27 Flogger family and the Su-24 Fencer – and also by modification to older designs. There are some 1400 Floggers operational with

Frontal Aviation and these include both Flogger-B and G air superiority fighters and Flogger-D and F ground attack fighters. Almost as numerous are late-model MiG-21 Fishbeds (1300) which are all-weather air superiority fighters, with secondary ground attack capabilities. Since its service introduction in 1959 as a clear-weather, short-range point-defense fighter, the MiG-21 has been continually upgraded to improve its all-weather and payload/range capabilities. Another example of the evolutionary process is provided by the Su-17 Fitter-C, D and H (650 operational). These are variable-geometry modifications of the earlier fixed, swept-wing Su-7 Fitter-A (200 remain in service). Finally there are some 400 of the formidable (by Soviet standards) Su-24 Fencer interdiction aircraft, which can cover targets throughout most of Western Europe.

In addition to its tactical fighter aircraft, Frontal Aviation controls a large force of battlefield helicopters and has its own reconnaissance, transport and ECM support aircraft. Nearly 70 percent of Frontal Aviation's units are deployed in Europe or the western USSR, where there are a large number of airfields to accommodate them. This is in contrast to the NATO powers, which face an acute shortage of military airfields (for example RAF Germany operates from only four). The Soviet Union is supported (but with what degree of enthusiasm is open to doubt) by her Warsaw Pact allies. They can add some 2400 tactical aircraft to the Soviet strength, but many are elderly and their greatest contribution is likely to be the air defense of rear areas against NATO interdiction aircraft.

Isolation of the battlefield from reinforcement and resupply by interdiction of enemy lines of communication is an attractive aim. In practice it has often proved very difficult to accomplish, as the USAF campaign against the Ho Chi Minh Trail during the Vietnam War bears witness. However in a European war transport targets will be more vulnerable and even a comparatively short delay in feeding reinforcements into the battle area may prove to be crucial. The Soviet army is especially vulnerable in this respect, as its divisions have less staying power than their NATO equivalents and Soviet doctrine requires that they be replaced regularly by fresh divisions from the rear. Therefore any disruption of roads, railways, bridges or staging areas may result in the attack losing momentum.

Interdictor aircraft will be employed on offensive counter-air missions against enemy airfields. They can also directly attack reinforcements moving up to the battle area. These troops are likely to be less prepared to meet air attack than those already deployed. SAM and AA fire will be less intense and forces on the move will offer a better target than those dispersed over the battlefield.

Although NATO's strategy is one of 'flexible response', so that a conventional (i.e. non-nuclear) attack will be met at first with conventional defenses, it is becoming increasingly recognized that NATO's

Above: MiG-23 Flogger tactical fighters overfly Warsaw Pact forces.
Above right: The Panavia Tornado is designed for low level interdiction.
Right: The versatile F-4 Phantom fighter in USAF service.

numerical inferiority may force the alliance into the use of tactical nuclear weapons to stem a Soviet breakthrough. Whether the Soviet marshals would countenance the first use of nuclear weapons to precipitate the collapse of NATO forces on the central front is open to doubt. They certainly appear to show little reluctance in contemplating fighting in a nuclear, bacteriological or chemical (NBC) warfare environment. Whatever the imponderables about the use of such weapons, it is certain that many NATO and Warsaw Pact aircraft can use them. They include the Soviet Su-24 Fencer, Su-17 Fitter and MiG-27 Flogger. NATO nuclear-capable aircraft are the F-111, F-4, Jaguar, Tornado and F-104.

The characteristics generally demanded of an interdiction/strike aircraft are good range and payload, the ability to evade air defenses by flying at low level and following the contours of the terrain and the capability of operating in all weather conditions. The pre-eminent example of such a warplane in the USAF's armory is the General Dynamics F-111. The F-111 was designed to

meet a controversial requirement, calling for a multi-role aircraft to undertake close air support and interdiction for the USAF combined with fleet air defense for the US Navy. In the event only the interdiction version entered service, together with the FB-111 strategic bomber.

The F-111 is a two-seat, variable-geometry wing fighter-bomber, powered by two Pratt & Whitney TF-30 afterburning turbofans. The variable-sweep wing enables the F-111 to operate from relatively short runways, yet it can reach supersonic speed at low altitude and Mach 2.5 above 60,000ft. In the fully-developed F-111F version the powerplants are TF-30-P100 turbofans each developing 25,100lbs of thrust with afterburning. Takeoff weight is 85,000lbs and the aircraft can carry a 6000lb bomb load over a combat radius of 1000 nautical miles. Alternatively a maximum warload of 24,000lbs can be lifted to a radius of 350 nautical miles. All tactical versions of the F-111 span 63ft (unswept), with a length of 73ft 5in and a 20mm M-61A Vulcan rotary cannon is standard armament.

There are four tactical versions of the F-111 in service with the USAF, plus the strategic FB-111. The F-111A was the initial production version for TAC and 86 remain in service. This version forms the basis of the EF-111A ECM aircraft, 42 of which are to be rebuilt

The US GBU-15 electro-optically guided glide bomb (above) makes possible precision attack from stand-off ranges.

from F-111A airframes. The B model was to have been the US Navy's fighter and the C is a variant of the A supplied to the Royal Australian Air Force. The F-111D, E and F all incorporated progressive improvements to the powerplants and navigation and attack avionics. Further upgrading is in prospect (including improvements to offensive and defensive avionics and provision of more advanced weapons) to keep the F-111 fully effective into the 1990s.

The process of improving the F-111's target acquisition and weapons capability has already begun, with the introduction of the Pave Tack weapons aiming system which is used in conjunction with such precision-guided munitions (PGM) as the GBU-15 glide bomb and Maverick TV-guided ASM. Pave Tack is a pod containing a forward-looking infra-red (FLIR) system, which presents the weapons system officer with a picture of the target area by day or night. He can then acquire his target and release weapons against it, further assisted by the Pave Tack pod's laser range-finder and designator.

The USAF's second interdictor strike aircraft is the ubiquitous F-4 Phantom multi-role fighter. Although a less capable aircraft in the specialized interdiction role (combat radius with 6000lbs of bombs is 350 nautical miles, compared with the F-111's 1000nm radius with the same load), the F-4 is available in greater numbers.

However this classic fighter is now past its prime and is being replaced by the General Dynamics F-16 in the tactical fighter wings. A specialized and much modified strike version, the F-16E, is competing with the F-15E to meet the USAF's requirement for a new attack aircraft. Another possible contender is the highly-secret Lockheed CSIRS (covert survivable in-weather reconnaissance/strike) fighter, which uses Stealth technology. However this is at present a high-risk research program, with only 20 aircraft in prospect. The US Navy can also take part in an interdiction campaign with its carrier-based Grumman A-6E Intruders.

America's NATO allies contribute to the Alliance's interdiction/strike capabilities, notably with the Panavia Tornado, which in 1982 began to enter service with the air arms of the UK, Germany and Italy. In the RAF, Tornado GR Mk 1s replaced the six squadrons of Vulcan B Mk 2 bombers scheduled to disband in 1982 and will supplement the Buccaneer S Mk 2 force. The Buccaneer was originally a shipboard strike/attack aircraft which was pressed into RAF service to fill a gap created by the cancellation of the TSR-2 and F-111K programs. It has proved to be extremely successful, although one unforeseen setback was the grounding of the entire force in 1980 due to fatigue problems. This has resulted in the numbers in service being reduced. Despite its age (first flight 1958) the Buccaneer is a stable, maneuverable and relatively fast (Mach 0.9) weapons platform for interdiction/strike at low level and its payload/range characteristics are impressive. Buccaneers have recently been given a measure of self-defense capability by the fitting of Westinghouse AN/ALQ-101 ECM jamming pods and Sidewinder AAMs. Their weapons load of 16,000lbs can include Paveway laser guided bombs.

Yet it is the Tornado which will give the NATO European allies a significant ability to carry out long range interdiction/strike. With the RAF it will upgrade an existing force, but for West Germany and Italy it represents a new capability in comparison with the Lockheed F-104 Starfighter which it will replace. The UK requirement is for 220 Tornado GR Mk 1 interdictor/strike aircraft, with a further 165 Tornado F Mk 2 air defense interceptors. West Germany needs 212 aircraft for the Luftwaffe and 112 for the Navy's maritime attack squadrons, while Italy plans to acquire a total of 100. By late 1984 400 had been delivered, with the manufacturing workload being divided amongst the three participating nations. Conversion training is also a co-operative effort and the Trinational Tornado Training Establishment has been set up at Cottesmore in the UK.

Tornado is a compact, variable-geometry aircraft, which accommodates a crew of two seated in tandem. Power is provided by two efficient and economical Turbo-Union RB.199 turbofans, each giving 16,000lbs thrust with afterburning. Wingspan (in the fully forward position) is 45ft 7in and length 54ft 9in, with maximum loaded weight 58,400lbs. Maximum speed ranges from Mach 1.1 at low level to Mach 2.2 above 60,000ft. Tactical radius flying a lo-lo-lo profile is 450 miles and external weapons load is 16,000lbs. A built-in armament of two 27mm Mauser cannon is standard. The landing run is impressively short at some 500ft. Tornado therefore combines performance and agility with the range/payload characteristics usually associated with far more staid aircraft.

A very comprehensive and sophisticated avionics fit assists the Tornado crew. The heart of the system is a central computer, which can store navigational and mission data and display it on request. Navigational aids include an inertial system and doppler radar. A terrain-following radar allows the aircraft to fly at high speed and low level automatically maintaining a pre-determined height (typically 200ft) above the ground. There is also a ground mapping attack radar, which provides pilot and navigator with computer processed information. The final stages of the attack are facilitated by a nose-mounted laser rangefinder. Weapons release can be automatically controlled by the central computer. Finally much of the turbulence and buffeting associated with low level flying is damped out by the

Tornado's Command and Stability Augmentation System.

A low flying Tornado will present a difficult target to enemy air defenses, and their problems will be compounded by the aircraft's ECM equipment, which includes a radar warning receiver, Sky Shadow jamming pods and chaff and flare dispensers. Tornado also has teeth and an unwary Soviet interceptor could find himself on the receiving end of its 27mm cannon or AIM-9L Sidewinder missiles. A wide range of offensive armament may also be carried, embracing free fall conventional and nuclear bombs, PGMs, anti-armor and anti-radar missiles, the RAF's JP233 anti-airfield cluster bomblet dispenser and the Luftwaffe's similar MW-1 weapon.

Frontal Aviation's interdiction/strike fighter, the Sukhoi Su-24 Fencer, is in many ways a smaller and lighter version of the F-111, although it is less technologically advanced. It is the first Soviet tactical fighter to carry a second crewmember and this reflects an increased emphasis on all-weather capability and weapons' management over such ground attack aircraft as the MiG-27. The Su-24 is the least known of the present generation of Soviet warplanes and perhaps for this reason it has become as much of a 'bogey' in the minds of Western defense planners as has Backfire.

Fencer has a variable-geometry wing, with a sweep-back angle of 16 degrees in the full-forward position, increasing to 68 degrees when fully swept. Span with wings in the forward position is 56ft 10in and length 72ft 10in, with takeoff weight being in the region of 65,000lbs. Power is provided by two afterburning turbofans, which produce an estimated 19,500lbs of thrust each. Performance includes a maximum speed of Mach 2 at 36,000ft reducing to Mach 1.2 at sea level, with combat radius in the order of 700 miles (assuming a hi-lo-hi profile). The two crew members are seated side-by-side in a rather cramped forward cockpit, with an attack and probably a terrain-following radar in the nose. A feature of the design is the rugged under-carriage, optimized for operations from short, rough forward airfields. The built-in armament consists of a twin-barrel GSh-23 23mm cannon and there are seven external hardpoints, but no internal bay. Weapons load is some 12,500lbs and may be made up of free-fall bombs or ASMs, including AS-7, AS-9, AS-11 or AS-12. AA-2 Atoll and AA-8 Aphid AAMs can be carried.

By making use of economical hi-lo-hi flight profiles, operating from forward bases and reducing its weapons load to 4000lbs, Fencer is able to operate over most of Continental Europe and much of the UK, particularly the important concentration of USAF and RAF air bases in East Anglia. Yet it is the classic interdiction targets which Fencer is most likely to seek out and thus fill the gap between the MiG-27 Flogger operating over the battlefield and the long-ranging Backfire.

The successful accomplishment of interdiction, counter-air, defense suppression or close-air support

The F-111 fighter-bomber provides the USAF with a formidable
all-weather attack capability (below). An F-111D of the 27th
TFW (Left) releases Mk 82 practice bombs. A SEPECAT Jaguar
tactical fighter of the Armée de l'Air maneuvers at low level
(below left).

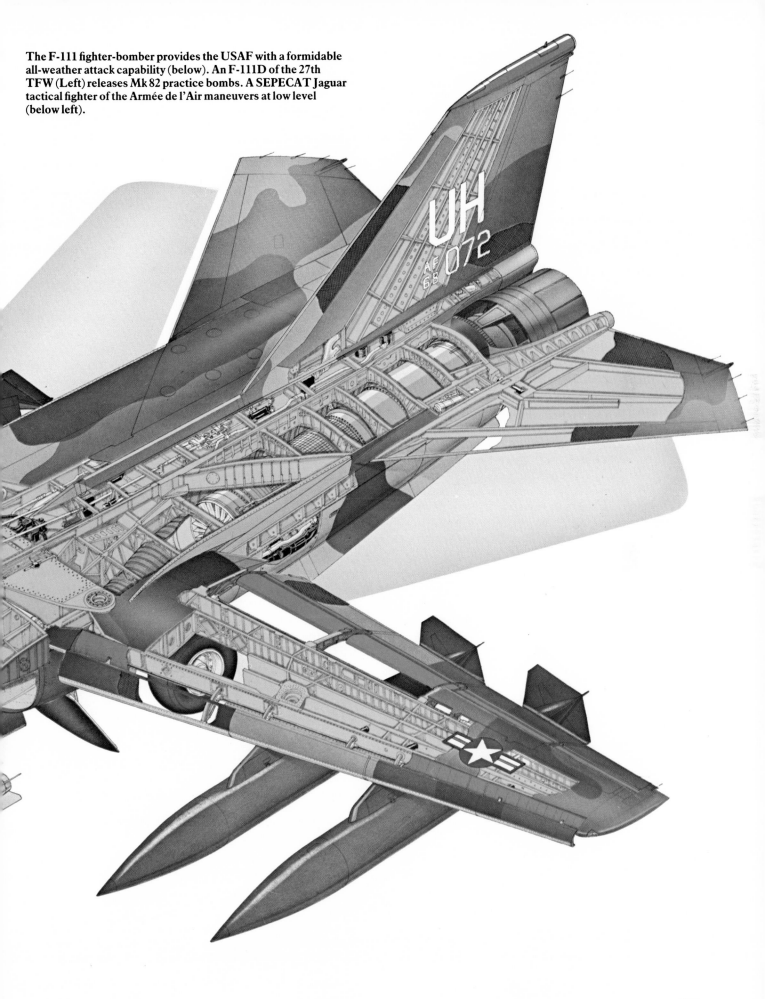

missions depends as much on the weapons employed as on the aircraft carrying them. There is a bewildering array of such weapons in service, both conventional and nuclear, although there is little information on the nuclear systems. The free-fall bomb is still in widespread use and the US Mk 80 series of low-drag, general purpose, high explosive bombs is in many ways typical. They are available in four main classes: the Mk 81 of 250lbs, the Mk 82 of 500lbs, the Mk 83 of 1000lbs and the Mk 84 of 2000lbs. The Mk 81, 82, and 83 can be fitted with a retarding tail device (when they are known as Snakeye bombs) which enables them to be released at low level without ricocheting off target or damaging the releasing aircraft in the blast. Fuzing can also be varied according to the mission, the options including proximity, for an airburst over the target, instantaneous on impact, or short and long delays.

Alternatives to high-explosive bombs include firebombs and cluster bomb units (CBUs). The latter are dispensers filled with a large number of small munitions, which on release are scattered over a wide area. They are thus very effective against dispersed targets. CBUs can be loaded with antitank, antipersonnel or antimateriel munitions, according to the anticipated target. This idea has been extended to large dispenser pods attached to the aircraft which eject submunitions. The RAF's JP233 anti-airfield weapon is such a system, dispensing both concrete-penetrating submunitions and antipersonnel devices to hamper repair work. West Germany's MW-1 is similar, but it is a multi-purpose weapon and can be most effective against enemy tank concentrations.

Unguided rockets, because they can be fired in salvos, have a high probability of hitting a target on the first firing pass. They are usually carried in pods, in the case of the US 2.75in FFAR (folding fin aircraft rocket) holding seven or 19 rockets. Warheads can be antitank, fragmentation, smoke (for target marking) or white phosphorous.

Despite the number and variety of unguided weapons in current use, it is the precision-guided munition that has made the greatest impact on modern air warfare. Laser and electro-optically guided bombs have made possible a hitherto unprecedented degree of precision in tactical bombing. This is perhaps best illustrated by an episode in the Vietnam War. The Thanh Hoa bridge had defied the best efforts of US strike aircraft to destroy it since 1965, but when laser-guided bombs were used against it in 1972 the bridge was severely damaged during the first attack. The Paveway family of laser-guided bombs and Walleye TV-guided glide bomb are both in US service. They are to be followed by the GBU-15 glide bomb, which may have TV or imaging infra-red guidance which is not dependent on good light conditions.

The 'stand-off' capability of glide bombs is particularly useful against heavily defended targets. Significantly the USAF pulled out of the JP233 program

(which was to have been a joint UK/US venture) because it disliked the attacking aircraft having to overfly its target. The answer to this problem is the air-to-surface missile, which has a better stand-off capability than the glide bomb, but it is also far more expensive. The widely-used Hughes AGM-65 Maverick has a range of some 14 miles and can use TV, laser or imaging infra-red guidance. An altogether more specialized ASM is the anti-radiation missile, such as the Shrike or Standard ARM, which homes onto radar emissions. It is particularly useful for defense suppression and an advanced new missile, the AGM-88 HARM (high-speed ARM) is being developed. Other interesting new lines of development include the Wasp millimeter-wave radar guided mini-missile for anti-armor use, which can be carried in 12 round pods and the laser-guided Hypervelocity missile, which relies on kinetic energy rather than a conventional warhead to knock-out the enemy tank.

Little is known about Soviet developments in PGMs although it is reported that Frontal Aviation has laser-guided bombs in service. Tactical ASMs include the radio-command guided AS-7 Kerry, with a range of six miles. Soviet aircraft are also armed with bombs and unguided rockets and Frontal Aviation almost certainly also uses chemical and bacteriological weapons (the US holds stocks of nerve-gas bombs as a deterrent).

However destructive a weapon may be, it will be of little use unless it is delivered accurately and therefore navigational and aiming systems are of great importance in attack aircraft. All-weather operations are particularly demanding in this respect. Radar provides much of the information needed, including ground mapping, terrain avoidance, height above terrain and the acquisition, tracking and ranging of ground targets. However radar emissions can betray the presence of the attacking aircraft and they may also be jammed. So various alternative navigation/attack systems are under development, including millimetric radar, which is harder to detect and jam than the current radars operating on centimetric wavelengths.

Infra-red imaging equipment can provide a TV-type picture of the landscape in virtually all weathers, although cloud and rain will degrade its performance. The US LANTIRN (low altitude navigation and targeting infra-red system for night) is being developed to provide single-seat F-16 and A-10 aircraft with all-weather attack capability. It combines FLIR with a terrain-following radar and laser target designation. Low-light level television (LLTV) can perform the same function as FLIR on a clear night, but it would be even more affected by adverse weather. Inertial navi-

F-16A tactical fighters of the 56th TFW fly in echelon formation (above right). The F-15 Eagles (right) are much heavier and more powerful, although both fighters undertake the air superiority role. The A-10A attack aircraft can locate targets marked by laser, using the Pave Penny tracker (far right).

gation systems can direct an aircraft to a predetermined target with no external source of reference. The aircraft's starting point is precisely determined and fed into a computer, all subsequent movement is recorded by sensors and information on the aircraft's position and directions to the target or to a 'waypoint' are displayed to the crew.

Weapons aiming systems rely on a computer to calculate the impact point for bombs, rockets or gunfire, taking account of the velocity of the attacking aircraft, the slant range to the target, the aircraft's attitude in flight and the ballistic characteristics of the weapons. Most modern attack aircraft make use of laser rangefinders and targets can also be marked by laser for attack by laser-guided weapons. Laser designation can be used by ground controllers to indicate a target for attack by PGMs, unguided or 'dumb' bombs, rocket or cannon fire during close air support sorties. Target

indication, weapons release instructions and steering commands are projected onto a head-up display (HUD), which is basically similar to the traditional gunsight, but provides the pilot with navigational and flight instrument data as well as weapons release instructions. Thus the pilot can complete his attack without having to look down into the cockpit for essential information.

The air superiority – or counter-air mission, as it is often called – is crucial to the successful conduct of tactical air warfare. Air superiority forces seek to gain a sufficient degree of domination over their opponents to allow friendly air and ground operations to be carried on without undue interference. The virtual destruction of the enemy's aircraft and weapons systems is an ideal that is seldom achieved – the 1967 Arab-Israeli War being a rare instance, accomplished by an Israeli pre-emptive attack in the opening hours of the conflict. In

practice, however, air superiority operations will be much more localized both in time and space, for example seeking to provide cover for a newly-established bridgehead during a river crossing, or clearing the path for a force of attack aircraft. A certain amount of enemy air activity must perforce be tolerated, but it cannot be allowed to deflect air or ground forces from their objectives.

The air superiority fighter may be called on to escort a force of attack aircraft or to patrol over a sector of the battlefield and its rear areas to keep the skies clear of enemy aircraft. It therefore requires good range or endurance. As it is required to engage high-performance enemy aircraft in air-to-air combat, it must be agile and fast. Finally as its primary role is air combat it must be heavily armed with AAMs and cannon. Not all air superiority fighters follow this design philosophy, which is particularly hard to fulfil satisfactorily because

the demands of endurance and performance are to a large extent conflicting. An entirely different view of the air superiority fighter is exemplified by such aircraft as the Soviet MiG-21 and US Northrop F-5 (which significantly is not in front-line service with the USAF). This doctrine calls for large numbers of lightweight, high performance aircraft in the belief that weight of numbers will tell over a smaller force of individually more capable aircraft. The Soviet Union has always favored numbers over quality, a position it has been forced into by the US pre-eminence in technology.

Air superiority is numbered amongst the roles of the versatile McDonnell Douglas F-4 Phantom, although this aircraft is now giving way to the more modern F-15 and F-16. The USAF flies three fighter versions of the Phantom, the F-4C, F-4D, and F-4E (plus the specialized F-4G for defense suppression and RF-4C tactical reconnaissance aircraft). The F-4 was originally deve-

The West German Luftwaffe plans to equip its Tornados with the MW-1 submunition dispenser (above). Weapons aiming is assisted on modern warplanes by the head-up display (inset) which projects flight data and weapon aiming commands into the pilot's field of view.

Above: A Danish Air Force F-16B two-seat trainer.
Right: The F-16's sidestick control column makes its cockpit layout particularly distinctive.

loped as a two-seat shipboard fighter for the US Navy and such was its outstanding performance that it was adopted by the USAF. The first F-4Cs became operational in 1964 and for more than a decade the F-4 was the backbone of the tactical fighter force. Its achievements during the war in Southeast Asia ranged from air-to-air combat, through tactical bombing to defense suppression.

The initial USAF Phantom, the F-4C, was similar to the US Navy's F-4B with added air-to-ground attack capability. It was followed by the F-4D, which had an improved bombing computer and gunsight. The definitive F-4E introduced built-in gun armament (a 20mm M-61 Vulcan cannon) thus correcting a major shortcoming and the wing was fitted with leading edge slats to improve maneuverability. The F-4E spans 38ft 5in, is 63ft long and maximum takeoff weight is 59,000lbs. Power is provided by two 17,900lbs thrust J79-GE-17 turbojets with afterburning, giving a maximum speed of Mach 2.4. Service ceiling is 70,000ft and combat radius 900 miles. Air-to-air armament in addition to the M-61 cannon, comprises four AIM-7 Sparrow radar-guided AAMs and four infra-red AIM-9 Sidewinders. A wide range of bombs, rockets and ASMs can also be carried. Five of the NATO allies fly the F-4 (Spain, Greece, Turkey, West Germany, and Britain).

Unlike the F-4, the McDonnell Douglas F-15 Eagle was tailored to the air superiority mission from its inception. The F-15 became operational in 1975 and export customers include Israel, Saudi Arabia and Japan. It is a large aircraft for a single-seat fighter, spanning 42ft 10in with a length of 63ft 9in and maximum takeoff weight of 68,000lbs. The keys to the F-15's impressive performance are its two Pratt & Whitney F100-PW-100 turbofans each developing 23,900lbs of thrust with afterburning. Maximum speed is over Mach 2.5 above 36,000ft, yet fuel consumption is not excessive. When fitted with FAST (fuel and sensor tactical) pack conformal fuel pallets the ferry range is more than 3000 nautical miles. The large wing (608 sq ft) makes it highly maneuverable because wing loading is very low.

At first sight the F-15's armament appears to be no more effective than that of the F-4E, comprising four Sparrow and four Sidewinder AAMs and a built-in M-61 20mm rotary cannon. However both missiles have been progressively improved since their service introduction and replacements are now under development. A new 25mm rotary cannon was in prospect, but development problems led to its cancellation. Nevertheless the F-15 does offer a substantial improvement over the F-4E by virtue of its APG-63 pulse-doppler radar, which enables it to detect and engage low-flying targets with a greater chance of success.

Essentially a complementary design to the F-15, the F-16 Fighting Falcon was developed in response to the USAF's Lightweight Fighter program. The US requirement is for 1388 F-16s and the fighter is also in production in Europe for the air forces of Belgium, Denmark, the Netherlands and Norway. It has been blooded in action by the Israeli air force, which used it in the successful raid on Iraq's nuclear reactor in June 1981.

The F-16's powerplant is a single Pratt & Whitney F-100-PW-200 turbofan of 23,840lbs thrust with afterburning, essentially the same engine as that fitted to the F-15. Maximum speed is over Mach 2 at 40,000ft, reducing to Mach 1.3 at sea level. The F-16 is a small aircraft in comparison with the F-4, which it is gradually replacing in the USAF's Tactical Fighter Wings. Wingspan is 31ft and length 49ft 6in, with maximum takeoff weight at 33,000lbs. As with the F-4, the F-16 has dual air-to-air and ground attack capability. Its weapons load includes a built-in M-61 cannon, wingtip mounted Sidewinder AAMs (a second pair may be carried under the wing) and up to 12,000lbs of bombs. Tactical radius with a 3000lb bomb load is 340 miles.

A compact radar, the Westinghouse AN/APG-66, is mounted in the aircraft's nose. It is a multi-mode sensor, which can be used both in air-to-air and air-to-ground combat. Radar controls are stick and throttle-mounted and air-to-air radar information can be projected onto the pilot's HUD. The F-16's cockpit incorporates a reclining seat, angled 30 degrees to the rear, which increases the pilot's 'G' tolerance over conventionally mounted ejection seats. Another innovation is the side-stick control mounted on the right of the cockpit, which replaces the centrally-positioned control column. Compared to the F-4 (which is twice the weight), the F-16 has thrice the combat radius for the air superiority mission. It is highly maneuverable, acceleration and turn rates being better than the F-4's by 60 percent.

The F-16 is really only a lightweight fighter in comparison with its stablemate the F-15. The Lockheed F-104 Starfighter which the F-16 is replacing with many NATO air arms, more truly justifies this description. Originally intended as a clear weather interceptor, the Starfighter achieved an outstanding flight performance at the expense of payload and all-weather capability. The multi-role F-104G has undertaken the air superiority, interceptor, reconnaissance and ground attack roles with ten NATO air forces: Belgium, Canada, Denmark, West Germany, Greece, Italy, the Netherlands, Norway, Spain and Turkey. The F-104G spans 21ft 11in, is 54ft 9in long and maximum weight is 28,780lbs. It is powered by a single General Electric J79-GE-11A turbojet of 15,800lbs thrust with afterburning. Top speed is Mach 2.35 at 36,000ft and combat radius 745 miles. Built-in armament is a 20mm M61 Vulcan rotary cannon and weapons load is up to 4000lbs.

The Northrop F-5 series of lightweight fighters also serves with several NATO air forces and numerous Third World nations. The F-5A model is a supersonic (Mach 1.4) clear-weather fighter armed with wingtip-mounted AIM-9 Sidewinders, or a 6000lbs warload for ground attack. Power is supplied by two General Electric J85-GE-13 turbojets, each producing 4080lbs of thrust with afterburning. Maximum takeoff weight is 19,860lbs and dimensions are 25ft 3in span and 47ft 2in length. Versions of the F-5A serve with the air forces of Canada, Greece, the Netherlands, Norway, Spain and Turkey. The improved F-5E (with more powerful engines, increased fuel load and an APQ-153 radar) serves with the USAF and US Navy in the air combat training role. A further improvement the F-5G, powered by a single General Electric F404 turbofan (16,400lbs thrust with afterburning) has yet to fly, but a top speed of Mach 2 is predicted.

France's highly successful Mirage III series of fighters are multi-role aircraft which have been widely exported, but apart from those with the Armée de l'Air the only NATO Mirage IIIs are those serving with the Spanish and Belgian air forces. A tail-less, delta-wing aircraft, the Mirage III spans 27ft and is 49ft 3in in length. The IIIE version is powered by a 13,670lbs thrust SNECMA Atar 09C afterburning turbojet and has a maximum takeoff weight of 29,760lbs. Top speed is Mach 2.1 at 40,000ft and combat radius is 745 miles. Armament comprises two DEFA 30mm cannon, plus three AAMs. A simplified ground-attack version, the

Mirage 5, equips one French escadre (wing) and another flies the Mirage IIIR tactical reconnaissance aircraft. From 1984 the Mirage III was superseded by the Mirage 2000. This is a Mach 2.3 tail-less delta, which is to be built in three versions for the Armée de l'Air: a multi-role fighter, an interceptor and a two-seat interdictor-strike aircraft.

For many years the backbone of Frontal Aviation's tactical fighter force was the MiG-21 Fishbed. This fighter is now being replaced by the MiG-23 Flogger, but nevertheless many MiG-21s remain in service. The first production version, the MiG-21F Fishbed-C, entered service in late 1959. It was a true lightweight air superiority fighter with no all-weather capability, a short endurance and relatively light armament. Over the succeeding 20 years there have been numerous improvements to the basic design, aimed at improving its all-weather performance and suiting it to the tactical fighter-bomber role. A basic fault that has never been satisfactorily eradicated is the MiG-21's short endurance.

The aircraft has many positive virtues to offset its fundamental weakness. It is highly maneuverable for a fighter of its period, although in comparison with the F-16 it is inferior in rate and radius of turn and in acceleration. It is easy to fly and maintenance, refueling and rearming present few problems. The gun armament of the late-model MiG-21bis comprises a twin-barrel GSh-23 23mm cannon, which is reliable and effective. Missile armament, usually four infra-red AA-2 Atolls, is less satisfactory because these weapons are not maneuverable enough for modern combat. However the later AA-8 Aphid is a much better weapon.

The MiG-21's small size gives its pilot an advantage in combat because it is more difficult to pick up than larger Western fighters such as the F-15 or F-4. Details of the MiG-21bis (Fishbed-N) include a span of 23ft 6in, length 51ft 9in and maximum loaded weight of 22,000lbs. The powerplant is a 16,500lb Tumansky

The MiG-21 (top left) remains an important fighter with the Soviet air force and the Warsaw Pact allies. Many F-4 Phantoms continue to serve in NATO (top); a USAF F-4D leads a Luftwaffe F-4F (background) and RAF Buccaneer. The RF-4C (above) is used for tactical reconnaissance, this aircraft serving with the USAF's 363rd TRW. F-15 Eagles (left and above center) were designed from the outset for air-to-air combat and the view from the cockpit is particularly good.

R-25 afterburning turbojet, giving a maximum speed of Mach 2 at 36,000ft. Service ceiling is about 50,000ft and combat radius 300 miles. Rocket pods or AS-7 Kerry ASMs can be carried for ground attack, but generally weapons load is restricted by the need to carry drop tanks on the fuselage centerline or underwing.

The greatest number of tactical fighters in Frontal Aviation are now versions of the MiG-23 and MiG-27 family, codenamed Flogger by NATO. The MiG-23 is a variable-geometry wing, single-seat fighter which can successfully undertake a variety of roles, including interception, air superiority, battlefield interdiction and close air support. The initial production versions, designated Flogger-B, are primarily intended for the air-to-air roles with secondary ground attack capability. Early examples were powered by the Tumansky R-27 afterburning turbofan producing 22,500lbs thrust, but this was superseded by the 25,350lbs thrust R-29 in the mid-1970s. Maximum speed at sea level is Mach 1.1 increasing to Mach 2.2 at 36,000ft. Service ceiling is 55,000ft and combat radius 575 miles. Span is 46ft 9in (17 degrees sweep) reducing to 27ft 2in when the wing is fully swept (72 degrees) and maximum takeoff weight is 41,000lbs.

The MiG-23's High Lark radar is a considerable improvement over the MiG-21's 20 mile range Jay Bird, having a search range of more than 50 miles and limited 'look-down' ability. Armament initially comprised the AA-2 Atoll infra-red guided AAM and the radar-guided AA-2-2 Advanced Atoll. However these missiles have given way to AA-7 Apex medium-range, radar-guided AAMs and the IR AA-8 Aphid for dogfighting. Two AA-7s plus four AA-8s can be carried. Gun armament is the 23mm GSh-23 cannon and bombs or rocket pods for the ground-attack mission. A laser range-finder is mounted forward of the nose wheel for air-to-surface weapons ranging. Improvements to the Flogger-B have

This MiG-23 Flogger (above) carries IR AA-8 Aphid AAMs beneath the fuselage and larger AA-7 Apex AAMs beneath the wing. The most important NATO AAMs are the radar-homing Sparrow (top right) and the IR-guided Sidewinder (right). A USAF technician (below) works on an F-4E's APQ-120 radar.

resulted in the Flogger-G, which is also primarily an air-to-air fighter. The most noteworthy development is the provision of a pulse-doppler radar which can engage targets flying below the fighter.

The MiG-23 is in no real sense a successor to the MiG-21, but rather has filled a gap by providing a multi-role capability roughly comparable to that of the USAF's F-4 Phantom. A replacement for the MiG-21 in the air superiority and air defense roles became operational in 1984. The MiG-29 (Ram-L) is a twin-engined, twin-fin single-seater, similar in appearance to a scaled-down F-15 or MiG-25. Performance is likely to be in the order of a Mach 2.3 maximum speed at altitude and Mach 1.2 at sea level. The Ram-L/MiG-29 will have a 'lookdown/shootdown' capability and generally its performance will be similar to or better than that of the McDonnell Douglas F-18, except for range which is significantly less. If reports on this new Soviet fighter are substantially correct then the technological gap between NATO and Warsaw Pact aircraft will be rapidly closing by the end of the 1980s.

For a time during the 50s and early 60s it was believed that an air superiority fighter could rely on missiles alone. The C and D models of the Phantom had no internal gun armament and when combat experience in Vietnam showed this to be necessary they had to carry a podded 20mm cannon. This was unsatisfactory because the weapon was less rigidly fixed than on an internal mounting and accuracy suffered. Ammunition capacity was also less than most internal gun arrangements and the gun occupied a stores station which could more usefully be taken up by bombs or fuel. The deficiency was finally corrected with the F-4E and its built-in 20mm M61 cannon, capable of firing at 6000 rounds per minute.

Nevertheless missiles remain the fighter's primary weapon. During the air war in Southeast Asia AAMs accounted for 88 of the 137 North Vietnamese fighters claimed as destroyed. The tactical fighters' guns destroyed 40 MiGs, while seven were maneuvered into the ground and two claimed by defensive fire from B-52s' tail guns. Two of the missiles used in Vietnam are still in NATO service, albeit in improved versions: the AIM-7 Sparrow (50 victories) and the AIM-9 Sidewinder (33 victories).

The Sparrow is a medium-range missile, which can be effective up to 60 miles from the launch aircraft in its AIM-7F version. It makes use of semi-active radar homing, which means that the parent aircraft's radar must lock onto the target for the missile to guide onto it. In an active homing missile, such as the Hughes AIM-54 Phoenix carried by the F-14 Tomcat fleet defense fighter, the illuminating radar is carried in the missile itself. The AIM-9 Sidewinder makes use of infra-red guidance which homes onto a heat source which the seeker head has been locked onto before the missile is launched. Effective range is 6-10 miles and the latest AIM-9L Sidewinder can be launched from 'all-aspects', rather than from the target's rear as with earlier Sidewinders. Infra-red guidance can be decoyed away from a target aircraft's engine exhaust by flares or a jamming beacon and a natural heat source such as the sun can deflect the missile from its target. However the system has the advantages of robustness and relative simplicity and because it does not need radar guidance it can be carried by virtually any aircraft for self-defense and by advanced trainers in an auxiliary air defense role. A replacement for Sidewinder is to be produced by a European consortium and an active radar successor to Sparrow is under development in the USA.

The Soviet counterpart of the Sidewinder is the AA-2 Atoll, which makes use of infra-red guidance. An advanced version, the AA-2-2 probably exists in both IR and semi-active radar homing versions. Range is 3.5 miles, but Atoll's reliability has been poor when used in combat in Vietnam and the Middle East wars. The AA-7 Apex and AA-8 Aphid are supplanting the earlier missile, both types arming the MiG-23 and the AA-8 being carried on MiG-21s. There are two versions of both missiles, one semi-active radar homing and the other using IR guidance and both types are often carried by Soviet fighters. The medium range (20 miles) AA-7 is generally comparable to the Sparrow, while AA-8 is a small, maneuverable dogfighting weapon of some four miles range.

Radar is important in the air superiority mission, not only for illuminating targets for semi-active radar

homing missiles, but also for target acquisition and ranging. The Hughes APG-65 radar fitted to the US Navy F-18 Hornet illustrates the capabilities of a modern tactical fighter's radar. It is a multi-mode radar, providing weapons aiming information for use with the 20mm cannon, Sparrow and Sidewinder AAMs, or guided and ballistic air-to-ground weapons. The radar modes applicable to the air-to-air mission include velocity search for picking up targets at a range of up to 80 nautical miles. As the target closes the radar can provide range information using the range-while-search mode. Thereafter the radar switches to single target track for guidance of Sparrow missiles, while 'fire-and-forget' missiles (active radar homing or infra-red guided) allow the radar to use the track-while-scan mode, providing position information on targets while still searching for others. An automatic priority is allocated to targets by the radar and up to ten can be tracked at once. It is also possible to assess the strength of a raid by radar beam sharpening. For dogfighting targets are automatically acquired at ranges from ten miles down to 500ft. The radar can scan a narrow beam above and below the fighter, look forward along the aircraft's centerline, or scan the field of view of the HUD. A gun director mode indicates a target's relative motion during dogfighting.

Knocking out the enemy air force on his own airfields is an attractive idea, but the Israeli success in 1967 is unlikely to be repeated unless tactical nuclear weapons are used. Nonetheless, an enemy's air effort can be seriously blunted by a counter-air campaign against his airfields. This is especially true if, as in the case of NATO, he is somewhat short of airfields and those he has are crowded with warplanes, their support equipment and supplies.

Airfield attack will be one of the priority tasks for interdictor aircraft such as the F-111, Tornado and Fencer. Although they may carry conventional high explosive bombs or tactical nuclear weapons, it is more likely that their armament will be one of the specialized weapons developed for airfield attack. France's Matra Durandal is a direct descendant of the 'dibber' bombs used during the Six Days War. The weapon weighs 430lbs and up to 11 can be carried by the Jaguar, while the F-15E can lift a maximum of 22. The bomb is released over an enemy runway by a low-flying aircraft flying at up to 550 knots. Two braking parachutes are then deployed to decelerate the bomb and to pitch its nose downwards. The parachutes are then jettisoned and a rocket motor accelerates the weapon to a rate of some 850ft per second. It penetrates up to 16in through concrete and the 33lb warhead explodes after a one second delay. The French BAP 100 is a smaller weapon

An important US precision-guided munition is the TV-guided Maverick (inset top). The A-7Ds (left) with ventral dive-brakes extended carry Mk82 bombs. The primary weapon of the A-10A is its 30mm cannon. A-10As of the USAF's 355th TFW are shown (inset left).

(80lbs weight) than Durandal, but works on the same principle.

Britain and West Germany have elected to develop large dispensers for carriage beneath the aircraft which eject numerous submunitions over the target.

During the 1970s much was done to reduce the vulnerability of military airfields. Important airfields are now defended by concentrations of AA guns and SAMs, with possibly a combat air patrol of fighters overhead. A general 'toning down' of aircraft, equipment, buildings and runways themselves make airfields and targets on them difficult for an attacker to pick out from the surrounding terrain. Aircraft, support equipment, munition and fuel stores are not only dispersed, but are also often protected by shelters able to withstand anything but a direct hit from a heavy bomb.

Dispersed operations away from the main airfield offer one solution to the problem. Such tactics are especially associated with the V/STOL Harrier, which in wartime will operate from camouflaged sites well away from regular airfields. However, any warplane with a degree of STOL (short take-off and landing) capability can operate from such sites as suitable lengths of major highway. The disadvantage is the difficulty of providing remote sites with adequate supplies of fuel and munitions. Any major servicing will also be extremely difficult without well-equipped workshops. Finally if a dispersal site is discovered and attacked by enemy aircraft or heliborne commandos, its defenses could be far less effective than those of a permanent airfield.

Air defenses consist not only of interceptor aircraft, but also of ground based systems such as SAMs, AA artillery and their associated radars and command centers. It is therefore an important part of the air superiority mission to neutralize these. The USAF has gained a great deal of experience in defense suppression tactics, which it codenames Wild Weasel. The need for active defense suppression varies somewhat according to the penetration tactics adopted by the attacking force. The USAF, like most other NATO air forces, flies tactical strike/attack missions at medium level, covered by fighter and ECM escorts, and therefore required active suppression of ground based defenses. An alternative approach, adopted by the RAF, is to operate at high speed and low level, thus giving ground defenses only a fleeting opportunity to come into action.

Soviet ground-based air defense systems include AA guns ranging in size from 14.5mm up to 130mm, with the ZSU-23-4 quad-barrel 23mm gun and the twin 57mm ZSU-57-2 representing a particularly serious threat to low flying aircraft. SAMs vary greatly in operating altitudes and mobility, but in general provide good air defense cover at all altitudes and in all weathers. SA-4 medium to high altitude missiles are deployed at army and front levels, while divisions have SA-6, SA-8 and SA-11 SAMs operating at low-to-medium altitudes and the regiments have low-altitude SA-9 and SA-13 missiles. In addition to the ground forces' missiles, deeper penetrating tactical aircraft will have to cope with the Air Defense Force's SAM force which currently numbers some 10,000 launchers.

The tactics evolved for dealing with SAMs are an outgrowth of the air war in Southeast Asia. In 1965 'Iron Hand' bombing strikes were initiated against SAM launching sites and later that year specialized 'Wild Weasel' F-100F aircraft were introduced to deal with the SAMs while the strike force went for the main target. The F-105F was also assigned to this role and from this aircraft evolved the F-105G. This two-seat variant of the Thunderchief was fitted with special electronic equipment which enabled it to detect and home in on the emissions of SAM guidance radars. The SAM sites could then be attacked by anti-radiation missiles, which home onto the radar signals, or by conventional bombs, rockets and CBUs.

The F-105 no longer flies with the Air National Guard, but the front-line Wild Weasel units now operate the F-4G version of the Phantom. The F-4G is a modified F-4E fighter, 116 of which are to be converted for the defense suppression role. It is fitted with the APR-38 radar homing and warning system, which detects AA gun and SAM radar emissions. The system's computer will provide the position of the hostile transmitter and identify it as an AA radar, or SA-2, 3, 4, etc. as appropriate. The system will also assign threat priorities for up to 15 different radars. The computer will then provide weapons release data, or execute an automatic bombing run if desired.

The weapons carried by the F-4G include the AGM-45 Shrike and AGM-78 Standard anti-radiation missiles and the new AGM-88 HARM, which is under development for the defense suppression mission. The electro-optically guided AGM-65 Maverick provides a useful answer to such simple countermeasures as shutting down the transmitter. Other air-to-ground ordnance may include free-fall bombs, PGMs and CBUs. The F-4G can defend itself against enemy aircraft as it can carry three Sparrow missiles (the position of the fourth Sparrow being taken up by an ECM jamming pod) and AIM-9 Sidewinders. However one retrograde step is the deletion of the internally-mounted gun, as its position is needed for radar-warning antennae.

The most effective stand-off weapon of the Wild Weasels is the anti-radiation missile. The AGM-78 Standard ARM has a speed of Mach 2 plus and a range of 15 miles, while the AGM-54 Shrike's range is some ten miles. Both weapons were used operationally in Southeast Asia and are due to be replaced by the AGM-88 HARM (high-speed anti-radiation missile), which has an increased range, higher speed and a greater frequency coverage.

There is more than one way of skinning a cat and, if a direct assault on enemy air defenses can be costly and hazardous, then the subtler techniques of deception can often do the same job just as effectively. Electronic countermeasures can affect virtually all aspects of air operations, but electronic warfare (EW) is especially significant in the tactical air war and a number of specialized EW aircraft have been developed to provide ECM escort for strike/attack forces.

In general terms ECM can be either active or passive. Passive measures include the Stealth techniques already discussed and the use of radar warning receivers to alert an aircraft's crew to a hostile threat. The active approach seeks to jam enemy radars and communications, or to confuse the defenders by deception. The widespread use of ECM from World War II onwards has led to ECCM (electronic counter countermeasures), which seeks to make air defense radars immune from enemy jamming by such techniques as frequency agility. This involves a rapid and random switching of the frequency on which radars or radio communications sets operate to make the task of jamming formidably difficult.

The USAF is currently developing an ECM escort aircraft based on the F-111A airframe. Known as the EF-111A, this airborne tactical jamming system makes use of the ALQ-99 electronic warfare equipment, which was originally produced for the US Navy's EA-6B Prowler. However the EF-111A's ECM operation is more automated as the EF-111A carries only one systems' operator in contrast to the Prowler's three.

The US Navy's EA-6B Prowler is a much earlier system, which first entered squadron service with the US Navy in 1971. In essence it is a modification of the A-6 Intruder attack bomber, with a four-man crew in an enlarged cockpit. Its jamming system is the same as that fitted to the EF-111A, but instead of being internally mounted the transmitters are carried in self-contained underwing pods. Up to five pods can be carried, each of which has two jamming transmitters, and the Prowler also carries a communications jamming set. Although it is a carrier based naval aircraft, the Prowler's mission otherwise differs little from that of land-based ECM aircraft.

There has been very little published in the West about the Soviet Union's ECM equipment and capabilities. However this is one of the areas of military technology in which the Soviet Union is claimed to excel. It is thought that most Soviet warplanes carry internally-mounted ECM systems and a number of specialized EW aircraft have been identified. Frontal Aviation's standard ECM escort is the version of the Yak-28 known to NATO as the Brewer-E. The Yak-28 is a twin-engined, two-seat warplane which undertakes a variety of missions including attack, interception and reconnaissance. The Brewer-E is based on the attack version, with the weapons' bay housing ECM equipment. Its performance – Mach 0.85 at sea level, increasing to over Mach 1 at medium altitudes – suggests that it will accompany strike formations as ECM

A Soviet Yak-28 Brewer-E electronic warfare aircraft pictured in service with Frontal Aviation.

escort. The Soviet stand-off jamming system is carried by the Cub-B variant of the Antonov An-12 tactical transport.

Specialized ECM aircraft are only available in relatively limited numbers when compared with the hundreds of tactical aircraft which will operate over the European battlefield. Therefore most warplanes are fitted with their own ECM equipment, which varies in complexity and effectiveness according to the level of opposition anticipated.

The crudest method of jamming a hostile radar is by 'noise', in other words by blotting out the radar's signal by a stronger transmission on the same frequency. This can be spot jamming on a single frequency or barrage jamming over a wide range of frequencies. Noise jamming is relatively simple to implement, but it is also fairly easily countered by changing frequencies or by frequency agility. A more subtle approach seeks not to jam the enemy's signals, but to distort them. This is achieved by receiving the signal and retransmitting it in a modified or delayed form. Alternatively the enemy can be confused by generating a cluster of false target returns in which the genuine return is lost. Finally most tactical aircraft will be fitted with chaff and flare dispensers. A cloud of chaff – minute strips of aluminum foil often cut in lengths to match the radar wavelength – will break a radar lock on its target, while IR flares can decoy an IR missile from the aircraft's engine exhaust. There are also more sophisticated electro-optical jammers intended to decoy heat-seeking missiles from their target.

Air power's most direct contribution to the land battle is the close air support (CAS) mission, which provides firepower for ground forces in contact with the enemy. Targets include armored and soft-skinned vehicles, troops and field fortifications. Because of the dangers of attacking one's own forces in error, positive control of CAS aircraft is of the greatest importance. This can sometimes best be achieved by an airborne forward air controller, orbiting the battle area in a light aircraft, who can mark ground targets with smoke rockets and direct the bombing runs of the attack fighters. There will be many attractive targets to the rear of the enemy's forward troops and so battlefield interdiction will also be undertaken by tactical air forces.

The most formidable target on the battlefield is the tank and the USAF's standard attack aircraft, the Fairchild A-10A Thunderbolt II (unofficially dubbed the Warthog) has been specially developed to deal with enemy armor in the Central European theater. It is a relatively simple, single-seat aircraft intended to be available in large numbers (the A-10A-equipped 81st TFW is the largest fighter wing in the USAF with six 18-aircraft squadrons) and survivability is one of the keynotes of the design. The A-10A is relatively large, spanning 57ft 6in with a length of 53ft 4in and a maximum takeoff weight of 47,400lbs. Power is provided by two General Electric TF-34-GE-100 turbofans of 9065lbs thrust each, giving a maximum combat speed with warload of 443mph. Operational radius, allowing a loiter time over the target area of two hours, is 288 miles. Maximum warload is 16,000lbs.

The built-in armament of the A-10A comprises a 30mm GAU-8/A seven-barrelled rotary cannon, with a rate of fire of either 2100 or 4200 rounds per minute according to the pilot's selection. Ammunition load is 1350 rounds and so the gun is fired in short (typically two second) bursts. Each ammunition round has an armor-piercing cone of depleted uranium, backed by an incendiary charge, and it is reckoned to knock-out a tank with hits on the side or rear at a distance of 6000ft. Beyond gun range a favored weapon is the TV-guided Maverick ASM, up to six of which can be carried. Alternative armament loads may include bombs, CBUs, or laser-guided bombs.

The A-10 has been designed to absorb considerable

battle damage and be able to return to base. The cockpit area is protected by a titanium shield which can withstand hits from a 37mm shell. Fuel tanks and their associated 'plumbing' are protected and are self-sealing and the engines are mounted high on the rear fuselage so that they will be partly shielded from groundfire. The ammunition tank is armored and hydraulic flying control systems are duplicated with manual reversion. Finally the aircraft's structure is particularly strong and it is claimed that the A-10 can lose one engine, half a tail and two-thirds of one wing and still remain in the air.

The most serious criticism of the A-10A is its lack of an all-weather capability. Because of the well-known vagaries of the European climate, there is a danger that the A-10 force may be grounded by bad weather and in winter daylight hours are in any case limited. A two-seat night and adverse weather variant of the A-10 was produced to cope with these conditions, but after evaluation it was decided to improve the single-seater. This will be achieved by fitting the LANTIRN system, which consists of a pod-mounted FLIR for navigation and targeting and a radar pod for terrain following.

The Warthog's predecessor in front-line service with the USAF, the Vought A-7D Corsair II, was an altogether more conventional aircraft. Although it has now retired from the regular squadrons, the A-7 remains an important aircraft with the Air National Guard, equipping 14 squadrons, and it is still the US

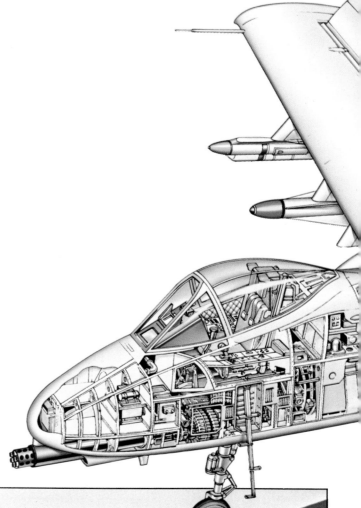

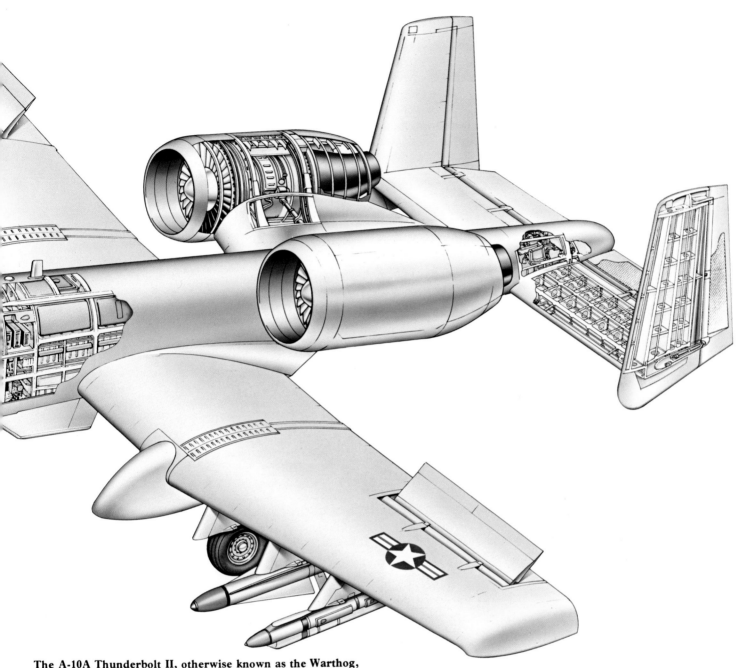

The A-10A Thunderbolt II, otherwise known as the Warthog, is a specialized anti-tank and close air support aircraft (cutaway artwork). The RAF Buccaneer S Mk 2Bs (left) belong to No 208 Squadron based at Lossiemouth in the UK.

Navy's standard shipboard light attack aircraft. The A-7D spans 38ft 9in and length is 46ft 2in, with a maximum takeoff weight of 42,000lbs. It is powered by a 14,250lbs thrust Allison TF-41A-1 turbofan, which gives a maximum speed of 663mph at 7000ft and a combat radius of 556 miles. The built-in armament comprises a 20mm M61A-1 rotary cannon with 1000 rounds of ammunition and the external ordnance load is up to 9500lbs. In addition two Sidewinder AAMs can be carried on fuselage pylons for self-defense. The A-7D's capabilities as an attack aircraft are due to a highly accurate navigation and weapons delivery system, which provides the pilot with navigational information and weapons release instructions projected onto a

cockpit HUD. A central computer is fed with information from an inertial navigation set, doppler radar and attack radar.

Close air support is also undertaken by the USAF's multi-role F-4 and F-16 fighters. An altogether more specialized aircraft is the AC-130 gunship, developed for night fire-support in Vietnam, which is still in service with the regular air force and AFRES. A conversion of the standard C-130 tactical transport, AC-130s are fitted with a broadside armament of 7.62mm and 20mm multi-barrelled guns, supplemented in the later AC-130H model by a 40mm cannon and a 105mm howitzer. The aircraft is also fitted with an array of target acquisition sensors, including radar, low-light

TV, IR detection equipment and night observation starlight scopes. A computer instructs the pilot to orbit his target at the appropriate angle of bank to concentrate the cone of fire from his side-mounted armament onto the target. Although a very effective system in Southeast Asia, the AC-130 is vulnerable to interception and can only operate in areas where the enemy air threat has been eliminated.

Forward air control of CAS sorties by an experienced airman accompanying the ground forces became a standard operational procedure in Western air forces during World War II. This not only ensures that enemy positions are clearly marked for the CAS aircraft, but also that the army commander's requirement has been realistically assessed by an airman with recent combat experience who understands the limitations and problems of CAS. As a logical extension of this practice, forward air control from an aircraft over the battlefield is now widespread in the US forces.

The aircraft used for FAC include the Cessna 0-2 development of the twin-engined Skymaster light aircraft, with underwing hardpoints for target marking rockets. This aircraft has a maximum speed of 200mph and a range of more than 1000 miles. Although good visibility for ground observation is more important in a FAC aircraft than performance, a more capable aircraft than the 0-2 is really required for the European battlefield. This is available in the guise of the Rockwell OV-10A Bronco, a two-seat twin-turboprop counterinsurgency aircraft developed for service in Vietnam. The Bronco combines excellent crew visibility with a good performance (maximum speed 280mph) and the ability to carry a weapons load of 3600lbs in addition to four built-in 0.30in machine guns, so that it can itself undertake light attack missions. A further increase in the performance of FAC aircraft has resulted from converting jet aircraft to this task. The USAF has modified Cessna A-37 attack aircraft to OA-37 configuration for service with reserve units and the US Marine Corps has similarly converted two-seat Skyhawks as OA-4Ms.

Undoubtedly the most interesting and original CAS aircraft serving with the United States' NATO allies (and also with the US Marine Corps) is the RAF's B Ae Harrier V/STOL fighter, the only land-based fighter of its type in operational service. The Harrier's vertical takeoff capability enables it to operate from dispersed sites close behind the battlefield, so that requests for air support can be quickly met. It is also independent of vulnerable and conspicuous permanent airfields, although as already noted the demands of resupply and maintenance of a relatively complex aircraft present other problems.

Three front-line RAF units currently operate the Harrier, Nos 3 and 4 squadrons at Gutersloh, Germany and No 1 squadron at Wittering in the UK. The latter squadron is assigned to NATO's ACE Mobile Force with a reinforcement role for NATO's flank areas. The

An A-37B Dragonfly light attack aircraft (above) of the USAF. The AC-130 (top) carries a broadside armament of 20mm cannon and 40mm Bofors.

operational US Marine Corps units are VMA-231 and VMA-542 at Cherry Point, North Carolina, and VMA-513 at Yuma, Arizona. The Marines pioneered the use of the Harrier (designated AV-8A in US service) in air-to-air combat, developing the use of vectored-thrust in forward flight, or 'viffing', to force conventionally powered fighters into overshooting.

The RAF's Harrier GR Mk 3 is powered by a 21,500lbs thrust Rolls-Royce Pegasus 103 vectored thrust turbofan, which gives a maximum speed of Mach 0.95. Maximum weight for vertical takeoff is 18,000lbs, increasing to 23,000lbs for a short takeoff. The Harrier is small, spanning 25ft 3in and is 45ft 8in long. Tactical radius is 400 miles and warload is 5000lbs of ordnance, plus two 30mm Aden cannon. Navigational equipment includes an inertial nav/attack system and a laser ranger and marked target seeker is fitted.

The AV-8B (Harrier GR Mk 5) will offer a significant improvement in payload/range over the present machine. It is a developed version of the original Harrier, built by McDonnell Douglas in co-operation with British Aerospace for the US Marines (336 required) and the RAF (60 required). It has a larger wing with leading-edge root extensions to improve the rate-of-turn. Other refinements include a raised cockpit with better visibility, six underwing stores stations (the AV-8A has four), the Hughes Angle Rate Bombing System with TV and laser spot tracking and a pod-mounted 25mm rotary cannon.

Complementing the Harrier in RAF service, the SEPECAT Jaguar (built jointly by Britain and France) operates primarily in the battlefield interdiction role, but it can also undertake close air support, tactical reconnaissance, airfield attack and tactical nuclear strike. Jaguar was designed from the outset for low-level operation, with the capability of destroying its target during the first pass. Powered by two Rolls-Royce Turboméca RT172 Adour turbofans of 7140lbs thrust with reheat, Jaguar has a maximum speed of Mach 1.1 at 1000ft. Range with external fuel tanks flying a lo-lo-lo sortie is 564 miles. It spans 28ft 6in and is 50ft 11in long, with a maximum takeoff weight of 32,600lbs. It can carry an external weapons load of up to 10,000lbs on five hardpoints and built-in armament is two 30mm Aden cannon. An overwing mounting for two Sidewinder or Matra Magic AAMs has been tested, but they are not fitted to RAF or French air force Jaguars.

The heart of Jaguar's avionics is the inertial NAVWASS (navigation and weapons' aiming subsystem), which provides navigational and weapons aiming data on a HUD. It also drives a moving map display in the cockpit. Five squadrons in RAF Germany are equipped with the Jaguar and three fly the type from the UK. Two Jaguar squadrons operate in the tactical reconnaissance/strike role. In the Armée de l'Air the Jaguar equips nine escadrons of the Force Aérienne Tactique.

Close air support aircraft do not need to be as complex as the Jaguar. Advanced trainer aircraft, such as the Macchi MB326, Fouga Magister, Saab 105, B Ae Hawk and Franco-German Alpha Jet, have a limited capability in combat roles. This can be enhanced by modifying the trainer into a light attack aircraft, as in the case of the A-37 variant of the USAF's Cessna T-37, or the Strikemaster version of the Jet Provost. Any advanced training aircraft used for weapons instruction can assume a secondary combat role if necessary. West Germany has put its 175 Alpha Jet trainer/light attack aircraft into first-line service with three of its Jagdbombergeschwadern, whereas France uses the type in the advanced training role.

For many years the Soviet air force neglected close air support, preferring to rely on artillery and surface-to-surface missiles for fire support, while Frontal Aviation provided fighter cover. However during the 1970s as part of the general increase in the effectiveness of Soviet tactical air power the ground support capabilities of Frontal Aviation were significantly upgraded. However control of attack aircraft is not as flexible as in NATO, with army requests for air support being filtered through air force liaison officers and requiring approval at many levels of command. Although this procedure can be shortcircuited in an emergency, its speed cannot compare with that of the FAC system employed by Western forces. The reluctance to delegate authority to junior levels of command is a recurring weakness in the Soviet system.

The most capable attack fighters in Frontal Aviation service at present are the MiG-27 Flogger-D and -J versions of the MiG-23 air-to-air fighter. A major change from the MiG-23 is the recontouring of the nose to improve the downward view from the cockpit. The air interception radar is replaced by a small ranging radar, a laser rangefinder and doppler radar to measure ground speed. The MiG-23's variable engine inlets are replaced by large fixed inlets and the afterburning is simplified. These modifications are designed to increase range at medium and low altitudes at the expense of Mach 2 performance, unnecessary for the attack mission. The undercarriage is modified for rough field operation, and a rocket-assisted takeoff pack can be fitted. Built-in armament is a single 23mm rotary cannon and the weapons load is 6600lbs. Performance includes a maximum speed of Mach 1.1 at sea level and a combat radius of 575 miles. A version of the MiG-23 known as Flogger-F is fitted with the new nose but lacks the other features of the MiG-27. It has been supplied to Warsaw Pact satellite air forces and exported to Africa and the Middle East.

The Sukhoi Fitter family of strike fighters offers another instructive example of the Soviet practice of progressively modifying an existing design to meet new requirements. The Su-7 Fitter-A is a swept-wing fighter-bomber, which served in quantity with Frontal Aviation in the 1960s and has not yet retired. It is a stable aircraft at low level, where it attains a maximum speed of Mach 1.1. However the Su-7 lacks effective navigation and weapons aiming avionics and its payload/range characteristics are poor.

Rather than replace the Su-7, the Soviet Union has modified the Fitter's wing with variable-geometry outer panels. These give some of the advantages of a true variable-sweep wing, but avoid the associated aerodynamic problems. The new aircraft, designated Su-17 (Fitter-C), was also fitted with a more powerful engine, the 24,250lbs afterburning AL-21F. It is undoubtedly an improvement over its predecessor, offering a better airfield performance and tactical radius, with nearly double the Su-7's warload. The later Fitter-D has a terrain avoidance radar and laser ranger and marked target seeker installed, thus improving another fault of the Su-7. Fitter-G is a further advance in this respect and probably carries laser-guided PGMs.

A replacement for the Su-17 emerged from the same bureau. The Su-25 Frogfoot is a specialized air support aircraft. It is a single-seat, subsonic aircraft powered by two turbojets mounted in the wing roots. A multi-barrel cannon is fitted and there are 10 underwing ordnance pylons. According to American reports, the Su-25 entered service in 1984 after a period of evaluation with the Soviet forces in Afghanistan. The inevitable comparisons with the USAF's A-10 are somewhat misleading as the Soviet aircraft is both smaller and lighter.

Mirage 2000 prototypes escort a Mirage 4000, one of Dassault's new generation of fighters for the Armée de l'Air.

AIR DEFENSE

The defense of friendly air space from intruders is a vital task alike in peace as in war. Air defense units maintain a constant alert 24 hours a day, 365 days a year. They are therefore better prepared than most elements of the armed forces to switch from a peacetime footing to all-out war. However this advantage is counterbalanced in the West by the serious neglect of air defense forces, which have for years operated elderly aircraft and missiles. Not so in the Soviet Union, where air defense – or more properly aerospace defense – enjoys a high priority in manning and equipment.

Ground based and airborne elements of an air defense system work very closely together and therefore C^3 (command, control and communications) are of the greatest importance. Normally ground radars provide the first warning of attack, although with the increasing deployment of airborne early warning (AEW) and control aircraft this emphasis is shifting. Once a threat has been recognized interceptors can be scrambled to deal with it. An alternative which results in an even quicker reaction time is to have the interceptors already airborne on combat air patrol (CAP). This expedient can be valuable if an attack is anticipated with some degree of certainty, but as a normal operational procedure it is very wasteful.

The responsibility for the defense of the air space of the United States and Canada is entrusted to the North American Aerospace Defense Command (NORAD). This arrangement between the Canadian and US governments, integrates early warning, C^3 and interceptor forces for space and atmospheric defense into a single organization. Nerve center of the command is the underground operations complex in Cheyenne Mountain, Colorado, where a computerized system manages all space surveillance, missile launch warning and aircraft early-warning systems.

Unfortunately, these sophisticated systems, often termed the air defense ground environment (ADGE) are not complemented by an up-to-date interceptor force. Most current USAF interceptor aircraft are 20 years old, with weapons and radar of limited use against low-flying aircraft. These shortcomings have been recognized and a modernization program is underway to equip the regular USAF fighter interceptor squadrons (FIS) with the F-15 Eagle and assign E-3A AWACS (airborne warning and control system) aircraft to North American air defense.

During the 1960s and 70s the Soviet manned bomber threat was, quite correctly, considered to be less significant than that from missiles. Consequently the USAF's air defense force was run down from a peak strength of over 40 regular squadrons in the late 1950s to its present level of six regular squadrons, backed by part-time ANG units. However, as the Soviet strategic bomber force has not disappeared and indeed may shortly introduce a new and effective inter-continental range manned bomber, the cutbacks have probably gone too far.

The newest USAF interceptor aircraft is the F-15 Eagle, an aircraft of the 1st TFW being shown here (top). The F-106A (center right) is still an important USAF interceptor. The aircraft are backed by ground-based radars (top right). Two squadrons of Lightning interceptors contribute to the air defense of the United Kingdom (above).

In 1979 the USAF phased out its Aerospace Defense Command (ADCOM) as a separate operational headquarters, although the function and authority of NORAD's Cheyenne Mountain headquarters (the Aerospace Defense Center) remained unchanged. ADCOM's radars, control centers and interceptors are now managed by Tactical Air Command, while SAC is responsible for missile warning and space surveillance sensors.

The Air National Guard provides a further 10 squadrons, four with F-106s, four with F-4s and two with F-101s. In addition the Canadian Armed Forces assign three squadrons of newly-purchased CF-188 Hornet fighters to NORAD, replacing the long-serving and now outmoded CF-101B Voodoo.

The Western European members of NATO do not have so clearcut an air defense problem as that of the North American partners. West Germany in particular is likely to find that her territory becomes the battleground in the early stages of World War III. Therefore her air defense is likely to merge with the air superiority mission.

The West German Luftwaffe operates two wings (JG 71 and JG 74) of F-4F Phantoms in the air superiority/air defense role. These are bolstered by two squadrons of Phantom FGR Mk 2s with RAF Germany and USAFE F-4E and F-16A units. The United Kingdom's air defense interceptor force comprises five squadrons of Phantom FG Mk 1s and FGR Mk 2s, plus two squadrons of shorter-range Lightning F Mk 6s. All are capable of inflight refueling. France's air defense command can operate within the NATO air defense ground environment, although France has no forces assigned to the alliance in peacetime. The Armée de l'Air's interceptor force comprises four wings operating the Mirage IIIC and Mirage F1 interceptors. These were joined by the Mirage 2000 from 1984 onwards. Spain's air defense command operates a single wing each of the Mirage III, Mirage F1 and F-4C Phantom.

If the NATO powers have in general neglected air defense forces, the Soviet Union by contrast has devoted considerable resources to this task. The interceptors, surface-to-air missiles and ground environment of the Soviet air defenses constitute an independent service, quite distinct from the air force. It is the largest air defense force in the world, with 10,000 SAMs, over 5000 early-warning and height-finding radars and 2500 manned interceptors.

Mainstay of the USAF's interceptor force, the Convair F-106A Delta Dart first entered service in 1959. It is a single seat, all-weather interceptor of tail-less delta configuration. Power is provided by one 24,500lbs afterburning Pratt & Whitney J75-P-17 turbojet, which gives the F-106A a maximum speed of Mach 2.3 at altitude. The F-106A spans 38ft 3in and is 70ft 7in long, with a takeoff weight of 38,700lbs. Rate of climb from sea level is 39,800ft per minute and combat ceiling is 52,000ft.

The F-106A is fitted with a highly-automated MA-1 weapons control system, which directs interceptions and weapons release. Armament comprises a single AIR-2A Genie unguided air-to-air rocket, which carries a nuclear warhead and has a range of about six miles, plus four AIM-4 Falcon AAMs. These can either be AIM-4Fs with semi-active radar guidance, or AIM-4Gs with IR homing, both having a range of seven miles. The missiles are carried in an internal weapons bay and, as first produced, this was the F-106's sole armament. However, as with the F-4 Phantom an internal gun armament was later thought to be necessary and a 20mm M-61 cannon was fitted under the Sixshooter modernization program.

France's Mirage F1C all-weather, single-seat interceptor differs from other members of the Mirage family in abandoning the tail-less delta formula for a high-mounted swept wing and horizontal tail surfaces. It is powered by a SNECMA Atar 09K-50 turbojet, which develops 15,875lbs thrust with afterburning. The Mirage F1 spans 27ft 7in, is 49ft 2in long and has a maximum takeoff weight of 32,850lbs. Performance includes a maximum speed of Mach 2.2 and a service ceiling of 65,000ft. Built-in armament consists of two 30mm cannon. Up to three Matra R530 or Super R530 AAMs, with alternative IR or semi-active radar guidance, can be carried, with Sidewinder or Matra Magic AAMs mounted on the wingtips. The Mirage F1's replacement will be the Mirage 2000 delta-winged interceptor, which will have a lookdown/shootdown capability.

The United Kingdom's primary interceptor is the ubiquitous Phantom, but two squadrons of the older BAe Lightning F Mk 6 remain in service. This swept-wing, single-seat fighter is powered by two Rolls-Royce Avon Series 300 turbojets, each delivering 16,300lbs thrust with afterburning. Unusually the engines are mounted one above the other, rather than side-by-side. The Lightning spans 34ft 10in, is 55ft 3in long and has a loaded weight of 49,000lbs. Maximum speed is over Mach 2 and ceiling is 60,000ft. A weakness of the design is its limited endurance, which has been somewhat alleviated in the F Mk 6 by fitting a large ventral fuel tank. Armament comprises two 30mm Aden cannon and two IR homing Red Top AAMs of seven miles range. In an emergency the RAF plans to use its Hawk T Mk 1 weapons trainers as point defense interceptors, armed with Sidewinder AAMs.

The RAF's next interceptor, due to enter service in 1985, is the Panavia Tornado F Mk 2, the air defense variant of the Tornado GR Mk 1. This two-seat aircraft is generally similar to the Tornado GR 1, but it has an elongated nose housing a Ferranti Foxhunter air interception radar with a range of some 100 nautical miles.

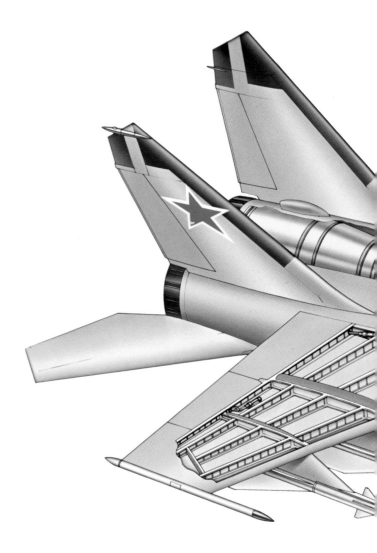

Performance includes a maximum speed of Mach 2.2 and a maximum ferry range (with full fuel load) of over 2000 miles. Built-in armament consists of a single 27mm Mauser cannon, with two Sidewinder short-range AAMs on wing pylons. Four medium-range Sky-flash AAMs, which have the ability to snap up or down to engage both low and high flying targets, are recessed under the fuselage.

Interestingly the variety of interceptors produced by the Soviet Union alone is almost as great as those built by the various NATO nations. The MiG-23 interceptor is the same aircraft as that flown by Frontal Aviation. It is now, in terms of numbers in service, the most important aircraft in the Soviet air defense force. In the 1960s this position was held by the now-superseded MiG-21, which, however, still serves as an interceptor with the Warsaw Pact satellites, and as a tactical fighter with Frontal Aviation.

The delta-wing Su-15 Flagon, unlike the MiG-21 and MiG-23, is a specialized interceptor unsuited to any

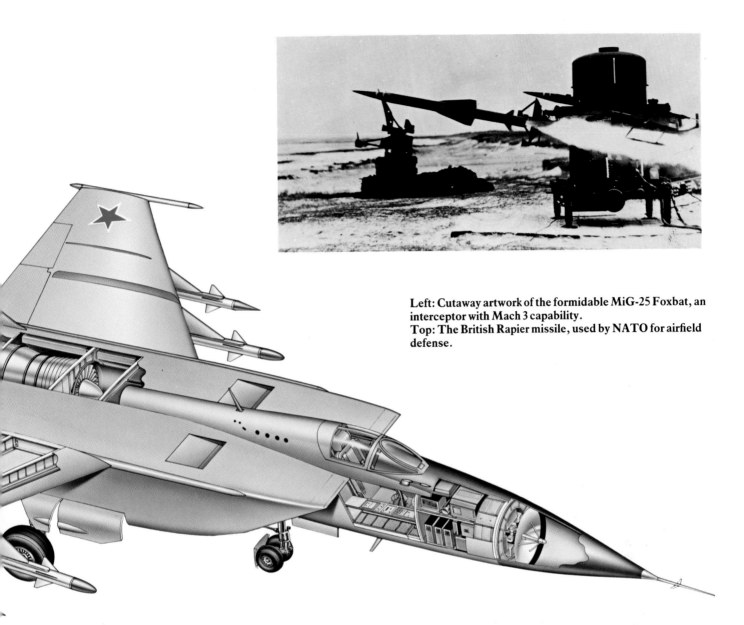

Left: Cutaway artwork of the formidable MiG-25 Foxbat, an interceptor with Mach 3 capability.
Top: The British Rapier missile, used by NATO for airfield defense.

other role. Some 700 of these single-seat, twin-engined fighters serve with the Soviet air defenses. The Flagon was originally envisaged as a progressive development of the earlier Su-9 and Su-11 Fishpot, with a larger and more capable radar. However it emerged as a considerably heavier aircraft, powered by two Tumansky R-13 turbofans developing 16,000lbs thrust with afterburning. Maximum speed is over Mach 2 at altitude, service ceiling is 55,000ft and combat radius 400 miles. Maximum takeoff weight is around 45,000lbs and dimensions include a span of 34ft 6in and a length of 70ft 6in. Armament consists of two 14 mile range AA-3 Anab AAMs carried underwing, one infra-red guided the other semi-active radar homing.

The Su-9/Su-11 Fishpot, precursor of the Flagon, is still in service, with perhaps as many as 600 being operational. Powered by a 22,000lbs afterburning Lyulka AL-7F turbojet, the Su-9 has a maximum speed of Mach 2.1 and a service ceiling of 65,000ft. Its delta wing spans 27ft 8in and overall length is about 60ft. The Su-11 is essentially similar, except that a modified nose

houses a more powerful Skip Spin radar. Because of its less capable radar the Su-9's armament is limited to four AA-1 Alkali 'beam-riding' AAMs, whereas the Su-11 carries two semi-active homing Anabs.

In many ways the most impressive interceptor in current service with the Soviet air defenses, the MiG-25 Foxbat-A was almost certainly designed to combat the fast, high-flying B-70 Valkyrie bomber. The MiG-25 is powered by two Tumansky R-31 turbojets, which give 27,000lbs of thrust each with afterburning. Maximum speed in clean condition is Mach 3, which is reduced to Mach 2.8 when external stores are carried. Ceiling is in the region of 75,000ft and the initial rate of climb is 30,000ft per minute. Maximum takeoff weight is 82,500lbs, the span is 46ft and length 73ft 2in. Operating at up to 250 miles from base, the MiG-25 can carry four AA-6 Acrid AAMs, a mix of two IR and two semi-active radar homing being typical. The semi-active homing AA-6 has a range of some 50 miles, while the IR version's range is half this.

Notwithstanding its impressive performance, the

SOVIET SAM (SA-2)

Foxbat is to a large extent an aircraft without a mission. SAC never received the B-70 and instead adopted low-level penetration tactics. The counter to these is an interceptor with radar and missiles having a lookdown/shootdown capability. These characteristics have been built into a new two-seat variant of the MiG-25, code-named Foxhound, which entered service in 1982. It has a radar reputedly based on F-14 Tomcat technology acquired from Iran and snap-up/snap-down AA-9 AAMs.

Long range is always desirable in an interceptor, but for the Soviet Union with its long Arctic frontier it is of paramount importance. So it is not surprising that the largest fighter in service anywhere – the Tupolev Tu-28P Fiddler – guards these inhospitable wastelands. With a maximum takeoff weight of 85,000lbs, the Tu-28P spans some 65ft and is 85ft in length. Two crew members are carried, seated in tandem in the forward fuselage behind the powerful 'Big Nose' radar. The powerplant is two Lyulka AL-21F turbojets, developing 24,500lbs of thrust with afterburning. Maximum speed is Mach 1.8 and service ceiling 60,000ft. Tactical radius is some 800 miles. The all-missile armament comprises four AA-5 Ash missiles of 18 miles range carried underwing. Their guidance can either be IR or semi-active radar homing, but the latter system is probably of shorter range.

The Yak-28P Firebar fulfils the same role as Fiddler in the less important Soviet air defense districts. In performance it falls between the Tu-28P and Su-15. A swept-wing aircraft, the Firebar has two 13,000lbs Tumansky R-11 afterburning turbojets, one mounted under each wing. Maximum speed is Mach 1.3 and service ceiling is 55,000ft. It is armed with two AA-3 Anab AAMs, in the usual mix of one IR and the other radar guided. Soviet tactics may require that those missiles are salvoed simultaneously to present the target bomber with a difficult problem in countermeasures. A new Soviet long-range interceptor is due to enter service by 1985. A twin-engined aircraft with two crew members, it has provisionally been identified as the Su-27.

Air-to-air missiles for the air defense mission are in general larger and longer ranging than those carried by the air superiority fighter. However many missiles have been found to be useful in both roles, notably the AIM-7 Sparrow. The most sophisticated AAM in service anywhere in the world is undoubtedly the AIM-54 Phoenix, carried by US Navy's F-14 Tomcat. Its range is over 100 miles, with most of the flight controlled by semi-active radar homing and an active radar seeker providing guidance for the last 12 miles. The AIM-54A's speed is over Mach 5 and the warhead is 130lb high explosive with proximity and impact fuzing. The

Soviet AA-6 Acrid carried by the MiG-25 is a Mach 4.5 missile with a range of up to 30 miles. However, this limitation is due to the tracking range of the Foxfire radar and missile ranges of up to 50 miles may be possible with an improved radar.

A serious problem arising from the use of long range missiles is the positive identification of the target as hostile. The standard IFF equipment, used by air-to-air and ground-to-air weapons systems, interrogates a radar contact electronically. If the aircraft is friendly a coded response is returned. However, the lack of a correct response cannot alone be positive proof that the radar contact is hostile. It may be a neutral, or a friendly aircraft with unserviceable IFF equipment.

The long-term solution seems to be to fit the interceptor with an electro-optical magnification device 'slaved' to the radar, to allow visual identification at increased ranges. An interim arrangement, which has been successfully tried on F-14s and F-15s, is to mount a telescope alongside the HUD. This allows an F-14-sized target to be picked up at 22 miles and positively identified at about half this distance. The more sophisticated magnification systems include the USAF's TISEO (target identification system, electro-optical), which is already fitted to some F-4Es, and the Tornado F Mk 2's VAS (visual augmentation system). The range of these can be 30 miles in ideal conditions.

Interceptors' radars should have good range, the ability to deal with several targets at the same time, resistance to ECM jamming and be capable of picking out low-flying targets as small as cruise missiles from the clutter of ground radar returns. It is symptomatic of the neglect of air defense forces by the USAF that the most capable system currently in US service is the AWG-9 fitted to the Navy F-14A Tomcat. It has a maximum range of 170 nautical miles against a bomber size target and can track up to 24 targets at once and simultaneously engage six of them. The Foxhunter radar fitted to the British Tornado F Mk 2 is less costly than the AWG-9. It has a 100 nautical mile range and can handle multiple targets. Resistance to ECM jamming is especially good.

The MiG-25's Foxfire radar's 54 nm search range does not compare very favorably with the latest Western types. However, as Soviet interceptors operate under rigid ground control, maximum radar range is not so important as for NATO interceptors. In general Soviet radar technology lags behind that of the NATO powers, the Foxfire lacking such refinements as transistors and printed circuitry. However, resistance to jamming is considered to be good. The MiG-23's High Lark radar has a search range of 46 nautical miles and that for the Skip Spin fitted to the Su-15 and Yak-28 is 22 nautical miles. The Tu-28P's Big Nose radar's search range is 32 miles.

While the interceptor is the main offensive weapon of air defense forces, providing defense in depth, the surface-to-air missile is useful as a last ditch defense and

The Soviet Union deploys an extensive range of ground-based air defense systems, including the Galosh anti-ballistic missile (top left) and the SA-3 Goa (left), a mobile medium-to-low altitude surface-to-air missile.

for point protection of such high value targets as airfields. Mobile SAMs also contribute to the air defense of armies in the field. SAMs normally operate in a predesignated missile zone, backing up an air interception zone.

Missile belts are part of the air defenses on NATO's Central Front in Europe, the standard area defense missiles being the MIM-14B Nike Hercules and MIM-23B Improved Hawk. Nike Hercules is a long-range SAM, which for many years was deployed as part of the North American air defenses. It was phased out of American service in the 1970s but remains in use by the United States' European and Far Eastern allies. The MIM-14B is a two-stage missile powered by solid propellant. Its length is 41ft and launch weight is 10,000lbs. Either a conventional or nuclear warhead can be fitted and range is about 90 miles.

The Hawk low and medium altitude SAM is widely used by the US armed forces and the NATO allies. Most Hawks in current service are the MIM-23B Improved Hawk, which has a maximum range of 25 miles.

The UK has deployed the Bloodhound Mk 2 50-mile range SAM as an area defense weapon to guard the vulnerable East Anglian air bases. This is backed up by the shorter range BAe Rapier which provides low-level, point defense for the RAF and USAF airfields in the UK and also the bases in RAF Germany. Rapier's range is about four miles and guidance is command to line of sight, the operator keeping his sight on the target onto which the missile is then automatically guided.

The Soviet Union makes extensive use of SAMs for air defense, quite apart from the mobile tactical systems which provide air cover for armies. The elderly SA-1 Guild provides the primary missile defense for Moscow, with two rings of launchers deployed around the city. The SA-1 first entered service in the mid-1950s and is believed to use active radar homing. Range has been assessed at about 30 miles.

The SA-2 Guideline has for long been the standard Soviet air defense SAM. It is deployed throughout the USSR and has been exported. It was used extensively by the North Vietnamese during the Southeast Asia conflict. It is a medium altitude missile, with a range of 30 miles. As more SA-10 missiles are deployed, the SA-2 force will be gradually reduced. The SA-10 is the latest strategic air defense SAM to be deployed by the Soviet Union. It has a range of over 60 miles and is effective at low, medium and high altitudes. In view of the current SAC penetration tactics, the low altitude capability of the SA-10 is especially valuable and it may also be effective against cruise missiles.

Medium to high altitude coverage is provided by the SA-5. This 185 mile range missile entered service in 1963 and is now operational at more than 100 launch complexes with deployment continuing. It is complemented by the SA-3, a low to medium altitude point defense missile of 12 mile range.

The most exotic surface-to-air missiles are undoubtedly the anti-ballistic missile systems. The United States' Safeguard site was dismantled in 1975. This used the 460-mile range Spartan missile for destruction of incoming missiles or warheads outside the earth's atmosphere. It was backed up by the shorter-range (25 miles) Sprint, which was a fast reaction missile intended to pick off those warheads which had evaded the Spartans. Both missiles carried nuclear warheads. Research into ABM systems continues and they may be reintroduced to defend MX launch sites. The Soviet Union at present deploys 32 ABM-1B Galosh missiles in defense of Moscow (up to 100 are allowed under the 1972 SALT treaty). Two new ABMs are under development, SH-4 and SH-8, similar in concept to the Spartan/Sprint combination and the Soviet Union continues to develop and deploy the sophisticated radars on which the ABMs depend for targeting information.

The interceptors and SAM forces are the offensive elements of air defense, but they cannot function effectively without the information provided by ground based radars and control centers. The air defense ground environment (ADGE) in its turn is dependent on good communications to relay data to interceptors and missile sites and also to exchange information between control centers. The ADGE has been extended into space to provide early warning of ballistic missile attack and surveillance of the numerous space satellites.

The North American continent's first line of defense against attack by aircraft or cruise missiles is the

The US air defenses are to be improved with E-3A AWACS aircraft (top), supplementing the ground radars of the DEW line stations (above).

DEW (distant early-warning) Line of radars which stretches from Alaska to Greenland. There are at present 31 radars in this chain, but the number is being reduced to 13. All are linked to the NORAD Combat Operations Center at Cheyenne Mountain. Improvements will replace the existing radars with a mixture of long-range radars, with shorter-range unattended radars filling gaps in the coverage. A second radar chain, the Pine Tree Line, follows the border between the United States and Canada.

Further coverage of North American airspace is provided by the Joint Surveillance System, which is shared by the Federal Aviation Authority and USAF. In all there are 83 sites in this network. The seaward approaches to the United States are to be covered by two over-the-horizon backscatter (OTH B) radars from the mid-1980s. This advanced system, which has yet to be proved operationally viable, will provide all-altitude detection out to 1000 nautical miles from the coast. It achieves this outstanding range by bouncing radar waves off the ionosphere, a technique which is not usable in polar regions to replace the DEW Line radars. Cuba presents a particular problem to the US air defenses, as a Soviet ally within the Western Hemisphere. Consequently a balloon-borne long-range radar, based at Cudjoe Key, Florida, maintains a special watch in this direction.

Early warning of missile attack is provided by three BMEWS (ballistic missile early warning system) radars at Clear, Alaska, Thule, Greenland, and Fylingdales in the United Kingdom. Early warning satellites are also used for this purpose and the Safeguard system's perimeter acquisition radar remains operational and is capable of detecting incoming ICBM warheads. Submarine-launched ballistic missiles can be detected by two Pave Paws radars covering the Atlantic and Pacific. A limited FSS-7 radar covers the Gulf of Mexico.

Two answers to the airborne early warning problem – the Soviet Tu-126 Moss with 'mushroom' radome (above left) and the RAF's 'duck-bill' Nimrod AEW Mk 3 (left and above).

The European NATO allies maintain a network of surveillance radars and associated command and communications systems. The coverage of the NATO air defense ground environment (NADGE) embraces Norway, Denmark, West Germany, the Netherlands, Belgium, Italy, Greece and Turkey. The separate UKADGE is linked to this network and France also exchanges information with the other NATO members, but does not allow them to control her interceptors or missiles. The NATO systems are designed to cope with high levels of air activity and they use automatic data processing to improve reaction times. All control centers are connected and interoperable so that information is shared. NATO is also aware of the threat to its radars from enemy action and some of these are mobile units, which are more difficult to target.

The greatest weakness of a ground based radar is its limited detection range against low flying aircraft. Radar beams follow a straight line and, as the earth's surface is curved, a low-flying aircraft soon falls below the horizon. Even under optimum conditions, detection range will only be some 60 nautical miles, giving only a short time to react to a threat. Hence the development of AWACS (airborne warning and control system) aircraft, which, by carrying the radar aloft, greatly extend the coverage against low-flying aircraft. An

The USAF fulfils this mission with the Boeing E-3A Sentry, a derivative of the Boeing 707 airliner which carries its APY-1 radar in a large rotating radome atop the fuselage. The USAF plans to buy at least 40 E-3As

and NATO will acquire a further 18. With a span of 145ft 9in and length of 152ft 11in, the E-3A has a maximum takeoff weight of 325,000lbs. Power is provided by four Pratt & Whitney TF33-PW-100 turbofans of 21,000lbs thrust each. Maximum speed is 530mph and service ceiling 35,000ft. Endurance is over 11 hours and this can be extended by inflight refueling. The normal crew complement is 17. The immense amount of information gained from the radar is handled by operators using computer processing. Data can be transmitted to ground stations or interceptors by voice radio and data link. The E-3A is fitted with the Joint Tactical Information Distribution System (JTIDS), which can provide secure communications between all air defense elements.

The UK has its own early-warning aircraft, the Nimrod AEW Mk 3, which is due to become operational in 1985. It is a conversion of the maritime reconnaissance Nimrod MR Mk 1, fitted with radar antennae in the nose and tail. Eleven aircraft will replace the elderly Shackleton AEW Mk 2s which currently provide the RAF with AEW. The Nimrod AEW Mk 3 will be fully interoperable with the NATO E-3A fleet and compatible with the NATO air defense ground environment. It differs from its American counterpart in being designed from the outset to carry out maritime surveillance, as well as AEW roles. However, the E-3A has been modified to give it a measure of sea surveillance capability.

Although it is often regarded as the Soviet equivalent to the E-3A, the Tupolev Tu-126 Moss is in fact a much earlier aircraft. It became operational in about 1970, some two years before the RAF's Shackleton AEW Mk 2s, and the first E-3As were not delivered until 1977. Therefore it is unlikely that the Soviet aircraft would be as capable as the E-3A, even discounting the acknowledged Soviet backwardness in electronics. The Tu-126's ability to detect low flying aircraft is assessed as only marginally effective over water and nonexistent over land. However, this may be an evaluation of the aircraft in a role for which it was never designed. Perhaps the Moss is simply an airborne radar picket, intended to extend the range of ground based radars against aircraft at medium and high altitudes. As such it would complement the Tu-28P in operations over the Soviet Union's Arctic frontiers.

The Tu-126's design is based on that of the Tu-114 airliner, with its radar mounted above the fuselage in an installation similar to that of the E-3A. Power is provided by four Kuznetsov NK-12MV turboprops of 15,000shp, giving a maximum speed of 460mph. Span is 167ft 8in and length 188ft, with a takeoff weight of 365,000lbs. Service ceiling is 33,000ft and endurance is an incredible 20 hours, which can be further extended by inflight refueling. Only a small number of Tu-126s are in service (less than 20). A new Soviet AEW aircraft is reported to be under development, possibly based on the Ilyushin Il-86 wide-bodied airliner.

An RAF Jaguar GR Mk 1 fitted with a reconnaissance pod flies over the West German countryside. This aircraft serves with No 2 Squadron at Laarbruch.

RECCE AND ELINT

Air reconnaissance is an indispensible preliminary to many military operations, as the knowledge it makes available about enemy forces and intentions may form the basis of a commander's plan of action. Tactical air reconnaissance is primarily intended to provide timely information of immediate use to the commander on the battlefield. However, the longer term aims, of building up an overall view of an enemy's military strength and industrial capacity so that his war-fighting capability may be accurately assessed, are equally important. This strategic reconnaissance task may also be carried out by aircraft, although air reconnaissance is only one of many information sources available to intelligence officers.

Reconnaissance aircraft use many different sensors to carry out their diverse missions. The visual observation of the crew is often valuable and their comments can be recorded for later analysis. The camera is of course still a primary reconnaissance sensor and it is used both for area and pin-point coverage. Imagery can be recorded on conventional photographic film, or an infra-red picture can be obtained which will reveal much that is hidden from the naked eye. A further alternative is to record a radar picture. This data can be stored aboard the reconnaissance aircraft until its return to base, or transmitted direct to a battlefield headquarters, thus giving a commander 'real time' information. Reconnaissance is not confined to visual imagery, however, as electronic intelligence (ELINT) is a very important aspect of this activity. ELINT aircraft monitor enemy radio and radar transmissions, so that the performance of equipment and operational procedures can be assessed and an electronic order of battle can be built up.

The introduction of reconnaissance satellites has tended to diminish the importance of the strategic reconnaissance aircraft, but these nevertheless continue in service. This is because they can be speedily deployed to cover unexpected contingencies and can reconnoiter areas which would not justify the expense of satellite coverage. Since Powers' U-2 was shot down in 1960, it is unlikely that American aircraft have overflown Soviet territory, but they certainly operate around the Soviet borders using stand-off systems to gather intelligence. They have also covered the territory of other potential adversaries, an activity publicized in 1981 when North Korean SAMs unsuccessfully attempted to shoot down a Lockheed SR-71.

The United States' strategic reconnaissance aircraft operate within Strategic Air Command, as one of their functions is to provide the command with targeting information. The 55th Strategic Reconnaissance Wing flies Boeing RC-135 aircraft, primarily used for ELINT, from Offutt AFB, Nebraska. The 9th SRW is based at Beale AFB, California, and operates one squadron of Lockheed SR-71A Blackbirds and a second of Lockheed U-2s. The 9th SRW has detach-

ments flying from Mildenhall in the UK and Kadena AB on Okinawa. Other airfields are regularly used for strategic reconnaissance flights, including Hellenikon AB in Greece and Eielson AFB in Alaska.

The Lockheed SR-71 Blackbird is a high-performance, high altitude reconnaissance aircraft, which carries a crew of two, the pilot and reconnaissance systems officer (RSO). It has a loaded weight of some 170,000lbs and spans 55ft 7in, with a length of 107ft 5in. Power is provided by two Pratt & Whitney JT11D-20B turbojets, which can operate continuously on afterburner producing 32,500lbs of thrust each. Maximum speed is over Mach 3 and operating altitude is between 80,000ft and 100,000ft. Maximum fuel load is some 80,000lbs of special JP-7 and the Blackbird operates with KC-135Q tanker aircraft. The nose-mounted sensors can cover 100,000 square miles in one hour and can be changed to suit the mission. A typical sortie will last for 2½ hours, but this can be extended to four hours giving a mission radius of some 4000 miles.

The SR-71's high operating altitude and Mach 3 plus speed make great demands on crew and aircraft alike. The pilot and RSO wear astronaut-style pressure suits for safety in the aircraft and in the event of an ejection. The SR-71 requires great skill from its pilot since very precise flying at Mach 3 is virtually impossible – at this speed the radius of a turn is 90 miles. High airspeeds also cause the aircraft's skin to heat, with temperatures varying from 450 degrees Farenheit up to 1100 degrees F. The aircraft's distinctive black paint scheme helps deal with this problem, as it radiates heat more effectively than natural metal, and the fuel is also used for cooling. After landing the aircraft is literally

The Lockheed U-2 strategic reconnaissance aircraft has been in US service since the late 1950s, an early U-2B being pictured (above left). The USAF's standard tactical reconnaissance aircraft is the RF-4C Phantom, an aircraft of the 10th TRW based at Alconbury in the UK is pictured (above).

too hot to touch and because of the heating problem over 90 percent of the structure and skinning is titanium. The engines too are quite distinctive, as they operate as turbojets at low airspeed and as ramjets at high Mach numbers.

The SR-71 originated as the YF-12A experimental interceptor, which first flew in 1962. The project was highly classified and the SR-71's existence was not officially confirmed until 1964. Blackbirds entered service in January 1966 and it is believed that 31 were built. Two of these were converted to SR-71B pilot trainers and one of these has been lost in an accident.

The Lockheed U-2, which entered service with the USAF in 1957, still equips the 9th SRW's 99th Strategic Reconnaissance Squadron. A number of the squadron's aircraft are U-2Cs, which are used for electronic reconnaissance. This version is powered by a 17,000lbs thrust Pratt & Whitney J75-P-13 turbojet, which gives a cruising speed of 460mph. Operating altitude is about 80,000ft and range (which is well over 4000 miles) can be increased by gliding flight between intermittent bursts of engine power. The high aspect-ratio, glider-like wing spans 80ft and the fuselage length is 49ft 7in. Electronic reconnaissance equipment is carried in an 8ft long canoe-like fairing atop the fuselage. Most of the current U-2 fleet are U-2R variants, a much larger aircraft than the C, with a

lengthened fuselage and larger wing, which is increased in area by over 70 percent. The nose section houses various interchangeable reconnaissance packs. Twenty-five U-2Rs have been produced by rebuilding earlier airframes.

The MiG-25 represents the Soviet Union's equivalent to the SR-71 and two reconnaissance versions, Foxbat-B and Foxbat-D are currently in service. The aircraft can operate as high as 80,000ft at a maximum speed of Mach 3.2. Shortly after its introduction into service in 1971, four Foxbat-Bs were detached to Egypt and flew reconnaissance missions over the Israeli-occupied Sinai peninsula without being intercepted. Similar detachments have operated from Syria and Libya and Soviet-based Foxbat-Bs have overflown Turkey and Iran. The aircraft has also made shallow penetrations of NATO airspace, overflying West Germany, Denmark and Norway. However with the deployment to Europe of the F-15, the MiG-25 has lost much of its immunity, but it continues to operate effectively over less-well defended areas and as a stand-off system.

Foxbat-B differs little from the interceptor MiG-25 apart from equipment changes for its new role. The large Foxfire radar is replaced by a battery of cameras, a sideways-looking airborne radar (SLAR), plus ground-mapping doppler and forward-looking radars for navigation. The cameras are installed in oblique pairs, angled to port and starboard at angles of 15 and 45 degrees, with the fifth mounted vertically. Foxbat-D is equipped primarily for ELINT and has a larger SLAR, in addition to electronic monitoring equipment. Some 150 Foxbat-B and D reconnaissance aircraft have been

Above:The SR-71 Blackbird is a Mach 3-plus strategic reconnaissance aircraft serving with the USAF's 9th SRW at Beale AFB, California.
Right: Although obsolete, the Saab Lansen continues to serve the Swedish Air Force in the target-towing and ECM roles.

produced for service with Frontal Aviation.

Until the early 1970s the Soviet Union also operated the Yak-25RD Mandrake, a high-flying, single seat strategic reconnaissance aircraft. This had a 72ft span unswept wing and operated above 60,000ft over a range of more than 2000 miles. Recent reports have indicated that a belated successor to Mandrake is being tested. Identified as Ram-M, this aircraft is broadly similar to the Lockheed U-2, but has twin vertical tail surfaces. Echoing the practice of both Britain and Germany before World War II, the Soviet Union apparently uses civil flights by aircraft of Aeroflot for clandestine reconnaissance missions. In November 1981 a Soviet airliner overflew the Groton Shipbuilding Yard in Connecticut, where Trident submarines are made.

In contrast to the highly-specialized strategic reconnaissance aircraft, tactical reconnaissance machines are generally modifications of standard fighter and attack aircraft. This allows these aircraft to undertake a secondary strike/attack role and simplifies maintenance, by keeping the number of aircraft types in service to a minimum. Some air forces take this philosophy a stage further and simply install self-contained reconnaissance pods on otherwise unmodified aircraft. Although this simplifies switching the reconnaissance aircraft to another role it does not solve the problem of

crew training. Tactical reconnaissance is a highly skilled operation and aircrew proficient in the art will have little time to train for an equally specialized secondary mission. The best compromise is to assign tactical reconnaissance units a secondary tactical nuclear strike role, as this mission most closely resembles their primary task.

The USAF's standard tactical reconnaissance aircraft is the RF-4C version of the Phantom. A total of 505 was built between 1964 and 1974 and the aircraft now serves with TAC's 363rd Tactical Reconnaissance Wing at Shaw AFB, SC, and the 67th TRW at Bergstrom AFB, Texas. The 363rd TRW is scheduled to become a tactical fighter wing with the F-16, but it will retain a single squadron of RF-4Cs. In Europe the RF-4C serves with the 10th TRW at Alconbury in the UK and 26th TRW at Zweibrücken in West Germany. One squadron of the 18th TFW at Kadena, Okinawa, operates the RF-4C in the USAF's Pacific Air Forces.

The first reconnaissance version of the Phantom was the US Marines' RF-4B, a straightforward con-

version of the F-4B with a modified nose housing vertical and oblique cameras. The RF-4C, based on the F-4C, has a more comprehensive range of sensors. There are three camera stations, that in the nose usually being a forward-looking oblique camera, with a fan of three low-level cameras in the center position and a panoramic camera mounted vertically aft. However, there are numerous permutations, which can be matched to high or low level missions by day or night. For night photography photoflash cartridges are ejected from the rear fuselage to provide illumination.

The RF-4C also carries an infra-red linescan sensor, which records the heat signatures of objects on the ground. It can, for example, penetrate camouflage and locate hidden vehicles. IR can show which aircraft on an airfield have recently been fueled or had their engines running. It can even reveal traces of aircraft which have recently taken off, as their presence remains as a heat shadow on the hardstanding. Radar reconnaissance is undertaken by a nose-mounted forward-looking radar and a sideways-looking airborne radar, which scans to either side. The SLAR is able to pick out moving targets, such as truck convoys, using doppler techniques. The RF-4C is currently being modified to incorporate a data link, to transmit the SLAR picture to a ground station 30-50 nautical miles away. This eliminates the delays in getting the results of a sortie to the commanders who requested it.

Accurate navigation is essential for effective tactical reconnaissance and the RF-4C is accordingly fitted with an inertial navigation set, navigation computer and radar altimeter. Some aircraft also have the very

Among the most useful reconnaissance sensors available to NATO is infra-red linescan (right). It is capable of producing a thermal picture of the terrain overflown by day or night (below). The most important Soviet tactical reconnaissance aircraft is the Fishbed-H version of the MiG-21, shown (below right) in Polish service.

accurate LORAN long-range navigation equipment. A data annotation device records the aircraft's position, altitude and other performance parameters on the film as it is exposed. The RF-4C carries no defensive armament, but can be fitted with ECM jamming pods. It can also carry a tactical nuclear weapon on the centerline station for its secondary strike role. Otherwise the external stores stations carry auxiliary fuel tanks with a total capacity of 1340 gallons, supplementing the internal tankage of 1889 gallons. This gives a radius of 513 miles for a low-level mission, or 673 miles at high altitude.

The USAF has supplemented the RF-4C with the Lockheed TR-1A, a stand-off, tactical reconnaissance aircraft based on the U-2. A total of 35 is on order and one squadron is deployed at Alconbury in the UK to cover the NATO central region. The TR-1A spans 103ft and is 63ft in length. Power is provided by one Pratt & Whitney J75-P-13B, which gives a cruising speed of 430mph. The aircraft can operate at altitudes of 90,000ft and range is over 3000 miles. Operating at high altitudes, the TR-1A's advanced, synthetic aperture, sideways-looking radar can detect ground activities several hundred miles to the side of the aircraft. Therefore a TR-1A operating over NATO territory can warn of movements deep in Warsaw Pact territory, without having to evade the enemy defenses. The aircraft carries a variety of interchangeable sensors in the nose bay and in wing pods, the maximum payload being almost two tons. The aircraft's endurance is up to 12 hours, although sorties of this length would make great demands on the pilot, who has to wear an uncomfortable pressure suit throughout the flight.

Many of the European NATO Allies make use of pod-mounted reconnaissance systems flown on tactical fighters. A typical example is the RAF's tactical reconnaissance Jaguar, which carries a pod-mounted camera and IR-linescan. Two RAF Jaguar squadrons specialize in reconnaissance; No 2 Squadron at Laarbruch in RAF Germany and No 41 at Coltishall in the UK. The aircraft are standard Jaguars, the inertial navigation system being especially useful. Reconnaissance cameras are housed in two rotatable drums within the pod, which swivel to expose the camera ports during photography. The front drum contains two side-mounted and one forward-looking oblique camera, while the second drum has two oblique cameras for low-level work, or a single vertical camera for use at medium altitudes. This combination gives horizon-to-horizon coverage and a data conversion unit obtains the aircraft's position from the navigation computer and annotates it onto the film. The IR-linescan is especially useful in poor light and darkness and it too has the aircraft's position automatically marked on the film. At the end of a sortie the film is rapidly processed so that within ten minutes it is being examined by interpreters. The results of their examination, together with the pilot's report, can be passed on within half an hour of the aircraft landing.

France's Armée de l'Air has a single reconnaissance wing, the 33e Escadre de Reconnaissance based at Strasbourg, with three component squadrons flying Mirage IIIR and Mirage IIIRD aircraft. These are variants of the Mirage IIIE multi-role fighter, fitted with five nose-mounted cameras suitable for high, medium and low altitude reconnaissance. The Mirage IIIRD is more advanced, with IR sensors and doppler navigation equipment. Both types are currently being replaced by the Mirage F1CR (62 on order). This reconnaissance version of the F1C interceptor has provision for inflight refueling and carries cameras, IR sensors, forward-looking radar and an inertial navigation system.

West Germany's Luftwaffe operates the RF-4E version of the Phantom, 88 of which were delivered in the early 1970s. They serve with Aufklarungsgeschwader 51 at Bremgarten and AK52 at Leck. Essentially the reconnaissance systems are those of the RF-4C, but the

basic airframe is that of the F-4E.

Apart from the MiG-25, which is apparently used for both tactical and strategic reconnaissance, the Soviet Union's main battlefield reconnaissance aircraft is the MiG-21R or Fishbed-H. This carries cameras and probably also IR linescan in a ventral pod and has small pods on the wingtips for electronic sensors.

Because tactical reconnaissance aircraft often operate in a high threat area, particularly when battlefield reconnaissance is required, unmanned remotely piloted vehicles (RPVs) or autonomously-guided drones have been developed for this task. They range from quite complex turbojet powered vehicles to expendable mini-RPVs which are little more advanced than radio-controlled model aircraft. The most widely used turbojet powered drone in NATO is the Canadair CL-89, which serves with the British, Canadian, West German, French and Italian armies. The CL-89 is launched from a ramp, follows a preprogrammed flight path and returns to friendly territory homing onto a beacon, where it parachutes back to earth. Either cameras or IR linescan can be carried.

During the war in Southeast Asia the USAF made extensive use of air-launched Teledyne Ryan AQM-34 reconnaissance drones, which were derived from the Firebee target drone. More than 20 variants were manufactured to undertake high, medium and low altitude missions by day and night. Guidance was either by radio command from an airborne or ground control

post, or by a pre-programmed flight plan. The sensors were cameras or IR linescan and data could be transmitted to a ground or airborne relay station. The launch aircraft was a DC-130 variant of the Hercules, with recovery by parachute. Sometimes Sikorsky CH-3 helicopters retrieved the AQM-34 in the air after parachute deployment. This system is no longer in use, although it it believed that drones are in storage and could be returned to service quickly.

Rotary-winged drones have been evaluated as battlefield reconnaissance systems and as tethered platforms intended to raise sensors several hundred feet above their operating vehicles and relay visual or radar data to them. In West Germany Dornier developed the Do34 Kiebitz, which was fitted with a battlefield reconnaissance radar. Other rotary wing systems have been developed with low-light TV, still and TV cameras and IR sensors.

The basic reconnaissance tool remains the camera. For fast low-level work they need to use lenses of short focal length to give the widest angle of view. Often they are mounted in fans to give the maximum coverage. Higher flying aircraft can use a camera with a longer focal length lens to give a good image size. Various

310

problems arise because of aircraft vibration and variations in temperature can also affect the quality of a photograph. Because the aircraft is moving during the exposure, a technique known as image movement compensation is used, which moves the film at the same speed as the object it is photographing so that the image will not be blurred.

The film used for photographic reconnaissance is usually black and white, but color film can be useful if this provides a greater contrast. A further alternative is color infra-red film, which is useful for penetrating camouflage. Of more use is the IR linescan sensor. This builds up a heat picture of the terrain, which can be recorded on tape or film for later analysis.

Photography and thermal imaging can be supplemented by radar reconnaissance. Sideways looking radar is especially effective because it makes use of synthetic aperture techniques. This means in simple terms that the distance an aircraft travels can be used as though it were a very long radar aerial and so images of a very high resolution are obtained.

The results are of little use, however, unless they are accurately interpreted and the information is speedily disseminated to the commanders who will make use of it. These problems have long been recognized, but solutions are not always easy to find. Early RF-4Cs were fitted with film cassettes which could be ejected in flight to users on the ground, but the system was found to be unworkable and was discontinued.

The ideal system is one that provides the commander on the ground with 'real time' information, for by the time an aircraft has returned to base and its film has been processed the tactical situation may have radically altered. The transmission of the SLAR imagery, which is now possible, helps to achieve this capability. SLAR is not defeated by cloud, haze and smoke, but the images it produces, although they are sharp, often cannot be identified because they are radar blips and not a photographic image. The USAF has used SLAR in conjunction with TEREC (tactical electronic reconnaissance) a system, which can identify a target associated with a radio or radar emitter, as many military targets will be. Clearly this is not a complete answer. One promising development is the AN/UXD-1 system which is being tested by the USAF. This enables high quality photographs to be transmitted to a ground station within ten seconds.

In spite of the development of advanced sensors and stand-off capabilities, direct visual observation by a reconnaissance crew is valuable in many situations. One way to ensure that tactical targets are hit soon after they are located is for the reconnaissance aircraft to rendezvous with the strike force and lead it to the target. The reconnaissance aircraft can then round off its mission by photographing the results. Another possibility is that the reconnaissance crew can report their visual observation by voice radio, provided that communications links are not jammed.

A Canadair CL-289 reconnaissance drone (top) is launched from its ground vehicle. After following a preprogrammed flight path to its objective, it is recovered by parachute (right), automatically-inflating airbags absorbing the landing impact.

Where it is not essential that reconnaissance imagery be received and processed rapidly (and this applies especially to strategic reconnaissance), a number of techniques can be employed to gain the maximum information from the material. Hidden details can be brought out during film processing. Computer technology can be used to assist in interpretation of photographic, IR and SLAR imagery, by automating target searches and corellating the photo images with map references. If the imagery is presented in digital form, then data processing can be used to sharpen images or alter contrasts to assist in identification and interpretation.

Because modern armed forces are so dependent upon radars and radio communications, electronic intelligence-gathering or ELINT is today as important as visual reconnaissance. ELINT aircraft operate on the borders of a potential enemy's territory scanning the wavelengths for electronic emissions. Every signal can be classified and identified, so that a picture can be built up of the opponent's air defenses, showing, for example, the positions of radars and control centers or the radio wavelengths used to communicate with enemy fighters. This information will be essential in planning one's own electronic-countermeasures, quite apart from the intelligence which can be gathered about enemy dispositions.

ELINT can make a valuable contribution to virtually every aspect of defense intelligence. ELINT aircraft have 'captured' the telemetry transmitted from Soviet missiles under test, so that the US intelligence agencies can accurately assess their performance. If the accuracy of Soviet missiles is known with some degree of certainty, then American planners can devise a basing system for their ICBMs which will defeat the opposition. In the absence of such intelligence, resources may be wasted on a needlessly sophisticated basing system. Alternatively deterrent forces may be put at risk by presenting the adversary with an ICBM force he will be able to knock out.

At the tactical level, ELINT aircraft can enable a comprehensive library of enemy electronic systems to be built up. This means for example that a hostile warship using its search radar can not only be detected, but the radar itself can be identified and this will provide a clue to identifying the class of ship. The same information can be applied to the defense suppression mission, as every hostile radar emission will identify the SAM or AA gun which it is serving.

ELINT gathering is a highly classified activity and, although the aircraft types employed can be identified, the equipment they use and the way they operate is shrouded in secrecy. The USAF's ELINT aircraft are the Boeing RC-135s of the 55th Strategic Reconnaissance Wing at Offutt AFB, with aircraft operating on detached service to virtually all parts of the world. The RC-135 is basically a modified KC-135 Stratotanker. It has a range of over 5000 miles and is fitted with an airborne refueling receiver. The crew complement for the early RC-135C variant was quoted as 18, four of whom were the flight deck crew.

Ten versions of the RC-135 have been identified, each with a different combination of sensors, and indeed equipment variations occur within individual sub-types. The specific missions of these aircraft are not known, but each has its own permutation of SLAR and forward-looking radars, HF, VHF and UHF antennae, plus a range of distinctive and mysterious aerials and radomes.

The US Navy undertakes its own ELINT, which is primarily intended to gather data on Soviet naval electronic systems. Two fleet air reconnaissance squadrons carry out these missions; VQ-1 covers the Pacific from Agana on Guam, while the Atlantic and Mediterranean are the responsibility of VQ-2 at Rota in Spain. Both squadrons operate a mixture of EA-3B Skywarriors and EP-3E Orions, the former being able to operate from aircraft carriers.

Lockheed EP-3Es are conversions of early-model Orion ASW aircraft and about a dozen are in service. They carry a 15-man mission crew, and can accommodate a complete relief crew for maximum efficiency on a 17 hour mission. An extensive range of detection and monitoring equipment is fitted, including an ALR-60 communications interception and recording system, an ALD-8 direction finding system, an ALQ-110 radar signal collection system and a frequency measuring receiver.

The Douglas EA-3B is a development of the A-3 Skywarrior attack aircraft, which entered US Navy Service in 1956. Although now obsolete in its original nuclear-strike role, the type continues to serve in small numbers in the tanker, reconnaissance and ECM roles, as well as for ELINT. The EA-3B carries a crew of seven, four more than the other variants. Power is provided by two Pratt & Whitney J57-P-10 turbojets, each developing 10,500lbs of thrust. Maximum speed is Mach 0.83 at 10,000ft, ceiling 41,000ft and range 2900 miles. Wingspan is 72ft 6in, length 76ft 4in and maximum takeoff weight 84,000lbs.

Two European NATO members operate small ELINT forces, using conversions of ASW patrol aircraft. The RAF has three Nimrod R Mk 1s in service for this task. They seve with No 51 Squadron, which is based at Wyton in the UK. The West German Navy has had five of its 20 Breguet Atlantic ASW aircraft converted for ELINT tanks. They are primarily concerned with Soviet naval activities in the Baltic and operate alongside the standard ASW Atlantics with Marinefliegergeschwader 3 'Graf Zeppelin' at Nordholz.

Electronic intelligence is greatly valued by the Soviet Union. Soviet aircraft seek this information on a routine basis and by monitoring NATO exercises. They also attempt to trigger a reaction from defense forces by provocative intrusions into national airspace, as they can learn much by monitoring the result. An ELINT version of the Antonov An-12 transport, the Cub-B, has been produced in addition to the ECM Cub-C. These aircraft may operate with Soviet Naval Aviation, as many Soviet ELINT sorties are concerned with naval operations. Another Soviet transport aircraft converted for ELINT work is the Ilyushin Il-18 Coot-A. It carries a large antennae fairing beneath the fuselage, as well as numerous radomes and aerials. Coot-A has operated around NATO central region and has probed the UK's air defenses.

Two older Soviet ELINT systems are converted bomber aircraft. They are probably less efficient than the modified transports, as they do not have the same amount of space for equipment and its operators. They are the Bear-E variant of the Tu-20 and the Badger-E and F versions of the Tu-16, both of which serve with Soviet Naval Aviation.

As with strategic reconnaissance, the introduction of ELINT or Ferret satellites has not made the aircraft systems unnecessary, but has rather provided a complementary source of intelligence. The satellites can cover areas deep in enemy territory, while the ELINT aircraft can cover such activities as naval exercises more effectively – if necessary by provoking a response from defensive systems.

The RAF's first VC 10 K Mk 2 in-flight refueling tanker, which was converted from a standard VC 10 airliner, pictured during testing.

TRANSPORT AIRCRAFT

Above: A USAF C-130E Hercules demonstrates the parachute container delivery system, which can dispense up to 16 one-ton loads in flight.
Above right: The cavernous hold of the C-5A Galaxy is accessible via a hinged nose section. A Roland fire unit exemplifies the bulky loads that can be accommodated.

The modern transport aircraft has made it possible to airlift troops, their equipment and supplies over enormous distances at a speed hitherto unprecedented in warfare. Air transport operations can be strategic, involving the movement of forces between theaters of operations, or tactical airlift within the theater itself. A further aspect of tactical airlift is battlefield mobility, although this is more satisfactorily regarded as part of army aviation and is fully dealt with in the following chapter.

The advantages of air transport are obvious. Because of its speed of reaction, reinforcements can be rapidly lifted to a theater of operations from their peacetime stations, thus reducing the expense of permanent foreign garrisons, such as the US Army in Europe. Movement by air across the Atlantic is reckoned in hours, whereas by sea it would take days and even then the port of disembarkation could be far from the battlefield. However, air transport has definite limitations. The movement of large bodies of troops by air presents few problems, but without their weapons and equipment they are of little use. Even the massive C-5A Galaxy transport can only carry two main battle tanks and so clearly the airlift of an armored division from the USA to Europe would present problems.

One answer is the dual basing system for forces normally based in the United States, which would be needed in Europe in the event of war. These formations have equipment positioned both in the United States and in Europe, so that only the men need to be airlifted across the Atlantic. This is of course very expensive, as the cost of equipping these formations is doubled and the prepositioned equipment must be carefully stored and maintained.

During the American involvement in the Vietnam War no less than 98 percent of all supplies were transported by sea. This was despite strategic airlift operations on a massive scale. USAF Military Airlift Command's flying hours for 1967 alone were equivalent to 8750 flights around the world and the number of troops carried could have manned 85 US Army infantry divisions. The Vietnam statistics are probably misleading to some degree when applied to a war in Europe, because a massive amount of construction work was necessary in Southeast Asia and the materials inflated the sealift figures. Nevertheless, it indicates the basic problem of airlift operations, which are efficient in moving men, but unable to carry heavy equipment or gasoline and ammunition in sufficient quantity.

The US is especially concerned with the problems of mobility over large distances. Forces normally based in the USA may be required to reinforce NATO units in Europe or to bolster the US troops defending South Korea, while a further eventuality is the Rapid Deployment Force's movement to the Middle East, where no US Army or USAF forces are permanently stationed. All of these movements may have to be made at short notice. In studying these contingencies, planners have had to balance the advantages and shortcomings of airlift, prepositioning of equipment and sealift. Air transport is fast and flexible, but its capacity is limited and its use is dependent on the availability of friendly airfields. Prepositioning, as well as being expensive, is inflexible, while sealift offers great capacity at the expense of speed and some flexibility. The planners' conclusions are that airlift will transport some 90 percent of the combat forces put into action during the first 30 days of the operation, with some equipment being prepositioned. In an extended conflict sealift will deliver between 90 and 95 percent of all supplies.

The availability of staging posts overseas may be of crucial importance in airlift operations. Inflight refueling can go some way to make transport aircraft independent of the need for intermediate landings. Nonstop airlift operations across the Atlantic are quite feasible, of course, although in any case NATO controlled airfields are available on Iceland and the Azores. However, an airlift to the Middle East would require staging posts and supporting tanker aircraft would themselves require overseas bases. A related problem is the need to obtain permission to overfly foreign airspace. This has to be applied for through diplomatic channels well in advance and it could be refused. Thus air barriers can be created, which will require additional fuel to fly around with a consequent reduction in payload. These barriers can even make a proposed air route impassable.

The United States strategic airlift capability comprises some 350 Lockheed C-5A Galaxy and Lockheed C-141B Starlifter transport aircraft of Military Airlift Command. In an emergency the Command can call upon approximately 460 civil passenger and cargo aircraft of the Civil Reserve Air Fleet (CRAF). These could carry 95 percent of military personnel requiring airlift, but only 35 percent of cargo. Cargo capabilities are to be increased by fitting wider doors and strengthened floors to civil transports in future. The capabilities of the regular forces are also being enhanced. The entire C-141A Starlifter fleet has been modified to C-141B standard, with fuselage lengthened by 23ft 4in and flight refueling capability added.

The USAF's strategic transports are flown by seven military airlift wings of the regular air force. These are supported by associate wings of the Air Force Reserve, which provide air and ground crews to supplement the regulars.

The C-5A Galaxy was designed from the outset to carry bulky items of military equipment. Its lower cargo deck can accommodate 16 light trucks, or 270 troops, while the upper deck can seat a further 75 troops. The C-5A is powered by four General Electric TF-39-GE-1 turbofans, which give a maximum speed of 571mph at 25,000ft. Range is 6500 miles when carrying maximum fuel plus an 80,000lbs payload. With a maximum takeoff weight of 764,500lbs, the Galaxy spans 222ft 8½in and is 247ft 10in long. Its runway requirements are comparatively modest for its size, the C-5A needing an 8000ft takeoff run and half that for landing. A flight crew of seven is normally carried.

The Lockheed C-141B Starlifter, 270 of which are in service, is the USAF's workhorse strategic transport

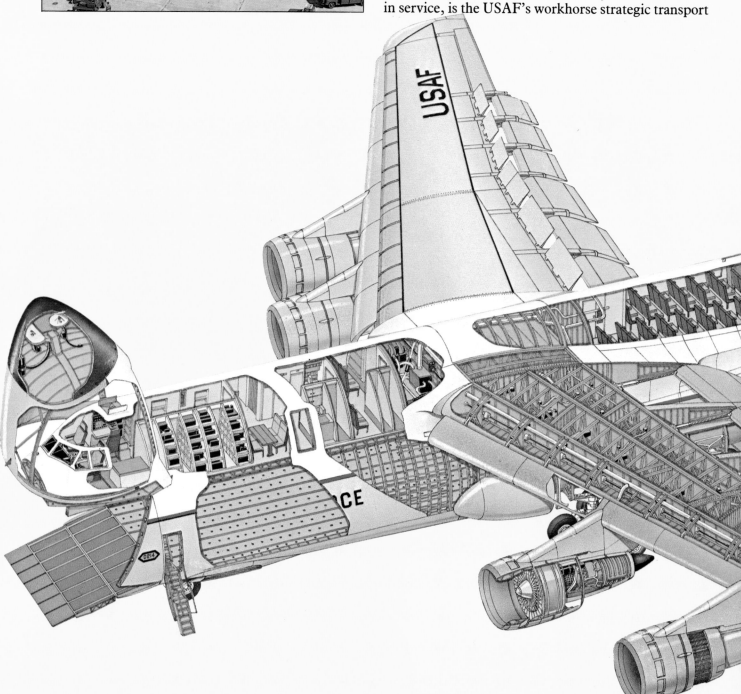

with good range and payload characteristics, the former enhanced by inflight refueling when necessary. The stretched aircraft is 168ft 4in long, with a wingspan of 159ft 11in and maximum takeoff weight of 324,900lbs. Power is provided by four Pratt & Whitney TF-33-P-7 turbofans of 21,000lbs thrust each. Cruising speed is 512mph and ceiling 45,000ft. With a 74,200lbs payload the Starlifter's range is 3200 miles. A flight crew of seven is carried and in addition to cargo the C-141B can carry troops or be converted to an aerial ambulance for medical evacuation.

The USAF's CX requirement calls for a new out-size-cargo transport which will be able to fly such equipment as tanks, self-propelled artillery and infantry fighting vehicles from bases in the USA direct

The USAF's C-5A Galaxy is Military Airlift Command's largest transport aircraft and is able to lift a maximum payload of over 220,000lbs (above left and below).

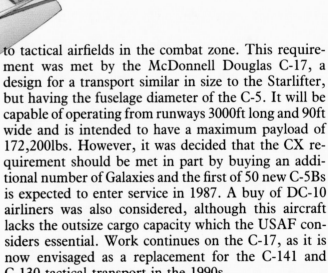

to tactical airfields in the combat zone. This requirement was met by the McDonnell Douglas C-17, a design for a transport similar in size to the Starlifter, but having the fuselage diameter of the C-5. It will be capable of operating from runways 3000ft long and 90ft wide and is intended to have a maximum payload of 172,200lbs. However, it was decided that the CX requirement should be met in part by buying an additional number of Galaxies and the first of 50 new C-5Bs is expected to enter service in 1987. A buy of DC-10 airliners was also considered, although this aircraft lacks the outsize cargo capacity which the USAF considers essential. Work continues on the C-17, as it is now envisaged as a replacement for the C-141 and C-130 tactical transport in the 1990s.

A strategic transport force is more of a luxury than a necessity for the Soviet Union, which does not have to move its forces over large areas of ocean to reach the probable battlefields of World War 3. However, the vast extent of the Soviet homeland makes air transport within its frontiers very useful. With expanding Soviet influence in such troubled areas as the Middle East, Africa, Southeast Asia and Central America, a long-range airlift capacity has become necessary to support Soviet client states and associates in distant regions. Nevertheless, Military Transport Aviation remains

primarily concerned with supporting Soviet ground forces and with transporting the airborne divisions. At the beginning of 1985, Military Transport Aviation had a strengh of some 600 medium- and long-range transport aircraft, more than 180 of which were long-range Ilyushin Il-76 Candids and Antonov An-22 Cocks. In addition the Soviet Union can make use of the total resources of Aeroflot, which would add about 1300 long- and medium-range passenger and cargo aircraft to the military transport fleet. Aeroflot could also provide several thousand short-range transports and helicopters.

The Ilyushin Il-76 is really a successor to the Antonov An-12 Cub tactical transport, but because it has twice the payload and range it can be used for strategic airlift. This was demonstrated when weapons were sent to Ethiopia in late 1977. Although similar in size to the C-141B Starlifter, the Il-76 is more powerful. It is also able to use rough tactical airstrips, unlike the C-141, and can operate comfortably from a 5000ft runway. The Il-76 has a maximum payload of 88,200lbs and can lift this over a distance of more than 3000 miles. Maximum range is over 4000 miles, but unlike the US transports the Il-76 cannot be refueled in flight. Power is provided by four 26,450lbs Soloviev D-30KP turbofans, which give a maximum cruising speed of 466mph. Wing span is 165ft 8in and length 152ft 10in, with a maximum takeoff weight of 375,000lbs. A flight crew

of six is carried and many aircraft carry a defensive armament of two radar-directed 23mm cannon in a manned tail turret.

The massive Antonov An-22 Cock is the Soviet Union's heavylift strategic transport, with some 50 in military service and an equal number with Aeroflot. It can accommodate main battle tanks, or the tracked launch vehicle for twin SA-4 surface-to-air missiles, as part of its 175,000lbs maximum payload. The An-22 is turboprop powered, with four 15,000shp Kuznetsov NK-12MV engines driving massive 20ft diameter contra-rotating propellers. These give a maximum speed of 460mph, with a service ceiling of 25,000ft. Range with a payload of 100,000lbs is 6800 miles. With a maximum takeoff weight of 550,000lbs, the An-22 spans 211ft 4in and is 189ft 7in long. Surprisingly in view of its bulk, the An-22 has been designed to operate from rough, unprepared airstrips. This reflects the Soviet concern with tactical airlift in support of ground forces, with strategic airlift being only secondary. In World War 3 the Soviet strategic transport fleet is likely to be used for the rapid movement of forces from outlying military districts to the battlefronts. The An-22 could also be used to fly heavy equipment into a bridgehead seized by the airborne divisions.

Tactical airlift is concerned primarily with the logistic support of the fighting armies. Urgently-needed supplies and reinforcements can be more

Top left: The mighty An-22 Cock provides the Soviet Union with the backbone of its strategic heavy lift transport capability. Its maximum payload totals 175,000 pounds.
Above left: With a range of some 4000 miles, the turbofan-powered Il-76 Candid provides further long-range capability.
Above: A C-7A Caribou transport demonstrates the technique of low-level parachute extraction.

rapidly carried to the front by air than by land transport. Airborne forces operating behind enemy lines, or pockets of resistance surrounded by an advancing enemy, can only be resupplied by air and if necessary they can be evacuated by the same means. Tactical transports will provide an essential link between the strategic airlift of forces into the theater of war and the battlefront, by ferrying troops from the secure 'airheads' in rear areas to tactical airstrips in the combat zone.

The USAF's tactical airlift commitment is carried out by 14 squadrons of Lockheed C-130 Hercules transports of Military Airlift Command. Until 1974 these assets were controlled by Tactical Air Command, reflecting the close co-operation between the tactical airlift squadrons and the ground forces they support. However, the change in command represented a rationalization of resources and a recognition that the Hercules' 4600-miles maximum range could make it a useful supplement to the strategic transport force in an

emergency. MAC's regular peacetime strength can be doubled by the 51,000 reservists of the ANG and AFRES trained in air transport duties. Over 300 tactical transport aircraft, including C-130s and the older Fairchild C-123 Providers and the DHC C-7 Caribou, are in service with the ANG and AFRES.

The Lockheed C-130 Hercules entered USAF service in December 1956 and over 1000 have been built for the American services alone. The aircraft has been exported to over 50 countries, including among the NATO allies Belgium (12), Canada (33), Denmark (3), Greece (12), Italy (14), Norway (6), Portugal (5), Spain (12), Turkey (8) and the United Kingdom (66). The C-130E version is powered by four 4050shp Allison T-56A-7 turboprops, which give a maximum cruising speed of 368mph. Maximum payload is 45,000lbs, which can be carried over a range of 2400 miles. Take-off weight is 175,000lbs and dimensions are 132ft 7in wing span and 97ft 9in length. The C-130H, an improved version with more powerful engines, remains in production. Deliveries of new C-130H aircraft have been made direct to Air National Guard squadrons, as part of the modernization of the reserves begun in the 1970s.

Among the European NATO members the UK and France have the largest transport forces, partly as a result of their continuing commitments in former colonial territories. The RAF has four tactical transport squadrons equipped with the Hercules and based at Lyneham and a single strategic transport squadron flying 4200 miles range VC 10 transports from Brize Norton. Thirty of the standard Hercules C Mk 1 are being 'stretched' by an extra 13ft 4in fuselage section. Redesignated Hercules C Mk 3, they have a 40 percent increase in cargo capacity and 92 paratroops can be lifted instead of the C Mk 1's 64. These forces are primarily committed to NATO, but they also support operations outside the Alliance's area. France's tactical transport force flies the Franco-German C.160 Transall, which equips Escadre de Transport 61 at Orleans-Bricy and is replacing the elderly Noratlas with ET64 at Evreux. The Transall C.160 also equips three transport wings of the Luftwaffe. Powered by two Rolls-Royce Tyne Mk 22 turboprops of 6100shp, it has a range of 2830 miles with a 17,650lbs payload.

The An-12 Cub remains the mainstay of Soviet Military Transport Aviation, with over 400 in service. Most are based in the western military districts of the USSR. Powered by four 4000shp Ivchenko AI-20K turboprops, the An-12 has a maximum cruising speed of 400mph. With a 22,000lbs payload, the An-12's range is 2100 miles. Maximum payload is 44,000lbs and up to 100 troops can be accommodated. However, because the cargo cabin is unpressurized, it has to fly at low altitudes when carrying troops, thus reducing range. Maximum takeoff weight is 134,500lbs and dimensions include a span of 124ft 7in and a length of 108ft 6in. Twin 23mm cannon are carried in a manned tail turret.

Various methods can be used by tactical transports to deliver supplies to forward areas. The preferred method is to land and unload, as this avoids the complications and expense of parachute systems and allows the maximum load to be delivered. The landing fields used are likely to be primitive 3500ft dirt airstrips, constructed with the minimum of labor. They can present problems to the modern transport pilot, used to operating from 10,000ft concrete runways. For example a turboprop using reverse thrust can create a cloud of dust over the entire landing area. The problem is exacerbated at night, when airstrip lighting will be considerably less efficient than that of a permanent airfield. Even without dust clouds, an unsurfaced airstrip will tend to blend into the surrounding landscape. Yet all these problems are comparatively insignificant when compared with the dangers of enemy artillery or AA fire, or air attack. For this reason, the aircraft will keep their time on the ground to a minimum.

If conditions on the ground are too dangerous to allow the transport to land, supplies can be parachuted. The USAF's Low-Altitude Parachute Extraction System (LAPES) used with the C-130 requires the pilot to overfly the airstrip at a speed of 130 knots and a height of only five feet. A drogue parachute, attached to a special sled-like cargo pallet, is trailed from the rear cargo hatch. As the canopy deploys, it pulls the pallet and its cargo out of the aircraft and onto the runway where it skids to a halt. This method is accurate and fast, but it can be very dangerous for personnel on the airstrip and the low-flying aircrew must be careful to avoid obstacles on the ground.

A similar system to LAPES, the Ground Proximity Extraction System (GPES), was safer. It made use of an arrestor system on the airstrip, which engaged a hook attached to the cargo pallet after the aircraft touched down. The pallet was pulled out and the aircraft meanwhile accelerated and took off. The real disadvantage of GPES was that because it required special ground equipment, it lacked the flexibility of LAPES and so only a few sets of the system were produced.

If the landing zone is obscured by cloud or mist, parachute drops can be made from medium altitude guided by ground radar. However, very precise flying is required of the transport's crew if the loads are not to be hopelessly scattered. Three tactical airlift squadrons in MAC are equipped with the adverse weather aerial delivery system (AWADS). This comprises a very accurate ground-mapping radar carried by the C-130 and linked to the aircraft's flight control instruments. AWADS is thus independent of ground radars, which even if they are available in the right place, are vulnerable to enemy action. It is also more accurate than ground-controlled drops.

The USAF's parachute container delivery system is in fact a one ton load of fuel, food or ammunition lashed to a pallet and then covered by a shroud. The C-130 carries up to 16 of these, which are placed on rollers on the floor of the cargo compartment. Over the dropping zone the pilot opens the rear loading doors and lowers the cargo ramp, while the loadmaster releases the restraining lashings. The pilot then pulls up the aircraft's nose, allowing the pallets to roll out gently and be parachuted.

Evacuation of the wounded from the battle zone to permanent hospitals is an important task for military transport aircraft. Just as the helicopter enables the wounded to be removed from the battlefield to medical care as soon as possible, so aeromedical airlift operations can clear the wounded from field hospitals. This not only ensures better attention for the wounded at permanent and well-equipped hospitals remote from the war zone, but it also relieves the burden of caring for them from the overworked medical teams in the field.

The USAF operates a special unit for this role, the 375th Aeromedical Airlift Wing based at Scott AFB, Illinois. It flies the C-9A Nightingale, a version of the DC-9 airliner, specially-equipped and carrying doctors and nurses to care for the patients in flight. Detachments of the unit are based at Rhein-Main in West Germany and Clark AB in the Philippines. Standard transport aircraft can also be used in this role, including the C-141 Starlifter. During the Vietnam War Lockheed C-141As flew 6000 such missions between 1965 and 1972.

The twin-turboprop Transall C.160 (right) is flown by the air forces of France and West Germany. This view of the VC 10 K Mk2 (below) shows its underwing refueling pods and the third refueling point beneath the rear fuselage. The An-12 Cub (bottom right) is being replaced by the Il-76 as the standard Soviet tactical transport, but over 400 remain in service.

Army airborne forces are of course a priority claimant for military airlift resources. However, they make great demands on what will undoubtedly be a scarce asset in wartime. During the US exercise 'Bright Star' in 1981 it was found that it would take 10-14 days to deploy one of the US Army's two airborne divisions to Egypt, although an airborne brigade could be rushed to the area in 48 hours. This gives some idea of the magnitude of the problem of using airborne forces on a large scale. A US light infantry division, which could be used as an air landing force rather than a true airborne formation, would require 1230 C-5A and C-141B sorties to transport to Europe. With the USAF transport fleet presently available this would take several weeks to accomplish.

A more realistic approach would be to use smaller units to reinforce troops already in the theater of operations at short notice. For example, a 600-man paratroop force with its equipment can be airlifted to Europe from the USA in ten C-141B Starlifters. This would involve an eight hour flight with a drop into the battle area. The UK may be better placed to employ its airborne troops in this manner, but it will require a force of 21 Hercules C Mk 1s to lift a battalion to its drop zone. One weak-

The Soviet Union employs airborne troops on a large scale and currently maintains seven airborne divisions. They are well equipped with BMD amphibious assault vehicles, giving them better mobility and firepower than the paratroops of the NATO nations. The Soviet Union is therefore equipped to undertake large-scale airborne assaults, using paratroops, reinforced with air landing forces once airfields have been secured. As Military Transport Aviation does not have MAC's transoceanic reinforcement role, Soviet airborne troops are likely to enjoy a higher priority for airlift resources than their US counterparts. In addition to the airborne divisions, the Soviet Union has a number of air assault brigades, which can be used for small scale assaults on key objectives, such as nuclear weapon storage sites.

Raids against high value targets behind enemy lines will be made on a much smaller scale by highly-trained Special Forces troops, who will require air support to infiltrate enemy territory, to supply them during their operations and finally to evacuate them. The USAF maintains three squadrons trained and equipped primarily to support Special Forces operations. They are the 1st Special Operations Squadron (SOS) at Clark AFB in the Philippines, the 7th SOS at Rhein-Main in West Germany and the 8th SOS at Hurlburt Field, Florida, all flying the MC-130E version of the Hercules. Code-named Combat Talon, the mission of these aircraft is the covert infiltration and recovery of Special Forces from enemy territory.

The helicopter is also very useful in special operations. The USAF's 1st Special Operations Wing at Hurlburt Field, which experiments in and teaches the air aspects of unconventional warfare, flies the Sikorsky

CH-3E, the Bell UH-1N and Sikorsky HH-53. The latter helicopter has been extensively used on special operations, as well as in its primary role of combat rescue. During the Vietnam War, in November 1970, HH-53s carried a force of raiders to the Son Tay prison camp, 23 miles from Saigon. Their mission was to release American PoWs. The plan was boldly conceived and brilliantly executed, but intelligence had failed to discover that all the prisoners had been removed to other camps. In May 1975 HH-53s and the similar CH-53 (intended for special operations, but lacking the rescue helicopter's inflight refueling capability) participated in the operation which led to the release of the crew of SS *Mayaguez*, an American freighter illegally

The USAF's standard tactical transport aircraft is the C-130 Hercules. A C-130E (above) of the 36th Tactical Airlift Squadron overflies Mount St Helens. Strategic airlift is undertaken by the C-5A Galaxy and C-141 Starlifter (left). The C-5A has its nose visor raised. All USAF C-141As have been modified to C-141B standard (above right) by 'stretching' the fuselage by 23ft 4in.

seized by Cambodian gunboats.

These successful air operations should be set against the much publicized failure to release the US hostages from Tehran in April 1980. The helicopters employed in this mission were RH-53s – a similar design to the HH-53 but with the primary mission of minesweeping. Operating from the carrier USS *Nimitz*, three of the eight machines became unserviceable before reaching the desert landing strip which was to be the jumping-off place for the rescue mission. This led to the abandonment of the mission, which required six helicopters to transport the Special Forces troops to Tehran. The failure was exacerbated when one of the helicopters collided with a supporting Hercules transport taking off from the desert strip.

The Iranian debacle was due to a failure in planning and sheer misfortune, rather than to any fundamental weakness in equipment. It is very likely that helicopter operations will support clandestine missions in Europe during World War 3. CH-53s are based at Sembach in West Germany, ostensibly to transport mobile radars, but it is probable that they have a secondary special operations role. Soviet special forces troops controlled

by the KGB and GRU (military intelligence) will operate extensively behind NATO lines in World War III. They will be supported by transport aircraft of Military Transport Aviation and by the assault helicopters of Frontal Aviation.

Air refueling operations are one of the most valuable of air force support functions. Tanker aircraft are 'force multipliers', enabling tactical aircraft to operate at extended ranges, or for longer periods and with a heavier warload. Their contribution to strategic bomber operations is vital and indeed all USAF tanker aircraft are controlled by SAC. Tanker aircraft will enable the NATO air forces in Europe to be rapidly reinforced with tactical fighter squadrons from the USA and Canada in the event of war. However, because air refueling is such a useful adjunct to a variety of combat and support missions, tanker aircraft will be very scarce assets in war. Their allocation will be carefully controlled and it is unlikely that tanker support will be available for every mission that could benefit from it.

At present the USAF's aerial refueling force comprises 615 Boeing KC-135 tanker aircraft, including 128 assigned to the Air National Guard and AFRES. All these aircraft are controlled by SAC and have the primary mission of supporting strategic air operations. However, a proportion of the tanker force can be detailed to support tactical air operations. All strategic bomber and C^3 aircraft are capable of being refueled in flight, as are the great majority of tactical fighter aircraft, reconnaissance, airborne control aircraft, strategic transports and the tankers themselves. SAC is currently upgrading its capabilities by introducing the new KC-10 Extender tanker/transport, which is especially valuable for supporting the overseas deployment of tactical fighters, and by extending the service life and efficiency of the KC-135s by a re-engining program.

The KC-135 Stratotanker family bears a striking resemblance to the Boeing 707 airliners and in fact the military and civil aircraft are parallel developments, with a common ancestor in the Boeing Model 367-80 of

1954. Powered by four Pratt & Whitney J57-P-59W turbojets each developing 13,750lbs of thrust with water-injection at takeoff, the KC-135A has a cruising speed of around 530mph at 35,000ft. Maximum takeoff weight is 316,000lbs, wingspan is 130ft 10in and length 134ft 6in. Total fuel capacity is 31,200 gallons, housed in integral wing tanks, underfloor fuselage tanks and a rear fuselage tank. The KC-135A can fly out to a radius of 3000 nautical miles to offload 24,000lbs of fuel, or it can supply 120,000lbs of fuel at a 1000nm radius. As many KC-135s are fitted with an air refueling receiver system these operating radii can be extended by the tankers themselves being refueled in flight. Operating at maximum weight the KC-135A will require nearly 14,000ft of runway for takeoff.

The KC-135A is operated by a crew of four, comprising two pilots, a navigator and a boom operator. The cabin can be used for personnel or cargo transport, with accommodation for up to 160 troops, or 83,000lbs of cargo. This is useful for overseas deployment of tactical squadrons, allowing maintenance personnel and ground equipment to be carried. Fuel is transferred by means of a boom fitted beneath the rear fuselage. This is lowered, telescopically extended and then maneuvered by the boom operator until it connects with the refueling receptacle in the receiver aircraft. Fuel can then be transferred at the rate of 5850lbs per minute. Two rows of lights are mounted beneath the forward fuselage to provide the receiver aircraft with aid in lining up with the tanker.

The KC-135Q version of the Stratotanker (56 produced by modifying KC-135A airframes) provides tanker support for the SR-71 Blackbirds and has a special fuel system capable of handling the JP-7 fuel

used by the aircraft and TACAN equipment to facilitate aerial rendezvous. Apart from the exotic SR-71 all USAF units assigned to NATO are converting to JP-8 fuel from JP-4. The new fuel is to be standardized for all NATO aircraft, thus contributing to interoperability and also to safety, as it has a higher flashpoint than JP-4. Another development that will contribute to compatibility between the NATO air arms is the fitting of a hose drum unit to the belly of KC-135As. This means that aircraft of the US Navy and of the NATO allies, who all use the probe-and-drogue refueling system, can refuel from USAF KC-135s without prior notice. Without this installation, a drogue unit has to be fitted to the boom before takeoff if probe-equipped aircraft are to be refueled.

The most significant modification in prospect for the KC-135A is its re-engining with license-built versions of the French SNECMA CFM-56 turbofan giving 60 percent more power for 25 percent less fuel. Plans call for 344 of the existing fleet to be so modified by 1988, receiving the new designation KC-135R. The advantages of the program are that takeoff performance will improve, engine noise levels will be reduced, and most significantly, because the tanker's engines will consume less fuel, it will have more available to pass on. It is estimated that the KC-135R will be able to offload up to twice as much fuel as it predecessor and its improve takeoff characteristics will allow it to operate from four times as many bases.

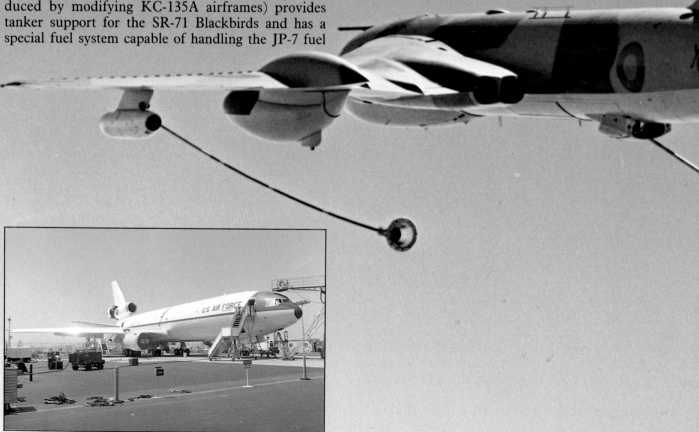

A USAF KC-135A Stratotanker (above) refuels the first C-141B conversion during development trails. An RAF Victor K Mk 2 tanker streams its three hose and drogue refueling units (below). The USAF's KC-10A Extender (below left) combines the duties of cargo transport and tanker aircraft.

The KC-135 tanker will soldier on into the 21st century, but it will be supplemented by up to 60 McDonnell Douglas KC-10A Extenders, a tanker/cargo version of the civil DC-10 airliner. By early 1985 60 such aircraft had been ordered, being flown by the 32nd ARS at Barksdale AFB, Louisiana, and the 9th ARS at March AFB, California. The KC-10A is intended to reduce the US forces' reliance on overseas staging posts – a weakness demonstrated during the 1973 Arab-Israeli War when many countries denied landing rights to USAF supply flights bound for Israel. The Extender will be able almost to double the range of a fully-loaded C-5 Galaxy, or accompany an overseas fighter deployment, refueling the aircraft and carrying maintenance men and their equipment.

The KC-10A is powered by three 52,500lbs General Electric CF6-50C2 turbofans, which give it a maximum cruising speed of 595mph. Range with maximum cargo carried is 4370 miles and at a maximum takeoff weight of 590,000lbs an 11,000ft runway is required. Fuel load is 117,500lbs in underfloor tanks in the fuselage, plus 238,565lbs in wing tanks. This can be transferred using either a boom, or a hose and reel unit, both of which are fitted on all aircraft. The cabin can accommodate up to 80 passengers, plus a crew of five, or up to 169,400lbs of cargo. Operating out to a radius of 1900nm, the KC-10A can offload 200,00lbs of fuel.

The US Navy and Marines, in common with several NATO air forces, use the probe-and-drogue method of aerial refueling. This involves the tanker aircraft trailing a hose with a drogue on the end. The receiver aircraft then maneuvers to engage the drogue with the

An HH-53B Super Jolly Green Giant rescue helicopter (top) maintains a low hover while winching a rescued airman aboard. In order to improve the helicopter's night rescue capability, this HH-53 is fitted with Pave Low III sensors (above).

refueling probe attached to his aircraft. Once the connection is made fuel is transferred. The KA-6D modification of the Intruder is used as a shipborne tanker aircraft while the Marines use the KC-130F and R. Attack aircraft also use the buddy refueling technique. This involves aircraft flying in pairs, one fuel-laden aircraft carrying a hose and drogue unit in a refueling pod, which is used to transfer fuel to the second attack aircraft to extend its range. This technique is also used by several NATO air forces, for example the RAF's maritime attack Buccaneers and the Marineflieger's Tornados.

In Europe the RAF maintains a tanker force comprising two squadrons of Victor K Mk 2 tankers (16 aircraft). These converted strategic bombers are fitted with a three-point hose and drogue refueling system. The Falklands Crisis revealed the inadequacy of so small a force and a small number of Vulcan bombers and Hercules transports have consequently been converted to tanker aircraft. This is a stopgap measure pending the availability of VC 10 tanker aircraft, which are due in service in the mid-1980s to supplement the Victors. Nine Super and Standard VC 10 airliners are undergoing conversion. France's Armée de l'Air maintains a single squadron of C-135F tankers, which are similar to the USAF's KC-135As, but equipped for probe-and-drogue refueling. Additionally 15 of the new production C.160 Transall transports will have provision for a hose-and-drogue unit to be fitted, ten aircraft actually being thus equipped initially.

An interesting answer to the shortage of tanker aircraft was put forward by the Boeing Company in 1981. It was suggested that a civil tanker reserve force be created by converting airliners as tankers. British Airways' Boeing 757s due to be delivered in 1983 could be converted at a cost of £44 million. More ambitiously, a NATO reserve tanker force could be created by modifying the Boeing 737s flown by the airlines of European NATO powers. The disadvantage of such schemes, apart from finding the money from slender defense budgets, is in finding the time to train civil crews up to the necessary level of competence in a specialized branch of military aviation.

At present the Soviet Union lags behind NATO in provision of inflight refueling for tactical aircraft. Some 30 modified M-4 Bison bombers serve with Long Range Aviation and a further 70 Tu-16 Badgets provide Naval Aviation with tanker support. Whether the introduction of the Ilyushin Il-76 tanker version reported to be under development will increase Soviet use of this support service remains to be seen. Unlike the United States, the Soviet Union has no worries about intermediate landing facilities when moving her forces within the Soviet block. However, her increasing involvement in the Third World may act as a spur to developing a larger tanker force. The Soviet air force (in common with the USAF and RAF) is reportedly interested in acquiring a large subsonic aircraft which could serve in transport, maritime reconnaissance, cruise-missile carrying and tanker roles.

Combat rescue is a valuable activity quite apart from its humanitarian aspects and the beneficial effect that an efficient rescue organization will have on aircrew morale. Military aircrew represent a considerable investment in costly and time-consuming training and experience. Therefore any effort made to recover aircrew from enemy territory or the sea is sound military policy, as much as an act of humanity. The United States maintains a considerable force of rescue aircraft divided between the US Coast Guard, concerned primarily with air/sea rescue around the American coasts and the USAF's Aerospace Rescue and Recovery Service, (ARRS) which is part of Military Airlift Command. The Coast Guard, which will be embodied into the US Navy in time of war, operates C-130 Hercules for long-range search and rescue (SAR) and Sikorsky HH-52A and HH-3F helicopters.

ARRS has a combat rescue role, extensively practiced during the war in Southeast Asia where 3883 lives were saved. The aircraft used then, the HC-130 variants of the Hercules and the HH-3 'Jolly Green Giant' and HH-53 remain in service. It is a moot point whether the successes obtained over the jungles of Southeast Asia could be repeated in the hostile environment of Central Europe or even over the deserts of the Middle East. Nevertheless, the USAF maintains six squadrons ostensibly for this task, although two US-based units are primarily concerned with supporting SAC's ICBM sites. The HC-130 Hercules are equipped with spacecraft reentry tracking systems, search radars for ocean surveillance and inflight refueling equipment to extend the range of their accompanying helicopters.

The HH-3E is a twin-engined, all-weather rescue helicopter, powered by two 1400shp General Electric T58-GE-10 turboshafts. Rotor diameter is 62ft, fuselage length 54ft 9in and maximum loaded weight 21,500lbs. The HH-3E has a maximum speed of 166mph and a range of 625 miles, which can be extended by inflight refueling. It is fitted with a rescue hoist, which has a 240ft cable able to lift loads of 600lbs. The later HH-53 is a derivative of the US Marine CH-53 heavy assault helicopter. It is armed with three 7.62mm Miniguns each with a maximum rate of fire of 4000rpm, which are used to suppress hostile groundfire during rescue missions. In addition it is extensively armored. Maximum weight is 42,000lbs and a crew of up to eight is carried – pilot, co-pilot, flight mechanic and five pararescuemen to assist survivors and man the armament. The HH-53's 600-mile range can be extended by flight refueling.

The HH-53s are scheduled to be replaced by HH-60D Night Hawk variants of the US Army's UH-60A Black Hawk, with the older helicopters reverting to the troop transport/special operations role. The HH-60D will operate at night and at low level, using terrain-following radar and FLIR in an attempt to evade enemy defenses during its rescue missions. Should this fail, the helicopter is armed with three Miniguns and may be given Stinger anti-aircraft missiles and Hellfire antitank missiles. It is equipped for inflight refueling. An interim model, the UH-60E, is likely to be used by Special Forces units to gain experience in operating the helicopter. The USAF's experience in combat rescue is unrivalled, most nations merely having a US Coast Guard-style search and rescue organization, usually equipped with helicopters.

The AH-64 Apache is the US Army's latest attack helicopter. Armed with Hellfire advanced anti-tank missiles it can fight in all weathers by day or night.

330

ARMY AVIATION

The helicopter will be a major participant in the land battles of World War 3. The US Army is the world's largest user of helicopters, with 9000 of its 10,000 aircraft being rotary-wing machines. A wide range of Army helicopter roles has been developed to the point where virtually all land operations make use of helicopter support.

These roles encompass battlefield mobility for infantry, resupply of ammunition and fuel, and heavy lift for engineer and artillery units. The helicopter has been used for casualty evacuation since the Korean War. Its use for scouting and surveillance is almost as old, whereas the electronic warfare helicopter is a much more recent development. However, it is the armed helicopter, with its ability to attack enemy troops and more significantly armor, which has made the greatest impact on modern tactics. Primarily because of its importance in the antitank role, the helicopter has itself become the target of enemy air forces; attack helicopters and close air support aircraft will both operate in the anti-helicopter role over the battlefield.

The most serious criticism levelled at the army helicopter is its vulnerability to groundfire. The statistics for Vietnam, the first conflict in which helicopters were used on a large scale, would seem to bear this out, with over 16,000 helicopters brought down by enemy fire or in accidents. Yet to put this figure into perspective, it should be remembered that helicopters were used in great numbers at a very high sortie rate. During the Lam Son 719 operation into Laos in February/April 1971 helicopter losses were 107 machines, but this was only one helicopter for every 4000 sorties flown.

It would nonetheless be futile to deny that helicopters will suffer a high loss rate in battle. This can be alleviated in several ways. Making use of terrain masking and other cover and co-ordinating helicopter actions with artillery fire and close air support sorties will help. Improvements in design make the latest generation of helicopters less vulnerable to groundfire, by the use of armor, self-sealing fuel tanks and 'redundant' structures and controls. Redundancy means designing an airframe in such a way that if a primary load-bearing member is hit, others will take up the load and the structure will not fail. The same philosophy will result in duplicated control runs, as widely separated as possible in the aircraft, so that if one is severed the second will take over its function.

The standard US Army troop transport helicopter is the Bell UH-1 'Huey', with about 4000 in service. Most of these are the UH-1H variant, which is similar to the UH-1Ds used in Vietnam except for its more powerful engine. Most US Army divisions have a combat aviation battalion and infantry divisions have several troop lift helicopter companies with a strength of between 20 and 25 UH-1s. Air Cavalry units rely exclusively on helicopter transport. The UH-1 carries two pilots plus a squad of infantry. The UH-1H is powered by a 1400shp Lycoming T53-L-13 turboshaft and has a maximum speed of 127mph at maximum weight. Range is 318 miles and payload is nearly 4000lbs. Maximum takeoff weight is 9500lbs and dimensions include a rotor diameter of 48ft and a fuselage length of 41ft 1in. The 220cu ft volume cabin accommodates up to 14 troops, two of whom may be gunners manning 7.62mm M60 machine guns mounted by the doors. The UH-1H can also be fitted with mine dispensers and used to lay minefields more rapidly and safely than ground vehicles.

The stalwart UH-1s are in the process of being supplemented by the Sikorsky UH-60A Black Hawk, with the planned total buy of the new helicopter standing at 1107 machines. However, the US Army will continue to rely heavily on the UH-1Hs until the end of the century. By 1984 some 500 UH-60As had been delivered to the US Army, its intended roles being troop transport and medical evacuation. This helicopter has been designed to operate with the minimum of attention from groundcrew in the field, under one hour of maintenance being required for one hour of flight during the first year of service. It is a rugged helicopter able to absorb considerable battle damage, for example the main rotor can withstand a hit from a 23mm cannon shell. In the event of a crash, the helicopter's cabin can resist loads of up to 20 G and a 2500ft per minute (28mph) impact is reckoned to be survivable.

The UH-60A carries a crew of three and 11 fully-equipped infantrymen. It is powered by two General Electric T700-GE-700 turboshafts which deliver 1560shp each. Maximum cruising speed at sea level is 160 knots and endurance is 2-3 hours. Maximum takeoff weight is 20,250lbs, fuselage length is 51ft and rotor diameter 53ft. An External Stores Support System (ESSS) is being developed, primarily to allow the UH-60A to carry two 450 gallon and two 270 gallon external fuel tanks for ferrying. This will give the helicopter a transatlantic range, staging through the Azores. Alternatively 16 Hellfire antitank missiles or mine dispensers can be carried on the ESSS.

Several NATO armies operate UH-1 troop transports including those of West Germany, Italy, Spain and Turkey. However, the UK and France fly the jointly produced Aérospatiale/Westland Puma. The British examples are operated by the RAF with one squadron in the UK and a second in Germany. France's Pumas are flown by five Régiments d'Hélicoptères de Combat of the Army's Aviation Légère de l'Armée de Terre (ALAT), alongside antitank and reconnaissance Gazelles and Alouette II and IIIs. The Puma is flown by two pilots and can carry up to 20 troops. It is powered by two Turboméca Turmo IVB turboshafts of 1400shp each, giving a maximum speed of 170mph. Range is 365 miles and service ceiling is 15,000ft. Maximum weight is 14,770lbs and dimensions include a fuselage length of 46ft 2in and a rotor diameter of 49ft 3in.

The standard Soviet assault helicopter is the Mil Mi-8 code-named Hip by NATO. Helicopter opera-

The Soviet Mi-6 Hook heavy transport helicopter (top) can carry small armored vehicles in its cabin. It is here fitted with auxiliary wings to offload the rotor in forward flight. The Bell UH-1 'Huey' (above) was the workhorse troop transport helicopter of the Vietnam War and it remains one of the most important aircraft in service with the US Army. This picture shows a helicopter crew chief in action with the door-mounted M60 machine gun.

tions in support of ground forces have increased in importance as a result of Soviet combat experience in Afghanistan and new units have been formed and existing ones strengthened. The Hip can carry 28 fully-equipped troops or up to 8800lbs of cargo in its cabin, which has rear-loading clamshell doors enabling loads such as small vehicles or antitank guns to be carried. The Mi-8 is armed for laying down suppressive fire during a helicopter assault; the Hip-C carries 128 57mm rockets in four packs mounted on outriggers, while the Hip-E increases this to 192 rockets in six packs, plus four AT-2 Swatter antitank missiles and carries a flexibly-mounted 12.7mm machine gun in the nose.

The Mi-8 is powered by two 1700shp Isotov TV-2 turboshafts (replaced by the 1900shp TV-3 in later aircraft), which gives it a maximum speed of 145mph and a range of 260 miles. Maximum takeoff weight is 26,500lbs and main rotor diameter is 69ft 10in, with a fuselage length of 60ft 1in.

The Hip is supplemented by the Mi-24 Hind-A, which is primarily an assault transport helicopter with a heavy ground attack and anti-armor armament. It has been developed into the more specialized Hind-D and E gunship helicopters. However, in its assault transport form it is a formidable enough machine, which can carry a squad of eight fully-armed troops, in addition to 128 unguided 57mm rockets, four AT-2 Swatters and a

A US Army CH-47 Chinook medium lift helicopter (below) supplies a mountain-top position. The British Army Air Corps Lynx AH Mk 1 (bottom left) can be armed with Tow missiles in the anti-tank role, but here carries unguided air-to-ground rockets. The West German Heeresflieger is eqipped with HOT-armed Bö 105 anti-tank helicopters (bottom).

nose-mounted 12.7mm machine gun. Hind-A is powered by two 1700shp TV-2 turboshafts (later aircraft have the 1900shp TV-3) and has a maximum speed of around 200mph. Loaded weight is around 22,000lbs and both rotor diameter and the length of the fuselage is 56ft. Hind-A carries a crew of four, comprising two pilots, a gunner in the glazed nose and a loadmaster in the cabin.

Soviet helicopter assault forces will be used to capture key points on the battlefield such as bridges or other bottlenecks. They will probably be used in conjunction with close support aircraft and artillery, or possibly in the aftermath of a tactical nuclear strike. The troops airlifted will be drawn from the motorized infantry divisions, as the Soviet army has no equivalent to the US Army's air cavalry units. Hind-As will probably be used to spearhead such a heliborne assault, suppressing ground fire and dropping troops to secure a landing zone for the following Mi-8s and Mi-6 Hooks carrying heavier equipment.

Most troop transport helicopters also undertake the casualty evacuation role. The US Army assigns special medical evacuation units to this task. They are equipped with the UH-1H, which can carry six litters plus a medical attendant. Rapid evacuation of casualties from the battlefield has considerably reduced the number of fatalities among seriously wounded troops. In Vietnam over 370,000 casualties were evacuated by helicopter and the death rate of those reaching US hospitals was 2.6 percent in contrast to the World War II figure of 4.5 percent. The UH-60A has the same capacity as the UH-1H in the medical evacuation role, while the Soviet Mi-8 can carry up to 12 casualty litters.

The US Army's standard medium helicopter is the Boeing Vertol CH-47 Chinook, some 450 of which are in service. These can be used in the troop transport and casualty evacuation roles, carrying 44 troops or 24 casualty litters. However, they are more usually employed as cargo carriers. The CH-47C version can lift a maximum payload of 19,100lbs and can carry a 15,000lb load over a radius of 30 nautical miles. An extensive rebuilding program is underway, which is intended to extend the service life of the CH-47 fleet and to improve the helicopter's performance, payload and maintainability. A total of 436 CH-47A, B and C model Chinooks are to be remanufactured as CH-47Ds, giving them an increased airframe life equivalent to that of a new aircraft. This force is to be increased by a further 91 CH-47Ds, which are to be newly built.

The first rebuilt CH-47D was delivered to the US Army in May 1982. The D variant is powered by two Avco Lycoming T55-L-712 turboshafts of 4500shp each, driving twin rotors. The 30ft long cabin is the same for all Chinook variants, but the maximum externally slung load has increased in weight from the C's 22,700lbs up to 28,000lbs. Maximum speed is 160 knots at sea level and a 14,000lbs internal load can be carried over a 100 nautical mile radius. Loaded weight

Soviet Frontal Aviation's helicopter armory includes the Mi-8 Hip (right) and Mi-24 Hind-A (bottom) assault helicopters and the Hind-D gunship (below).

is 53,500lbs and dimensions include a fuselage length of 51ft and a rotor diameter of 60ft. The Chinook is operated by a crew of three – two pilots and a loadmaster.

Because the Chinook will usually run out of cabin space before its maximum load is reached, it generally carries its cargo slung beneath the fuselage. This idea has been further developed in the design of the CH-54 Tarhe helicopter, which is in effect a flying crane. Some 80 of these heavy-lift helicopters are in US Army service, performing such specialized duties as positioning heavy artillery, recovering shot down helicopters and aircraft and lifting armored vehicles and engineers' bulldozers and graders. During the Vietnam War these machines recovered some 380 crashed aircraft. The CH-54 has a forward cabin housing three crewmen, including an aft-facing crew member who controls the helicopter when underslung loads are being picked up or landed. Aft of the cabin a boom runs back to the tail rotor, with the engines mounted on top of this structure. There is no main cabin as such, but a detachable pod can be fitted to house passengers or equipment.

The Tarhe is powered by two 4500shp JFTD-12A-4A turboshafts which drive a 72ft diameter main rotor. The fuselage length is 70ft 3in and overall height is 25ft 5in, giving a ground clearance of 9ft 4in beneath the boom. Maximum weight is 47,000lbs, giving a maximum lift capacity of 25,000lbs although 20,000lbs is a more usual load. Speed is 126mph and range is 230 miles.

Among the United States' NATO Allies several countries operate Chinooks, including Canada, Greece, Italy, Spain and the United Kingdom. The RAF's 33 Chinook HC Mk 1s are primarily intended to provide logistical support for the Army, with secondary roles as troops transports and for casualty evacuation. They may also support dispersed site operations by Harrier aircraft. France's ALAT has no helicopter heavier than the Puma, but the West German Army's Heeresflieger has a force of 110 Sikorsky CH-53Gs. These are formed into medium helicopter regiments with one attached to each of the three army corps. Each regiment can move a lightly-equipped battalion in a single lift.

The Soviet Union's Mil Mi-6 Hook heavy lift helicopter was the largest helicopter in the world at the time of its entry into service at the end of the 1950s and perhaps as many as 400 remain in use. It has a maximum takeoff weight of 93,700lbs with a payload of 26,000lbs. Dimensions include a fuselage length of 108ft 10in and main rotor diameter of 114ft 10in. The Mi-6 is fitted with stub wings to offload the rotor and by using a rolling takeoff rather than a vertical liftoff it can increase its maximum payload. Power is provided by two 5500shp Soloviev D-25V turboshafts, giving a maximum speed of 186mph and a range of over 600 miles with an 8800lbs payload. In the troop transport role 65 men can be carried. However artillery pieces or armored vehicles are more usually carried and Mi-6s were used in this way during the fighting between Ethiopia and Somalia in the Ogaden in 1978. A flying crane version of the Mi-6, the Mi-10 Harke, can lift even heavier loads, although fewer than 100 are in service with Frontal Aviation.

The Mi-6's successor in the mid-1980s is likely to be the Mi-26 Halo, a 110,000lbs machine with about twice the payload of the Hook. It is powered by two 11,400shp Soloviev D-136 turboshafts, driving a large eight-bladed main rotor. The Mi-26 like its predecessor will operate in concert with troop carrying machines during a heliborne assault, lifting armored vehicles, artillery and perhaps SAMs into the landing zone.

At the other end of the scale from the massive heavy-lift helicopters are the small rotorcraft used for battlefield reconnaissance. These need to be small and agile so that they can make maximum use of terrain masking and nap of the earth flying techniques for cover. In future many will be fitted with mast-mounted sights carried above the rotor, so that they can remain behind cover while observing. Scout helicopters work

in conjunction with antitank helicopters, identifying targets and directing attacks. They observe the effects of shellfire for artillery units and scout for armored and infantry formations. They are also useful as liaison machines and as airborne command posts.

The US Army currently operates two types of observation helicopter, the Hughes OH-6A Cayuse (1000 in service) and the Bell OH-58 Kiowa (2000 in service). The OH-6A, which does not at present serve in Europe, is the smaller of the two. It has a maximum loaded weight of 2700lbs, a fuselage length of 23ft and rotor diameter of 26ft 4in. Power is provided by a 317shp Allison T63-A-5A turboshaft, giving a speed of 150mph and a range of 380 miles. Crew comprises a pilot and observer, with accommodation for two passengers. An armament of one 7.62mm XM-27 machine gun with a rate of fire of 4000 rounds per minute is carried.

The larger OH-58A Kiowa, which serves with the US Army in Europe, has a maximum loaded weight of 3000lbs, a fuselage length of 32ft 7in and rotor diameter

The agile OH-6A scout helicopter (above) serves with US Army units based in the United States and Far East. The CH-54A Tarhe flying crane (left) is invaluable for recovering crashed helicopters and supporting engineer and artillery units. The West German CH-53G medium-lift helicopters (below) can each carry 38 fully-equipped troops.

of 35ft 4in. It is powered by a 317shp Allison T63-A-700, giving a speed of 138mph and range of 300 miles. In addition to its crew of two, three passengers can be carried. Armament is optional, but can include two XM-27 machine guns. The OH-58C version has the more powerful (420shp) Allison 250-C20B engine and is fitted with 'non-glint' windows and infra-red suppressors on the engine exhaust.

The US Army plans to modify 720 OH-58A Kiowas under the army helicopter improvement program (AHIP) to produce a scout capable of working with the AH-64 Apache advanced attack helicopter. The OH-58 AHIP will carry a mast-mounted sight above the rotor, fitted with a TV camera for daylight operation, imaging IR for night observation and a laser rangefinder and designator. Using the laser, the OH-58 AHIP will be able to mark targets for the AH-64's Hellfire antitank missiles, or for Copperhead laser-guided artillery shells. Other improvements to the OH-58A include fitting the more powerful Allison 250-C30R, increasing payload by 550lbs and an armament of Stinger anti-aircraft missiles to provide prototection against attack helicopters and CAS aircraft.

The most important scout helicopters in service with the European NATO armies are the Anglo-French Gazelle and West Germany's Bö 105. The Gazelle serves with ALAT in both the reconnaissance and anti-tank roles (armed with HOT antitank missiles). The UK's Army Air Corps uses the Gazelle for observation and liaison. Powered by a 590shp Turboméca Astazou turboshaft, the Gazelle has a speed of 190mph and a range of 415 miles. Maximum loaded weight is 3970lbs and dimensions include a fuselage length of 31ft 3in and a rotor diameter of 34ft 5in.

West Germany's Heeresflieger uses the Bö 105 for observation and antitank duties and it also serves in the Netherlands. It is powered by 400shp Allison 250-C20 turboshafts and has a maximum speed of 165mph and 400 mile range. With a maximum weight of 5070lbs, the Bö 105 has a fuselage length of 28ft and a rotor diameter of 32ft 3in. It can carry four troops, plus the pilot, and in the antitank role it carries six HOT missiles.

Surprisingly, the Soviet Union has no equivalent to NATO's large forces of scout helicopters. This deficiency is as much a result of differing operational philosophies, as of the apparent inability of Soviet designers to produce a small and agile scouting helicopter.

NATO's reliance on timely intelligence of enemy moves is reflected in the various electronic reconnaissance helicopters and fixed wing aircraft in service with the US Army or under development. The Gruman OV-1 Mohawk is a twin-turboprop fixed wing reconnaissance aircraft which provides battlefield reconnaissance at division level. Operated by a crew of two, the Mohawk can fly from short and roughly-surfaced airstrips close to the battlefront. It carries various sensors, including SLAR, cameras and infra-red. Some Mohawks have been modified for electronic reconnaissance. Powered by two 1400shp Lycoming T53-L-701 turboprops, the Mohawk has a top speed of 290mph and a range of over 900 miles. Maximum loaded weight is 18,100lbs and dimensions include a span of 48ft and a length of 41ft.

An altogether more specialized Army fixed-wing aircraft is the Beech RU-21 Ute, which is used for signals intelligence. By monitoring enemy radio transmissions, information on his order of battle can be gleaned and preparations made to jam his signals traffic.

The RU-21 Ute is derived from the Beechcraft King Air executive transport. It is powered by two UAC 500shp PT6A-20 turboprops, giving it a speed of 250mph and a range of 1160 miles. Maximum weight is 9650lbs, span is 45ft 10in and length 35ft 6in. The crew comprises two pilots and two electronic systems operators. Prominent antennae are fitted to the wings and rear fuselage forming part of the radio intercept equipment.

The specialized attack helicopter was the outcome of experience in Vietnam, where it was found necessary to provide heavily-armed escorts for troop-carrying UH-1s and CH-47s. A two seat attack helicopter, the AH-1G Huey Cobra was produced, using the power-plant and transmission system of the UH-1. Armed with a turret mounted 7.62mm GAU-2B minigun (later superseded by the XM-28) and a 40mm grenade launcher, the AH-1G entered combat in 1967 and was quick to prove its worth. It was used defensively to escort other helicopters and lay down suppressive fire during landing operations, carrying up to 76 FFAR unguided 2.75in rockets. It was also used in offensive roles, hunting for enemy troops and providing close air support when the enemy was too close to friendly forces to allow the use of USAF CAS aircraft. The great advantages of the AH-1G were its agility, its ability to use ground cover and the excellent visibility from its cockpit.

The AH-1G's characteristics were found to be admirably suited to the antitank helicopter role in Europe and approximately 100 AH-1Gs were modified to AH-1Q standard by fitting the BGM-71 TOW antitank missile. These aircraft retained the chin turret, with 7.62mm gun and grenade launcher. However, they were only an interim solution and the US Army has standardized on the improved AH-1S, over 900 of which had entered service by 1984. It replaced the Huey Cobra's 1250shp Lycoming T53-L-13 power-plant with the more powerful 1825shp T53-L-703, giving sufficient reserves of power to accelerate from the hover to 150 knots in 11 seconds. The nose turret armament is retained and the stub wings can carry eight TOW missiles, plus two 19-rocket FFAR pods.

Basic characteristics of the AH-1S include a maximum takeoff weight of 10,000lbs, a fuselage length of 44ft 5in and a main rotor diameter of 44ft. Cruising

Above: Guns and rocket pods on stub-wing attachment points augment the nose-turret armor of this early model AH-1G HueyCobra gunship.

speed is 120 knots, rate of climb is 1600ft per minute and range 275 nautical miles. Armament is to be upgraded by replacing the 7.62mm minigun and grenade launcher with either an M197 three barrel 20mm cannon, with a rate of fire of 750 rounds per minute, or the 30mm Hughes Chain Gun (700 rounds per minute).

The TOW antitank missile has a maximum range of 12,300ft and is effective down to 200ft. The missiles are aimed by the gunner using a chin-mounted sighting turret giving a ×2 or ×13 magnification. This optical sight is to be augmented by a FLIR sight to give a limited night fighting capability. The gun turret can be controlled by both pilot and gunner using helmet mounted sights and a fire control computer, linked to a laser tracker, provides weapons release instructions for rockets and gunfire impact points projected onto a HUD.

AH-1 battle tactics depend on nap-of-the-earth flying and use of ground cover. The terrain of Central and Southern Germany where they will operate is especially suited to such tactics. Because of dense AA defenses surrounding Soviet armored formations, the AH-1s will seek to engage from long range and they will co-ordinate their tactics with friendly artillery and A-10 aircraft. As the territory that they will fight over is the same as that which they use for peacetime training, AH-1 crews will have the considerable advantage of good local knowledge of the terrain. Normally they will operate in groups of five, directed by three OH-58 scouts. Short-range, high-powered radio transmissions are difficult to jam, but AH-1 crews keep the use of radio to a minimum by careful preflight briefing and the use of hand signals.

The AH-1S has a limited ability to fly and to fight at night. The new FLIR-Augmented Cobra TOW sight (FACTS) will give the gunner a night-firing capability, but the pilot needs to wear image-intensifying night goggles. As these need to be refocused if he wants to look away from his instruments and out of the cockpit, the system is rather inflexible. A much better night fighting capability will be provided by the Hughes AH-64A Apache, which is due to become operational in 1985.

The AH-64A offers a great deal more than the ability to fly nap-of-the-earth sorties at night or in bad weather, however. It will be armed with up to 16 Rockwell Hellfire laser-guided missiles giving it a 'fire-

A Hughes AH-64 Apache attack helicopter firing Hellfire ATGW. Note how it uses the cover of the trees, making it a difficult target.

and-forget' capability, unlike the TOW which has to be guided to its target from the launch helicopter. Used in this way, the AH-64A will remain behind cover while its target is designated by laser from the ground or from a scout helicopter. The Apache can then launch its Hellfires from cover, lobbing them over the intervening terrain to the designated target.

The Apache is powered by two General Electric T700-GE-701 turboshafts rated at 1690shp each. Maximum speed is over 150 knots, rate of climb is 1300ft per minute and endurance is over two hours. With a maximum weight of 14,000lbs, the AH-64A has an overall length of 56ft 9in and a main rotor diameter of 48ft 8in. Apart from the Hellfire missiles, armament options include a 30mm Hughes Chain Gun with 1200 rounds of ammunition and up to 76 unguided 2.75in FFAR rockets.

The Apache's night fighting ability is due to the Pilot's Night Vision Sensor (PNVS) and the gunner's Target Acquisition Designation Sight (TADS). The PNVS comprises a FLIR which presents an IR image of the terrain in front and to the side of the helicopter. This is displayed on a monocle sight, which the pilot can position in front of either eye, and flight instrument data is also projected onto the sight. The PNVS makes possible nap-of-the-earth flying at night and in poor visibility. It is complemented by TADS, which gives the gunner a day and night target sight, plus a laser tracker, target designator and rangefinder.

Apache has numerous built-in survivability features, which should help to reduce its vulnerability. It has a low silhouette in profile and a small head-on cross section. The main and tail rotors are quieter than those of most helicopters and the engine's IR signature is reduced by a 'black hole' suppressor. Crew seats are armored, as are key engine components and fuel cells. Each of the four rotor blades can withstand a hit by a 23mm cannon shell and the main gear box will continue to function for up to an hour after losing its oil.

The antitank helicopter has been developed independently of the United States by three major European NATO Allies. The British Army Air Corps is basically organized into two-squadron regiments, with one squadron flying 12 Gazelle scouts and the other (when re-equipment is completed in the mid-1980s) with 12 TOW-armed Westland Lynx AH Mk 1s. The five AAC regiments serving with British Army of the Rhine in Germany have all re-equipped, while UK-based units continue to fly Westland Scouts armed with the Nord SS-11 missile.

West Germany's Heeresflieger plans to equip three antitank regiments with the PAH-1 (Bö 105P) helicopter, 212 of which are on order. Each regiment will have a strength of 56 helicopters, with a regiment assigned to each of the three army corps. The PAH-1 is armed with six Euromissile HOT 13,000ft range antitank missiles and German crews have achieved a success rate of better than 90 percent during practice firings. The basic tactical unit of PAH-1s is the seven-

aircraft Schwarm and a daily sortie rate of up to five per aircraft is anticipated.

France's main antitank helicopter is the HOT-armed Gazelle, which serves alongside the older SS-11-armed Alouette III in the six Régiments d'Hélecoptères de Combat (RHC). Each RHC has three antitank-helicopter escadrilles and some 160 Gazelles are on order to equip them. France and West Germany may co-operate to produce a new antitank helicopter armed with advanced antitank missiles and with a night and adverse weather capability.

The heavily-armed Hind-D and -E variants of the Mi-24 represent the Soviet Union's nearest equivalent to the NATO antitank attack helicopters. They carry the pilot and gunner in individual cockpits in the nose section, with a four-barrel 23mm cannon mounted beneath the nose. Otherwise the armament is similar to that of Hind-A, namely four 32-round 57mm rocket pods and four AT-2 Swatter antitank missiles. The 1.5 mile range Swatters are replaced by the tube-launched AT-6 Spiral on the Hind-E, with range increased to some 5.5 miles. The Hind gunship's weapons aiming sensors are believed to include radar, low light TV and a laser rangefinder. As the gunships retain the troop carrying capabilities of the earlier Hinds, they are far more flexible machines than the NATO attack helicopters.

CONCLUSION

The possible causes and likely outcome of a third World War have provided the opportunity for many knowledgeable and distinguished strategists to construct scenarios that correspond to their own particular theories. The most popular, perhaps, is that of a Soviet offensive in Western Europe's Central Region, using the element of surprise as a 'force multiplier' to achieve a rapid result. Yet even if peaceable negotiation had failed to secure the Soviet Union its demands, the level of NATO forces – especially given their likely reinforcement after a period of international tension – might well make such an action unwise.

If past history is any guide, a likely trigger for World War 3 is a confrontation at sea, where superpower involvement in localized disputes can bring opposing maritime forces into close proximity. Past events in the Middle East and even the South Atlantic could, in retrospect, have provided the flashpoint for a global conflict – and the fact that most Third World countries have furnished their armories with the assistance of either the United States or Soviet Union makes some degree of superpower involvement probable rather than possible.

Air action in World War 3 is likely to follow closely the course of the conflict on land and/or sea, with army and naval aviation to the fore. Although it is comparatively unlikely that the use of air power *per se* would be the one single factor to precipitate global war, incidents such as the shooting down of Korean Air Lines Flight 007 in 1983 remind the observer that the Soviet Union guards its airspace jealously and is ever vigilant in its outlook. The high level of Soviet air defenses reflects continued American development of the manned bomber, the Soviets relying more on their ICBM stock than a fleet of largely obsolete aircraft.

As far as the two superpowers' air forces are concerned, it is a common generalization that the

Below: The US Defense Satellite Communications System is the primary Department of Defense comsat network, carrying communications for the three services. In World War 3, the war in the air may easily expand into space.

Above: Blooded in the Falklands War of 1982, the vertical take-off Sea Harrier proved a versatile and potent shipborne strike fighter with great potential for the future.

Below: US armor maneuvers on the North German plains, an area considered one of the likely battlegrounds on which World War 3 might be fought.

United States' lead in technology is canceled out by the Soviets' superior numbers. With Vietnam a not so distant memory for many serving US pilots, however, it is likely that the USAF's combat readiness will, in the short term at least, be greater than that of their adversary. The employment of Aggressor Squadrons to test their pilots' abilities against simulated Soviet tactics will have helped retain this edge. Elsewhere in NATO, however, the constituent air forces' lack of standardization could well work against them: the Warsaw Pact air forces are, in contrast, equipped almost totally with Soviet designs.

It is more than possible that World War 3 in the air may expand into space – and there is little doubt that the United States leads in this potential theater of war. The Soviet insistence that President Reagan's 'Star Wars' concepts be included in any future strategic arms limitation talks indicates how seriously the Kremlin views the possibility – and, while it can be difficult to separate fact from fiction, it is certain that

Above: A Soviet *Moskva* class helicopter carrier operating a variable-depth sonar installation over her stern.

both sides currently employ numerous electronic intelligence (ELINT), reconnaissance and communications satellites. It would not only be advantageous to eliminate these in time of war, but the destruction of strategic weapons by orbiting anti-ballistic missile systems as envisaged by President Reagan leads logically to more offensive possibilities. The launching of earth-targeted warheads from space, as postulated by the Soviet Union's Fractional Orbit Bombardment System (FOBS), is outlawed at present, but the detection of such an attack would obviously pose major problems to the already overloaded early warning systems now in service.

In addition to the multifarious weapons listed in this volume, many new systems are currently under development that may well have some bearing on a future conflict. Laser weapons, predictably, are among these. Currently utilized in range-finding applications, the race is on to be the first to employ them as weapons of destruction on land, sea and air. Two 'alternatives' to the tactical nuclear bomb, meanwhile, have been suggested in the neutron bomb (which, although nuclear, has the advantage of leaving buildings and matériel intact) and fuel air explosive (FAE) devices.

The nuclear imbalance favoring the Soviet Union is to some extent counterbalanced by the fact that most

US nuclear missiles have multiple warheads. The importance of the nuclear submarine now lies in its second-strike capability, that is to say retaliatory action should a pre-emptive strike by the enemy have incapacitated land-based weapons. That said, the varying methods of submarine detection and warfare available to East and West alike are more numerous and potent than ever before, and submarines' ability to remain undetected for indefinite periods must perforce be questioned.

It has often been remarked that in a nuclear war there can be no winner – and, while a conventional assault with the benefit of surprise might yield territorial gains, it only takes one battlefield commander to cross the nuclear threshold and take the conflict into a new dimension. In the final analysis, however, and whatever the tactical and technological pros and cons, the human being is always the weakest link in the chain. And, while it is inevitably assumed that the Soviet Union as likely aggressor will have the element of surprise on its side, it is the Western soldier, sailor and airman who, by virtue of his (usually) voluntary status and superior training, is encouraged to act on his own initiative. And it is this factor that the West will rely upon to redress the numerical balance.

Sikorsky CH-53E Super Stallion, latest version of the US Navy and Marine Corps assault transport helicopter.

Acknowledgements

The publishers would like to thank Adrian Hodgkins who designed this book and Ron Watson who prepared the index. The Royal Ordnance Factory, the US Defense Department, the US Army, Navy, Air Force and Marines kindly supplied many of the illustrations; in addition, the following agencies and individuals should be credited:

AP Worldwide 15 top
Avions Marcel Dassault 290-291
Bison Picture Library 15, 16, 18, 45, 63 top, 98 bottom, 259, 266, 285, 309
Bremer Vulcan 192-193 bottom
British Aerospace 89 both, 171 lower, 267 top, 286, 294-295, 300, 301, 302-303, 306 both, 314-315, 326-327
Michael Badrocke 318-319 artwork
Bundesmarine 144, 148-149 top, 177 top
Canadair 93, 204 all three
Canadian Defence Forces 18, 23, 58-59, 62 top, 67, 73 top, 77 bottom, 99 bottom, 111 top, 114-115
ECPA 130, 136-137, 146, 170, 177 bottom, 203
FMC Corporation 51 bottom, 71 bottom
General Dynamics 126-127, 138-139, 143, 276 both
V. Graham 210-211
Harco Corp 72 top
Hughes 67 top, 90, 330-331
Robert Hunt Library 45 bottom
Italian Navy 208
Japanese Maritime SDF 121

John Jordan 231 artwork
Mike Lennon 196, 229 lower
Lockheed 321
MARS 20, 39, 42-43, 50 top right, 57, 60 bottom, 65 below right, 69 both, 77 top
Martin Marietta 86
Martin Corporation 258, 260-261
McDonnell Douglas 171 top, 197
Charles Messenger 112
Messerschmitt-Bolkow-Blohm 274-275, 334-335 bottom
Ministry of Defence, London 26-27, 28, 29 top, 44, 54, 55 both, 64 bottom, 74-75, 79, 98 bottom, 104, 105, 106, 107 top, 108 top, 122-123, 132-133, 212-213, 216, 224-225, 292 bottom, 310 bottom
MoD via MARS 166
Nippon Steel Tube 218-219
Novosti 12, 13, 113
PPL 134 both, 142, 140-141, 160-161, 186 bottom, 215 bottom, 232
John Roberts 142-143, 162-163, 206-207 all artwork
Rockwell International 268
SAAB Scania 307 top
Scott Lithgow 146-147
Shorts 87 top right
Sikorsky 214-215 top
Société ECA 214 top left
Swan Hunter 190-191
TASS 224 bottom
C&S Taylor 164-165, 180-181, 185, 220-221, 233
VFW-Fokker 323 top, 338-339
Vought Corp 79
Westland Helicopters 202, 334 bottom
World Wide Photos 236